THE REFORMATION PARLIAMENT
1529–1536

The opening of Parliament in 1523
From the Wriothesley Garter Book in the Royal Library, Windsor
reproduced by gracious permission of Her Majesty the Queen

THE REFORMATION PARLIAMENT
1529–1536

STANFORD E. LEHMBERG
Professor of History, University of Minnesota

CAMBRIDGE
AT THE UNIVERSITY PRESS
1970

Published by the Syndics of the Cambridge University Press
Bentley House, 200 Euston Road, London N.W. 1
American Branch: 32 East 57th Street, New York, N.Y. 10022

Library of Congress Catalogue Card Number: 70–85723
Standard Book Number: 521 07655 2

Printed in Great Britain by
Alden & Mowbray Ltd at the Alden Press, Oxford

CONTENTS

PREFACE

The Reformation Parliament, which met in seven sessions during the years from 1529–1536, was clearly one of the most important assemblies ever to gather in England. Pickthorn may have exaggerated when he called it 'the most important Parliament in English history':[1] the Long Parliament of the seventeenth century and that which passed the great Reform Bill of 1832 are obvious competitors for such recognition. But Bishop Stubbs wrote that the Reformation Parliament, 'both on account of its length and for the importance of its acts, may deserve the title of the Long Parliament of Henry VIII',[2] while Froude believed its work to be 'of larger moment politically and spiritually than the achievements of the Long Parliament itself'.[3]

The chief work to which Froude referred was, of course, Parliament's rejection of papal authority in England, thus establishing the independence of the Anglican Church and opening the way for Henry VIII's divorce and remarriage. But although Parliament's primary concern may have been for regulation of the Church, other matters did not escape its attention. Indeed its economic, social, and legal reforms would have earned prominence for the Parliament had it never passed an ecclesiastical measure. Further, this intense activity effected a change in the nature of Parliament itself, giving it 'a permanent place of political importance and, so to speak, finally incorporat-[ing] it in the English system of government'.[4]

It may seem surprising that so significant a Parliament has not before now received thorough study. Some work has of course been done, particularly by G. R. Elton and the late A. F. Pollard, who was engaged in collecting material relating to the Parliament at the time of his death. Perhaps other historians

---

[1] Kenneth Pickthorn, *Early Tudor Government: Henry VIII*, 133.
[2] William Stubbs, *Seventeen Lectures on the Study of Medieval and Modern History and Kindred Subjects*, 269.
[3] J. A. Froude, *History of England from the Fall of Wolsey to the Defeat of the Spanish Armada*, I, 191.
[4] G. R. Elton, *The Tudor Constitution*, 229.

have been deterred by the lack of adequate documentation. There is no Journal of the Commons, whose records begin only in 1547. The Lords' Journals are incomplete and in any case of limited usefulness. No private diaries, and only a handful of letters mentioning Parliament, survive. There is, fortunately, considerable parliamentary material in the *Chronicle* of Edward Hall, himself a member of the Commons, and the dispatches of the ubiquitous Spanish ambassador, Eustace Chapuys, yield valuable if sometimes misunderstood or distorted information. His original dispatches have been consulted throughout this study; they provide a somewhat fuller account than the summaries in the *Calendar of State Papers, Spanish,* or *Letters and Papers of Henry VIII,* through which most historians have known the envoy's reports. These dispatches, preserved in the Haus-, Hof-, und Staatsarchiv, Vienna, are referred to in the notes that follow as Chapuys MSS.; they are written in French, with considerable use of cipher, fortunately decoded in the margin at the time of receipt. Drafts of bills have been utilized to show the various stages through which important pieces of legislation passed and the hands which worked on them. Few of these are dated. I have fitted them together as seemed most probable, but I would readily concede that other interpretations and datings are possible. The original acts preserved in the House of Lords Record Office show, among other things, which House of Parliament first passed each bill and what provisos were added. Finally, the statutes of the Parliament constitute its principal memorial. They are readily available in the printed *Statutes of the Realm* but have been infrequently read and inadequately used. Even when all these sources are carefully studied the Parliament remains a jig-saw puzzle with half the pieces missing. I have thought it better to see what can be done with these inadequate materials than to abandon the Parliament, but readers are warned not to expect the sort of racy day-to-day narrative produced by Sir John Neale for Elizabeth's Parliaments. Henry VIII's will never provide that.

Although I have been more concerned with the activities and accomplishments of Parliament than with a Namierite analysis of its membership, I have devoted some attention to its composition. Biographical information concerning members of the Commons is being collected by the History of Parliament Trust in associa-

tion with the Institute of Historical Research, London. I am
grateful to Professor S. T. Bindoff, editor of the early Tudor
section of the *History of Parliament*, and to Mr E. L. C. Mullins,
secretary to the editorial board, for allowing me to examine the
draft biographies which were written before 1963, and to Dr
R. J. W. Swales for assistance in locating them. For several
reasons I did not feel that I could ask for a subsequent renewal
of this privilege, but I have been able to collect considerable
further information on my own. Material which I have taken
from the typescript drafts at the History of Parliament Trust is
clearly identified in the footnotes by the symbol H.P.T. Since I
believe one of the failings of much recent parliamentary history
to be neglect of the House of Lords, I have devoted a chapter
to its composition. The Convocation of the Province of Canterbury, which met concurrently with Parliament and was involved
in considerable interplay with the two Houses, also receives
some analysis and has been brought into the narratives where
appropriate.

My aim throughout the narrative chapters has been to give a
full, balanced picture of the Parliament's work, as if seen through
the eyes of the members themselves. I have therefore mentioned
virtually all the statutes passed during these years. No doubt a
more selective approach, such as Neale used, would have produced a more palatable book, but I thought it would be false
to convey a one-sided, distorted view of parliamentary activity
and accomplishments. As a further means of attempting to
recreate the feeling of the participants I have quoted liberally
from the sources. In most cases I have retained their original
spelling, although I have made punctuation, capitalization, and
the use of i and j, u and v conform to modern practice. Occasionally I have corrected silently what I take to be errors in the
original. Modernized spelling is used in all quotations from the
statutes themselves, primarily because variations exist in the
originals: the printed *Statutes of the Realm* reproduce the spelling
of the Parliament Rolls, but the original acts at the House of Lords
Record Office differ considerably in orthography. It seemed
pointless to collate the two and hardly justifiable to adopt one
version over the other. I regret that the footnotes are so cumber-
some. Since virtually all quotations are from the manuscript
sources I have necessarily cited the manuscripts, but I have also

thought that scholars who do not have access to the original papers should be given a reference to the summary in the *Letters and Papers of Henry VIII* or one of the other Calendars of State Papers, if such a summary exists. This practice has doubled the length of many notes, but I hope that it may prove more useful than manuscript citations alone.

A considerable portion of this study was completed while I held fellowships granted by the John Simon Guggenheim Memorial Foundation and the University of Texas Research Institute. Only those who have tried to write while beset by the pressure of classes and committees will appreciate the extent of my gratitude. My debts to others are many. The Clerk of the Records, Mr M. F. Bond, and his assistants Mr Stevens and Mr Cobb treated me with unusual courtesy during my days at the House of Lords Record Office. Dr Rath, then general director of the Vienna archives, and Mr Wing, assistant librarian of Christ Church, Oxford, kindly arranged for the microfilming of documents in their care. I have, as always, received efficient and co-operative attention at the British Museum and Public Record Office, as well as at the University Libraries in Austin, Cambridge, and London. I am particularly grateful to Professor Elton for his careful comments on an earlier draft of my work. Finally, I thank my students and family for their help and forbearance while this study was in progress.

S. E. L.

Austin, Texas
July, 1968

LIST OF ABBREVIATIONS

A.H.R.: *American Historical Review*
B.I.H.R.: *Bulletin of the Institute of Historical Research*
B.M.: British Museum
C.C. 306: Christ Church, Oxford, MS. 306
Chapuys MS.: Manuscript dispatches of Eustace Chapuys, in Haus-, Hof-, und Staatsarchiv, Vienna, Staatenabteilung England, Karton 4, 5, 7
C.S.P., Milan: *Calendar of State Papers, Milan*
C.S.P., Spn.: *Calendar of State Papers, Spanish*
C.S.P., Venetian: *Calendar of State Papers, Venetian*
D.N.B.: *Dictionary of National Biography*
E.H.R.: *English Historical Review*
G.E.C.: G. E. C[okayne], *The Complete Peerage*, new ed.
H.P.T.: History of Parliament Trust
L.J.: *Journals of the House of Lords*
L.P.: *Letters and Papers of Henry VIII*
P.R.O.: Public Record Office
S.R.: *Statutes of the Realm*
S.T.C.: numbered items listed in A. W. Pollard and G. R. Redgrave, *Short-Title Catalogue of English Books, 1475–1640*
T.R.H.S.: *Transactions of the Royal Historical Society*

Unless otherwise stated all references in the *Letters and Papers of Henry VIII* and in the various Calendars of State Papers are to item numbers rather than page numbers.

Counties and Boroughs represented in the Reformation Parliament

Counties are shown in italic. Boroughs are numbered within each county to correspond to numbers on the map. See at foot for key to the Cinque Ports, shown by the letters A–G on the map.

Bedfordshire
1. Bedford

Berkshire
1. Reading
2. Wallingford
3. Windsor

Buckinghamshire
1. Buckingham
2. High Wycombe

Cambridgeshire
1. Cambridge

Cheshire

Cornwall
1. Bodmin
2. Dunheved
3. Helston
4. Launceston
5. Liskeard
6. Lostwithiel
7. Truro

Cumberland
1. Carlisle

Derbyshire
1. Derby

Devonshire
1. Barnstaple
2. Dartmouth
3. Exeter
4. Plymouth
5. Plympton
6. Tavistock
7. Totnes

Dorset
1. Bridport
2. Dorchester
3. Lyme Regis
4. Melcombe Regis
5. Poole
6. Shaftesbury
7. Wareham
8. Weymouth

Durham

Essex
1. Colchester
2. Maldon

Gloucestershire
1. Bristol
2. Gloucester

Hampshire
1. Portsmouth
2. Southampton
3. Winchester

Herefordshire
1. Hereford
2. Leominster

Hertfordshire

Huntingdonshire
1. Huntingdon

Kent
1. Canterbury
2. Rochester

Lancashire
1. Lancaster
2. Preston

Leicestershire
1. Leicester

Lincolnshire
1. Grantham
2. Grimsby
3. Lincoln
4. Stamford

London and Middlesex
1. London

Norfolk
1. Bishop's Lynn
2. Norwich
3. Thetford
4. Yarmouth

Northamptonshire
1. Northampton

Northumberland
1. Berwick
2. Newcastle-on-Tyne

Nottinghamshire
1. Nottingham

Oxfordshire
1. Oxford

Rutland

Shropshire
1. Bridgnorth
2. Ludlow
3. Shrewsbury
4. Wenlock

Somerset
1. Bath
2. Bridgwater
3. Taunton
4. Wells

Staffordshire
1. Newcastle-under-Lyme
2. Stafford

Suffolk
1. Dunwich
2. Ipswich
3. Orford

Surrey
1. Blechingly
2. Gatton
3. Guildford
4. Reigate
5. Southwark

Sussex
1. Arundel
2. Bramber
3. Chichester
4. East Grinstead
5. Horsham
6. Lewes
7. Midhurst
8. Shoreham
9. Steyning

Warwickshire
1. Coventry
2. Warwick

Westmorland
1. Appleby

Wiltshire
1. Bedwin
2. Calne
3. Chippenham
4. Cricklade

I

THE CAUSES AND THE SUMMONS

On 9 August 1529, Henry VIII commanded the issue of writs summoning peers to a Parliament and ordering the elections of members of the Commons.[1] The Parliament was not to meet until 3 November: a long interval, but one reflecting the time necessary for preparing documents and holding elections rather than any unusual deliberation.[2]

Parliament had not met for six years. Thomas Wolsey, the great cardinal who had managed Henry's affairs for more than a decade, preferred to rule without parliamentary interference, no doubt partly because of his troubles with the Parliament of 1523. In that assembly, summoned to provide money for Wolsey's war with France, there had been unusual opposition, with even Wolsey's protégé Thomas Cromwell arguing that the conquest of Thérouanne had cost his Majesty 'more than twenti suche ungracious dogholes cowld be worthe unto hym'[3] and Wolsey himself haranguing the Commons only to be greeted by 'a mervailous, obstinate silens'.[4] Supply was finally granted—a shilling in the pound on lands and goods during each of the succeeding four years, with reductions for the less wealthy—but only after protracted debate of great bitterness.

I amongist other [Cromwell wrote a friend] have indured a Parlyament which contenewid by the space of xvij hole wekes, wher we communyd of warre, pease, stryffe, contencyon, debatt, murmure, grudge,

[1] Printed in Thomas Rymer, *Foedera*, xiv, 302–6, from Close Roll, C 54/398, m. 10 dorso, P.R.O. Cf. *L.P.*, iv, iii, 5837.
[2] Dr J. J. Scarisbrick asserts (*Henry VIII*, 236–7) that the writs were not sent out until early October. He cites no source; presumably he interprets the letter of 6 October from Gardiner to Wolsey, mentioned below, as implying that writs had not yet been dispatched. This may be its meaning, but other explanations are also possible; in any case Gardiner mentioned only a small number of writs. For my view that the interval was not unusual, see Sir Maurice Powicke and E. B. Fryde, eds. *Handbook of British Chronology*, 2nd ed., 535, which shows an interval of three months between the summons and assembly of the Parliaments of 1510, 1512, and 1515, with two months in 1542 and (after the final prorogation) in 1545. Cf. A. F. Pollard, *Wolsey*, 241–2.
[3] R. B. Merriman, *Life and Letters of Thomas Cromwell*, i, 39; *L.P.*, iii, ii, 2958.
[4] William Roper, *The Lyfe of Sir Thomas Moore, Knighte*, 18.

riches, poverte, penwrye, trowth, falshode, justyce, equyte, discayte, oppressyon, magnanymyte, actyvyte, force, attempraunce, treason, murder, felonye, consyle, and also how a commune welth myght be edeffyed and contenewed within our realme. Howbeyt in conclusion we have done as our predecessors have bene wont to doo, that ys to say as well as we myght, and lefte wher we began.[1]

This seemingly mild end masked continuing resentment which was to cause the failure of Wolsey's 'amicable grant' of non-parliamentary revenue in 1525.

But it was not Wolsey who decided to summon Parliament in 1529. By August twin calamities had brought his meteoric career to a fiery decline. In June had come the failure of the league in which Wolsey, now allied with France, had attempted to combat the threat of an Italian conquest by Charles V, the king of Spain and Holy Roman Emperor. The Imperial victory at Landriano brought the papacy under Charles' control and revealed the futility of the cardinal's foreign policy. An even more disastrous blow was Wolsey's failure to secure the divorce from Catherine of Aragon which Henry had perhaps desired as early as 1514 and eagerly sought since 1527.[2] When a legatine court opened at Blackfriars in May 1529 the king confidently assumed that a favourable judgment would be pronounced within a matter of weeks, but on 23 July Cardinal Campeggio, Wolsey's fellow judge, adjourned the trial without a decision. The court never reconvened; instead the pope revoked the case to Rome, where Charles could prevent any settlement harming Catherine, his aunt. Wolsey, foreseeing his doom, had not failed to tell the pope that such action would utterly alienate the king and bring ruin for himself,[3] but Clement VII had no power to help. He was (to borrow his own figure of speech) caught between the anvil and the hammer, and could only play for time.[4]

Henry's intentions in calling a Parliament so soon after the break-down of the divorce hearings are not immediately clear. It has often been implied, particularly in superficial narratives, that he had in mind the great scheme of ecclesiastical nationaliza-

[1] SP 1/28, fol. 153, P.R.O.
[2] See Betty Behrens, 'A Note on Henry VIII's Divorce Project of 1514', B.I.H.R., XI (1933–1934), 163–4. Garrett Mattingly has cast considerable doubt on the story of this project; see his Catherine of Aragon, 320–1.
[3] A. F. Pollard, Wolsey, 234.
[4] Benet, Casale, and Vannes to Wolsey, Rome, 9 July, in L.P., IV, iii, 5762.

tion which Parliament was ultimately to carry through, or that he planned to move in carefully measured stages against the papacy.[1] There is no evidence, however, to support such an assumption, and every reason to believe that Henry's aims were not yet so clearly defined or far reaching. He had not, by 9 August, received news of the actual advocation to Rome, although he may have suspected it. He was certainly not ready to break with the pope, and he does not seem to have conceived any particular method of putting pressure on Rome. One is tempted to think that, not knowing where to turn now that Wolsey had failed him, he summoned Parliament in the vague hope that its members might suggest a solution.

More specifically, he probably intended Parliament as a stage for action against Wolsey.[2] The king must have been eager to vent his irritation, while the councillors who would benefit from the cardinal's fall, notably the dukes of Norfolk and Suffolk and Anne Boleyn's father, Viscount Rochford, cannot have missed an opportunity to inveigh against him. It may be more than a coincidence that as early as 1 July Thomas Darcy had composed a long series of articles which could be used in attainder proceedings,[3] and further charges by John Palsgrave may be of about the same date.[4] Darcy, who had opposed Wolsey's policy in the north for years, even went so far as to draft a proclamation urging all who had been injured by the cardinal's negligence and inordinate vainglory to present their evidence before a group of special commissioners.[5] Nothing came of that project, but word of the plan to prosecute Wolsey in Parliament spread rapidly. On 4 September Eustace Chapuys, who had just arrived in England to take up his post as Imperial ambassador, reported that the whole purpose of Parliament was to take away the chancellor's seals from the cardinal, although this could be done equally well without parliamentary sanction.[6] A month later Du Bellay, the French

---

[1] See, for instance, G. de C. Parmiter, *The King's Great Matter*, 113: 'The significance of the step [summoning Parliament] was unmistakable; Henry was appealing from the pope to his people.'

[2] This argument has been advanced by Arthur Ogle, *The Tragedy of the Lollards' Tower*, 178.

[3] *L.P.*, IV, iii, 5749.   [4] *Ibid.* 5750.   [5] *Ibid.* 5749, sec. 3 (ii).

[6] Chapuys MS., fols. 212–13 (*C.S.P., Spn.*, IV, i, 135; not in *L.P.*). Chapuys, who had been born about 1489 in Annency, Savoy, entered the service of Charles V in 1527 after a decade as chancellor to the bishop of Geneva. In 1529 Charles sent him to replace the scheming Don Inigo de Mendoza as ambassador at the English

ambassador, wrote that Wolsey would lose his power entirely 'par ce Parlement'.[1] On 6 October Stephen Gardiner, whom Henry had recently appointed his secretary, ordered Wolsey to send him the writs for elections in five of the shires: as chancellor the cardinal was still legally responsible for issuing the documents but was allowed no opportunity to meddle in the elections, which were entrusted to Norfolk's direction.[2] Small wonder that Wolsey had begun writing pitiful letters to Henry, crying for mercy and signing himself 'your most prostrate poor chaplain, T. Cardinalis Ebor., miserimus'.[3]

Despite these plans Wolsey's condemnation was not in the end reserved for Parliament. Henry, who seems to have spent the month of September debating how to deal with the cardinal, finally offered him the alternative of indictment in the King's Bench on a charge of violating the statute of praemunire. Wolsey had much to gain from such a move, since attainder could mean death while the penalty in a praemunire suit was limited to loss of property, and Henry too preferred to avoid the spectacle of a parliamentary hearing. He was evidently feeling some twinges of remorse at the fall of his faithful servant—Anne Boleyn, who hated Wolsey, reportedly made Henry promise not to give him an audience, for she thought that the king could not help taking pity on him[4]—and he may have realized that an airing of complaints against the cardinal would inevitably reflect on the king who had acquiesced in his activities. Accordingly, on 9 October an indictment against Wolsey was drawn up by the attorney-general, Christopher Hales; Wolsey was allowed to name proctors, so as to avoid a personal appearance in court; they acknowledged that he had procured bulls to make himself legate, and had in other ways violated the fourteenth-century statutes of provisors and praemunire; and on 30 October Wolsey was found guilty. All his goods and possessions were declared forfeit.[5]

court; Chapuys arrived late in August and was presented to Henry on 14 September. His dispatches form one of the major contemporary sources for the period from 1529 to his retirement in 1545. Chapuys was a humanist and corresponded with Erasmus. He died in 1556, leaving a considerable fortune for the foundation of colleges in Annency and Louvain. See Mattingly, 'A Humanist Ambassador', *Journal of Modern History*, IV (1932), 175–85; Mattingly, *Renaissance Diplomacy*, 242–6; and L.P., VIII, preface, xliv–xlv.

[1] L.P., iv, iii, 5983.   [2] Ibid. 5993.   [3] Ibid. 5999.
[4] Du Bellay's dispatch, 17 October, in *ibid.* 6011.
[5] Ibid. 6035; A. F. Pollard, *Wolsey*, 244–5; Ogle, *The Lollards' Tower*, 178–9.

The tottering cardinal had now fallen completely from political power, as Chapuys wrote,[1] but Henry softened the blow by allowing him to retain a considerable household at Esher and by restoring to him the archbishopric of York.

Four days after the court's sentence the Reformation Parliament assembled. It is unlikely that the king intended any further action against the cardinal, and it may be true, as Ogle argued, that from Henry's point of view the Parliament met 'in a vacuum, with nothing of consequence before'.[2] The chief councillors, however, were not so easily satisfied; they feared that Wolsey might somehow regain Henry's favour, and knew that such a turn of events would end their power and place their very lives in jeopardy. Chapuys, with his usual perspicacity, wrote Charles that more execrable things would surely be said against Wolsey in Parliament, since those who had raised the storm would not rest until his ruin was complete.[3] And there were other uses to which Parliament could be put. Catherine of Aragon, who felt that Henry held the Lords and Commons 'tous a sa main', feared that action against her was brewing there.[4] Chapuys heard that Parliament was to inquire into the conduct of the realm's finances; he thought that it might outlaw the reception of future papal legates in England.[5]

Members of the Parliament itself had their own reasons for welcoming the session. They must have shared the general animus against the fallen cardinal, but for them hatred of the over-mighty churchman was but one aspect of the anti-clerical sentiment which was boiling throughout the realm. Fabyan's *Chronicle* sums up their intentions neatly in its succinct entry under 1529, 'A Parliament for ennormities of the cleargy'.[6]

Since concern for clerical abuses was not new, it may be helpful to follow this theme through the previous Parliaments of the

---

[1] Chapuys MS., fols. 214–22 (*C.S.P., Spn.*, IV, i, 194; *L.P.*, IV, iii, 6026). This dispatch is printed in full, with an English translation, in William Bradford, *Correspondence of the Emperor Charles V*, 256–98.

[2] Ogle, *The Lollards' Tower*, 179.

[3] Chapuys MS., fol. 221ᵛ (*C.S.P., Spn.*, IV, i, 304).

[4] Chapuys MS., fol. 209ᵛ (*C.S.P., Spn.*, IV, i, 235); dispatch of 21 September. The same point is repeated in a dispatch of 8 October, Chapuys MS., fols. 196–9 (*C.S.P., Spn.*, IV, i, 274).

[5] Chapuys MS., fol. 209ᵛ (*C.S.P., Spn.*, IV, i, 235); repeated in a dispatch of 27 September, *C.S.P., Spn.*, IV, i, 257.

[6] Robert Fabyan, *The New Chronicles of England and France*, 699.

Tudor period. As early as 1489 there had been opposition to the abuse of benefit of clergy, which placed those in holy orders outside the reach of the secular courts, and Parliament had ordered that clerks convicted of murder or other felony be branded on the thumb.[1] In 1512 Henry VIII's second Parliament had enacted that murderers and thieves in minor orders should be deprived of benefit of clergy; probably to appease the bishops in the House of Lords, the statute carried a proviso that it should remain in force only until the next Parliament.[2] Clerical objections increased after Pope Leo X's pronouncement in 1514 that no laymen could have jurisdiction over clergymen, and early in 1515 the abbot of Winchcombe, Richard Kidderminster, preached a famous sermon at Paul's Cross attacking the 1512 statute and upholding the validity of papal decrees in England.

Meanwhile the activities of churchmen and ecclesiastical courts had been called to the attention of Englishmen by the celebrated Hunne affair. Richard Hunne, a London tailor of Protestant leanings, had been sued by the rector of Whitechapel for refusing to give the usual mortuary fee after the burial of his dead baby. He countered the suit with a praemunire charge against the church court in which he had been arraigned, arguing that it sat by authority of a papal legate and thus, as a foreign court, could have no jurisdiction over English subjects. The clergy, not to be outdone, then cited Hunne for heresy and committed him to prison in the Lollards' Tower of old St Paul's, where he was found dead in December 1514. Although the churchmen asserted that he had committed suicide they could not convince a coroner's jury, and despite his privileged status as a cleric Dr Horsey, the bishop of London's chancellor, was brought to trial at King's Bench. The bishop's comment that any London jury would condemn a clergyman though he were innocent as Adam bears testimony to the general clamour.

In this unsettled atmosphere the Parliament of 1515 had assembled. A bill was immediately introduced to restore to Hunne's children the property which had been forfeited when their father was posthumously found guilty of heresy, and the Commons petitioned the king for reform in the matter of mortuary fees. An attempt was also made to extend the 1512 statute against benefit of clergy.

[1] 4 Henry VII, c. 13.   [2] 4 Henry VIII, c. 2.

Before action could be taken attention was diverted by the repercussions of Kidderminster's sermon. Hearing of it, Henry, always interested in theological disputes, determined to have the matter argued in his presence at Blackfriars, with the abbot defending his position and Dr Henry Standish upholding the validity of the statute. The only direct outcome was clerical indignation against Standish; he was summoned before Convocation to explain his views, which that orthodox assembly might well regard as heretical. The king again intervened by convoking a court at Blackfriars, where the judges, peers, and some members of the Commons charged the entire Convocation with praemunire. Wolsey was able to save his position only by making a humble apology and partial submission. The episode bears a marked resemblance to the more sweeping submission of the clergy in 1532, for which it helped prepare the way.

In the end precedents and bitterness were the chief legacies of the Parliament, which the king speedily dissolved on Wolsey's advice. Nothing came of any of the proposed ecclesiastical reforms; the statute of 1512 was allowed to lapse; and in what may have been a political compromise Standish was preserved from the hands of the Church and Horsey from temporal punishment.[1]

Still the issues raised in 1515—Hunne, mortuary dues, benefit of clergy, praemunire, and the independence of the Church generally—were not forgotten. They may have been submerged during the Parliament of 1523, which was almost entirely occupied with Wolsey's demands for money, but they rose and assumed new meaning in 1529. Hatred of Wolsey led naturally to complaint against the Church which he had headed, while the failure of the legatine court to grant the king's divorce reopened the question of papal jurisdiction in England.

All of these matters must have been in the minds of the parliamentarians as they converged on London in November, and of the king and his advisers as they prepared for the session.

[1] On this series of events see Ogle, *The Lollards' Tower*, 11–169; J. S. Roskell, *The Commons and their Speakers in English Parliaments, 1376–1523*, 319–20; Edward Hall, *Hall's Chronicle*, 573–80.

2

THE MOST MALIGNED COMMONS

Perhaps no House of Commons has been so maligned as that which assembled in 1529. Nearly every sort of special interest has been alleged. Simon Fish must have been referring mainly to the Lords when he claimed that the wealthy, corrupt clergy were stronger in Parliament than the king,[1] but Clement Armstrong, a contemporary critic, specifically charged that the Commons was made up of enclosers, graziers, forestallers and regraters, and lawyers whose singular greed had 'distroyed the welth of the king and his lordes and common people'.[2] The power of the lawyers as 'rulers in [the] Commen Howse' angered another writer sufficiently for him to petition the king against them.[3]

The most common complaint, however, was the opposite one: that the House was subject to undue royal influence. Even a writer generally so favourable to Henry as Bishop Burnet wrote that 'there had been great industry used in carrying elections for the Parliament, and they were so successful, that the king was resolved to continue it for some time'.[4] Chapuys reported Catherine of Aragon's belief that Henry held the Commons in his hand and added that they had all been bribed and won over.[5] The chronicler Edward Hall, himself a burgess for Wenlock, Shropshire, commented that 'the most parte of the Commons

[1] *A Supplicacyon for the Beggers*, quoted in William A. Clebsch, *England's Earliest Protestants, 1520–1535*, 242. Fish's tract was probably written some months before the summoning of Parliament.

[2] *A Treatise Concerninge the Staple and the Commodities of this Realme*, quoted in R. H. Tawney and Eileen Power, *Tudor Economic Documents*, III, 121. Professor S. T. Bindoff believes that this treatise was written between 1533 and 1535; see his article, 'Clement Armstrong and His Treatises of the Commonweal', *Economic History Review*, XIV (1944), 68. Armstrong (or Ormeston or Urmeston) was probably a brother of Robert Ormeston, under-clerk of Parliament from 1515 to 1547. Cf. A. F. Pollard, 'The Under-Clerks and the Commons Journals (1509–1558)', *B.I.H.R.*, XVI (1938–1939), 145–7.

[3] SP 2/Q, fols. 138–40, P.R.O. (*L.P.*, VII, 1611 [3]).

[4] Gilbert Burnet, *The History of the Reformation of the Church of England*, I, 84.

[5] Chapuys to Charles V, 9 December 1529, in Chapuys MS., fol. 250, 'yl sont tous gagnez et practiquez par le Roy' (*C.S.P., Spn.*, IV, i, 228).

were the kynges servauntes'.[1] The most damning charges came from John Fisher's early biographer:

In this Parlement the Common Howse was so parcially chosen, that the king had his will almost in all things that himself listed; for where in old time the king used to direct his brieffe or writ of Parlement of every cittie, borrough, and corporat towne within this realme, that they amonge them should make election of two honest, fitt, and skilfull men of their own number to come to this Parleament; the same order and forme of the writt was now in this Parleament observed; but then with every writte there came also a private letter from some one or other of the king's counsellors, requesting them to chuse the persons nominated in their letters, who fearing their great authority, durst commonly chuse none other.

The Parliament thus included 'fewe other then roystinge courteours, servingmen, parasites, and flatters of all sortes, . . . lightly furnished ether with learninge or honestie'.[2] Perhaps this was what Sir Thomas More meant at his trial when he contrasted the power of one Parliament, 'God knoweth what manner of one', with the authority of all the councils of Christendom.[3] The rebels in the Pilgrimage of Grace voiced similar complaints.

Most of these charges may be partially explained by either bias or context. Chapuys' sources of information were not always reliable, and he naturally accepted suggestions favourable to Catherine's side; Fisher's biographer was an Elizabethan Catholic divine who spent most of his adult life abroad; Edward Hall was trying to demonstrate why the Commons were willing to cancel Henry's obligation to repay a loan. Still, the strictures are substantial enough to merit attention. Only an analysis of the actual membership of the Commons can show to what extent, if any, they are correct.

I

In 1529 there were 310 members of the Commons: 74 knights of the shire, elected from 37 counties, and 236 burgesses representing 117 parliamentary boroughs.[4] All these were double-member

---

[1] Edward Hall, *Hall's Chronicle*, 767.   [2] [Richard Hall,] *The Life of Fisher*, 68.
[3] Harpsfield's *Life of More*, quoted in R. W. Chambers, *Thomas More*, 243.
[4] This reckoning counts London and the other county boroughs as boroughs. The figures are calculated from the list printed in the *Return of Members of Parliament*, Part I, 368–71. The actual returns, sent by sheriffs to the Chancery, do not

constituencies save London, which was by tradition allocated four seats. Since the Parliament lasted so long, a number of by-elections were necessary to fill vacancies created by death or removal to the House of Lords. In all, we know the names of at least 335 members, with about ten further doubtful cases.

As is well known, the enfranchising of boroughs was determined by precedent and the chances of history, not by any logical scheme. Few new parliamentary boroughs were created in the early Tudor period, but since 1491 seven towns had gained representation: Buckingham, Lancaster, Preston, Thetford, Oxford, Berwick, and Dunheved, which had formerly been joined to its Cornish neighbour Launceston.[1] There appears to have been no special reason for these creations, except perhaps local pressure, but they did serve in some slight measure to redress the over-representation of the south. Wiltshire, with sixteen enfranchised boroughs, stood far ahead of its nearest rival, Sussex, which had nine. Eight towns in Dorset returned burgesses; Cornwall, its representation not yet swollen by later Tudor grants, had seven enfranchised towns, as did Devon and the misnamed Cinque Ports. Surrey had five parliamentary boroughs, all other counties four or less. Wales as yet returned neither knights of the shire nor burgesses, although it was to be granted this privilege by a statute of 1536.[2]

Throughout the counties a uniform franchise applied, the forty-shilling freehold established by statute in 1430.[3] The vote was thus given to all the moderately well-off landowners; inflation had not yet rendered forty shillings an insignificant sum, and the later multiplication of freeholds, created especially by regarding ecclesiastical and other life-time offices as freeholds, had not yet begun.

But in 1529 details of the franchise were of little more than theoretical interest, since we know of no election in which rival

survive for the Reformation Parliament; the names in the official *Return* are taken from SP 1/56, fols. 2–10, P.R.O., where the counties are arranged geographically rather than alphabetically. Although this list is probably of 1529 it notes members who died or were knighted through May 1532. See A. F. Pollard, 'Thomas Cromwell's Parliamentary Lists', *B.I.H.R.*, IX (1931–1932), 37–8, 43.

[1] Cf. the list of members for 1491 printed by Winifred Jay in *B.I.H.R.*, III (1926), 168–75, and the earlier lists in the official *Return*. There are no full lists of members for the Parliaments held between 1492 and 1529, although we do know the names of a few members. The case of Thetford is given further consideration below.

[2] 27 Henry VIII, c. 26.   [3] 8 Henry VI, c. 7.

candidates were actually presented to the voters. A few contested elections of Henry's reign have left records,[1] and more may have occurred without throwing down permanent traces. But the political realities evidently lay behind the scenes rather than at the polls. In the absence of definitive records we can perhaps learn something from studies of other periods. Professor Neale has shown that virtually all Elizabethan elections were settled in advance, by discussions between the leading landowners, and Professor Edwards has extended the argument back to the fifteenth century.[2] If there was but one great family in a county matters were simple: that family could name the knights of the shire. If there were two prominent landlords each could fill one seat, as the Greys and the Hastings did in the Leicestershire election of 1529.[3] Three or more families could sometimes agree on rotation of seats or find mutually acceptable candidates. Only if such pre-election manipulation failed were contests likely to occur.

Influence was also the dominant factor in determining elections within boroughs. Here a wide variety of franchises and electoral arrangements prevailed, but in practice most borough elections seem to have been controlled by the municipal corporation. Two of London's four burgesses were named by the aldermen and two by the commonalty, meeting in the court of common council; a common council burgess was obliged to vacate his seat if named an alderman.[4] At York election was by the mayor, aldermen, sheriffs, and council of twenty-four.[5] The Chamber of Exeter nominated that city's burgesses.[6] Cambridge had an enormously complicated procedure for indirect election: the

---

[1] One of these was the Hampshire election of 1539. See Elton, 'Thomas Cromwell's Decline and Fall', *Cambridge Historical Journal*, x (1951), 163.

[2] Sir Goronwy Edwards, 'The Emergence of Majority Rule in English Parliamentary Elections', *T.R.H.S.*, 5th ser., xiv (1964), 175–96; Sir John Neale, *The Elizabethan House of Commons*, 69–70.

[3] One knight of the shire for Leicestershire, Sir Richard Sacheverell, had married the widow of Edward, Lord Hastings, while the other, Sir William Skeffington, was a protégé of Thomas Grey, marquis of Dorset. Skeffington, called 'the Gunner' because of his skill in artillery, was appointed Lord Deputy of Ireland in 1530 and must have been absent from most of the Parliament's sessions. (*D.N.B. sub* Skeffington; H.P.T. biographies.)

[4] Helen Miller, 'London and Parliament in the Reign of Henry VIII', *B.I.H.R.*, xxxv (1962), 128; A. F. Pollard, 'Thomas Cromwell's Parliamentary Lists', 38.

[5] Angelo Raine, ed., *York Civic Records*, iii, 119.

[6] Wallace T. MacCaffrey, *Exeter, 1540–1640*, 222.

mayor and aldermen chose one representative, the commonalty another; these two named eight men; the eight made a final selection of burgesses.[1] Elections in High Wycombe, a borough of middling size, were made informally in the borough court, the mayor and bailiffs dominating.[2] At Old Sarum the seven qualified landowners may have met in the middle of fields to go through the formality of holding an election. The borough had been depopulated for centuries but was to continue returning burgesses until 1832.[3] Gatton, Surrey, had only one elector, Sir Roger Copeley; one of his eighteenth-century successors indulged in a very English political joke by erecting a Doric 'Town Hall' with an urn inscribed 'Salus populi Suprema Lex' for his private elections.[4]

Although virtually all of these boroughs were open to political manipulation, it should be emphasized that there is no extant proof of direct royal intervention in the elections. The frequently repeated story that Henry wrote with his own hand to the residents of Colchester, requesting the return of a candidate whom he had nominated, refers to 1522 rather than 1529 and is otherwise exaggerated.[5] Henry may have asked the duke of Norfolk and some other courtiers to use their influence for him in certain areas; Gardiner's letter to Wolsey, already mentioned, suggests that special attention was paid to the elections in Nottinghamshire, Derbyshire, Bedfordshire, Buckinghamshire, Hampshire,

[1] Neale, *Elizabethan House of Commons*, 249–50; C. H. Cooper, *Annals of Cambridge*, I, 272, 422; Edward Porritt, *The Unreformed House of Commons*, I, 70.
[2] L. J. Ashford, *The History of the Borough of High Wycombe from its Origins to 1800*, 111.
[3] Sir Lewis Namier, *The Structure of Politics at the Accession of George III*, 2nd ed., 76.
[4] Cottonian MS. Caligula B. vi, fol. 373, B.M. (*L.P.*, x, 816); Neale, *Elizabethan House of Commons*, 185; Ian Nairn and Nikolaus Pevsner, *Surrey*, 216.
[5] The statements in H. A. L. Fisher, *The History of England from the Accession of Henry VII to the Death of Henry VIII*, 291, and Porritt, *Unreformed House of Commons*, I, 372, are based on H. A. Merewether and A. J. Stephens, *A History of the Borough and Municipal Corporations of the United Kingdom*, II, 1093, where the date is given as 1522. The ultimate source is printed in W. Gurney Benham, ed., *The Red Paper Book of Colchester*, 26; it does not say clearly that the king named candidates but only that the municipal officials proceeded to hold an election 'accordyng to the tenour and effect of the Kyng's wryght dyrected unto them by the shyryfe of Essex, and accordyng to the accomplyschement of a letter dyrected to them from the Kyng's Grace for the same purpose'. In 1529 at least one of the burgesses for Colchester, Richard Rich, was named 'at the command and special desire of the Earl of Oxford', not of the king. See [Henry Harrod], *Report on the Records of the Borough of Colchester*, 15. I have to thank Dr D. E. D. Beales for this reference.

and the town of Southampton.[1] Henry may, later in the Parliament, have encouraged his opponents to stay away, although the four cases specifically mentioned by Chapuys in 1534 all refer to members of the Lords.[2] By 1534 Thomas Cromwell was certainly trying to influence by-elections for the king,[3] and he did considerable politicking in 1536.[4] Three years later he was able to write the king that he 'and other your dedicate conseillers be aboutes to bring all thinges so to passe that your Majestie had never more tractable Parliament'.[5] But in 1529 Cromwell had no such power—he had to work hard, as we shall see, at finding a seat for himself—and there was no other general factotum to handle such matters. Direct royal pressure seems to have been negligible, perhaps because there was no channel through which it could be exercised effectively during the interval between Wolsey's fall and Cromwell's rise.

2

Most of the knights of the shire fit a common pattern, that of the courtier-cum-local magnate. Royal favourites or administrators could seldom obtain a county seat without local lands and ties. Conversely, few men prominent in their shires but hardly known at court represented counties. This is not to say that royal influence was necessarily used to find seats for favourites. It reflects, rather, the structure of Tudor society: most of the greater landowners—those who were likely to be knights of the shire—had spent some time serving the king at court, fighting with him in France, or assisting him in governing the realm.

A few examples will help demonstrate this common type. Sir

[1] L.P., iv, iii, 5994.   [2] Ibid. vii, 121.
[3] SP 1/74, fol. 26, P.R.O. (L.P., vi, 31). The unsigned letter to Cromwell, dated only 9 January but placed by the editors of L.P. under 1533, probably refers to the election of a member for Huntingdonshire following the death of Sir Nicholas Harvey; see A. F. Pollard, 'Thomas Cromwell's Parliamentary Lists', 42–3n.
[4] SP 1/82, fols. 59–62, P.R.O. (L.P., vii, 56) is a list of the parliamentary seats vacated by death, with notes on their disposition, evidently prepared for Cromwell in May 1536; it is mentioned by A. F. Pollard, 'Thomas Cromwell's Parliamentary Lists', 43. See also L.P., x, 815, 817, 852, 903, 916, 1063.
[5] Cottonian MS. Titus B. I, fol. 260, B.M. (L.P., xiv, i, 538); cf. Elton, 'Thomas Cromwell's Decline and Fall', 160–1.

John Russell, who represented Buckinghamshire, had been a gentleman of the privy chamber since 1506, when he was about twenty years old. Soon after Henry VIII's accession Russell became a favourite of the young king; he was a captain in the expedition to France, 1513; he accompanied Henry to the Field of Cloth of Gold in 1520; he was made knight-marshal of the household in 1523 and was employed in embassies to France and Italy.[1] The career of Sir Giles Strangeways, knight of the shire for Dorset, was virtually identical; following his education at the Middle Temple he was an esquire for the body and was in France with the king in 1513 and 1520. His local ties were perhaps stronger than Russell's. By 1529 he had already served three terms as sheriff of Somerset and Dorset, where he was a justice of the peace and vice-admiral.[2]

It is surprising that Sir Thomas Neville, who was a brother of the great Kentish landowner Lord Bergavenny and had been Speaker of the Commons in 1515, did not secure re-election in 1529.[3] Perhaps, having managed such a troubled session, he was not eager to sit again. In any case the two seats for Kent went to half-brothers, Sir Henry and Sir Edward Guildford. Their father, Sir Richard, had died on a pilgrimage to Jerusalem after serving Henry VII as master of the ordnance. Sir Edward, as constable of Dover Castle and warden of the Cinque Ports, was more prominent locally than his brother, but Sir Henry ranked higher at court; he was comptroller of the household and one of the few granted lodgings in the king's house by the Eltham Ordinances of 1526. Both brothers took part in the masque of Robin Hood with which the king celebrated New Year's Day, 1510; Sir Henry served as master of the revels on several other occasions and had his portrait painted by Holbein.[4] Sir Edward may have been the prime mover in the Kent election, for we know that he had a neighbour set aside the revenue from his timber sales 'against the day of choosing Knights for the Shire'.[5] He supervised the education of John Dudley, whose father had been attainted and executed in 1510. Dudley married Guildford's

---

[1] *D.N.B.* Russell later served as lord high admiral and lord privy seal; he was ennobled in 1550 as the first earl of Bedford. [2] *H.P.T.* biography.
[3] *D.N.B.*; J. S. Roskell, *The Commons and their Speakers in English Parliaments, 1376–1523*, 317–20. Neville lived until 1542. [4] *D.N.B.*; *H.P.T.* biographies.
[5] *L.P.*, Addenda, 1, i, 235. The *L.P.* editors placed this undated letter in 1523, but it may refer to the 1529 elections.

daughter Jane and succeeded to the parliamentary seat vacated by Guildford's death in 1534.[1]

There are other parallel careers. Sir Thomas Cornwall, Sir Marmaduke Constable, Sir Nicholas Carew, and Sir Anthony Wingfield all fought in the French campaigns of 1513; all retained court connections while serving as sheriff in their home counties. Cornwall, who was illegitimately descended from the Plantagenets, spent most of his time in his native Shropshire and was a member of the Council in the Marches of Wales.[2] Constable's father had preceded him as a knight for the body and member of Parliament for Yorkshire. Carew's ancestors had represented Surrey, and Wingfield's Suffolk, for a century.[3] Other members with one foot planted firmly at court and the other in a county were Sir William Parr (Northamptonshire), Sir William Kingston (Gloucestershire), Sir Nicholas Wadham (Somerset), Sir Edward Ferrers (Warwickshire), and Sir William Barentyne (Oxfordshire).[4] Sir William Gascoigne, one of the knights for Bedfordshire, differed only in being of an older generation. Born about 1468, he had been a knight for the body to Henry VII, in attendance at both the coronation of Elizabeth of York and the funeral of the king. He served Wolsey as comptroller of the household and continued in favour under Cromwell, receiving lands in Bedford following the dissolution of the monasteries. His father and grandfather had preceded him in Parliament; his great-grandfather was the judge said to have committed Henry V, while prince, for contempt of court.[5]

In a few cases men lacking county power themselves were returned to Parliament through the influence of stronger local magnates. Sir Richard Sandys, for instance, owed his election in Hampshire to his brother Sir William, Baron Sandys of the

---

[1] *Return of Members of Parliament*, Addenda, xxix. John Guildford, a nephew of the knights for Kent, was given one of the seats at Gatton although he was not yet twenty years old.

[2] H.P.T. biography.

[3] *D.N.B.*; [Josiah C. Wedgwood], *History of Parliament: Register of the Ministers and of the Members of Both Houses, 1439–1509*; G. R. Park, *Parliamentary Representation of Yorkshire*, 16n.

[4] *D.N.B. sub* Kingston; H.P.T. lives of Parr, Wadham, Ferrers, and Barentyne; Elton, *Star Chamber Stories*, 35, on Barentyne. Parr's sister Catherine was to become Henry VIII's last wife.

[5] Wedgwood, *History of Parliament, sub* Gascoigne; *Victoria County History, Bedfordshire*, III, 24, 166, 235–7; Sir Thomas Elyot, *The Book Named the Governor*, ed. S. E. Lehmberg, 114–15.

Vyne, in whose household he probably lived.[1] Sir Richard Weston, a court favourite and under-treasurer of the Exchequer, probably gained his seat in Berkshire through the patronage of Charles Brandon, duke of Suffolk, who was the greatest landowner in the county and must have known Weston at court.[2] Sir William Coffyn, whose lands lay in Devon, would hardly have been named a knight for Derbyshire but for his marriage to the daughter of a Vernon of Haddon Hall.[3] The duke of Norfolk may have helped procure the election, in Norfolk, of Sir Roger Townshend and Sir James Boleyn. Both were Norfolk men but not from the highest reaches of county society: Sir Roger was primarily a lawyer and second-rank administrator, while Sir James was Anne Boleyn's uncle and thus a distant relative of the great duke as well as younger brother of the earl of Wiltshire. In Middlesex, where administrative acumen was more important than broad acres, both knights of the shire were active in administering the lands of the duchy of Lancaster. Robert Wroth, the more prominent, was well connected at Enfield and probably helped nominate Richard Hawkes, an immigrant from Worcestershire.[4]

As was natural, court ties counted most in the shires nearest London, while great landowners without significant court connections were most likely to be returned from the distant north and west. Examples of this latter sort are Sir Christopher Dacre of Cumberland and the two members for Cornwall, Sir Piers Edgcombe and Sir Richard Grenville. Dacre, the younger brother of Lord Dacre of the North, spent most of his life fighting the Scots; Edgcombe was the greatest landowner in the vicinity of Plymouth; Grenville, of an old Cornish family, was to become the most important man in the county by the end of the Parliament. But even they were not without court connections. In 1523 Henry VIII had suggested Dacre's nomination to Parliament in a letter to Lord Dacre. Edgcombe's father had been an intimate friend of Henry VII, and Grenville was close to Sir Francis Bryan, a member of the Boleyn circle at

[1] H.P.T. biography.
[2] *D.N.B. sub* Weston; Miller, 'The Early Tudor Peerage, 1485-1547' (M.A. thesis, University of London, 1950), App. D and map.
[3] A. F. Pollard, 'The Reformation Parliament as a Matrimonial Agency and Its National Effects', *History*, xxi (1936-1937), 225.
[4] H.P.T. biographies.

court.[1] Indeed the less prominent knights of the shire for Westmorland and Wiltshire may be more representative of those country gentry who lacked direct ties to the court.[2]

Several county members enjoyed special relationships with the king. The case of Sir John Blount, knight for Shropshire, is unique: his daughter Elizabeth was the mother of Henry VIII's illegitimate son, Henry Fitzroy.[3] Sir William Fitzwilliam, who sat for Surrey, was even closer to the king. Since the age of ten he had been brought up with Henry, whose martial tastes and love of sport he shared. A naval leader, administrator, and ambassador, he had no long association with Surrey but gradually accumulated land and influence there. In his election, perhaps more than in any other, one suspects royal pressure, but there is as yet no evidence to show just how it may have been brought to bear.[4]

It should be emphasized that court connections were perfectly normal for members of the parliamentary classes and did not guarantee support of the king's policies. Sir George Throckmorton, who sat for Warwickshire, had a court background as squire for the body and member of the king's spears; he had for a time been attached to Wolsey's household; but in the Reformation Parliament he openly opposed anti-papal measures. He hated Thomas Cromwell, who imprisoned him after the Pilgrimage of Grace, and he may have helped topple Cromwell in 1540. He was allied through marriage with the recusant Vaux family, and his heirs remained loyal to the Roman Church.[5] During the Parliament he dined often at the Queen's Head Tavern with Sir William Essex, Sir Marmaduke Constable, Sir William Barentyne, and Sir John Gyfford. These men seem to have formed the core of an opposition group; in 1533 their

---

[1] Wedgwood, *History of Parliament,* sub Dacre; A. L. Rowse, *Tudor Cornwall,* 227–8; A. L. Rowse, *Sir Richard Grenville of the* Revenge, 26–47; H.P.T. biographies of Edgcombe and Grenville.

[2] On the Wiltshire members see Bindoff, 'Parliamentary History, 1529–1688', in *Victoria County History, Wiltshire,* v, 122.

[3] Blount died before March 1531 (A. F. Pollard, 'Thomas Cromwell's Parliamentary Lists', 40). In 1536 his widow objected to the county election, in which her son George was not chosen (SP 1/104, fol. 117, P.R.O. [*L.P.,* x, 1063]).

[4] *D.N.B.* sub Fitzwilliam; *L.P.,* xi, 202 (37). It is very difficult to disentangle the two Sir William Fitzwilliams active during this period. That this is the M.P. is indicated by Thomas Cromwell's parliamentary list of 1534, which mentions 'Mr. Treasurer' of the household. Fitzwilliam held this office from about 1531.

[5] *L.P.,* iv–xiii, *passim;* H.P.T. biography.

activities were questioned by Cromwell, who encouraged Throckmorton to stay at home and meddle little in politics.[1] Another member who had led a normal courtier's life, Sir John Brydges of Gloucestershire, also opposed the break with Rome. He later found favour under Mary, serving as lieutenant of the Tower and supervising the burning of Bishop Hooper at Gloucester. He was created first Baron Chandos in 1554.[2]

It would be tedious to cite further examples, interesting though the individual biographies of additional members might be, and the general pattern should by now be clear. The knights of the shire were typical members of the most prominent non-noble class, great country landowners with court connections and administrative experience, frequently related by marriage to peers as well as to other wealthy gentlemen. Most were inclined to support the king, whose problems they understood and whose interests they shared, but they were not subservient and could on occasion oppose his policies.

3

A quite different pattern emerges among the burgesses of 1529. A few borough members, it is true, were of the same class as the knights of the shire. Sir Ralph Ellerker, for instance, had been knighted at Flodden in 1513 and was a prominent landowner in the East Riding of Yorkshire. He might have obtained a county seat but was sheriff of Yorkshire in 1529 and had to content himself with election at Scarborough.[3] Roger Corbet, who was sprung from one of the oldest families in Shropshire and had links with the duke of Suffolk, Lord Windsor, and the Vernons of Haddon, failed to manœuvre himself into a county seat—he was no match for Sir Thomas Cornwall and John Blount. Perhaps to allay his disappointment, he was named sheriff and returned as a burgess for Truro in Cornwall.[4] Sir John

---

[1] *L.P.*, xii, ii, 952.
[2] *D.N.B. sub* Brydges. Brydges was allied by marriage to the Grey de Wilton, Hastings, and Bray families.
[3] *D.N.B.*; Park, *Parliamentary Representation of Yorkshire*, 293.
[4] H.P.T. biography. It was probably during the Parliament that Corbet married the daughter of Andrew Windsor, who was elected to the Commons for Buckinghamshire but immediately went to the Lords. (A. F. Pollard, 'The Reformation Parliament as a Matrimonial Agency and Its National Effects', 225).

Raynesford, like his father, was primarily interested in warfare and had fought with the king in France. He gained election at Colchester, possibly with the assistance of the earl of Oxford.[1] It is more surprising that Sir John Seymour, father of Henry VIII's third wife and of Protector Somerset, was a burgess for Heytesbury rather than a knight of the shire for Wiltshire. In 1529, he had, of course, not risen to the prominence he was to acquire by 1535, when the king visited him at Wolf Hall.[2]

But these are exceptional cases. Most of the parliamentary burgesses were actually residents of the towns they represented, where they were often prominent merchants and nearly always active in civic administration. That this type was dominant is of considerable interest, for Sir John Neale has shown that only fifty-three out of a sample of 447 members of the Parliament of 1584 were primarily merchants or borough officials.[3] The vast majority of the borough members in Elizabeth's later Parliaments were country gentlemen.

Such complete calculations are not yet possible for the Parliament of 1529. A sample of nearly one hundred burgesses for whom biographical information is available indicates, however, that there were at least two active borough residents for every country gentleman. If lawyers, courtiers, administrators, and clients of noblemen who obtained borough seats are added to the country gentlemen and this total set against the number of active residents, the proportion of townsmen drops to just over one-half: hardly in accord with fifteenth-century statutes which prescribed residential qualifications for membership, but much higher than the ratio of townsmen to gentry later in the sixteenth century.

Even under Elizabeth London preserved its independence. Its election procedures, designed to insure that the more ordinary merchants as well as the aldermen were represented, have already been mentioned. In 1529 the aldermen elected a former mayor

---

[1] H.P.T. biography. We know that the earl of Oxford nominated the other burgess for Colchester, Richard Rich: Harrod, *Records of the Borough of Colchester*, 15.

[2] *D.N.B. sub* Jane and Edward Seymour; A. F. Pollard, *England under Protector Somerset*, 9. The second member for Heytesbury, Robert Seymour, was doubtless a relative although not one of Sir John's ten children.

[3] Neale, *Elizabethan House of Commons*, 147. By contrast, more than three-fourths of the known burgesses in 1422 were residents: Roskell, 'The Social Composition of the Commons in a Fifteenth-Century Parliament', *B.I.H.R.*, XXIV (1951), 155.

and the City's recorder. Sir Thomas Seymour, an exporter of wool and cloth, had been warden of the Mercers in 1509 and mayor in 1526; no relation of the Seymours of Wolf Hall, he was sheriff during the riots of Evil May Day, 1517, and was thereafter disliked by the commons for his repressive policies.[1] The recorder was John Baker, a lawyer who continued to sit in Parliament until 1558 but never again represented London. Speaker of the Commons in 1545 and 1547, Baker probably resigned his London seat in 1535, when he was appointed attorney general of the duchy of Lancaster, and was succeeded by the new recorder, Sir Roger Cholmeley.[2]

The common council members are rather more interesting. Paul Withypoll held one of the seats, He was active in the Merchant Tailors and Merchant Adventurers, and was reported by Stephen Vaughan to have special knowledge of the Netherlands. Although prominent enough to be an alderman, he refused election in 1528 and paid a fine of £100. Throughout the Parliament he effectively promoted the City's interests in the Lower House. John Petyt, who was elected to the other common council seat, 'was one of the fyrste that with Mr. Fryth, Bylney, and Tyndale cowght a sweetnes in Godes worde. He was . . . free of the Grocers, eloquent and wel spoken, exactly sene in hystores, songe, and the Laten tongue.' In 1529 he opposed the bill to release the king from repaying forced loans. It is said that Petyt was imprisoned for possessing heretical books which Sir Thomas More found in his house; this is possible, for parliamentary privilege did not extend to immunity from the Crown, but seems unlikely. In any case Petyt died before January 1533, when his will was proved in the Prerogative Court of Canterbury. Some orthodox priests are reported to have poured 'sope ashes' on his burial plot to show that God would not suffer grass to grow upon the grave of such a heretic.[3]

---

[1] Seymour was in bad health during the later years of the Parliament and probably ceased to attend in 1534, but he was evidently not replaced. Miller, 'London and Parliament in the Reign of Henry VIII', 144-5; H.P.T. biography; R. W. Chambers, *Thomas More*, 147-51.

[2] H.P.T. biography. The returns also list a John Baker as burgess for Bedford; it may be that the recorder was elected by two constituencies but preferred to sit for London.

[3] This account of Petyt's career is drawn from the reminiscences of John Louthe, archdeacon of Nottingham, sent to the martyrologist John Foxe in 1579 and printed in J. G. Nichols, ed., *Narratives of the Days of the Reformation*, 25-8. See also the note in *ibid.* 295-99, and Leland Miles, 'Persecution and the *Dialogue of*

Petyt's seat was filled by William Bowyer, a wealthy draper. But Bowyer was named an alderman in 1534, thus forfeiting his right to represent the commonalty.[1] Another by-election, held on 27 October 1533 returned Robert Pakington, 'a man of good substaunce, and yet not so riche as honest and wise'.[2] Pakington, who had been born in Worcestershire, migrated early to London, where he prospered as a mercer and exporter of cloth. Thomas Cromwell occasionally consulted him about trade with the Dutch; Stephen Vaughan urged Cromwell to 'cherisshe hym and geve hym thankes', for 'the Kyng hathe no truer subject ne honester man of a marchant in his realme'.[3] Edward Hall called Pakington 'a man of great courage and one that could speak and also woulde be h[e]arde', adding that while in Parliament he 'talked somewhat against the covetousness and crueltie of the clergie'. But he was a religious man. He used daily, Hall wrote, 'at foure of the clock winter and sommer to rise and go to masse at a churche then called Saint Thomas of Acres'. On 13 November 1536, 'a great mistie morning such as hath seldome be[en] sene', he was 'sodenly murdered with a gonne' while on his way to church. Although a number of labourers standing at the end of Soper's Lane had seen him leave his house and heard the clap of the gun, 'the dede doer was never espied or knowen'. Hall suspected that Pakington had been murdered by the clergy, as Hunne had been twenty-two years earlier. John Foxe claimed that the Dean of St Paul's, Dr Incent, confessed on his death-bed that he had hired an Italian to perform the murder for sixty crowns. While Foxe may not be reliable, it is clear that Pakington was one of the more Protestant parliamentarians and a thorn in clerical flesh. His funeral sermon was preached by the great reformer Robert Barnes.[4]

Comfort: A Fresh Look at the Charges Against Thomas More', *Journal of British Studies*, v (1965), 21.

[1] A. F. Pollard, 'Thomas Cromwell's Parliamentary Lists', 38; *Return of Members of Parliament*, Part I, App., xxix.   [2] Edward Hall, *Hall's Chronicle*, 824.

[3] SP 1/90, fol. 212, P.R.O. (*L.P.*, VIII, 303; IX, 346.)

[4] Edward Hall, *Hall's Chronicle*, 824; Nichols, *Days of the Reformation*, 296–7; H.P.T. biography. Holinshed and Stow have it that a man hanged at Banbury for felony confessed to murdering Pakington: John Stow, *The Survey of London* (Everyman ed.), 234. Pakington's brother Augustine was hired by Tunstall while bishop of London to buy up at Antwerp all the unsold copies of Tyndale's New Testament, so that they could be burned; Augustine probably realized that the transaction would give Tyndale the money he needed for publication of a new and better edition. Edward Hall, *Hall's Chronicle*, 762–3.

York, the second city in the realm, offers us the strange case of the displaced recorder. Like London, York could usually be counted on to return two of its leading citizens to Parliament.[1] Elections were made by the mayor, aldermen, sheriffs, and council of twenty-four; on 27 September 1529 'the said persons by vertue of the King's writt in the same county [did] elect and [choose] the right worshipfull Richard Page, esquyer, recorder of the said city, and George Lawson, esquyer and oone of the aldermen of the same city, for to be citizens of the King's High Court of Parlement'.[2]

Page's situation was curious. Although he had been recorder of York since at least 1527, he was neither resident nor learned in the law. Instead, he had been a servant of Wolsey and remained one of the knights of the king's chamber, sufficiently favoured to receive several grants of land formerly held by the cardinal. He was not popular in York and was finally persuaded to resign as recorder in 1533, since he had not been able to attend to the city's legal affairs. It is doubtful that he sat in Parliament at all; the civic records contain no reference to his replacement, but by 1531 they speak of Master Lawson and Master Jackson as citizens of the Parliament.[3] Lawson and Jackson are also named in the parliamentary list, probably made in 1529, which is printed in the official return. Although Henry VIII is not likely to have insisted on Page's election in 1529, he or Wolsey may have helped secure the appointment as recorder from which it sprang.

The other members for York were of the normal type. George Lawson was already a leading burgess. In 1530 he served as mayor and was knighted; he had been connected with the central government as treasurer of Berwick and a member of the duke of Richmond's council.[4] Peter Jackson, who replaced Page, was a former sheriff and mayor. He died in 1532 and was succeeded by another alderman, George Gayle.[5] Gayle was especially active in pressing for the passage of legislation favouring York, which was experiencing bad times economically. Trouble with fish-

[1] Twenty-four of the twenty-eight M.P.s for York, 1509–1603, were aldermen: A. G. Dickens, 'Tudor York', in *Victoria County History, The City of York*, 139.

[2] Raine, *York Civic Records*, III, 119.

[3] *Ibid.* 151, 153, 135; *L.P.*, IV, 6516 (7), 6748 (5). Page was also controller of customs in the port of London and surveyor of kerseys at London and Southampton: *ibid.* III, 2106; IV, 4124 (17).

[4] Dickens, 'Tudor York', 117.   [5] Raine, *York Civic Records*, 76, 135, 146.

garths in the Humber and Ouse was alleviated by an act of 1532, while novel tolls exacted by Hull, the port through which flowed most of York's foreign trade, were regulated in 1536. The city's longest dispute was with the earl of Rutland, who claimed that the city was obligated to pay him £100 a year. This, too, was resolved in 1536.[1]

The cities of Norwich and Bristol followed York in size and were enjoying somewhat greater prosperity. Both returned local men to Parliament. Edward Rede and Reginald Lytilprow were aldermen of Norwich: Rede had served the first of three terms as mayor in 1521, while Lytilprow was to be named mayor in 1532. The two men were among the most outspoken supporters of the Reformation. Rede, who had several disputes with the Norwich cathedral chapter, seems to have been strongly anti-clerical and to have sympathized with Bilney, who was martyred during Rede's mayoralty in 1531.[2] Lytilprow, a mercer, had known Thomas Cromwell for years and continued to write him detailed, sycophantic letters about affairs in Norwich throughout the life of the Parliament.[3] The representatives of Bristol were less prominent. Richard Abingdon, a haberdasher, became mayor in the last years of the Parliament, while the obscure Thomas Jubbes was the borough's recorder.[4]

The seven coastal towns which clung to the outdated title Cinque Ports were also amazingly consistent in choosing local men. Their representatives in Parliament were sometimes called 'barons', although they were not peers. Virtually all the men chosen were jurats (the local equivalent of aldermen) and former or future mayors. They were commonly merchants, shipowners, importers, or fishermen.[5] The exception was Richard Gibson,

[1] 23 Henry VIII, c. 18; 27 Henry VIII, c. 3 and c. 32. The compromise agreement reduced York's payment to £40. For instructions to the burgesses for York see Raine, *York Civic Records, passim*.

[2] *L.P.*, IV, i, 655; V, 372, 522, 560, 569; H.P.T. biography.

[3] *L.P.*, V, 913, 1526, 1641; VI, 284, 441; VII, 779, 796; IX, 308; X, 97, 595; Addenda, I, i, 602; H.P.T. biography. A. F. Pollard suggested that Lytilprow's marriage to a Blount from Shropshire resulted from an acquaintance made during the Parliament: 'The Reformation Parliament as a Matrimonial Agency and Its National Effects', 225.

[4] E. W. W. Veale, ed., *The Great Red Book of Bristol*, Part IV, 9, 117; D. Hollis, ed., *Calendar of the Bristol Apprentice Book, 1532–1565*, Part I, 83 and *passim* (for apprentices to Abingdon); *L.P.*, VI, 433 (iv).

[5] Members of this type included John Boys, Vincent Engeham, and Thomas Wingfield of Sandwich; John Bunting of Romney; Richard Calveley, Thomas

who represented Romney although a citizen and merchant tailor resident in London. Gibson was an official of the court for over thirty years, charged with providing costumes for masques and canvas for tents. His greatest accomplishment was the sumptuous tent-city at the Field of Cloth of Gold. But even Gibson had some association with his borough. He had been a jurat of Romney since 1524 and was perhaps named to Parliament so that he could effectively present the town's private bill for inhabitants of Romney marsh.[1]

Since it has been suggested that only a handful of 'men of trade' sat in Tudor Parliaments,[2] a generalization which we know to be true of Elizabeth's reign, the occupations of burgesses are of considerable interest. Most of those who were active borough residents seem to have made their way in commerce. As might be expected, many were engaged in some aspect of the cloth trade. Henry Hamplyn of Exeter, William Stumpe of Malmesbury, John Batenor of Lewes, William Webb of Salisbury, and John Bird and Thomas Whelpley, both of Bath, were mercers; John Bond of Coventry and Nicholas Rand of Northampton were drapers; Robert Hayward of Leicester was a wool merchant; Robert Bowyer of Chichester exported kerseys; Nicholas Dey of Southampton had been a tailor.[3] At least three brewers sat in Parliament, along with a cobbler and a rope-maker.[4]

But the largest occupational contingent in Parliament, if one excludes the country gentlemen, was that of the lawyers. In

Shoyswell, and John Durant of Hastings; Thomas Ensing and George Lowys of Winchelsea; John Fletcher, Nicholas Sutton, and Richard Inglet of Rye; Robert Nethersale and John Warren of Dover. H.P.T. biographies.

[1] The bill passed the Commons in 1534 but was rejected in the Lords, where Cranmer complained that it would reduce tithe payments: *L.J.*, I, 79; Harleian MS. 6148, fol. 43ᵛ, B.M. (*L.P.*, VII, 592); H.P.T. biography. Gibson died in October 1534 and was succeeded by John Marshall, not a local man and perhaps a nominee of Anne Boleyn's brother, Lord Rochford, who was Lord Warden of the Cinque Ports. On the whole, however, the warden seems to have enjoyed very little patronage.

[2] *Ibid.*; MacCaffrey, *Exeter, 1540–1640*, 258; H.P.T. biographies. The *Return* lists Nicholas Rous for Northampton, but A. F. Pollard plausibly suggested that this was an error for Rand: 'The Reformation Parliament as a Matrimonial Agency and Its National Effects', 223. The members for Reading were probably also in the wool trade; see Arthur Aspinall *et al.*, *Parliament through Seven Centuries: Reading and Its M.P.s*, 20, 35–36. [3] Bindoff, 'Parliamentary History, 1529–1688', 112.

[4] John Brydges of Canterbury, John Taylor of Hastings, and William Chard of Bridport; George Hayward of Bridgnorth; Richard Furloke of Bridport. H.P.T. biographies.

all, we know of more than forty burgesses who practised or had studied law, and at least eleven of the knights of the shire were likewise members of an Inn of Court.[1] Some of the parliamentary lawyers, such as John Mawdelyn of Wells, John Mille of Southampton, Anthony Babington of Nottingham, and William Honychurch of Tavistock, were prominent residents of their boroughs. Others were members of local gentry families: Christopher Jenny, a burgess for Dunwich, was the younger son of Sir Edmund Jenny, who had represented the borough under Edward IV and Henry VII.[2] John Guildford, burgess for Gatton, and two young Cornishmen, Richard Bryan of Lostwithiel and James Trevyniarde of Liskeard, probably served in Parliament while studying at one of the Inns.[3]

A number of lawyers had local connections but were in the administrative service of great landowners, who helped arrange their election. Thomas Brokesby, who assisted the Hastings family in its quarrel with the Greys, had the earl of Huntingdon to thank for his position as recorder of Leicester and for his return to the Commons. Sir Edward Bray, a nephew of the great Sir Reginald, lived in Lewes but probably owed his election for that Sussex borough to the duke of Norfolk. The earl of Arundel nominated two of his legal officers, Richard Sackville and Thomas Prestall, to the seats for Arundel; their effectiveness as a parliamentary team may have been limited by their dispute over lands which Prestall's father had leased from Arundel college. William More had the help of Sir Thomas Arundel of Lanherne in his election at Shaftesbury, and William Grimston may have been a client of Sir John Rogers at Wareham. Both, however, were natives of the West Country.[4]

Court connections may have been of use to several legally trained burgesses. Coventry would probably have returned its recorder as a matter of course, but Roger Wigston had served

---

[1] The burgesses are too numerous to list; the knights of the shire are: Lincoln's Inn: Sir Everard Digby, Sir Piers Edgcombe, Sir Roger Townshend, Richard Hawkes; Gray's Inn: Robert Wroth; Middle Temple: Richard Knightley, Sir Nicholas Wadham, Sir George Throckmorton, Sir Thomas Audley, Sir Andrew Windsor; Inner Temple: Thomas Bonham. Roskell calculated that about a fifth of the M.P.s in 1422 were lawyers: 'The Social Composition of the Commons in a Fifteenth-Century Parliament', 165.

[2] Wedgwood, *History of Parliament*, *sub* Sir Edmund Jenny; May McKisack, *The Parliamentary Representation of the English Boroughs during the Middle Ages*, 108.

[3] H.P.T. biographies.   [4] H.P.T. biographies.

the king as a receiver-general and was to be active in the Council for the Marches of Wales. Humphrey Wingfield, the first burgess to become Speaker of the Commons, had been in Wolsey's employ and was a member of the king's learned counsel; he could have been elected at Yarmouth, however, on the strength of his position in Norfolk alone. Two Londoners probably were under the patronage of relatives who held Exchequer offices: both Robert Southwell, who sat for Lynn, and Jasper Fyllol, elected at Dorchester, were later prominent assistants of Thomas Cromwell in the dissolution of the monasteries.[1]

The numerous Wiltshire boroughs offered unparalleled opportunities for what Pollard happily termed 'legal carpet baggers'. In 1529 these parliamentary migrants included John Baldwin, a future chief justice and the father-in-law of Robert Pakington, the murdered mercer of London; John Hynd, the builder of Madingley Hall, who missed election at Cambridge although he had been recorder there; Nicholas Hare, a future judge and Speaker of the Commons; William Horwood, later solicitor-general; Edmund Knightley, member of a great Northampton-shire family, who earlier sat for Reading; Robert Coursone, in time to be a baron of the Exchequer; and Thomas Polstead, a brother of Cromwell's receiver-general, who was by-elected in 1533.[2] Their parliamentary seats proved good stepping-stones to future prominence.

Several of the Wiltshire boroughs belonged to the bishop of Winchester, who would normally have been able to name his officers and retainers as burgesses. In 1529, however, Wolsey had just surrendered the bishopric. The resulting power vacuum was filled by the Crown, by local interests, or simply by the aspiring lawyers themselves. Wolsey had also controlled the

---

[1] *D.N.B. sub* Wingfield; *L.P.*, IX, 283–4, 523, 846; X, 213; H.P.T. biographies. Fyllol's father was a lawyer living in Dorset, which he regularly represented in Parliament during the fifteenth century (Wedgwood, *History of Parliament, sub* Fillol).

[2] A. F. Pollard, 'Thomas Cromwell's Parliamentary Lists', 40; Bindoff, 'Parliamentary History, 1529–1688', 112, 117; Aspinall, *Parliament Through Seven Centuries*, 34; *D.N.B. sub* Baldwin, Hynd, Hare, Knightley. The boroughs in question were Hindon, Downton, Wilton, Bedwin, and Cricklade. It may be noted that Hare, like Bromley, remained a religious conservative and was favoured by Mary. He had three sisters who married Reformation Parliament burgesses for Cambridge, Hindon, and Windsor: A. F. Pollard, 'The Reformation Parliament as a Matrimonial Agency and Its National Effects', 225.

borough of Taunton in Somerset, for which the rising Thomas Cromwell gained his seat. Cromwell's election is of unusual interest, and we are fortunate in knowing a good deal about it. Ralph Sadler, Cromwell's clerk, first approached the duke of Norfolk to see if the king wished Cromwell to enter Parliament— as a former servant of Wolsey, Cromwell was eager to forge a new attachment at court—and was told 'that his highnes was veray well contented ye should be a burges, so that ye wolde order yourself in the saide rowme according to such instructions as the saide Duke of Norffolk shall gyve you from the king'. But Cromwell did not ask Norfolk to provide his seat. Instead he had Sadler see whether his friend Thomas Rush could make available one of the seats for Orford, Suffolk, an area which Cromwell knew well through his work for Wolsey's college at Ipswich. No doubt Rush would have been happy to oblige, but it was too late. Sadler did not speak to him until after 1 November, by which time Orford had named Erasmus Paston, a member of the great letter-writing family, and Richard Hunt. Cromwell then fell back upon a second line of attack and had Sadler ask Sir William Paulet, who controlled the lands of Winchester during the vacancy of the see, 'to name [him] to be one of the burgesses for one of my lordes townes of his busshopriche of Wynchester'. Here Cromwell was successful, perhaps with the further help of the other burgess for Taunton, William Portman, a local man who was later to become chief justice. Cromwell's name was slipped in, possibly by being inserted in a blank return which Paulet held, one day before the Parliament met.[1] It is intriguing to speculate how different Cromwell's career, or for

---

[1] Sadler to Cromwell, 1 November [1529], Cottonian MS. Cleopatra E. iv, fol. 178, B.M. (*L.P.*, iv, App., 238), printed in R.B. Merriman, *Life and Letters of Thomas Cromwell*, I, 67–8; Elton, *The Tudor Revolution in Government*, 77–80. As Elton noted, both Merriman and *L.P.* err in reading Oxford for Orford. Cromwell's efforts to enter Parliament must have been common knowledge in Wolsey's household; George Cavendish says, erroneously, that Cromwell took the place of a son of Sir Thomas Rush, 'a special friend of his': *The Life and Death of Cardinal Wolsey*, in *Two Early Tudor Lives*, ed. Richard S. Sylvester and Davis P. Harding, 115. The availability of the seats at Taunton, Downton, and Hindon to Crown nominees is attested to by a list of government officials to be elected in 1536. The names, written on a slip of paper, are attached to Catherine of Aragon's will, Cottonian MS. Otho C. x., fol. 216, B.M. (*L.P.*, x, 40 [ii]). There is no evidence to support the view of A. J. Slavin, in *Politics and Profit: A Study of Sir Ralph Sadler, 1507–1547*, 20–2, that Cromwell tried to buy seats from Norfolk and Rush. It was a matter of connection and influence, not money.

that matter the course of the Parliament itself, might have been had he failed.

The Parliament might not have been greatly changed without Edward Hall, but our knowledge of it would be substantially reduced had the chronicler not found a seat. Hall had been born in London; he was probably the best educated parliamentarian, having attended Eton and King's College, Cambridge, as well as Gray's Inn. He felt particular hostility to Wolsey and favoured such Protestants as Bilney and Tyndale. He later supported the divorce and Henry's policies generally. How he came to be elected a burgess for Wenlock remains a mystery, since he is not known to have had lands or a patron in Shropshire.[1]

Hall was not the only member who had attended a university, but the number was quite small. Nicholas Hare and John Hynd had spent some time at Cambridge before proceeding to the Inns of Court, while Richard Tracy and Geoffrey Lee held degrees from Oxford. Tracy's father was a Wiltshire justice of the peace who had adopted Lutheran views; his Protestant will became famous and was declared heretical by Convocation in 1532.[2] Lee's brother Edward succeeded Wolsey as archbishop of York. The family was on intimate terms with Sir Thomas More and with the Poles, who probably arranged Lee's election at Portsmouth.[3] Although a few other members may have received university training, the size of the Oxford and Cambridge group remains minuscule, especially when compared to the large university coterie in Elizabeth's later Parliaments.[4] The universities, of course, changed their outlook considerably during the century. Before the Reformation they were concerned mainly with educating churchmen, and it is not surprising that our parliamentarians found training at the Inns of Court more useful.

While it is not easy to place the Commons of 1529 in political groups, it is interesting to note the large circle centred around Sir Thomas More. More himself could not sit in the Lower House, since as chancellor he presided over the Lords, but four sons-in-law, a brother-in-law, and several other associates did

[1] *D.N.B.*; H.P.T. biography.
[2] Clebsch, *England's Earliest Protestants*, 107-8, 245; *D.N.B.* Tracy sat for Wotton Basset, Wilts.   [3] H.P.T. biography.
[4] Neale calculated that there were about 150 university men in the Parliaments of 1584 and 1593: *Elizabethan House of Commons*, 302-3.

find seats. Sir Giles Alington, one of the knights for Cambridge-shire, was the husband of More's foster daughter Alice Middleton. It was in Alington's private chapel at Willesden that More's two younger daughters were married, Elizabeth to William Dauntsey, whose father was one of the knights for Oxfordshire, and Cecily to Giles Heron, son of the late treasurer of the chamber and a ward of More's. In 1529 William Dauntsey and Heron were the burgesses for Thetford, Norfolk: a curious business, since Thetford returned members to no other Parliament during Henry's reign. The borough belonged to the duchy of Lancaster, of which More was chancellor, so he was presumably responsible for the return of his young sons-in-law.[1] Just why the borough was thus temporarily enfranchised is unclear. More may have wished to provide experience for his protégés, or the duke of Norfolk may have suggested that their presence could prove useful.

Norfolk may have had something to do with the Thetford election, for he had influence in the area. It is nearly certain that he was responsible for the election at Bramber, Sussex, of William Roper, More's future biographer and husband of his beloved daughter Margaret. The second member for Bramber, Henry See, shared chambers with Roper at Lincoln's Inn and was evidently an intimate of More's household at Chelsea, since a list of parliamentarians prepared by Cromwell in 1533 refers to him, along with Roper and Dauntsey, as 'of Chelchythe'.[2] John Latton, a burgess for Oxford, is also described as of Chelsea. He may have been a member of More's circle; we know only that Cromwell asked for his re-election in 1536.[3] John Rastell, More's brother-in-law, probably owed his election at Dunheved to that Cornish leader Sir Richard Grenville.[4] A man of many talents, Rastell had helped garnish the roofs of the banqueting hall at the Field of Cloth of Gold, had devised pageants for the

---

[1] Chambers, *Thomas More*, 109, 183; A. F. Pollard, 'Thomas Cromwell's Parliamentary Lists,' 37. When More became lord chancellor on 26 October 1529 he resigned the chancellorship of the duchy and was succeeded by Sir Thomas Audley, but the elections should have been held earlier.

[2] SP 1/99, fol. 234, P.R.O. (*L.P.*, IX, 1077), printed by A. F. Pollard, 'Thomas Cromwell's Parliamentary Lists', 31–43. See was active in the city of York's dispute with Rutland; his death during the plague of 1537 cut short an unusually promising legal career. H.P.T. biography. [3] *L.P.*, X, 903.

[4] Rowse, *Tudor Cornwall*, 228. Dunheved was a borough of the duchy of Cornwall, so there may have been Crown influence also.

City and the court, and had been an early advocate of English colonization. He was most active as a lawyer and printer.[1]

Several other burgesses may be reckoned as peripheral members of More's group. Edward Madyson, burgess for Hull, married William Roper's sister, whom he probably met during the Parliament.[2] Robert Fisher sat for Rochester, where his brother John was bishop. More had long enjoyed a cordial relationship with Bishop Fisher, whom he was to join in tragic death before the dissolution of Parliament, and he probably knew Robert at Lincoln's Inn.[3] Geoffrey Lee's ties have already been noted, but it may be added that in 1504 More had dedicated his life of Pico della Mirandola to Lee's sister Joyce, a nun at Aldgate.[4] There is, finally, Geoffrey Pole, who sat for Wilton. We know that More relished the scholarly company of Geoffrey's brother Reginald, the future Marian archbishop, and used to show him examples of his daughter Margaret's fine Latin prose.[5]

An even larger circle of parliamentarians was associated with the duke of Norfolk. Norfolk acted as the king's chief adviser during the interval between the fall of Cardinal Wolsey and the rise of Thomas Cromwell, and he enjoyed the greatest share of parliamentary patronage. In a memorandum of 1536 Norfolk listed six boroughs in Sussex as being under his control—Horsham, Shoreham, Steyning, Lewes, Reigate, and Gatton, 'where Sir Roger Copley dwelleth'—and he noted, less precisely, his influence in the counties of Norfolk and Suffolk.[6] In 1529 most of the burgesses for these towns were the duke's servants or clients. Another servant, George Gyfford, was elected at Midhurst.[7] The powerful Boleyn group had blood ties with Norfolk as well as a common interest in securing Henry's divorce. Its members included Sir James Boleyn, Anne's uncle and a knight

---

[1] Chambers, *Thomas More*, 141; *D.N.B.*; H.P.T. biography.
[2] A. F. Pollard, 'The Reformation Parliament as a Matrimonial Agency and Its National Effects', 225.
[3] Chambers, *Thomas More*, 215–16; H.P.T. biography.
[4] S. E. Lehmberg, 'Sir Thomas More's Life of Pico della Mirandola', *Studies in the Renaissance*, III (1956), 70.
[5] Chambers, *Thomas More*, 182.
[6] Cottonian MS. Caligula B. VI, fol. 373, B.M. (*L.P.*, x, 816). Norfolk, curiously, was not certain that Reigate returned burgesses to Parliament. Reigate and Gatton are actually in Surrey, not Sussex.
[7] The second member for Midhurst, John Bassett, was a servant of the earl of Arundel, as was one of the burgesses for Portsmouth, Francis Dingeley. H.P.T. biographies.

of the shire for Norfolk, as well as two leaders of the Lords: her father, the earl of Wiltshire, and her brother, Viscount Rochford.

The More and Norfolk circles illustrate the sort of connections which can be traced in Parliament. It would not be difficult to find others;[1] one must remember what a small society the upper classes formed in the early sixteenth century and how thoroughly its members were intermeshed through friendships and marriages. But these groups also show us the danger of supposing that men's opinions were necessarily shaped by their connections alone. It would be easy, for instance, to suppose that the More–Fisher–Pole circle formed a solid phalanx opposing religious reform. In fact Roper had undergone a severely Lutheran phase, while Rastell held to Protestant views even at the time of More's death.[2] In 1529 the political situation was still fluid. Men like More and Norfolk were still working in harmony. Nothing could be more misleading than an attempt to determine the views of the Commons at the opening of Parliament on the basis of their later affiliations and actions.

4

Members of the Commons were entitled to pay during sessions and while travelling to and from London. Burgesses could claim two shillings a day, knights of the shire twice that sum.[3] Normally these payments imposed little strain on any save the smallest borough, but the unprecedented length of the Reformation Parliament meant equally unprecedented bills running to as much as £70 for each burgess. Professor Pollard once calculated that the total cost of the Parliament to the counties and

[1] For instance, the burgesses for Southwark—Sir John Sylsterne or Shilston and Robert Acton—were protégés of Charles Brandon, duke of Suffolk, whose family had long controlled the borough. Shilston had married Brandon's sister Anne: A. F. Pollard, 'The Reformation Parliament as a Matrimonial Agency and Its National Effects', 222–3.

[2] Chambers, *Thomas More*, 186–7, on Roper; H.P.T. biography of Rastell. Rastell was also anti-clerical, opposing the collection of tithes from the London poor (*L.P.*, x, 247).

[3] These rates had applied since the fourteenth century: A. F. Pollard, *The Evolution of Parliament*, 2nd ed., 406. York was probably unique in paying its members £10 between them when they set out for London, but it expected them to be accompanied by liveried servants 'for the honour and worship of the city'. Raine, *York Civic Records*, iii, 174; iv, vi.

boroughs approached £30,000, nearly a third of what they would have paid if a subsidy had been levied.[1] Many towns groaned under the burden; their officers would have agreed with Sir Thomas Smith when he said, 'What can a commonwealth desire more than peace, liberty, quietness, [and] few Parliaments?'[2]

There is little evidence relating to the payment of knights of the shire, but what there is suggests that they had a hard time collecting their pay. Perhaps most of them did not even try, thinking that they were well enough off to get by on their own. But it proved an expensive business. Sir Richard Grenville calculated that his attendance at Parliament cost him five hundred marks—more than £333—for five years.[3] Sir Richard Cornwall asked Cromwell's help in collecting his expenses, for he feared that the sheriff of Herefordshire would leave office without paying,[4] and after Cornwall died his wife and executors had to sue for payment of £30 16s. 'for parcelle of his wages'.[5] Robert Faryngton, whose father was a knight of Lancashire, also appealed to Cromwell: he had been studying at Cambridge but could not proceed to his doctorate because his father, who had been sending him money, had not been paid by the county and was impoverished.[6] The cost of maintaining two households over a long period of time could ruin even a wealthy man.

Many boroughs experienced difficulty in meeting the bills of their burgesses, especially after the earlier sessions had depleted their treasuries. Dover, for instance, was unable to pay John Warren in 1533 and could give Robert Nethersale only 40s. for sixty-three days. In 1535 the town paid off its old debts but allowed Warren only 10s. 6d. of the £3 2s. due him for the 1534 session.[7] In 1535 Sandwich still owed a considerable sum to the heirs of John Boys, who had died in 1533; they finally accepted a compromise payment of £10. Bridport, also unable to pay in 1535, gave William Chard 20s. and the right to hold a bridge-

---

[1] A. F. Pollard, 'An Early Parliamentary Election Petition', *B.I.H.R.*, VIII (1930–1931), 157.

[2] John Strype, *The Life of Sir Thomas Smith*, 192. The Parliament met about 484 days in all.

[3] H.P.T. biography.

[4] SP 1/55, fol. 167, P.R.O. (*L.P.*, IV, iii, 5962). *L.P.* places this at 28 September 1529, but the year is uncertain and is likely to be later.

[5] C 1/752/66, P.R.O. He died on 2 September 1533: *L.P.*, VII, 56n.

[6] SP 1/84, fols. 224–5, P.R.O. (*L.P.*, VII, 852).

[7] Egerton MSS. 2092–2093, *passim*, B.M., cited in H.P.T. biography.

house rent free for six years.[1] Even a prosperous city like Salisbury had trouble. In 1534 it escaped the payment of about £30 to Thomas Chaffyn by exempting him from the expense of being mayor, and in 1535 it had to spread the payment of £43 8s. to William Webb over three years. Webb, evidently sympathizing with the borough's plight, finally remitted the odd £3 8s.[2] One of the members for Lincoln, 'out of his zeal and love to the city', accepted £7 instead of the £11 3s. 4d. due to him in 1535. The city had already been faced with two bills of £45 4d. each, and the Parliament had another session to run.[3]

Fortunately for the boroughs, few members attended Parliament with absolute regularity. Romney had to pay John Bunting only £31 for the seven sessions. Rye's bill from John Fletcher was higher—nearly £48—but his fellow member Nicholas Sutton fell ill in 1532 and had to be paid for only fifteen days instead of the full 109. In all Sutton and his successor, Richard Inglet, received just over £30 in wages.[4] Canterbury was so pleased when John Brydges cut short his attendance in 1533 that it gave him 7s. for a new bonnet. Brydges also played the truant in 1534, gaining another bonnet worth 7s. 6d. 'for saving the wages that he should have had if he had ridden up'.[5] An act of 1515 had attempted to guard against premature departure of members by ordering that those who left without the licence of the Commons and Speaker should forfeit their wages, but this seems to have been ignored by the boroughs which might have profited from it.[6]

Other boroughs reduced their charges in other ways. Cambridge may have given its members only half the usual wage, for one of the borough records mentions a disbursement to Thomas Bracken and Robert Chapman 'after the rate of 12d. a day'.[7] Wycombe probably did not pay its members at all; we know that the burgesses named to Henry's first Parliament agreed not to claim their stipends, and their successors may well have had to

[1] H.P.T. biographies.
[2] Neale, *Elizabethan House of Commons*, 155; Bindoff, 'Parliamentary History, 1529–1688', 113–14.
[3] Neale, *Elizabethan House of Commons*, 155.
[4] H.P.T. biographies, based on Rye chamberlains' accounts, vol. III.
[5] Neale, *Elizabethan House of Commons*, 155; H.P.T. biography.
[5] 6 Henry VIII, c. 16.
[7] C. H. Cooper, *Annals of Cambridge*, I, 386.

make similar promises.[1] A number of other boroughs, particularly those which returned the legal carpet-baggers and other out-siders, likely avoided paying expenses. Professor Bindoff has suggested that economy may have helped dictate the election of so many recorders, who were often resident in London during the legal terms and might not expect additional pay.[2]

Two disputes over the election of members sprang from wage claims. Soon after the dissolution of Parliament the borough of Newcastle-under-Lyme, Staffordshire, filed a complaint in Chancery against John Pearsall, who had presented a £66 bill for service in the Commons. The borough alleged that it had duly elected its mayor, Richard Robinson, but when Robinson tried to take his seat he found that the sheriff had returned Pearsall's name in place of his. Pearsall's answer and the further replication and rejoinder throw little additional light on the case: Pearsall asserted that he had been properly elected, but he did admit that he failed to have his name entered in the appropriate book when he was absent from part of a session. Nor do we know the outcome. Still, the borough's intent to avoid payment of Pear-sall's wages is clear enough; if it had really objected to having him as burgess it would have complained sooner. The petition also alleges, with little vigour, that Richard Grey was improperly named to the other seat. Grey had died in 1533, leaving his daughter £8 6s. 4d. from his parliamentary wages if she could collect it.[3]

In the dispute at Weymouth both sides agreed on the facts. John Clerk was named to one of the borough's seats, but he was not especially eager to serve and allowed William Bond to take his place. The sheriff had not yet presented the return, so Bond's name was easily inserted. All would have been well had not Bond foolishly promised to serve in the Parliament, no matter how long it might be, for no more than ten days' wages. Little did he know what was in store for him! As one session followed another he grew increasingly irate, and in 1535 he petitioned Sir Thomas Audley, the lord chancellor, for an order granting him £44 in wages. Bond knew that he had no case at common law, and he is

[1] Ashford, *The Borough of High Wycombe*, 95.
[2] Bindoff, 'Parliamentary History, 1529–1688', 114.
[3] C 1/862/11–14, P.R.O.; A. F. Pollard, 'An Early Parliamentary Election Petition', 156–66.

not likely to have obtained relief in the Chancery, but again we cannot be certain of the verdict.[1] The borough must have rejoiced if it escaped without paying him the usual fee.

5

The length and expense of the Parliament, unique among Tudor assemblies, could not have been predicted in 1529. In all other ways the House of Commons appears perfectly normal. It contained great landowners, merchants, mayors, aldermen, recorders, lawyers, courtiers, administrators. Contrary to the allegations of Fisher's biographer, it was more freely elected than the earlier Parliaments directed by Wolsey or the later ones dominated by Cromwell. It reflected the influence of great magnates, but no more than other sixteenth-century Houses. It was well equipped to deal with the business which would come before it. In short, it formed a true microcosm of the classes in Tudor society from which it was drawn and which it represented. He who would indict the Commons must indict the realm as well.

[1] C 1/740/40–1, P.R.O.; A. F. Pollard, 'A Changeling Member of Parliament', *B.I.H.R.*, x (1932–1933), 20–7. Pollard noted that a borough could be fined £100 for failure to provide burgesses, although he knew of no instance in which such a fine was exacted during our period.

3

THE LORDS ASSEMBLED

The Upper House, composed of Lords temporal and spiritual, was superior to the Commons in dignity and antiquity. In framing legislation it was theoretically of equal weight with the king and Commons, since the assent of all three was necessary before a statute could be effective, and in practice its importance during our period was roughly equal to that of the Commons. Indeed the Reformation Parliament may be regarded as representing a balance between the Lords and Commons seldom achieved in English history. The House of Lords—that term was not in use prior to 1544, but the anachronism does little harm[1]—had earlier been the dominant body, and Wolsey's presence had insured that it would remain so until his fall. By the Elizabethan age the Commons had gained the upper hand, although they were not perhaps so eminent as they appear: Sir John Neale's concentration on the Elizabethan House of Commons has left the Lords sadly unchronicled and seriously underestimated. The power of the Commons increased in 1529 for obvious reasons: its members best gave voice to the anti-clericalism which proved useful to Henry, and after the rise of Thomas Cromwell the Lower House provided the natural forum for his intense parliamentary activity. But important bills continued to originate with the Lords, and the measures proposed by the Commons were very frequently modified in the Upper House. We can avoid serious distortion only by giving equal attention to the two chambers.[2]

I

The membership of the House of Lords during the Reformation

---

[1] Cf. Elton, *The Tudor Constitution*, 241n.

[2] There are understandable differences of opinion about a matter so little susceptible of quantification and proof as the relative importance of the Commons and Lords. Elton argues that the Commons enjoyed a period of primacy, although short and spurious, during the decade beginning in 1529; J. S. Roskell doubts that the medieval traditions of the Commons were substantially extended under the Tudors. See Roskell, 'Perspectives in English Parliamentary History', *Bulletin of the John Rylands Library*, XLVI (1964), 458, 475.

Parliament totalled 107. Of these, fifty were Lords spiritual and fifty-seven Lords temporal: the clerics formed a minority, but a substantial one. The following table sets out the size of the different groups.[1]

Composition of the Lords, 1529–1536

I. Lords spiritual	
1. Archbishops, bishops, and custodians of spiritualities	21
2. Abbots and priors	29
Total	50
II. Lords temporal	
1. Dukes	3
2. Marquises	2
3. Earls	13
4. Viscounts	1
5. Barons	38
Total	57
Total	107

The number of clergymen summoned to Parliament had remained practically constant for centuries, while the number of lay Lords fluctuated. The archbishops and bishops, since they

---

[1] These figures are drawn from three sources: the list of Lords summoned to Parliament in 1529, C 54/398, P.R.O., printed in Sir William Dugdale, *A Perfect Copy of all Summons of the Nobility to the Great Councils and Parliaments of this Realm*, 494–5, and in Thomas Rymer, *Foedera*, 2nd ed., XIV, 302–6; the list of Lords who paid the fee for entry into Parliament, printed in Dugdale, *A Perfect Copy of all Summons*, 497; and the lists of attendance in *L.J.*, I, 58–83, for the session beginning 15 January 1534. This is the only session for which the *L.J.* survives, although there is a copy of a fragment from the 1536 session, Harleian MS. 158, fols. 143–4, B.M. The prior of St John of Jerusalem, a layman, is reckoned as a temporal baron. Not all of these peers were eligible to sit at any one time; in 1529 the House consisted of 49 Lords spiritual and 51 Lords temporal, while in 1534 the numbers were 50 and 55 respectively. Temporal peers have been reckoned under the highest title which they held during the Parliament. Thus (for instance) Thomas Boleyn, summoned as Viscount Rochford but created earl of Wiltshire later in 1529, is counted as an earl. Detailed lists of the members in each category are given below, as each group is discussed. The table counts titles, not holders of titles. There were thus more than 107 individuals involved in the Parliament, since a number of peers died during its course and were followed by their heirs or (in the case of bishops and abbots) by new appointees.

were more concerned with temporal matters, tended to play a more important role than the abbots and priors even though there were fewer of them. Normally the two archbishops, fifteen English bishops, and four holders of Welsh bishoprics could expect to be summoned regularly.[1] Henry did not call the non-resident bishop of Worcester, Jerome de' Ghinucci, summoning instead a custodian of the spiritualities for that diocese. Another Italian, Cardinal Campeggio, evidently received a summons as bishop of Salisbury, but by 1535 both he and Ghinucci had been deprived in favour of the reformers Nicholas Shaxton and Hugh Latimer.[2] Rather surprisingly, George de Athequa, Catherine of Aragon's Spanish confessor who had been provided to the bishopric of Llandaff, is known to have been present on a few days in 1534. He cannot have taken an active part in Parliament, however, since he spoke no English.[3]

The natural leaders of the Lords spiritual were the archbishops of Canterbury. In practice their power was somewhat in eclipse until 1532, when William Warham died, for Warham was old and had doubts about Henry's divorce. His successor, Thomas Cranmer, effectively used the influence of his office in support of the king's policies. In the spring of 1534, when we can check on attendances in the only surviving Lords' Journal of this period, Cranmer was present for forty-one of the forty-six days. He doubtless helped secure the passage of Henry's ecclesiastical legislation in the Upper House.

The archbishops of York were much less active. When Parliament first met, the northern archbishopric was still in Wolsey's hands. Edward Lee, his successor, was a conservative but eager to avoid displeasing the king; he took little part in politics and never attended in 1534.[4] Wolsey was also bishop of Winchester, where he was followed by Stephen Gardiner, like Lee a conservative of great learning. Gardiner had been tutor to the duke of

---

[1] Archbishops of Canterbury and York; bishops of London, Winchester, Rochester, Norwich, Chichester, Exeter, Lincoln, Bath and Wells, Carlisle, Salisbury, Ely, Coventry and Lichfield, Hereford; Welsh bishops of Llandaff, St Asaph, Bangor, and St David's; custodians of spiritualities for Durham and Worcester.

[2] Campeggio, who had been one of the judges in the divorce trial at Blackfriars, did not leave England until 26 October (*L.P.*, IV, iii, 6050); he is included in the list of peers in 1534, although he never attended. This list, in *L.J.*, omits the bishops of Worcester and Hereford.

[3] *L.J.* for 1534; J. D. Mackie, *The Earlier Tudors*, 350.

[4] *D.N.B.*; Lacey Baldwin Smith, *Tudor Prelates and Politics, 1536–1558*, 305.

Norfolk's son and secretary to Wolsey; he probably played an important role in the earlier sessions of Parliament, for he was secretary to the king until 1534 and came to the Lords regularly that spring, but he later fell out with Cranmer and Cromwell. As the Parliament closed he found himself virtually powerless, if only temporarily so.

Prior to Wolsey's translation to Winchester in February 1529, the cardinal had held the bishopric of Durham *in commendam* with the archbishopric of York. Durham was left vacant for a year—it was asked to send a custodian of the spiritualities to Parliament in 1529—but it finally provided a convenient see for Cuthbert Tunstall, former bishop of London, whose orthodox views made his position in the capital uncomfortable. He obviously wished to have little to do with Parliament. John Stokesley, Tunstall's successor at London, actively supported the break with Rome and was probably one of the leaders of the Lords. Described by Hall as 'a man of great wytte and learnyng',[1] Stokesley attended Parliament with reasonable regularity. The great John Fisher of Rochester was a more awkward conservative than Tunstall: he could not be disposed of by translation to a distant see and ultimately became the only prelate to be executed during the life of the Parliament. In 1529 he was active in the defence of ecclesiastical privilege, but by 1534 he had been jailed for refusing the succession oath. The more pliable John Hilsey, a Dominican, followed him at Rochester and may have helped the government during the Parliament's last session.

Of the remaining bishops much the most active was John Clerk of Bath and Wells. Frequently sent on diplomatic missions to the Continent, he had been one of the agents in Wolsey's unsuccessful bid for the papacy. He generally supported Catherine of Aragon but attended the Lords assiduously, at least in 1534. John Longland, bishop of Lincoln, was present occasionally during the documented session, but the other English prelates never attended. Most of them—Veysey of Exeter, Sherburne of Chichester, and Nix of Norwich—were conservatives, and they probably found parliamentary business distasteful. John Kite of Carlisle argued for the king during Catherine's trial but was otherwise little involved in governmental affairs. The diocese of Ely was between bishops during the spring of 1534, for Nicholas

[1] Edward Hall, *Hall's Chronicle*, 783.

West had died in 1533 and lay buried in his beautiful chantry chapel. His successor, the royal chaplain Thomas Goodrich, was not consecrated until April. The aged Geoffrey Blyth, bishop of Coventry and Lichfield since 1503, also died during the life of the Parliament and was succeeded in 1531 by another royal chaplain, Rowland Lee, who spent most of his time in Wales but may have helped support his master's views. The Lords' Journal for 1534 makes no mention of the bishop of Hereford, possibly because the incumbent, Charles Booth, was too ill to attend. He died in 1535 and was followed by yet a third royal favourite, Edward Fox, who probably played a prominent part in the session of 1536. The three Englishmen who held Welsh sees—Richard Rawlins of St David's, Henry Standish of St Asaph, and Thomas Skeffington of Bangor—were even less in evidence than Athequa of Llandaff, but John Salcot or Capon, the Benedictine monk who followed Skeffington in April 1534, had been very active in Parliament as abbot of St Benet's Hulme and doubtless continued to lend his voice for the king. We know that he was present on the opening days of the 1536 session, when the only other bishops to attend were Clerk, Goodrich, and (surprisingly) Tunstall.[1]

The perceptive reader will already have realized how significantly the complexion of the bench of bishops changed during the course of the Parliament. In 1529 the prelates were, almost to a man, conservatives who would acquiesce in the divorce only reluctantly or, as in Fisher's case, not at all. By 1536 many of these orthodox bishops had died or had removed themselves from active intervention in politics, and the standard was carried by such reformers as Cranmer, Goodrich, Fox, Shaxton, and Latimer. In no other parliamentary group is such drastic alteration apparent. The king was of course acting normally in naming new bishops where vacancies occurred, and he could hardly have been expected to choose opponents of his policies. But he was

---

[1] Harleian MS. 158, fols. 143–4, B.M. Most of these bishops are noticed in the *D.N.B.* Dates of nomination, consecration, translation, and death may be found in the *Handbook of British Chronology*, ed. Sir Maurice Powicke and E. B. Fryde, 2nd ed., 209–80. See also Philip Hughes, *The Reformation in England*, 1, 75–8, and, especially for a discussion of the social standing of the bishops, J. J. Scarisbrick, 'The Conservative Episcopate in England, 1529–1535' (unpublished dissertation, Cambridge University), 1–80. Standish had been given his bishopric in 1518, presumably as a reward for his opposition to Kidderminster three years earlier; see above, Ch. 1.

extraordinarily fortunate in having so many positions to fill in such a short time.

2

Heads of the larger monasteries were also routinely summoned to the Lords.[1] Although changes in the list of religious houses represented were made only rarely, Henry VIII had earlier added to Parliament the abbots of Tewkesbury and Tavistock, and in 1534 he called the abbot of Burton-on-Trent also.[2] The surviving Lords' Journal for 1534 shows that a surprisingly large number of abbots took part in the work of the House: thirteen monastic clergy attended on fifteen days or more, as opposed to only four of the secular prelates.[3] The most assiduous were the abbots of Winchcombe, Waltham, Hyde, Westminster, St Augustine's Canterbury, St Albans, and Battle, all of whom were present on thirty or more days. The abbots of St Benet's Hulme, Colchester, Bury St Edmund's, Reading, Shrewsbury, and Cirencester attended less often but still with fair regularity. While the special circumstances of 1534 may account for some absences, most of them probably reflect disinclination to be bothered with Parliament. We may therefore regard those who attended regularly in 1534 as leaders of the monastic group in the Parliament, at least during its middle years. Fewer were active at its conclusion. Only four bishops and three abbots attended on the first two days of the 1536 session, for which we have a fragmentary copy of the Journal. Doubtless several more appeared later, but at least thirteen obtained the king's license to be absent.[4]

Little is known of Richard Munslow or Ancelme, the abbot of Winchcombe who attended with such regularity in 1534. Professor Knowles described him as 'a moderate conservative who ended his days as a prebendary of the new cathedral of

[1] During our Parliament these were: abbots of Westminster, St Augustine's Canterbury, St Albans, Bury St Edmunds, Glastonbury, Abingdon, Evesham, Gloucester, Ramsey, St Mary's York, Reading, Battle, Winchcombe, Bardney, Croyland, Shrewsbury, Tewkesbury, Cirencester, Malmesbury, Thorney, Selby, Peterborough, Hyde, St Benet's Hulme, Colchester, Waltham, Tavistock, Burton; prior of Coventry.

[2] William Stubbs, *Seventeen Lectures on the Study of Medieval and Modern History and Kindred Subjects*, 296.

[3] The attendances of Lords spiritual are tabulated below in Appendix A.

[4] Harleian MS. 158, fols. 143–4, B.M.

Gloucester'.[1] His predecessor, the redoubtable Richard Kidderminster who had argued against the limitation of benefit of clergy in 1515, had been the most distinguished English monk of his age; he retired as abbot in 1527 but lived until about 1532 and may have influenced Munslow's activities in the earlier sessions of Parliament.[2] Robert Fuller is, like Munslow, a shadowy figure. He was prior of St Bartholomew's, Smithfield, as well as abbot of Waltham, and this convenient London residence may help account for his faithful attendance upon the Lords.[3]

John Salcot or Capon, abbot of Hyde, was more prominent and can be reckoned as one of the chief supporters of official policy in the Upper House. He had been educated at Cambridge, where he later helped secure acceptance of Henry's divorce, and was translated to Hyde about 1530 from the abbacy of St Benet's Hulme, Norfolk. Early in 1534 he preached a scurrilous sermon vilifying Elizabeth Barton, the nun of Kent; it was probably as a reward for this service to Cromwell and for his loyalty to Anne Boleyn that he was given the bishopric of Bangor. He surrendered the abbey of Hyde in 1538 and was again, perhaps, rewarded for his co-operation by translation to Salisbury, where he remained until his death in 1557.[4] William Repps or Rugge, who followed Salcot at Hulme, was likewise a zealous supporter of the divorce and active in the Lords. The holder of a Cambridge doctorate, he helped codify conservative theology in the Bishops' Book of 1537. Like Salcot he received a bishopric, that of Norwich, but he was unwise enough to alienate most of its temporalities to the king in exchange for the revenues of Hyde, and in 1549 financial embarrassment forced him to resign. He died in the following year and was buried in Norwich cathedral.[5]

Heads of the great houses at Westminster, Canterbury, and St Albans were naturally expected to take part in Parliament. John Islip, abbot of Westminster from 1500 to 1532, is chiefly remembered as the builder of Henry VII's chapel and other embellishments of the Abbey. He was a member of the King's Council

[1] Dom David Knowles, *The Religious Orders in England*, III, 338.
[2] *Ibid.* 53–4, 91–5.   [3] Dugdale, *Monasticon Anglicanum*, VI, i, 58.
[4] *Ibid.* II, 432; Knowles, *Religious Orders in England*, III, 189. Salcot's sermon against the nun is summarized in *L.P.*, VII, 72 (3) and printed by L. E. Whatmore, 'The Sermon against the Holy Maid of Kent and her Adherents', *E.H.R.*, LVIII (1943), 463–75. Knowles speculates that it was 'prefabricated' in Cromwell's office.
[5] *D.N.B.*; Dugdale, *Monasticon Anglicanum*, III, 65.

and a supporter of royal measures; his funeral was the most magnificent ever accorded an abbot of Westminster. William Boston or Benson, his successor, was also a king's man. In 1534 he tried to persuade More not to stick at the oath of supremacy, and in 1540 he surrendered his house without complaint.[1] John Essex or Focke, of St Augustine's Canterbury, was more interested in classics and ancient British history than in politics. He probably supported the government and certainly made no trouble about the suppression of his abbey; he ended his days as a country gentleman at his manor of Sturry.[2] At St Albans Wolsey was followed by Robert Catton, his former prior, who was subservient to Cromwell but incurred the enmity of his monks because he lined the pockets of his friends at the expense of the abbey. He was deposed shortly before the dissolution of the monastery but had sat in the Parliament, and presumably supported the king, until its end.[3]

The abbots of Colchester, Reading, and Glastonbury may have formed the core of monastic opposition to Henry's divorce and ecclesiastical supremacy. Thomas Marshall or Beche, who was translated from St Werburgh's, Chester, to Colchester in 1533, subscribed to the oath of supremacy in 1534, but he clearly sympathized with More and Fisher and opposed the dissolution of the monasteries. When charged with high treason he lacked the courage to make a forthright profession of his convictions; he was nevertheless found guilty and executed in 1539. He cannot have been helped by his reported statement that the avaricious thirst of the king could not be quenched if the Thames ran with gold and silver.[4]

Hugh Cook, abbot of Reading, was inwardly a conservative but given to outward vacillation. In 1533 he had the bravery to affirm that marriage with a dead brother's widow was lawful, if allowed by a papal dispensation, but a few years later one of Cromwell's agents found him 'as conformable a man as any in

---

[1] Knowles, *Religious Orders in England*, III, 96–9; *D.N.B. sub* Islip; Dugdale, *Monasticon Anglicanum*, I, 277–9.

[2] Knowles, *Religious Orders in England*, III, 95.

[3] Elsie Toms, *The Story of St. Albans*, 66–7.

[4] Knowles, *Religious Orders in England*, III, 376–8. Dugdale, *Monasticon Anglicanum*, V, 605, errs in supposing Marshall and Beche to be two different men. Beche's Christian name is sometimes given as John (e.g. in Edward Hall, *Hall's Chronicle*, p. 652). See also Geoffrey Baskerville, *English Monks and the Suppression of the Monasteries*, 178.

thys realm'. Finally his association with the Pole circle brought him into suspicion, and he was hanged, drawn, and quartered after stoutly asserting his belief in papal supremacy.[1] The aged Richard Whiting of Glastonbury is a more attractive figure, for he had 'governed his monastery with great prudence and judgment'. Although he opposed the divorce he made no public stand against it or the king's supremacy, and it is likely that he shied away from Parliament, where he might have to compromise his conscience or run afoul of the government. But in the end he too was charged with treason, apparently on the weak ground that he had concealed the treasures of his abbey from the king's visitors. In 1539 he was hanged on Glastonbury Tor.[2]

Bury St Edmund's, the great Suffolk abbey, had been ruled by John Melford or Reeve since 1514. Although he attended Parliament with some regularity there is no reason to believe that he took a leading part in its work. Baskerville pictures him, perhaps too colourfully, as 'a merry old man, fond of the ladies, fond of his glass, fond of the gardens in his numerous country houses'. He did not long survive the surrender of his abbey but, as Baskerville suggests, he may have died of gout rather than grief.[3] One gets similar if more blurred impressions of the abbots of Cirencester, Shrewsbury, Burton, and Tavistock. They came to Parliament occasionally in 1534 but were of no real importance there.[4]

None of the other mitred abbots attended Parliament during the documented session. They may have come on other occasions, but they were not leaders in the Lords. Probably, as Fuller says of the prior of Coventry, they 'played at in and out', and declined to appear there.[5] Virtually all made no difficulty about surrendering their houses and were rewarded with liberal pensions; the exception is Clement Lichfield or Wych of Evesham, builder of the splendid tower which still stands, who was persuaded to resign in 1539.[6] John Wardeboys or Lawrence, abbot of Ramsey,

---

[1] Knowles, *Religious Orders in England*, III, 378–9, 491; Dugdale, *Monasticon Anglicanum*, IV, 32; Baskerville, *English Monks*, 175–7. Hall rather unfairly calls Cook 'a stubborn monk, and absolutely without learning' (*loc. cit.*).

[2] Dugdale, *Monasticon Anglicanum*, I, 7; Knowles, *Religious Orders in England*, 379–82.

[3] Dugdale, *Monasticon Anglicanum*, III, 115–16; Baskerville, *English Monks*, 189–90.

[4] Dugdale, *Monasticon Anglicanum*, VI, i, 176; III, 515, 35; II, 492; Baskerville, *English Monks*, 252–3 (on Blake of Cirencester).

[5] Quoted in Dugdale, *Monasticon Anglicanum*, III, 184.   [6] *Ibid.* II, 8–9.

not only surrendered his own monastery, but also used his influence to encourage the heads of other houses to submit. The equally co-operative abbots of Peterborough and Tewkesbury, John Borowe or Chambers and John Wick or Wakeman, were rewarded with bishoprics as well as pensions of two hundred pounds a year.[1]

Clerics who did not wish to attend Parliament themselves could still have their views represented, since one of the privileges enjoyed by the Lords but not by the Commons was the right to give proxies. As usual our principal evidence relates to the first session of 1534; it indicates that the abbots availed themselves of this right more than the bishops. Only two bishops sent proxies: Edward Lee of York gave his voice to three of the most active bishops—Stokesley, Gardiner, and Clerk, *conjunctim et divisim*—and Tunstall of Durham was also represented by Clerk. Fourteen abbots and priors sent proxies, although two of these fourteen attended occasionally themselves. The abbots of Hyde and Hulme (Salcot and Repps, both supporters of government policy) held by far the largest number of proxies, six and seven respectively. Other proxy holders were the abbots of St Alban's, Reading, and Waltham; the abbots of Gloucester and Cirencester and the prior of Coventry held proxies but gave their own voices to others, while two lay peers, the earl of Huntingdon and Lord Sandys, also served as deputies for clergymen. William Thornton, abbot of St Mary's, York, evidently sent a blank proxy. Since it was witnessed by Thomas Cromwell it must have been given to one or more of his supporters, most likely to the abbots of Hyde and Hulme.[2] In 1536 three bishops and ten abbots sent their proxies. Three of these were blank, and most of the others were made out to the abbots of Westminster, Waltham, and Bury.[3]

3

Since the Lords temporal composed a majority of the House, they could carry any vote which evoked a sharp division between

---

[1] *Ibid.* I, 363–7; II, 57.
[2] *L.J.*, I, 58. On the use of proxies see Vernon F. Snow, 'Proctorial Representation and Conciliar Management during the Reign of Henry VIII', *Historical Journal*, IX (1966), 1–26, and Miller, 'Attendance in the House of Lords during the Reign of Henry VIII', in *ibid.* X (1967), 325–51.   [3] Harleian MS. 158, fols. 143–4, B.M.

clergy and laymen. Such had not always been the case, for during the fourteenth century the Lords spiritual had occasionally dominated, and as late as the reign of Henry VII there had been forty-nine spiritual to twenty-nine temporal peers.[1] But by 1529 the clergy had begun the decline in relative strength which was to be capped by the disappearance of the abbots and priors as their religious houses were suppressed. As early as 1516 the judges had declared that the presence of the Lords spiritual was not essential.[2] Seventeenth-century theorists might argue the invalidity of acts opposed by all the clerics, but the Tudors had no such doubts.

The Lords spiritual would have retained their majority even in 1529 had not the king created five new temporal peers. It may be that Henry wished to strengthen his hand, and that of the lay element in the House, by granting baronial titles to Andrew Windsor, Thomas Wentworth, Edmund Bray, John Hussey, and Henry Pole; on the other hand, all were long-time servants of the king, and he doubtless regarded their promotion as a suitable reward. If his intention was to gain lasting support he failed miserably, for both Hussey and Pole became opponents of his policies and had to be executed shortly after the dissolution of Parliament.[3] Wentworth, Windsor, and Hussey cannot have known that they were to be elevated much before the Parliament actually assembled, for all three were elected to the House of Commons as knights of the shire. We do not know who replaced them in the Lower House. Pollard believed that no by-elections were held before December 1532, so the counties of York, Buckingham, and Lincoln may have gone under-represented for several years.[4]

[1] Elton, *Tudor Constitution*, 242.

[2] Luke Owen Pike, *A Constitutional History of the House of Lords*, 326.

[3] Pole, a brother of Cardinal Pole, became Lord Montague; the others retained their surnames as baronial titles. On these creations see MacCaffrey, 'England: The Crown and the New Aristocracy, 1540–1600', *Past and Present*, XXX (1965), 55; Miller, 'The Early Tudor Peerage, 1485–1547', *B.I.H.R.*, XXIV (1951), 89.

[4] A. F. Pollard, 'Thomas Cromwell's Parliamentary Lists', *B.I.H.R.*, IX (1931–1932), 38–9. Windsor's son William was elected to Parliament by the borough of Wycombe and Hussey's son Sir William by Grantham. Pollard speculated that William Windsor resigned his seat, preferring to attend in the Lords: a convenient supposition, since Cromwell's list names two other men for Wycombe, but unlikely. Sons of peers had no right to vote in the Lords unless the family held a secondary title available to them, and there is no contemporary evidence to show that eldest sons of peers could then, as now, sit on the steps of the throne.

Four other peers were raised to earldoms in 1529: a signal honour, but one which conveyed no new power in the Lords. It was on 8 December, a month after Parliament assembled, that Lord Clifford became the earl of Cumberland, Lord Hastings the earl of Huntingdon, Viscount Fitzwalter the earl of Sussex, and Viscount Rochford the earl of Wiltshire. Wiltshire's promotion was of course the most significant, since he was Anne Boleyn's father; Anne's brother, George, was also summoned to Parliament in 1533 with the title Lord Rochford. Two other sons of peers were called in 1533: Lord Maltravers, the earl of Arundel's heir apparent, and Lord Talbot, eldest son of the earl of Shrewsbury.[1] One further creation occurred during the Parliament, when the courtier John Mordaunt was made a baron in 1532.[2]

A few peers were not summoned in 1529. Thomas, second Lord Vaux of Harrowden, had been born in 1509, and although he succeeded to the title upon his father's death in 1523 he was presumably considered under age when Parliament first met. He took his seat at the beginning of the 1531 session. Edward Stanley, third earl of Derby, was the same age as Vaux but is not known to have entered Parliament until 1534. Edward Fiennes, Lord Clinton, probably never sat in the Reformation Parliament at all. Only seventeen in 1529, he was a royal ward and married the king's mistress, Elizabeth Blount. He lived into the reign of Queen Elizabeth, who named him lord high admiral and earl of Lincoln. Robert, fourth Lord Ogle, who was summoned normally in 1529, died about 1531; his son Robert was not called until 1539, again probably because of his youth. Edward Sutton, Lord Dudley, similarly received a summons in 1529 but died in 1532. John, his son and heir, was 'a weak man of understanding' who began almost immediately to alienate the family lands, finally selling even Dudley Castle. He was never called to Parliament, but his heir again received a summons in 1554. Poverty and mental incapacity joined to account for Dudley's absence from Parliament; poverty alone seems to have been the reason why Sir Henry Grey, half-brother and heir of Richard Grey, earl of Kent, who died in 1523, never assumed his title or attended in the Lords.

[1] *L.P.*, VI, 123.
[2] Information about titles, dates of creation, and relationship of peers, here and below, is taken from G. E. C[okayne], *The Complete Peerage*, new ed., hereafter cited as G.E.C.

There were two further irregularities. Lord Burgh apparently was not summoned in 1529 but took his seat all the same. Lord Ferrers, who had received a summons as early as 1509, was likewise not called in 1529, but the Journal for 1534 records his presence. The hereditary right to be summoned was becoming inalienable during the sixteenth century, but such ambiguities and special cases had not yet disappeared entirely. On the other hand, several peers were duly summoned although they obviously could not attend: Lord Berners and Viscount Lisle served in succession as deputies of Calais and were tied to their post on the Continent.[1]

The lay majority was emphasized by the regular attendance of the temporal peers. During the documented session in 1534 the average attendance of Lords temporal was just over twenty-two days, out of forty-six, while the average daily attendance of the Lords spiritual was only about twelve. To put it another way, the laymen attended 48 per cent of the meetings, on an average, and the clerics 26 per cent. Of course the times help account for the contrast: the bishops and abbots must have known that sweeping ecclesiastical legislation was to be considered in 1534, and they may have preferred abstention to opposition or forced acquiescence. It may be, too, that the lay Lords who supported the government were pressed to attend. Certainly there had been less distinction during the first session of the 1515 Parliament, when the average daily attendance of laymen was 34 per cent and of clergy 30 per cent. Still, the figures for 1534 are interesting in suggesting how completely the lay element could dominate the House.[2] These attendances are tabulated in Appendix B.

---

[1] G.E.C.; L.J.; Dugdale, *A Perfect Copy of all Summons*, 494–7; Miller, 'The Early Tudor Peerage, 1485–1547' (unpublished thesis, University of London), 11–18, 104–5; Lawrence Stone, *The Crisis of the Aristocracy, 1558–1641*, 53–4.

[2] L.J., 1, 58–83 (for 1529), 18–40 (for 1515). The count for 1515 is based on the thirty-six days for which the attendance is fully recorded; it is defective for at least six others. My figures differ somewhat from those in Helen Miller's thesis. She calculated that the total average daily attendance was 43 per cent during the first session of 1534, 35 per cent during the first session of 1515 (p. 165). The 1536 fragment does not permit any such calculation, since it covers only the first two days of the session. The temporal peers who attended then were the dukes of Norfolk and Suffolk, earls of Oxford, Rutland, Derby, Westmorland, Wiltshire, Sussex, and Huntingdon, Lords Audley, Rochford, Talbot, Dacre of Gisland, Ferrers, Cobham, Powys, Sandys, Vaux, Bray, and the prior of St John of Jerusalem (Harleian MS. 158, fols. 143–4, B.M.).

4

The three dukes were catapulted by their social prestige into parliamentary leadership if they cared to exercise it. The duke of Richmond, who ranked first in precedence, cannot have been of much importance except as a ceremonial adornment, for he was only ten years old when the Parliament began. Indeed, it is rather surprising that he attended so faithfully in 1534, when he was fifteen. The king's illegitimate son by Elizabeth Blount, he had been 'bred up' with Norfolk's son Henry 'in the castle of Windsor, . . . from whence they went together to study at Paris'; in 1533 he married Norfolk's daughter Mary. 'Very personable and . . . much cherished by our King', according to Lord Herbert of Cherbury, he disappointed Henry's expectations by dying in 1536. He was probably carried off by consumption, like Prince Arthur and Edward VI, although some suspected that Anne Boleyn and her brother had poisoned him.[1]

In the absence of a mature royal duke much responsibility devolved upon the shoulders of Thomas Howard, third duke of Norfolk. There can be no doubt that Norfolk was the most important adviser and administrator during the interval between Wolsey and Cromwell, both of whom he disliked. Norfolk's influence in both Houses of Parliament was enormous; in addition to controlling a number of seats in the House of Commons he was related to many of the leading peers, among them the earls of Sussex, Oxford, Derby, and Wiltshire, Viscount Lisle, and Lords Berners, Daubeney, and Dacre of the South. Both Anne Boleyn and Catherine Howard were his nieces; his son Henry, who was given the courtesy title earl of Surrey but never summoned to Parliament, was at one time the intended husband of Princess Mary, and later took to wife Frances Vere, daughter of the earl of Oxford. Norfolk himself had first wed Edward IV's daughter Anne, and after her death in 1512 he married Elizabeth Stafford, daughter of the duke of Buckingham whom Henry had executed in 1521 because of his all-too-direct descent from Edward III. It was Norfolk's misfortune to be haughty, violent, ambitious, and lacking in administrative skill; Professor Mattingly once described him, over-disparagingly, as 'the ponderous, cold-

[1] Edward Lord Herbert of Cherbury, *The Life and Reign of King Henry the Eighth*, 165; G.E.C.

hearted, chicken-brained Duke, moving sluggishly in the mists of the feudal past like some armoured saurian'. By 1531 or so Henry was relying on Thomas Cromwell instead of the duke to manage his affairs. But Norfolk retained more power than has sometimes been thought. Chapuys' dispatches emphasize his constant employment in ceremonial and diplomatic matters, and in the House of Lords no one, except perhaps Cranmer, could challenge his authority. Indeed a desire to meet Norfolk on common ground may be one reason why Cromwell accepted a peerage in 1536 rather than continuing to manage Parliament through the Commons.[1]

Charles Brandon, the duke of Suffolk, was a self-made man completely lacking in the noble lineage which Norfolk prized so highly. His father had been slain at Bosworth Field, where he was standard bearer to Henry VII, and Suffolk himself was primarily a military man. He was given his dukedom in 1515 as a reward for successfully commanding the vanguard at the battle of the Spurs, and in the following year he secretly married Henry VIII's sister Mary, who had just been released from a distasteful French marriage by the death of her first husband, Louis XII. Several obstacles—Henry's wrath and Suffolk's presumably valid previous marriage—were overcome with gifts of gold and papal bulls, and Brandon retained the king's favour. He may have been of some use to Henry in Parliament, for he supported the divorce and whatever else the king desired. But his real abilities ran in the direction of love and war, not politics and statecraft.[2]

Next to these three dukes ranked the two marquises. Thomas Grey, second marquis of Dorset, had spent part of Henry VII's reign in prison but gained favour with Henry VIII because of his skill at the joust. He was, like Suffolk, a military man employed in the wars with France and Scotland. In 1530 he died and was succeeded by his son Henry, who was only thirteen: too young to

---

[1] Mattingly, *Catherine of Aragon*, 265; Edward J. Tucker, *The Life of Thomas Howard, Earl of Surrey and Second Duke of Norfolk, 1443–1524*, 102; L. B. Smith, *A Tudor Tragedy: The Life and Times of Catherine Howard*, 24–35; *D.N.B.*; G.E.C. Lodovico Falier, the Venetian ambassador in London, described Norfolk as prudent, liberal, affable, and astute; small and spare in person, with black hair (*C.S.P.*, *Venetian*, IV, 694). It is unfortunate that the third duke has not attracted a biographer, for despite his limitations his career deserves further study.

[2] *D.N.B.*; G.E.C. The Suffolk title had belonged to the Poles until the attainder of Edmund de la Pole, third duke, in 1504.

attend Parliament. Henry married well, espousing first the earl of Arundel's daughter and then—after the death of Charles Brandon—Mary Tudor, duchess of Suffolk. Through her he acquired the Suffolk title and royal blood for his daughter, Lady Jane, who was to wear the crown for nine days. Finally executed by Queen Mary, he was fascinated by politics and might have learned much during the Reformation Parliament had he been old enough to take part.

The other marquis, Henry Courtenay, had the dubious honour of being the king's cousin. His father had been attainted in 1503 as a possible Yorkist claimant to the throne and remained in the Tower until Henry VII's death. Henry Courtenay himself enjoyed a period of popularity with Henry VIII, who granted him estates, offices, and titles: first the earldom of Devon, then in 1525 the marquisate of Exeter. He supported the divorce and was present regularly during the 1534 session of Parliament, but by 1538 his royal blood had undone him. Always a threat to the king, he appeared even more so when he drifted into a conspiracy with the Poles. After a trial by his peers he was beheaded on Tower Hill. Like Grey, he aimed too high and was dashed low by the revolving wheel of fortune.

Only nine earls were summoned in 1529, but by 1534 the ranks had been swelled to thirteen by the elevation of two barons and a viscount and the attendance of an earl who had been under age when Parliament began.[1] They were a vigorous group; twelve of the thirteen attended with decent regularity during our recorded session, and the earls could boast an average attendance of twenty-nine days, or 63 per cent. Perhaps their relative youth helped account for their diligence. Seven earls were in their twenties or thirties, while only one was over sixty. The average age was forty.

The attendances of Arundel, Oxford, and Wiltshire are particularly remarkable. William Fitzalan, eleventh earl of Arundel, was present on all but one day in the first session of 1534; he approved Henry's policies and bore the rod and dove at Anne Boleyn's coronation, but he had no special personal interests

---

[1] All of the dukes and marquises are mentioned in the text. The earls were: Arundel, Northumberland, Oxford, Essex, Rutland, Cumberland, Shrewsbury, Worcester, Westmorland (all summoned in 1529); Derby (under age in 1529); Wiltshire (summoned as Viscount Rochford); Huntingdon (summoned as Lord Hastings); Sussex (summoned as Lord Fitzwalter).

to care for. His son and heir, Lord Maltravers, was named for the king, his godfather; he also attended more than half the meetings of the Lords. John de Vere, fifteenth earl of Oxford, was doubtless associated with the duke of Norfolk in managing the House, for Oxford's daughter had married Norfolk's son. De Vere's role as crown-bearer at Anne's coronation symbolized his support of the king's new marriage, and his wife, 'a woman of hye witte and lovying to her frendes' although a commoner, was a friend of Cromwell.[1] Wiltshire had a more obvious parliamentary cause, but he had been active in government service long before the divorce was thought of and might have taken pains to be present regularly even if his daughter's position had not been at stake. His son, Lord Rochford, ranked just below him in attendance and may have helped popularize the Boleyn cause among the younger peers.

Intertwining marriage ties connected a number of the earls, who may have felt family pressures in the Lords or may simply have come to regard the House as something approaching a family club. Like Oxford, Edward Stanley, third earl of Derby, had married a daughter of the duke of Norfolk; it was his great-grandfather who had crowned Henry VII on Bosworth Field and married Henry's mother, Lady Margaret Beaufort. Derby's sister was the second wife of Robert Radcliffe, earl of Sussex, who had earlier been married to a daughter of Edward Stafford, the duke of Buckingham executed in 1521. Other daughters of the prolific Buckingham had married Ralph Neville, earl of Westmorland, and George Hastings, earl of Huntingdon, as well as the duke of Norfolk. Hastings was also related to Sussex's second wife and to George Talbot, fourth earl of Shrewsbury, an old, overworked, trusted fighter, whose first wife was Hastings' aunt. Shrewsbury's daughter had married Henry Percy, earl of Northumberland, who remained loyal to the king even when his mother and brothers supported the Pilgrimage of Grace. But the marriage was unhappy and Northumberland died without heirs two years after the close of Parliament, leaving virtually all his lands to the king and abandoning his title, which was taken up (as a dukedom) by John Dudley in 1551.[2] Henry

---

[1] Rowland Lee to Cromwell, 24 April 1533, SP 1/75, fol. 429, P.R.O. (*L.P.*, VI, 381).
[2] SP 1/101, fol. 135, P.R.O. (*L.P.*, X, 150); the lands were assured to the king by 27 Henry VIII, c. 47. G.E.C. calls Northumberland 'Henry the Unthrifty'.

Clifford, earl of Cumberland, was related by marriage to both Shrewsbury and Northumberland, for his first wife was Shrewsbury's daughter and his second Northumberland's sister. Like Northumberland he spent a good deal of his time fighting the Scots but managed to come to London for Parliament.

Two earls were connected by marriage to members of the Commons rather than the Lords. Thomas Manners, earl of Rutland, had taken to wife Eleanor Paston, daughter of Sir William and sister of Erasmus Paston, a burgess for Orford. Perhaps more important, Henry Somerset, earl of Worcester, was married to a sister of Sir William Fitzwilliam, the king's close friend who sat in the Commons for Surrey. Worcester had previously been married to Margaret, daughter of William Courtenay, earl of Devon, by Edward IV's daughter Katherine; he himself was illegitimately descended from Henry Beaufort, duke of Somerset and Lady Margaret's cousin.

The odd man out among the earls, at least in 1534, was Henry Bourchier, earl of Essex, who never attended a meeting of the Lords. It was ill health rather than opposition which kept him away; as he wrote to Cromwell, 'when I come into the air it driveth me into an ague, and then fall I ableeding'.[1] Perhaps he had caught a stubborn chill at Princess Elizabeth's christening, when he carried the basin.[2] Essex offered to send a proxy made out according to the king's pleasure and was in fact represented by the earl of Oxford. In 1533 Essex had also obtained leave of absence and given his voice to Oxford, but after the session began the king wrote requesting his personal attendance. Essex, however, did not come; he told Cromwell that he had been driven from his house by sickness and—interestingly but incorrectly—that he could not revoke his proxy.[3] In 1536 he again gave Oxford his proxy.[4] Essex died in 1540 of a broken neck suffered in a riding accident; he had no male heirs, and within a month his title had been appropriated by Thomas Cromwell. He could claim some Lancastrian blood and relationship to a fifteenth-century archbishop of Canterbury as well as to another Tudor peer, John Bourchier, Lord Berners, who gained fame for his translation of Froissart.

[1] L.P., VII, 23.   [2] Ibid. VI, 1125.
[3] SP 1/69, fols. 72–3, P.R.O. (L.P., v, 741); cf. SP 1/69, fol. 56, P.R.O. (L.P., v, 728).
[4] SP 1/101, fol. 235, P.R.O. (L.P., x, 231).

Like Essex, England's sole viscount never attended Parliament in 1534.[1] Arthur Plantagenet, Viscount Lisle, was serving as governor of Calais and could not return to London for the session. Lisle was the illegitimate son of Edward IV, but he obtained his title through marriage to the daughter of Edward Grey, Viscount Lisle, who died without male heirs. Since he was a conservative, it is just possible that Henry sent him to Calais to keep him out of the way. In 1540 he was imprisoned on suspicion of treasonous activities; he was declared innocent but died—of joy, it is said—before he could be released from the Tower. A good deal of his correspondence survives, and the letters sent to him, especially by John Hussey, are of some interest for their descriptions of affairs at home.[2]

5

The barons formed the largest single group of peers. Thirty-five were summoned in 1529; there were thirty-six in 1534 and thirty-eight who were eligible to sit at some time during the Parliament's life.[3] But the barons were not so important in Parliament as their numbers suggest. They had less prestige than peers with higher titles; three of them were sons of such peers, and probably amplified their fathers' voices rather than playing independent roles. And the barons did not come as regularly as men of higher rank: they had an average attendance of twenty-one days, as against twenty-nine for the earls and thirty-three for the dukes.[4]

[1] Three viscounts had been summoned in 1529, but the other two, Rochford and Fitzwalter, were promoted to earldoms.   [2] In the P.R.O., Lisle Papers, SP 3.
[3] This reckoning counts titles, not men; since some barons died and were succeeded by their sons during the course of the Parliament, there were actually more individuals involved. George Hastings, summoned as Lord Hastings but given an earldom in 1529, is omitted in this calculation and reckoned as one of the earls. The barons were: Lords Bergavenny, LaWarr, Dudley, Latimer, Conyers, Darcy, Mountjoy, Zouch, FitzWarin, Morley, Dacre of the South, Ogle, Berners, Stourton, Dacre of Gisland, Monteagle, Audley, Lumley, Scrope, Powys, Grey de Wilton, Cobham, Berkeley, Sandys, Daubeney, Montague, Hussey, Windsor, Talbot, Wentworth, Burgh, Bray, Mordaunt, Rochford, Ferrers, Maltravers, Vaux, and William Weston, prior of St John of Jerusalem.
[4] The two marquises and single viscount had lower average attendances—19 and 0 respectively—but their figures are artificially deflated by the unavoidable absence of Dorset and Lisle. In the Middle Ages the Lords spiritual were held to be barons, but they could not claim to be tried by their peers or take part in such trials if the death penalty could be inflicted. See Sir William Holdsworth, *A History of English Law*, 1, 358.

Not all of the barons merit our attention, but a number are of interest for a variety of reasons. George Neville, Lord Bergavenny, could claim precedence over the other barons even though there was some doubt about his hereditary right to the ancient title. His family stood high at court during the earlier part of Henry's reign; Sir Thomas Neville, Bergavenny's brother, had been Speaker of the Commons in 1515, while another brother, Sir Edward, gained prominence as a warrior and royal favourite. Lord Bergavenny had some bad days in 1521, when he was imprisoned with his father-in-law, the duke of Buckingham, but he weathered the storm and held a command in the French expedition of 1523. He was related to the earls of Arundel and Northumberland and to Lord Dacre of Gisland. His death in 1535 may have been fortunate, for he had been drawn into the Pole–Courtenay circle and was said to be planning a revolt in Kent and Sussex. His brother Edward did join the Poles and was beheaded in the purge of 1539.[1] Bergavenny's son-in-law, Lord Daubeney, took no part in these schemes and in 1538 received a higher title, earl of Bridgewater, rather than imprisonment. But his allegiance was doubtless to Norfolk, father of his second wife, not to the Nevilles.

William Dacre, called Lord Dacre of Gisland or of the North to differentiate him from Thomas Fiennes, Lord Dacre of the South, had the unusual distinction of being tried by his peers in 1534. It was an ordeal which Dacre sought to avoid, only to be told by the judges that he could not waive his right to such a trial, but in the end he was unanimously acquitted. His accusers turned out to be 'some mean and provoked Scottish men' who probably 'spoke maliciously' since Dacre, as Warden of the Western Marches, had harassed them in the Border country.[2] He may have been an argumentative sort, insistent on pressing his rights, for during the Parliament he was involved in an unsuccessful attempt to assert his precedence over Lord Morley.[3]

---

[1] Cf. Roskell, *The Commons and their Speakers in English Parliaments, 1376–1523*, 317–18; Miller thesis, 83–5; G.E.C. *sub* Abergavenny.

[2] Lord Herbert of Cherbury, *King Henry the Eighth*, 407–8; G.E.C. Lord Dacre's brother Christopher, who sat in the Commons as a knight for Cumberland, was also imprisoned briefly in 1534; see Wedgwood, *History of Parliament*, 248. The *Third Report of the Deputy Keeper of the Public Records*, App. II, 234–6, gives a detailed account of the trial, calendared from the Baga de Secretis, KB 8/6, P.R.O.

[3] *L.J.*, I, 79.

He was certainly a religious conservative: he protested against the Prayer Book of 1549, but his loyalty to Henry VIII prevented any overt opposition so long as the king lived. His wife was Shrewsbury's daughter, Lord Talbot's sister.

Two of the barons were among the few learned members of the House. Henry Parker, Lord Morley, had attended Oxford and translated Petrarch. He was also familiar with Machiavelli's *Prince*, which he recommended to his friend Thomas Cromwell as 'surely a very speciall good thing for youre Lordschip'.[1] In 1539 he printed an exposition of Psalm 94, which he turned into a tract against the papacy, but he later showed his innate conservatism by voting against the destruction of Latin service books and abstaining from the vote on the second Book of Common Prayer. His religious views, indeed, may have coincided with Henry VIII's: no popery but little Reformation.

The other learned baron was William Blount, Lord Mountjoy, who is chiefly remembered for his friendship with Erasmus. Mountjoy studied with the great humanist in Paris and later persuaded Erasmus to come to England, where Mountjoy acted as his patron. Although perhaps little better than a dilettante intellectually, Mountjoy could write elegant Latin letters such as the one telling Erasmus how the accession of Henry VIII had expelled avarice from the land.[2] He was often employed in war and diplomacy, serving also as master of the mint and steward of Cambridge University. His second wife was a Spanish lady attendant on Catherine of Aragon—Mountjoy was Catherine's chamberlain—and his fourth was a daughter of the old marquis of Dorset. Mountjoy died in November, 1534; his heir, Charles Blount, was only eighteen and probably did not attend the later sessions of the Parliament.

Several barons, although favourable enough to the king in 1529, drifted gradually into opposition. Sir John Hussey, raised to a barony in 1529 as a reward for his work as controller of the household, was having secret interviews with Chapuys by 1534.[3] He absented himself from the first session of that year, and in 1536 he asked to be excused from Parliament on the transparent grounds of illness. No doubt he sympathized too much with the

---

[1] Sir Henry Ellis, *Original Letters Illustrative of English History*, 3rd ser., III, 66–7. Cf. Lehmberg, *Sir Thomas Elyot, Tudor Humanist*, 87–8.

[2] Chambers, *Thomas More*, 70, 76, 100.   [3] *L.P.*, VII, 1206.

Princess Mary, whom he served as chamberlain; he was executed in 1536 on a charge of complicity in the Lincolnshire rising. Lord Darcy, a military leader who had been in great favour with the king, likewise stopped attending Parliament around 1534. In 1537 he was found guilty of delivering Pontefract Castle to the insurgents in the Pilgrimage of Grace and was executed on Tower Hill. Lord Lumley and Lord Latimer also took part in the revolt; they were pardoned, but Lumley's son was killed.[1] Henry Pole, Lord Montague, and Thomas West, Lord LaWarr, were two final believers in the old religion. Montague was beheaded in 1539, along with Exeter and Bergavenny's brother. LaWarr was spared but condemned to obscurity. As early as 1532 he had been excused from Parliament, ostensibly because of his poverty but in fact probably because of his bitter objection to the statute of uses and other official legislation. In 1534 and 1536 Lord Rochford—hardly a friend—held his proxy. Doubtless this arrangement was dictated by Cromwell, who witnessed the document.[2]

Sir William Weston, the prior of St John of Jerusalem, counted as a baron and signed as such when a group of peers wrote in 1530 urging the pope to grant Henry's divorce.[3] He had distinguished himself at the siege of Rhodes in 1522 and commanded a warship, sometimes called the first ironclad, at Crete in 1523. In 1527 he was named head of the Knights of St John in England, thus acquiring a seat in the Lords. He attended regularly and probably supported the king; he died in 1540 on the very day of the dissolution of his order.[4]

A few more barons may be mentioned in passing. Walter Devereux, Lord Ferrers, was one of the most regular attenders. A military man and chief justice of South Wales, he was later created Viscount Hereford; his great-grandson became Elizabeth's favourite, the Earl of Essex. Like Ferrers, Lords FitzWarin, Powys, and Berkeley were present on more than half the days of the documented session. FitzWarin—a Bourchier, but not closely

---

[1] Latimer's first wife was a sister of the earl of Oxford; his second, Catherine Parr, lived to be the last of Henry VIII's queens.

[2] *L.J.*, I, 58; Harleian MS. 158, fol. 144, B.M. A note on this MS. adds that the proxy remained with Cromwell. Thomas, Lord Vaux, may have been in sympathy with the opposition group, but outwardly he remained loyal to the king. His son was to be the well-known Elizabethan recusant.

[3] *L.P.*, IV, iii, 6513.   [4] *D.N.B.*

related to Lord Berners—was married to Daubeney's sister and was raised to the earldom of Bath in 1536. Edward Grey, Lord Powys, was an illegitimate descendant of Humphrey, duke of Gloucester, and had married Charles Brandon's illegitimate daughter Anne; his title lapsed when he died leaving only an illegitimate son. Thomas, sixth Baron Berkeley, had just succeeded to his title when Parliament met in January 1534 but died unexpectedly in September. Nine weeks later his wife, who was the earl of Huntingdon's daughter, gave birth to the fifth baron: the family was carried on but lost its voice in the Lords for two decades. Lord Cobham, a son-in-law of Lord Bray, supported the Reformation into Elizabeth's reign and lies buried under a magnificent tomb commemorating his 'defence of the Gospel'. William, Lord Sandys, had been ennobled only in 1523; he was an able administrator and builder of that charming Hampshire house, The Vyne. Both Lord Conyers and Lord Scrope were brothers-in-law of Lord Dacre of Gisland. Scrope attended only ten meetings of the House in 1534 despite the fact that a private bill concerning one of his manors was pending. Other peers—Lords Zouch, Burgh, and Monteagle—came less often, and eight barons not at all.[1]

6

The cost of attending Parliament may have kept some of the Lords away. In April, 1534—a week after the end of our documented session—Lord Latimer complained to Cromwell:

My being at everie prorogacion of the Parliament well nye thies foure yeres haith bene painfull, costlie, and chargeable to me, considering that I have not yett paide all paymentes to the Kinges Highnes for the levery of my landes, and have not paid all summes whiche I am bounde to pay for the performance of the willes of my lord my father and my lady my mother-in-lawe.[2]

He asked leave to be absent from the next session, promising to be ready for service against the Scots and currying Cromwell's

---

[1] Lords Audley, LaWarr, Dacre of the South, Berners, Stourton, Darcy, Hussey, and Wentworth.

[2] SP 1/83, fol. 69, P.R.O. (L.P., VII, 438). Latimer had served in the Commons during the session of 1529, but perhaps he did not collect the pay to which he was entitled there.

favour by sending him a gelding. Latimer was not one of the poorest peers, but he was licenced to stay home in 1536.[1]

John Tuchet, Lord Audley, could complain of financial distress with more justice. He was genuinely poor, and when he tried to improve his fortunes by investing in trade he lost heavily, allegedly through the craft of Lawrence Bonvisi. Audley also complained of palsy, but that was perhaps window-dressing; he was given leave of absence in 1531 after sending Cromwell a blank proxy. Like Audley, the 'unthrifty' earl of Northumberland was heavily in debt. He owed £10,000 to the king and £8,000 to Bonvisi's brother Anthony.[2] Viscount Lisle, too, was living in straitened circumstances.[3]

Most peers, however, were doing well enough during our period. After a laborious examination of inquisitions *post mortem* Helen Miller calculated that 27 per cent of the noble families increased their holdings by ten manors or more between 1485 and 1547, while 69 per cent retained essentially static amounts of land and only 4 per cent lost ten manors or more.[4] Most of the increments came after 1536, when at least half of the peers acquired monastic land, but there is no reason to believe that the peers as a class were experiencing hard times before the dissolution. The wealthiest, Arundel, had lands worth £2,200 a year in 1535. Norfolk, Derby, Dorset, Cumberland, and Huntingdon held more than eighty manors each. Bergavenny, who was not much better off than the average, had a yearly income of £1,622 in the 1520s. Miss Miller reckoned that only 18 per cent of the peers had fewer than twenty manors, and many of these received large revenues from office.[5]

Of course attendance at so long a Parliament could be a serious inconvenience to even the wealthiest peer. In 1531 Sir William Stourton, a member of the Commons, asked Cromwell to obtain a leave of absence for his father, Lord Stourton, who was 'so feble by reason of his grete age that he shall never be able with lyff to come half the way to London'. In fact Lord Stourton was nearly seventy, a considerable age in those days, and he had not been

---

[1] *L.P.*, x, 851.
[2] SP 1/68, fols. 115–16, and 1/69, fols. 67–70, P.R.O. (*L.P.*, v, 612, 734, 879).
[3] Miller thesis, 149.
[4] *Ibid.* 139; cf. Stone, *Crisis of the Aristocracy*, 160.
[5] Miller thesis, 110–52. On the economic troubles of the Elizabethan aristocracy see Stone, *Crisis of the Aristocracy*, 161.

on horseback for four years; his wife had lost her sight.[1] Lord Audley and, later, Lord Hussey also claimed that if they were forced to come to Parliament they would die on the way.[2] Lord Sandys, who was in his mid-sixties, excused his absence in 1534 on the grounds of age and sickness.[3] Lord Darcy thanked Cromwell for securing the king's licence so that he could 'tak my easse in my aygge and debelites'.[4] This was in November 1534, when the gout kept Lord Conyers at home.[5] But few peers were so infirm, and at least half of them had houses in London, many acquired during our period.[6] They were probably glad enough to have an opportunity of spending time in the bustling capital.

7

The peers had considerable help in conducting their deliberations. The chancellor of the realm presided over their sessions. The clerk of Parliament was responsible for scrutinizing writs of summons, filing petitions, engrossing bills, making up the rolls of Parliament, and keeping the unofficial Journal. The chief legal officers of England, summoned to the Lords by writs of assistance, were also available to advise the peers.

When the Reformation Parliament opened Sir Thomas More had just been appointed chancellor in Wolsey's place. Since he had been Speaker of the Commons in 1523 More had ample experience in parliamentary procedure; his flashes of wit must have enlivened the meetings of the Lords. He presided over four sessions of the Upper House, but grew increasingly apprehensive about its work, and on 16 May 1523—two days after the prorogation of Parliament, and the day after the Submission of the Clergy—he resigned the Great Seal. On the 20th it was given to Sir Thomas Audley, who had been Speaker of the Commons since 1529 and thus held the unique honour of presiding in turn over both chambers during the same Parliament.[7] Audley, a

---

[1] Cottonian MS. Titus B. 1, fol. 366, B.M. (*L.P.*, v, 626). Sir William also asked to be excused himself from the Commons, 'for it shulde be gretly for my proffithe', and he asked favour for the prior of Sherborne; he sent Cromwell twenty nobles to buy a tun of wine.

[2] SP 1/69, fols. 69–70, P.R.O. (*L.P.*, v, 701); SP 1/101, fol. 218, P.R.O. (*L.P.*, x, 206).   [3] SP 1/81, fol. 17, P.R.O. (*L.P.*, vi, 1556).

[4] SP 1/67, fol. 29, P.R.O. (*L.P.*, vii, 1426).

[5] SP 1/67, fol. 37, P.R.O. (*L.P.*, vii, 1439).

[6] Miller thesis, 151n.   [7] *L.P.*, v, 1075.

lawyer from Essex, was an avid supporter of the king and Cromwell, although he fell out with the Secretary briefly in 1535.
At the time of his elevation he was given the plate and lands
formerly belonging to Christ Church priory in London.[1] Neither
More nor Audley had a vote in the Lords, and they should have
conducted its meetings in a disinterested spirit. Still, they had
considerable scope for influencing the order of business or
direction of discussion. Audley, particularly, may have helped
smooth the course of court legislation.

The clerks, similarly, may have helped the king in inconspicu-
ous ways. Brian Tuke, who had been in Henry's service for
twenty years, had been clerk of Parliament since 1523; as Pollard
commented, 'he performed his official duties to the King's satisfaction, avoided all pretence to political independence, and
retained his posts until his death' in 1545.[2] After 1531 Edward
North was associated with Tuke in the clerkship, presumably
because Tuke was too busy in other positions to devote full time
to the Lords. North was later treasurer of the Court of Augmentations; he was ennobled by Mary and lived on into the reign of
Elizabeth, whom he twice entertained at his Cambridgeshire
house.[3] The clerk had a salary of £40, which Tuke and North
must have divided.[4]

The most important officers summed to the House of Lords
by writs of assistance were the judges of the King's Bench and
Common Pleas, the master of the rolls, the chief baron of the
Exchequer, the attorney general, and the solicitor general.[5]
Of these the attorney and solicitor appear to have been the most

---

[1] Lord Herbert of Cherbury, *King Henry the Eighth*, 371. Audley was originally
only Lord Keeper of the Great Seal, but was made lord chancellor in January
1533, presumably so that he could preside over Parliament: see A. F. Pollard,
'Wolsey and the Great Seal', *B.I.H.R.*, VII (1929–1930), 95. Audley was given a
barony in 1538.

[2] A. F. Pollard's biography of Tuke in *D.N.B.*   [3] *D.N.B.*

[4] A. F. Pollard, 'The Clerical Organization of Parliament', *E.H.R.*, LVII (1942),
31–58. See also A. F. Pollard, 'Fifteenth-Century Clerks of Parliament', *B.I.H.R.*,
XV (1937–1938), 137–61; A. F. Pollard, 'Receivers of Petitions and Clerks of
Parliaments,' *E.H.R.*, LVII (1942), 202–26; A. F. Pollard, 'The Clerk of the Crown',
ibid. 312–33. Ralph Pexsall, the clerk of the Crown, seems to have acted mainly
as a messenger between the two Houses.

[5] Cf. E. R. Adair and F. M. Grier Evans, 'Writs of Assistance, 1558–1700', *E.H.R.*,
XXVI (1921), 356–72. The judges and—at least after 1614—the attorney-general
were not eligible to sit in the Commons. The king's serjeants-at-law, secretaries
of state, and certain privy councillors were also sometimes sent writs of assistance.

active. Christopher Hales had sat in the Commons during the Parliament of 1523, but after his appointment as attorney general in 1529 he received writs of assistance calling him to the Lords and was paid by the Crown for his service there. It was his duty to conduct the trials of More, Fisher, and Anne Boleyn. He had previously been solicitor general; Baldwin Mallett followed him in that office but died in 1533 and was succeeded by the notorious Richard Rich. Rich, like Hales a close associate of Cromwell, had been elected to the Commons in 1529 for Colchester. There is no evidence that he resigned his seat, and he was later named Speaker of the 1536 Parliament, so he may have divided his time between the two Houses. His unscrupulous behaviour in the trials of More and Fisher has drawn much criticism from historians, but he seems to have been an efficient and tolerably honest administrator. He eventually gained the lord chancellor's seat and a barony.[1]

The chief justices, too, may have been fairly active in the Lords. Sir John Fitzjames, chief justice of the King's Bench, was a nephew of Richard Fitzjames, the bishop of London involved in the Hunne affair. He had been recorder of Bristol, attorney-general, and chief baron of the Exchequer. He must have regarded attendance in Parliament as an important duty, for in 1531 he went to the trouble of writing to Cromwell to say that he could not come because of a pain in his leg.[2] He may have sympathized with More and Fisher, since he maintained a discreet silence during most of their trials; he retired in 1538.[3] Robert Norwich and John Baldwin, successive chief justices of the Common Pleas, were probably less active in the Lords. Sir Richard Lyster, the chief baron of the Exchequer, and Dr John Taylor, master of the rolls, may have appeared occasionally. When Taylor died in 1534 Cromwell assumed his office, thus gaining a right to attend in the Upper House. Unfortunately we do not know if he ever exercised it.

8

As we cast a final glance at the Lords we may be struck by the

---

[1] On Rich see Walter C. Richardson, *History of the Court of Augmentations, 1536–1554*, 61–70.

[2] SP 1/60, fol. 12, P.R.O. (*L.P.*, v, 710). [3] *D.N.B.*

methods which the king might use in influencing their actions. He could allow, encourage, or even command his opponents to stay away, giving their proxies to royal appointees. Working through well-connected peers like Norfolk, he could apply the pressure necessary to transform Lords without strong convictions into active supporters of his policies. He could hold such threats over the churchmen that their opposition was tempered if not extinguished. He could appoint the chancellor and other non-noble servants of the House. All in all, he probably had more effective means of controlling the Lords than the Commons. What he could not do—and he never tried—was to turn the Lords into docile followers. As we shall see, they continued to oppose court legislation. On several occasions they granted Henry less than he wanted, later than he wanted it. In the Upper House as in the Lower, the parliamentarians gave effective voice to the sentiments of their countrymen.

4

THE CONVOCATION OF
CANTERBURY

By custom the Convocation of the English Church in the Province of Canterbury met concurrently with Parliament. Since the clergy insisted that they could not be taxed by Parliament, but might grant benevolences to the king by vote of their own assemblies, the tradition had its roots in financial necessity. This did not, however, limit the scope of their actions. The clerics, once gathered together, could discuss other matters affecting the welfare of the Church, and they were available for negotiations with the king and Parliament. During the years from 1529 to 1536 the interaction between Parliament and Convocation was so close that it would be folly for the historian to separate the two assemblies. Particularly in 1532, when the clergy were forced to make their famous Submission, no satisfying narrative can omit their debates. The activities of Parliament and Convocation ran parallel: they can be understood only if recreated in parallel.

Historically, church courts in England may be traced back to the Synod of Whitby in 664 or the Council of Hertford, called by Theodore of Tarsus in 673. These early assemblies had no consistent form, and laymen sometimes attended. Under the Norman kings ecclesiastical councils came to include only clergymen—bishops, abbots, priors, deans of cathedrals, and archdeacons. The thirteenth century saw the introduction of a representative element into the Convocation of Canterbury, as into Parliament: proctors of the lower clergy are first mentioned in 1256, and in 1283 it was explicitly stated that the inferior clerics in each diocese should send two proctors. By this time the Convocation of York had also established itself—there was never a national assembly of churchmen, but only the two provincial convocations—and soon after, each convocation separated itself into two houses, the bishops, abbots, and priors forming the upper house and the archdeacons and proctors the lower. Acts of Convocation required the assent of both houses; unlike parliamentary statutes, they were not submitted for royal ratification. Convocation

64

occasionally claimed equality with Parliament but never quite achieved it, partly because the bishops and abbots remained members of the House of Lords and partly because the resolutions of church councils did not directly bind laymen.[1]

Like the Reformation Parliament, Convocation has received its share of criticism. The complaint of the Commons, in 1532, that Convocation had the power to promulgate laws, constitutions, and canons without the assent of the king or laity, has found its way into most accounts of the period. Sir Thomas More's views are perhaps less well known. He argued that the clergy of each province should have met frequently to examine the state of the Church and, if necessary, reform it:

But in all my days, as far as I have heard, nor (I suppose) a good part of my father's neither, they came never together to Convocation but at the request of the king, and at such their assemblies, concerning spiritual things, have very little done. Wherefore that they have been in that necessary part of their duty negligent, whether God suffer to grow to an unperceived cause of division and grudge against them, God, whom their such negligence hath, I fear me, sore offended, knoweth.[2]

The clergy, he thought, were interested only in preservation of their temporal rights, not in making ordinances for the better performance of their spiritual duties.

While there is much truth in More's charge, it does not tell the whole story. Under Warham's leadership Convocation did pass a number of reforming canons in 1532, and it discussed additional ecclesiastical regulations. But the position of Convocation throughout our period was weak. The laity had been driven, partly by Wolsey, to despair of reform from within the Church and were ready to take matters into their own hands, in Parliament. Convocation could do little but fight a rearguard holding action, and when the clergy failed to defend the outposts of clerical privilege they were forced to retreat, shortening their lines and attempting to shore up secondary positions. Their battles will be chronicled in the succeeding narrative.

---

[1] Felix Makower, *The Constitutional History and Constitution of the Church of England*, 252–65. On the development of Convocation, especially in the thirteenth and fourteenth centuries, see also Dorothy Bruce Weske, *The Convocation of the Clergy*, *passim*.
[2] Sir Thomas More, *Apology*, quoted in A. F. Pollard, *Wolsey*, 191–2.

I

During our period the Convocation of Canterbury was potentially a slightly larger body than Parliament. A fortunately surviving list of the members of Convocation in 1529 shows that just over 500 clerics were summoned, while about 160 or 170 actually attended.[1] The upper house was considerably larger

Membership of Convocation, 1529

	Summoned	Attended
Upper house:		
Archbishop and bishops[2]	18	12
Abbots	151	50
Priors	200	46
Masters, etc.[3]	13	3
	382	111
Lower House:		
Archdeacons	52	35
Proctors of the clergy[4]	37	20
Deans of cathedrals[5]	11	3
Proctors of cathedral chapters[6]	20	3
	120	61
Total	502	172

[1] SP 1/56, fols. 60–82, P.R.O., printed in full in *L.P.* iv, iii, 6047 (1). The list, which is written in four or five different hands, does not give daily attendances, but has 'personaliter' before a number of names; it is uncertain whether the clergymen so identified attended on one given day—possibly at the opening of the session— or merely at some time during its course. Precise calculations are impossible because of the nature of the list. It does not mention the bishops, so that one can only guess how many of them attended, but it does include ten religious houses suppressed by Wolsey. It inflates the number of clergymen involved by enumerating positions rather than individuals: several men, including Peter Ligham, Richard Wolman, Humphrey Ogle, and William Glynn, held concurrently two or three offices which entitled incumbents to receive a summons. The list does not state clearly how many representatives of cathedral chapters attended, and its attendances are not always reliable. Peter Ligham, for example, is marked present in his capacity as proctor of the clergy for the diocese of Canterbury but not as a proctor for St David's; Richard Hilley, a proctor for Salisbury, is not marked present but probably attended since he had been given three proxies. (In one of

than the lower, although a smaller fraction of those qualified to attend it bothered to come. Defects in the list make it impossible to enumerate the classes of members precisely, but the accompanying table may be of some use if its figures are regarded as fallible approximations. The total figure of 172 in attendance is particularly misleading, since some individuals held two or three positions and thus are counted more than once.

The driving force in the upper house was the group of bishops and mitred abbots who sat also in the House of Lords. Since these clergymen have already received our attention, little needs to be added here. It may be, however, that these religious leaders were less docile in Convocation than in Parliament. Archbishop Warham was certainly willing to stand up to the king during the sessions of Convocation in 1531 and 1532; there is less evidence of his work in Parliament. Among the other bishops known to have been active in the earlier sessions of Convocation were Tunstall, Fisher, West, Longland, Veysey, Gardiner, and Clerk.[1] In 1533 Cranmer assumed direction of the house, and gradually Henry's other episcopal appointees took their seats;

these instances *L.P.* misspells his name as 'Hyller'.) Michael Kelly has analysed this list in his Ph.D. dissertation, 'Canterbury Jurisdiction and Influence during the Episcopate of William Warham, 1503–1532' (Cambridge University, 1963), 233n. Since the list is so imprecise it is not surprising that my figures differ slightly from his.

[2] The number of bishops who attended is a pure approximation. Wolsey and the three foreign bishops—Campeggio, Ghinucci, and Athequa—should clearly be excluded, and it is hardly likely that more than twelve of the remainder were present.

[3] This category includes masters of hospitals (e.g. St John's, Bridgwater; Burton St Lazarus), masters, deans, or rectors of colleges of priests (e.g. Warwick, Stoke, Ashridge), the commendatory of Titchfield, and the prior of St John of Jerusalem. The prior of St John was a layman, Sir William Weston, but since he did not attend little harm is done by referring to the members of Convocation collectively as clergymen.

[4] Only two proctors from each of the eighteen dioceses should have been named, but three are listed for Hereford.

[5] This includes St David's, which listed a precentor rather than dean. The archdeacon of Llandaff was head of the chapter there. The remaining cathedrals were monastic and had priors, not deans.

[6] Ten chapters named representatives, but seven of these are already listed in some other capacity and have been omitted here so as to avoid further inflation of numbers.

[1] This information is taken from Christ Church, Oxford, MS. 306, 27–61, a transcript of the acts of Convocation made for Archbishop Wake in the late seventeenth or early eighteenth century. This MS. is used effectively in Kelly's dissertation; it is referred to below as C.C. 306.

Convocation became less independent of the king and by 1536 had lost its importance, at least temporarily.

Members of Convocation, as of the Lords, had the right of giving proxies. In 1529 about a quarter of the absent clerics availed themselves of this privilege. The abbots of Hyde and Winchcombe, whose prominence in Parliament had been noted, held a number of proxies in Convocation and must have been active there too. Other members of the upper house who held several proxies were the abbot of St Mary Graces near the Tower of London, the abbot of St Mary Overey at Southwark, and the prior of the Holy Trinity, London. None of these had a seat in the House of Lords; they were probably named because of their presence in London, while the abbot of St Mary Graces had the additional attraction of being known in all the Cistercian houses since he was one of the visitors of the order.[1] Hugh Cook, abbot of Reading, and Anthony Kitchen, abbot of Eynsham, may also have been of some importance in Convocation. Kitchen lived on to achieve the dubious distinction of being the only Marian bishop to acquiesce in the Elizabethan religious settlement.

As the table indicates, relatively few of the priors or masters of collegiate churches and hospitals attended, and those who came probably played a minor role. Most of them were poorly educated and had little interest in national politics; their houses were small and could ill afford to maintain a representative in London. Doubtless the most active priors were the heads of the monastic cathedrals. We know that the priors of Canterbury, Winchester, Rochester, Bath, Ely, Norwich, and Worcester were present in 1529, and they may have provided support for their bishops or, in the case of the prior of Worcester, promoted the interests of the diocese in the absence of an effective prelate.[2]

2

The lower house was dominated by the archdeacons. Charged with the administrative and legal work of the Church, they understood well the significance of the proposals debated in Convocation. Many of the archdeacons summoned in 1529 were marked

[1] Knowles, *Religious Orders in England*, III, 249.
[2] Until 1535 Worcester was held by Ghinucci, a non-resident member of the Roman curia.

out for promotion. When Convocation assembled Gardiner sat in the lower house as archdeacon of Norfolk and Worcester, and Cranmer as archdeacon of Taunton. They did not stay there long, since Gardiner was made bishop of Winchester in 1531 and Cranmer archbishop two years later. Edward Lee, archdeacon of Colchester, received the archbishopric of York in 1531 but still attended the Convocation of Canterbury on occasion.[1] Stokesley was archdeacon of Surrey and Dorset before succeeding Tunstall as bishop of London. Rowland Lee, archdeacon of Cornwall, gained the bishopric of Coventry and Lichfield in 1534. Richard Sampson, who was a royal chaplain and dean of Windsor as well as archdeacon of Suffolk, became bishop of Chichester in 1536 and followed Lee at Coventry in 1543; he was an active supporter of Henry's policies, which he justified in several theological treatises. In 1539 John Bell, archdeacon of Gloucester, was made bishop of Worcester, and in 1541 William Knight, archdeacon of Huntingdon and Chester, was given the bishopric of Bath and Wells. William Glynn, a relative of the dean of Bangor and already archdeacon of Anglesey although he was still a student at Cambridge, became bishop of Bangor in 1555. Nicholas Hawkins, too, would have gained a see had he lived long enough. Archdeacon of Ely in 1529, he was named bishop of that diocese in 1533 but died in Spain, where he was resident ambassador, before he could be consecrated.[2]

A number of other archdeacons held important posts although they were never elevated to the bench of bishops. More will be said later of Richard Wolman, dean of Wells and archdeacon of Sudbury; it is possible that Henry might have given him a bishopric had he not died in 1537. Dr John Taylor, who was summoned to the Lords on a writ of assistance because he was master of the rolls, was archdeacon of Buckinghamshire and a prebendary of Lichfield and Westminster. Polydore Vergil, the distinguished Italian humanist and historian, sat in Convocation as archdeacon of Wells. Another learned archdeacon, John Chambre, had studied medicine at Padua. He was a charter member of the Royal College of Physicians and warden of Merton College, Oxford, but he also held ecclesiastical preferments as archdeacon of Bedford, precentor of Exeter, treasurer of

[1] C.C. 306, 44 (session of 1532).
[2] All of these clerics are noticed in the *D.N.B.*

Wells, prebendary of Lincoln, and canon of Westminster.[1] Nearly all of these active archdeacons supported the divorce, if with less enthusiasm than the archdeacon of Winchester. He was William Boleyn, Anne's cousin.[2]

Some archdeacons also served as proctors of the clergy within their dioceses.[3] Most of the other proctors were prominent diocesan officials, often wealthy pluralists. Peter Ligham, a proctor of the clergy for the dioceses of Canterbury and St David's, was Warham's dean of the Court of Arches—an important position, especially since the Commons were attacking the procedures of the court. Although he was a leader of the opposition to Henry in 1531, he later made his peace with Cromwell and received a prebend at St Paul's in 1533.[4] Another prebendary of St Paul's was Robert Ridley, proctor of the clergy in the diocese of London, who had studied in Paris and was one of the most scholarly opponents of the Reformation. He was an uncle of Nicholas Ridley the reformer; it is instructive to note what different opinions might be held by such close relatives. Robert Johnson represented the clergy of Rochester but was still studying civil law at Cambridge when the Convocation opened. He had perhaps fallen under the influence of Fisher, his bishop, for he later wrote a Latin treatise confounding the Protestant views of John Hooper. When Rochester cathedral was refounded in 1541 with a secular chapter he became one of its canons.[5] Nicholas Harpsfield, a proctor for the clergy of Winchester, had studied law at Bologna and was an officer in the Winchester ecclesiastical courts. He may have been as adamant a Romanist as his nephew, the early biographer of Sir Thomas More, for he gained no

---

[1] Chambre should not be confused with John Chambers, the Benedictine abbot of Peterborough, who also sat in Convocation and in 1541 became the first bishop of Peterborough. The *D.N.B.* gives biographies of both men.

[2] John and J. A. Venn, *Alumni Cantabrigienses*, Part I, I, 174.

[3] Among these were Glynn, proctor of the clergy for Bangor; William Cliff, archdeacon of London and proctor of the clergy for that diocese; Thomas Brerewood, archdeacon of Barnstaple and proctor of the clergy for Exeter; Richard Strete, archdeacon of Shropshire and proctor of the clergy for Coventry and Lichfield; Humphrey Ogle, archdeacon of Shropshire and proctor of the clergy for Hereford; John Booth, archdeacon of Hereford and proctor of the clergy for that diocese.

[4] John Le Neve, *Fasti Ecclesiae Anglicanae, 1300–1541*, V, 70–1. Ligham also held proxies for Archbishop Warham's nephew, the archdeacon of Canterbury, and for several other absent clerics.

[5] *D.N.B. sub* Nicholas Ridley, Robert Johnson.

further preferment in the Church and died obscurely in 1550.[1]
Dr John London, warden of New College, Oxford, sat in Convocation as a proctor for the diocese of Lincoln, where he was
treasurer of the cathedral. A time-server, he began and ended his
career prosecuting Lutherans but followed Cromwell during the
1530s. He is remembered chiefly for his visitation of the monasteries in 1538.[2] Rowland Philips, a proctor for the clergy of
Hereford, had considerable experience in Convocation, since
he had been Prolocutor of the lower house in 1523. He then
staunchly opposed Wolsey, and he remained an opponent of
government policy in 1531; he has been called the most eloquent
preacher of his age.[3] Another probable member of the opposition
group in the lower house was William Cliff, proctor for the
clergy of London and archdeacon of that diocese. Cliff evidently
found life in the capital uncomfortable, and in 1533 he followed
Tunstall north, exchanging his archdeaconry for that of Richmond in Yorkshire. In 1534 he became precentor of York
Minster; he was one of the authors of the conservative *Bishops'
Book*.[4]

Although few of the proctors were drawn from the ordinary
rectors and vicars who chose them, the elections appear to have
been conducted in a scrupulous, democratic fashion.[5] The parish
priests must have named men whom they could count on to
express their views—as well, perhaps, as men who would already
be in London and would need no further pay—and they seem
to have been well represented. It is notable that the proctors,
reflecting the generally conservative views of their electors,
formed the core of opposition to the divorce and supremacy.

Cathedral chapters were entitled to representation in the lower
house of Convocation, and deans of secular chapters could sit
there also. But few availed themselves of the privilege. If our
list is accurate, only half of the twenty cathedral chapters bothered
to name proctors. Most of these chose a representative who would
already be in attendance on Convocation: the cathedral prior, if it

[1] Harpsfield, *Life of Moore*, ed. E. V. Hitchcock and R. W. Chambers, clxxvi–clxxvii.
[2] Knowles, *Religious Orders in England*, III, 354–6.   [3] A. F. Pollard, *Wolsey*, 190.
[4] *D.N.B. sub* William Clyffe. Kelly believed that Ligham, Cliff, Philips, and Thomas
Pelles of Norwich were among the leaders of the opposition to royal supremacy in
1531 ('Canterbury Jurisdiction', 223–4).
[5] See Kelly, 'Canterbury Jurisdiction', 222n., a comment based on the register of
Geoffrey Blyth at the Lichfield Joint Record Office.

were monastic, an archdeacon, a proctor of the diocesan clergy, or a neighbouring abbot. In only three cases was a member of the chapter itself sent to Convocation: Dr John Smith sat for St Paul's, Brother William Basyng for Winchester, and Brother Walter Boxley for Rochester. Both Basyng and Boxley were later priors of their cathedrals, and Basyng lived on to be the first dean of Winchester under its secular foundation.[1]

Of the three deans who attended in 1529, one was Richard Wolman of Wells, who could also claim a seat as an archdeacon. The other two were of no special prominence: William Flesh-monger of Chichester, whose very name bespeaks his humble origins, and Gamaliel Clyfton of Hereford. To those should perhaps be added John Quarr, archdeacon of Llandaff, who under the curious constitution of that Welsh cathedral was head of the chapter. Six deans gave proxies. Richard Pace, the distinguished diplomatist and scholar who was dean of both St Paul's and Salisbury, was suffering from a severe nervous collapse through-out our period. Richard Sampson had been appointed his co-adjutor at St Paul's and may have represented him, but Pace did not actually give a proxy. Doubtless he was too ill.[2]

3

Convocation normally met at St Paul's, near enough to West-minster for easy communication with Parliament but distant enough for the clergy to assert their independence. Occasionally the meetings were transferred to Westminster Abbey. In 1523 Wolsey had called for such a move, to demonstrate that the assembly was his, not Warham's,[3] and in 1531 Warham himself ordered Convocation to the Abbey.[4] Since it had no regular meeting-place there it had to depend on the courtesy of the abbot and monks. The House of Commons probably met in the Chapter House at Westminster,[5] but Convocation may have used that

---

[1] Le Neve, *Fasti Ecclesiae Anglicanae*, v, 7; vi, 48, 41.
[2] *D.N.B.*; Le Neve, *Fasti Ecclesiae Anglicanae*, iii, 5; v, 7. The editors of *L.P.* had unnecessary doubts that Pace was dean of Salisbury as well as of St Paul's (*L.P.*, iv, 2699n).
[3] A. F. Pollard, *Wolsey*, 188–9.   [4] C.C. 306, 32.
[5] A. F. Pollard, *The Evolution of Parliament*, 2nd ed., 333. We cannot be certain where the Commons met before 1547; see Sir Goronwy Edwards, 'The Emergence of Majority Rule in the Procedure of the House of Commons,' *T.R.H.S.*, 5th ser., xv (1965), 181.

handsome chamber on days when Parliament did not meet. Otherwise the clerics had to be content with St Catherine's or St Dunstan's chapel.[1] The Chapter House of St Paul's was of course available when sessions were held there.

The bishops and mitred abbots, who sat in both Convocation and Parliament, must have found gatherings at the Abbey far more convenient, even if politically and psychologically less desirable. Because of their dual role some attempt was made to avoid conflicting meetings of the two assemblies. As a rule Convocation began its session one day later than the Lords, and it sat one day after the prorogation of Parliament. Convocation usually met only on Monday and Friday, although it could convene on other days as well when business was sufficiently urgent.[2] The Lords generally avoided Friday sessions, although they too could be driven to them if the press of work demanded.[3] Wednesdays were sometimes surrendered for meetings of the Council in the Star Chamber, which a number of ecclesiastical as well as lay officials were bound to attend.[4]

The two houses of Convocation could meet together, especially for the ceremonial opening of each session. Such joint meetings were conducted by the archbishop of Canterbury, who was also the presiding officer in the upper house. Since the archbishop frequently found it necessary to be elsewhere, he could appoint commissaries to preside in his absence; the bishop of London was, naturally enough, his most frequent deputy.

The lower house of Convocation, like the Commons in Parliament, elected a Prolocutor or Speaker. In 1529 they chose the dean of Wells, Richard Wolman. Wolman was learned enough— he had studied abroad and held a doctorate in civil law from Cambridge—but his primary qualifications lay elsewhere. His father had been in the service of John Howard, duke of Norfolk, and it was perhaps through the Howards that Wolman gained an introduction at court. In 1526 he became a royal chaplain and the king's master of requests; during Wolsey's absence he acted as an intermediary with the king in matters of ecclesiastical preferment. In 1527 Henry named Wolman his promoter in the early hearings of the divorce suit at Wolsey's home. Wolman

---

[1] Walter Farquhar Hook, *Lives of the Archbishops of Canterbury*, VI, 412.
[2] C.C. 306, *passim*.   [3] Cf. *L.J.*, I, 58–83.
[4] Cf. Stubbs, *Seventeen Lectures*, 270.

continued to favour the king, and after Cromwell's rise he cultivated the secretary's friendship; he was rewarded with numerous ecclesiastical positions, including the rectory of Ongar, Essex, and a canonry at Windsor.[1] Not all who dealt with Wolman liked him: the Italian merchant Peter de Bardis described him as 'impio . . . et ventricosissimo', knavish and big bellied, and he thought that Wolman deserved something worse than death.[2] But de Bardis was angry because nothing had come of his petition concerning a stolen cargo of rosin, and his views must be discounted. Wolman grew wealthy in the king's service and by 1532 could afford to give Henry a Christmas gift worth more than eleven pounds; he probably contributed two hundred pounds to the suppression of the Pilgrimage of Grace. He died during the summer of 1537 and was buried in the cloisters at Westminster Abbey, having left money for a market cross at Wells and an exhibition at Cambridge. It seems clear that he was a royal nominee, or at the very least that his election as Prolocutor was highly acceptable to the king. Wolman could not destroy the opposition group in the lower house, but he may have helped contain it.

4

The Convocation of York was far less important than that of Canterbury, and since it did not meet concurrently with Parliament we will have little need to examine its activities. As a rule its members gathered shortly after each session of the southern Convocation and agreed to whatever that body had granted. Constitutionally the Convocation of York was identical to its sister assembly, except that each archdeaconry, not each diocese, sent two proctors of the inferior clergy.[3] This change was designed to prevent the Convocation from being too small, but it remained tiny in comparison to the gathering in London. There were only three dioceses in the north—York, Durham, and Carlisle. The archbishopric of York was of course still held by Wolsey in 1529, and it was not effectively filled until the appointment of Edward Lee late in 1531. Durham, too, was vacant until Tunstall's arrival in 1530; John Kite, who was titular

[1] D.N.B. [2] SP 1/68, fols. 38–9, P.R.O. (L.P., v, 507).
[3] Makower, *Constitution of the Church of England*, 262.

bishop of Thebes, held Carlisle. Kite had been active in diplomacy during the years of Wolsey's supremacy and owed his preferments to the Cardinal's influence.[1] The north was even more conservative than the south, and with Tunstall there the Convocation of York could have proved very difficult. The abbots of great Yorkshire monasteries like Fountains could also have considerable influence if they opposed royal policies. Fortunately for the king and Cromwell, Edward Lee was willing to take great pains in smoothing the way for passage of unpalatable legislation,[2] and the king had ample reason to express satisfaction with Lee's services in 1533.[3]

5

In conclusion, much the same thing must be said of Convocation as of Parliament. Many members of each were fiercely independent and quite unafraid to voice their opposition to court-sponsored legislation. But the king had ways of influencing Convocation, either subtly through the mouths of bishops whom he had appointed and officials whom he had promoted or more bluntly, by threats and praemunire charges. Opposition was not silenced, and during the earlier years of our Parliament the views of the English clergy were elaborately ventilated in Convocation. But in the last analysis Convocation had to do more or less what the king wanted. The clergy were not popular with their countrymen, and public opinion as much as private pressure forced them to acquiesce in programmes desired by the king and parliament.

[1] *D.N.B.*   [2] Cf. *L.P.*, vi, 333, 367, 368, 437, 451, 486, 487, 491, 493.
[3] SP 1/76, fols. 63–4, P.R.O. (*L.P.*, vi, 493).

5

THE FIRST SESSION, 1529:
THE ANTI-CLERICAL COMMONS

A blaze of splendid pomp and medieval pageantry attended the opening of Parliament on 3 November 1529. The Lords and Commons had been summoned to Blackfriars, the great monastery in the City of London; it had been the scene of several Parliaments, most recently that of 1523, and had also provided room for the interrogation of Standish and the abortive trial of Henry's divorce suit.[1]

The king had spent the night at York Place, the magnificent palace which he commandeered from Wolsey. On the morning set for the opening of Parliament—a Wednesday—he came from Westminster by water, accompanied by numerous noblemen, with many barges and great boats following on the Thames. The entourage landed at Bridewell, a house near Blackfriars which Henry had built in 1522 for the entertainment of Charles V and his train.[2] There the king and nobles put on their Parliament robes and assembled for the ceremonial procession.

As the king set out for Blackfriars, probably about 11 o'clock,[3] he was surrounded by the great men of the realm. First came the knights, esquires, serjeants-at-law, and judges, two by two; then the bishops and abbots, flanked by heralds. Archbishop Warham and Sir Thomas More, wearing the chancellor's robe of scarlet furred with miniver, followed, More on the archbishop's left. Garter king of arms preceded the duke of Suffolk, who was earl marshal and bore his staff of office. After him came the marquis of Exeter carrying the king's sword and the marquis of Dorset bearing the cap of maintenance, an earlier gift of the pope. In the

---

[1] Blackfriars is described by Stow, *Survey of London*, 303–4. It lay near Puddle Dock and the present Blackfriars station, at the extreme west end of the City.

[2] *Ibid.* 351–2. Charles himself was lodged at Blackfriars, but his nobles were accommodated at Bridewell. Henry and Catherine had rooms there during the trial of their divorce case. From 1531 to 1539 the French ambassadors held the privilege of occupying the palace; it was given to the City of London in 1553. See Edward G. O'Donoghue, *Bridewell Hospital*, I, 1–89, *passim*.

[3] References to times of day are hard to come by; this was the hour when Elizabeth joined the parliamentary procession in 1584. See Neale, *Elizabethan House of Commons*, 349–50.

middle of the procession strode the king himself, wearing a crimson cloak lined in ermine; he was supported by his chamberlain, Lord Sandys. The earl of Oxford, as lord chamberlain of England, bore the king's train. Norfolk, the lord treasurer, came next, followed by the temporal peers arranged according to degree and seniority of title.

Once inside Blackfriars church the king took up his sceptre and proceeded to the choir, where a Solemn Mass of the Holy Ghost was sung by the choristers of the Chapel Royal. The spiritual Lords sat in the stalls on the south side of the richly ornamented church, the temporal Lords on the north; 'at the offering time the great estates went to attend upon the King's Highness, and after went to their stalls again'.[1]

After mass the scene shifted to the Parliament chamber. Chapuys says that this was the hall at the king's house—presumably Bridewell—which was connected to the priory church by a covered way.[2] We are unusually fortunate in having a contemporary picture of the opening of Parliament in 1523, so it is not difficult to visualize the setting.[3] Despite some changes in personnel the general arrangement must have remained the same in 1529.

The centre of attention was of course the king; our unknown artist has emphasized his importance by painting him larger than his subjects. Below the king, on the cloth of state, stood the two marquises bearing the cap and sword; to their left was the king's chamberlain. At the king's right hand, where Wolsey had claimed precedence in 1523, Warham now sat alone. Flanking the king, and standing behind the long settle or transverse railing, were More and Norfolk, as chancellor and treasurer.[4] On the king's

---

[1] This description is based on a MS. at the College of Arms, printed in Dugdale, *A Perfect Copy of all Summons*, 496. Some details have been drawn from Edward Hall, *Hall's Chronicle*, 764, and Harleian MS. 158, fols. 136–7, B.M. This last is catalogued as being from Henry VIII's reign but can be dated by internal evidence to Edward VI's last Parliament, 1553. There cannot have been much variation in the procedure during the Tudor period; cf. Neale, *Elizabethan House of Commons*, 349. Chapuys described the opening of Parliament in his dispatch of 8 November: Chapuys MS., fols. 224–7 (*C.S.P., Spn.*, IV, i, 221; not in *L.P.*).

[2] Chapuys MS., fols. 224–7.

[3] This drawing was made for Sir Thomas Wriothesley, Garter king of arms in 1523, and is part of the Wriothesley Garter Book in the Royal Library at Windsor. It is reproduced above as the frontispiece.

[4] In the picture these positions are filled by Tunstall, who delivered the opening address, and by two mysterious figures who are probably non-noble councillors

right sat the lords spiritual, on his left the lords temporal. Probably the bishops took the inner bench, with the mitred abbots behind them. Across from the bishops were the dukes who did not have places elsewhere; they can be identified by the four bars of miniver facing their gowns. Below the dukes sat the earls, whose robes bore three stripes, and below them the viscounts and barons, whose gowns had two bars. There are barons on the inner cross-bench in the painting—the premier baron, the prior of St John's, is distinguishable because of his unique robe—and on the bench behind the earls.

In the centre of the picture, forming a smaller square, are the judges and other officers summoned by writs of assistance; two of them are sitting on the highest wool-sack, which the chancellor occupied at ordinary meetings of the House of Lords. Below the fourth woolsack kneel the clerk of Parliament and the clerk of the Crown, writing their records in what must have been an exceedingly uncomfortable position. The Commons can barely be discerned at the lower edge of the painting; they are standing behind the bar and are led by their Speaker. It is impossible to identify the figures in the upper right-hand corner with any certainty, but Pollard believed that they were the eldest sons of peers, preceded by Garter king of arms.[1] If the picture can be taken as accurate in detail, it is interesting in showing not only the arrangement of the chamber but also the relatively small number of Lords and Commons present.

When all had ordered themselves Sir Thomas More made an eloquent oration explaining the causes which had moved the King to convoke Parliament. Edward Hall, who was probably among the throng standing outside the bar, has left us an account of the speech.[2] As he reports it, More began by comparing the king to a shepherd:

Like as the good shepard whiche not alonely kepeth and attendeth well his shepe, but allso forseeth and provideth for al thyng, which

---

(A. F. Pollard, *Evolution of Parliament*, 382). In 1523 Norfolk took the highest seat on the right-hand bench, where he can be recognized by his treasurer's staff; More was Speaker of the Commons and can be seen at the extreme bottom of the picture, towering over his colleagues.

[1] A. F. Pollard, *Evolution of Parliament*, 382.

[2] Edward Hall, *Hall's Chronicle*, 764. Chapuys' account (fols. 224–7) is quite similar. The speech is also reported in the Parliament Roll, C 65/138, m. 1, P.R.O., summarized in *L.P.*, IV, iii, 6043. The clerk called it long and elegant.

either may be hurtful or noysome to his floke, or may preserve and defende the same agaynst all peryles that may chaunce to come: so the kyng, whiche was the sheaperd, ruler, and governour of his realme, vigilantly forseyng thinges to come, considered how divers lawes before this tyme wer made nowe by long continuance of tyme and mutacion of thinges very insufficient and unperfight, and also by the frayl condicion of man, divers new enormities were sprong amongest the people, for the which no law was yet made to reforme the same, which was the very cause why at that tyme the kyng had somoned his High Court of Parliament.

The famous charges against Wolsey followed.

And as you se that emongest a great flocke of shepe some be rotten and fauty, which the good sheperd sendeth from the good shepe, so the great wether which is of late fallen as you all knowe, so craftely, so scabedly, ye and so untruly juggeled with the kyng, that all men must nedes gesse and thinke that he thought in himself, that he had no wit to perceive his craftie doyng, or els that he presumed that the kyng woulde not se nor know his fraudulent juggeling and attemptes; but he was deceived, for his Graces sight was so quike and penetrable, that he saw him, ye and saw through him, both within and without, so that all thing to him was open, and according to his desert he hath had a gentle correction, which small ponishment the kyng will not to be an example to other offendoures but clerly declareth that whosoever hereafter shall make like attempt or commit like offence, shall not escape with lyke ponyshment.

In conclusion the chancellor asked the Commons to choose an able person to be their common mouth and Speaker, and the clerk of the Parliament read out the names of the receivers and triers of petitions.[1]

Following the joint meeting the Commons adjourned to what Hall calls only the nether house—presumably another room at Bridewell, or perhaps the spacious chapter house at Blackfriars—

[1] C 65/138, m. 1, P.R.O.; A. F. Pollard, 'Receivers of Petitions and Clerks of Parliament', 202–6. These panels were made up of prominent men: the receivers were chancery clerks, including Wolman and Gardiner, while the triers included Warham, Norfolk, and a number of other Lords advised by several judges. But their duties, although important in the Middle Ages, were no longer of much significance. The receivers sorted the petitions addressed to the Lords—they had nothing to do with the Commons—and the triers may have acted as a committee of the Upper House to consider them. In addition the receivers, who sat on the lowest woolsack, were often employed as messengers carrying bills and other communications between the two Houses.

to choose their Speaker. They selected Thomas Audley, the junior knight of the shire for Essex. Audley, who was in his early forties, had studied law at the Middle Temple; he had already served at court as a member of Princess Mary's council, groom of the chamber, and chancellor of the duchy of Lancaster, but he was only beginning a political ascent which would ultimately bring him the chancellor's seal, a barony, and vast wealth.[1] If his abilities were undoubted, so was his loyalty to the king. He was probably a royal nominee, certainly a Speaker acceptable to Henry.

After this ceremonial opening Parliament was adjourned to Westminster, where it met again on Saturday, 6 November. The king and Lords, once more wearing their robes, sat in the Parliament chamber while the Commons presented their Speaker. As was usual, Audley delivered a speech praising the king and declaring his own insufficiency to perform the office. It was doubtless with reference to the punishment already meted out to Wolsey that he eulogized Henry's equity and justice, mixed with mercy and pity: no offence escaped punishment, but no extremity or undue rigour of the law went unmitigated. Audley's disclaimer of the wit, learning, and discretion necessary in so high a position was of course merely formal and was refuted by More, speaking for the king. Henry had known Audley to be wise, able, and discreet, and admitted him as Speaker.[2] The ceremony complete and both Houses now supplied with presiding officers, Parliament was ready to begin its work.

I

Meanwhile the Convocation of Canterbury was also organizing. Its ceremonies were similar to those of Parliament, and must have been only slightly less splendid. On 5 November Archbishop Warham had embarked at Lambeth Palace and taken a barge to

---

[1] D.N.B.; A. I. Dasent, *The Speakers of the House of Commons*, 124. Dasent reproduces a portrait of Audley seated behind the parliamentary mace, but it is obviously not contemporary and appears to be of considerably later date. The king paid Audley the usual fee—£100 per session—for his services as Speaker. Chapuys (*loc. cit.*) had the curious idea that Warham was originally chosen as Speaker, but rejected because of his age. Possibly he had mistaken a report that Warham had been considered for the chancellorship after Wolsey's fall.

[2] Edward Hall, *Hall's Chronicle*, 765; C 65/138, m. 1, P.R.O.

Paul's Wharf, from which he proceeded on foot to the cathedral. Within St Paul's, Bishop Tunstall celebrated another mass invoking the guidance of the Holy Ghost. After hearing a sermon in the lady chapel the clergy met in the chapter house; Warham, sitting on a raised platform, commissioned the bishops of London, Rochester, and Ely as his deputies, with authority to preside in his absence. He asked the chancellor of the Court of Arches, John Cocks, to examine the credentials of members and admonished the lower house to choose a Prolocutor; he then adjourned Convocation to the following Monday.

When the council next met the inferior clergy elected Richard Wolman their Prolocutor. Dr John Taylor, archdeacon of Buckinghamshire, presented Wolman to the prelates in a Latin oration. The Prolocutor, like the Commons' Speaker, gave a conventional excusatory speech, but Warham's commissaries admitted him to office. Convocation was adjourned to November 12, when it too would be ready for serious business.[1]

2

Since the great wether had already been separated from the fold, the Commons could not begin by taking action against him. Instead, they turned their attention, as More had requested, to laws made insufficient by passage of time and to new enormities lately sprung up among the people. This charge they interpreted as a mandate to consider the manifold abuses of the clergy.

Although we lack precise information about timing and names of speakers, we are fortunate in possessing considerable evidence of the anti-clerical storm in the Commons. Hall lists six great causes which 'sore moved' the House, and a number of surviving papers amplify and confirm the charges.

It is clear that legislation against clerical abuses was in the minds of many members of the House when Parliament assembled. In London, the Mercers' Company had framed five articles as a basis for redress of the City's grievances; four had to do with trade, but one bitterly attacked the priests. It urged Parliament 'to have in remembrans howe the kynges poore subgiectes, pryncipally of London, been polled and robbed without reason or conscience by th'ordenarys in probatyng of

[1] C.C. 306, 27–8.

testamentes and takyng of mortuarys, and also vexed and trobled by citacions with cursyng oon day and absoilyng the next day, *et hec omnia pro pecuniis'*—and all for money.[1]

These complaints from London formed the basis for two of Hall's six articles. The 'excessive fynes which the ordinaries toke for probat of testaments' were perhaps discussed first, and they generated much heat. Sir Henry Guildford, controller of the king's household and a knight of the shire for Kent, reported that he and the other executors of the estate of Sir William Compton, a courtier and military leader who had died of the sweating sickness in 1528, had been forced to pay Wolsey and Warham a thousand marks; 'after this declaration were shewed so many extorcions done by ordinaries for probates of willes' that Hall thought them 'to[o] muche to rehearse'.[2]

Hall's second cause was the 'great polling and extreme exaccion which the spiritual men used in takyng of corps presents or mortuaries'—close even verbally to the mercers' charge. Someone said that the clergy would leave a dead man's children to go begging or die from hunger rather than allow them to keep the cow which they owed as a mortuary fee. 'Such was the [priests'] charitie then.'[3] Another chronicle, copied later for Sir Simonds D'Ewes, adds that the churchmen made no distinction between the rich, who could well afford to pay for their funerals, and the poor, 'whose necessityes somtymes rather required relife'.[4]

Two further complaints were based on the worldliness of the clergy: they were employed as stewards and surveyors to bishops and abbots, and thus occupied farms, granges, and grazing lands; they sometimes kept tanning houses and dealt in wool, cloth, and other merchandise. In the former case they injured 'such as weare boren and bred up to be husbandmen', while in the latter they took business from temporal merchants and frequently raised prices by engrossing and regrating.

The Commons finally listed the inconveniences arising from pluralism and non-residency. Their fifth article charged that many of the beneficed clergy lived at court or in the homes of noblemen,

---

[1] Mercers' Company, Acts of Court, 1527–1560, fols. 24–5, quoted in Miller, 'London and Parliament in the Reign of Henry VIII', 144. For evidence that fees and citations were in fact burdensome see Margaret Bowker, *The Secular Clergy in the Diocese of Lincoln, 1495–1520*, 33–4, 149–51.

[2] Edward Hall, *Hall's Chronicle*, 765; cf. *L.P.*, IV, iii, 6183.

[3] Edward Hall, *Hall's Chronicle*, 765.   [4] Harleian MS. 158, fol. 145, B.M.

'so that for lack of residence both the poor of the parish lacked refreshyng, and universally all the parishioners lacked preaching and true instruccion of God's worde, to the greate perell of there soules'. The final cause of grief was to see an ignorant priest hold ten or twelve benefices while many 'great schollars' sat in poverty at Oxford and Cambridge, unable to share their knowledge.[1]

Before this time, Hall adds, no man dared to voice such complaints for fear of being called a heretic and losing all his possessions, since bishops were chancellors and had great power over kings. Now God had at last opened the king's eyes, and Parliament men could freely show their grievances and work for a reformation.[2]

After these complaints had been aired in the full House Audley appointed a committee of men learned in the law to draw up corrective statutes. We do not know the names of the committee-men, but it is almost certain that one of them was Thomas Cromwell: still acting privately, since he had as yet no government office, he was nevertheless important in the work of Parliament from the start. The committee probably included also one of the burgesses from London, perhaps the Protestant John Petyt.

Evidently the committee did not limit its discussions to the six abuses which had already been debated. Several surviving documents were probably presented to the committee, and two anti-clerical petitions may have originated with the committeemen themselves. All of these broaden and add to the grievances listed by the House.[3]

One paper probably considered by the committee was a memorandum concerning the proctors in the Court of Arches, the most important of the ecclesiastical tribunals.[4] There had originally been at least twenty of these proctors, who acted on behalf of suitors in the court, but the archbishop had misguidedly reduced the number to ten. Since some of these would always be

[1] *Ibid.*; Edward Hall, *Hall's Chronicle*, 765.
[2] Edward Hall, *Hall's Chronicle*, 765–6.
[3] None of these papers is dated, and it is possible that some or all of them are from a later session (1531 or 1532). I have placed them in 1529 because that seems to fit best the other available evidence. One would expect the papers, if written later, to make some reference to the legislation enacted in 1529.
[4] Cottonian MS. Cleopatra F. I, fols. 91–5, B.M. (*L.P.*, IV, iii, 6045).

absent or impotent, suitors would now suffer long delays and lack impartial justice unless the archbishop's order could be countermanded.

More interesting is a draft bill, undated but evidently from this session, relating to heresy trials.[1] Hall's complaint that criticism of clergymen often led to charges of heresy finds an echo here. The bill asserts that bishops and their officers 'perversly and uncharitably hathe and do arest and convent before them suche as either dothe preche, speke, or reason against the[ir] detestable and shamfull lyving, . . . and them in prison do kepe under the colure and name of heresy'; false articles are preferred against them, so that honest men 'remayne in perpetuall prison, or ellis [are] burned and utterly cast away forever'. The bill provides various remedies: citations for heresy are not to be made unless the bishop and his commissaries are free from private grudges; the accused is to be told the charges against him and the names of his accusers; at least two credible witnesses are to be required for conviction; the length of imprisonment is to be limited, and defendants are to be allowed their freedom on bail while awaiting trial.

It is likely that two anti-clerical petitions to the king were before the committee as well. The first starts from the complaints about mortuary dues and probate costs which had been voiced in the House; these charges are broadened and others added in the document.[2] The priests, it begins, collect certain sums of money for administration of 'sacraments and sacramentals'—the Eucharist, baptism, confession, marriage, and churching of women as well as burial—which should be freely ministered to the people. Judges, scribes, summoners, and other officials of ecclesiastical courts charge excessive fees for the probate of testaments. These judges also require great fees and rewards (an early version of the draft said 'bribes') so that nothing can be obtained in any church court without money. Clergy presented to benefices by the king and other lay patrons must pay excessive sums to the bishops and their officers in order to obtain letters of institution and induction. The ordinaries frequently confer benefices upon 'yong folks, calling them their nephewes'; the ordinaries take the profits from these offices, and the parishioners

---

[1] SP 2/N, fols. 20–2, P.R.O. (*L.P.*, vi, 120 [2]). Elton suggested that this document was of 1529; see his article, 'Parliamentary Drafts, 1529–1540,' *B.I.H.R.*, xxv (1952), 122. [2] SP 1/56, fols. 40–3, P.R.O. (*L.P.*, iv, iii, 6043 [7]).

'perisshe without doctrine or any good teching'.[1] Finally, an excessive number of holy days are kept with little devotion, causing idle workingmen to fall into 'abhomynable and execrable vices'.

This paper is written in a clerk's script, with a number of alterations in Cromwell's easily identifiable hand. Professor Elton has suggested that the document was devised by Cromwell's assistants,[2] but it is equally possible that it was put together by the committee, copied by a scribe, and then altered by Cromwell. The character of the changes may perhaps give some support to this hypothesis, for Cromwell consistently softened the harshest passages which may originally have reflected the bitter animosity of some parliamentarians. The first version spoke of ecclesiastical judges, for instance, as 'a sorte of ravenous woolvys nothing elles attending but there onelie pryvate lucres and satisfaction of the covetous and insaciable appetites of the said prelatis and ordynaries'; Cromwell deleted most of this and left the passage reading only, 'coveting so muche there pryvate lucres and satisfaction of the appetites of the said prelatis and ordynaries'.[3]

A second petition purports to present the views of the knights and burgesses 'in this present Parliament assemblid', and was probably drafted by the committee.[4] The first charge made here is the most interesting, for it is perhaps the earliest criticism made in Parliament about the legislative powers of Convocation. In its original form, before it had been recast by Cromwell, this article began:

First, albeit that the spiritual Lordes of this realme have a libertie and a voyce of assent in the makyng of eny your lawes and statutes of this

---

[1] The most glaring example of this practice was Wolsey's illegitimate son, Thomas Wynter, who held at least twelve ecclesiastical positions while studying abroad; hardly anyone bothered to maintain the pretence that he was the cardinal's nephew. See A. F. Pollard, *Wolsey*, 308–12. Warham's nephew, the archdeacon of Canterbury, presented quite a different case, for he was really the son of the archbishop's brother and was fully competent to perform the duties of his office.

[2] Elton, 'Parliamentary Drafts, 1529–1540', 119–20, and 'The Commons Supplication of 1532: Parliamentary Manœuvres in the Reign of Henry VIII', *E.H.R.*, LXVI (1951), 525. This document is Elton's draft 'B'; he agrees that it probably originated in 1529.   [3] SP 1/56, fol. 40ᵛ, P.R.O.

[4] SP 2/L, fols. 203–4, P.R.O. (*L.P.*, v, 1017 [3]). Elton is in agreement that this document (his draft 'A') was got up by a committee of lawyers in the Commons. A possible argument against dating the petition 1529 is its use of the phrase 'imperiall power' (and this is in the original text, not added by Cromwell). This sounds more like 1531 or 1532; if it is of 1529 it is either accidental or remarkable.

realme [since they sit in the Upper House of Parliament], yet neverthelesse they with the clergy in their Convocacion make lawes and ordynances wherby without your royall assent or th'assent of eny your ley subgettes they bynde your said ley subgettes in their bodies, possessions, and goodes.

The ordinances of Convocation are never openly proclaimed or published in the English tongue, so that obedient laymen break them through mere ignorance; such procedure tends to the 'dymyse, dymynucion, and derogacion' of the king's 'imperiall power, jurisdiccion, and prerogative royall'.

Further charges relate to the ecclesiastical courts. One repeats the complaint about proctors in the Arches. Another asserts that church courts, especially the Arches, charge excessive fees. There are three more points: the king's subjects, and poor persons in particular, are often summoned to appear in ecclesiastical courts without any lawful accusation, only to benefit the 'very light persons' employed as summoners; subjects are forced to answer, on oath and without counsel, unsupported charges suddenly made against them; subjects are frequently excommunicated for 'small and light causes,' and are put to great costs for absolution.

Almost certainly these petitions were not presented to the king. We do not know if they were before the entire House or not. In any case most of these criticisms were laid aside for the time being; the committee of lawyers, or perhaps the Commons themselves, if we can take Hall literally,[1] decided to concentrate on the immediate relief of the worst abuses. The lawyers framed only three statutes, dealing with three grievances which had been set out in the House: probates, mortuaries, and non-residence. Cromwell shrewdly filed away the petitions, perhaps looking to the future and the reopening of unresolved grievances.[2]

3

The Commons were evidently trying to be conciliatory in limiting

---

[1] Edward Hall, *Hall's Chronicle*, 766.

[2] It was probably after the end of the session, and very likely as late as 1531, that Cromwell had the draft copied, then reworked it by adding a preamble to emphasize the division between the clergy and the laity, softening some charges, sharpening the point of others, and ending with a stylistic flourish. SP 6/7, nos. 21 and 22, 206–36, P.R.O. (*L.P.*, v, 1016 [4]). Elton labels these drafts 'C₁' and 'C₂'; they are printed in full in Merriman, *Life and Letters of Thomas Cromwell*, i, 104–11.

their immediate goals, but they still encountered harsh opposition from the clergy in the Lords.

Matters did not begin so badly. The mortuaries bill passed the Lower House first, and when it was sent up to the Lords there was little outcry. 'The spiritual Lordes made a fayre face,' Hall reported, 'saying that surely priestes and curates toke more then they should, and therefore it were well done to take some reasonable ordre. Thus thei spake because it tuched them little.'[1]

Two days later the Lords received the bill limiting fees for probate of testaments. At this the bishops, especially Warham, 'both frowned and grunted, for that touched ther proffite'. Fisher made the most outspoken complaint, charging that the Commons' bills would bring the church 'into servile thraldome, lyke to a bound maid, or rather by little and little to be clean banished and driven out of our confines and dwelling places'. The Commons had called clergymen vicious, ravenous, and insatiable, Fisher said.

What, are all of this sort? Or is there any of these abuses that the clergie seeke not to extirpe and destroy? Be there not lawes alreadie provided against such and many moe disorders? Are not bookes full of them to be reade of such as list to reade them, yf they were executed? . . . These men now amonge us seeke to reprove the life and doings of the clergie, but after such a sort as they indevour to bringe them into contempt and hatred of the layetie, and so finding falte with other men's manners whom they have no authoritie to correct, omitt and forget their owne, which is far worse and much more out of order then the other.

He went on to remind the Lords of the troubles which Hus and Luther had brought to Bohemia and Germany. Men in those lands had 'almost excluded themselves from the unitie of Christes holy church'. Fearing a similar fate for England, Fisher urged the Upper House to 'resist manfully . . . this violent heape of mischeefe offered by the Commons'. If they did not, the Lords would 'shortly see all obedience withdrawn, first from the clergie, and after from yourselves [the lay aristocracy], wherupon will insewe the utter ruine . . . of the Christian faith, and in place of it . . . the most wicked and tyrannical government of the Turke'. All these mischiefs arose, he concluded, out of lack of faith.[2]

[1] Edward Hall, *Hall's Chronicle*, 766.
[2] [Richard Hall], *The Life of Fisher*, 69–70. Edward Hall has a briefer but similar account of the speech.

87

Fisher's speech met a mixed reception in the Lords. According to the bishop's early biographer, the duke of Norfolk reproved him 'half merrily and half angerly', commenting that the greatest clerks were not always the wisest men.[1] The Commons' reactions were more bitter. They soon heard that Fisher had charged them with lack of faith, and they imagined that he esteemed them all as heretics. A long debate ensued.[2] Finally the House determined to send Audley to the king with a 'grevous complaynt' against the bishop of Rochester.

A few days later the Speaker and thirty members of the Commons saw Henry at York Place. There Audley

very eloquently declared what a dishonour to the kyng and the realme it was to say that they which were elected for the wysest men of all the sheres, cities, and boroughes within the realme of England shoulde be declared in so noble and open presence to lacke faith, whiche was equivalent to say[ing] that they were infidelles and no Christians, as ill as Turkes or Sarasins, so that what payne or studie soever thei toke for the common wealth, or what actes or lawes soever thei made or stablished, shulde be taken as lawes made by panyms [pagans] and hethen people, and not worthy to be kept by Christian men.

Audley asked the king to summon Fisher and 'cause him to speake more discretely' of the Commons.[3]

According to Edward Hall, Henry too was displeased with Fisher's speech, and he promised to send for the bishop. At this the Commons' delegation departed. Some time later Fisher appeared before the king, accompanied by Warham and six other bishops: perhaps he believed the maxim about safety in numbers. We have several versions of what Fisher said at the interview. His early biographer has him stoutly upholding his words in the Lords. Since the common people daily injured and oppressed the

---

[1] Richard Hall, *Life of Fisher*, 70.

[2] Lord Herbert of Cherbury, *King Henry the Eighth*, 321-4, reports a very long discourse which he says was given in the Commons by 'one who had made use of the Evangelicks' doctrine so far, as to take a reasonable liberty to judge of the present times, and howsoever was offended that the Bishop rejected all on want of faith'. The speech emphasizes the variety of religious beliefs and ceremonies, concluding that virtue and love of God are the only essential parts of religion. It is difficult to believe that such deistic sentiments were expressed in 1529, and since the address is not mentioned in any contemporary source the presumption must be that Lord Herbert contrived it himself. It is reprinted in *The Parliamentary or Constitutional History of England*, III, 60-4.

[3] Edward Hall, *Hall's Chronicle*, 766.

Church, 'he thought himself in conscience bound to defend her all that he might'.[1] Edward Hall pictures Fisher as awkwardly trying to explain away his words; he had meant, he said, to accuse only the Bohemians, not the English Commons, of lack of faith. When the bishops confirmed that such had indeed been his meaning, Henry could do little but ask him to use his words more temperately. News of the audience was carried to the Lower House by Sir William Fitzwilliam, but the bishop's apologia pleased the Commons 'nothyng at all'.[2]

Despite their ruffled tempers the two Houses attempted to reach common ground by naming joint committees to consider the bills. In one of these sessions the bishops defended their customs on the grounds of prescription and usage; a gentleman of Gray's Inn—possibly Edward Hall—retorted, 'the usage hath ever ben of theves to robbe on Shoters Hill, ergo is it lawful?'[3] It was now the turn of the clergy to be offended that their tolls were termed robberies, but the Commons stood firm. The same speaker even told the archbishop that his excessive charges for probates and mortuaries were open theft. After several such meetings the temporal peers began to sympathize with the Commons, but they took no immediate action on the bills.

4

Meanwhile the two Houses turned their attention to finance. The king had not summoned Parliament to levy a tax, and he asked for none now. But he did wish the passage of a bill cancelling his obligation to repay the money which subjects had lent him upon privy seals, letters missive, or other obligations. The sums involved were considerable; during 1522 and 1523 alone Wolsey is said to have raised more than £350,000 in forced loans for the war with France.[4]

Although we have two contemporary copies of the bill,[5] there

---

[1] Richard Hall, *Life of Fisher*, 70–1.   [2] *Ibid.* 71; Edward Hall, *Hall's Chronicle*, 766.
[3] Edward Hall, *Hall's Chronicle*, 767. It has long been supposed that Hall was reporting his own words. The number of parliamentarians from Gray's Inn was not large; among the other possible speakers are Thomas Cromwell, John Guildford, John Hynd, Humphrey Wingfield, and Robert Wroth.
[4] F. C. Dietz, *English Government Finance, 1485–1558*, 2nd ed., 94, gives the figure as £352,231, but there is some doubt about his accuracy.
[5] SP 1/56, fols. 15–25 and 26–35, P.R.O. Both are identical to the statute as passed, 21 Henry VIII, c. 24; this is printed in Burnet, *Reformation of the Church of England*, I, App., 82–4, as well as in *S.R.*, III, 315–16.

is no evidence to show who composed it. Since it originated in the Lords, Norfolk may have been its principal architect. It was obviously a government measure, and it begins with a long preamble justifying repudiation of debt by calling attention to the 'inestimable costs, charges, and expenses which the King's Highness necessarily hath been compelled to support and sustain' in defence of the Church, the realm, and the catholic faith. Gilbert Burnet later called this prologue 'the highest flattery that could be put on paper';[1] it is of interest because it antedates Thomas Cromwell's entry into the government and shows that he was not the only believer in persuasion by preamble.

Burnet added that the courtiers had several aims in proposing the bill—they wished not only to assist the king but also to ruin Wolsey's friends, who had advanced large sums. This reasoning doubtless won some support for what was necessarily an un-palatable measure. Others were converted by the argument that the bill would discredit royal borrowing: once bitten subjects would be shy about responding to future loans, and the king would be entirely dependent upon Parliament for supply.[2] There seems to have been little opposition in the Lords, but not all members of the Commons were won over so easily. Hall reports that the bill was 'sore argued' in the Lower House,[3] and we know that John Petyt, one of the burgesses for London, spoke against it. 'I cannot in my conscience', he said, 'agree and consent that this bylle should passe, for I know not my neighboures estate. They perhaps borowed to lend the Kyng.' But Petyt was not totally opposed to remission: he knew his own condition and was ready to give the king freely what he himself had lent.[4] In the end the courtiers persuaded most of the other members, and the bill passed the Commons.[5]

News of it seems to have spread throughout the realm like wildfire. On 20 November Sir Thomas Seymour, the senior

---

[1] Burnet, *Reformation of the Church of England*, I, 83.
[2] *Ibid.*   [3] Edward Hall, *Hall's Chronicle*, 767.
[4] John Louthe's reminiscences on Petyt, printed in Nichols, *Days of the Reformation*, 25-6.
[5] It was in an attempt to explain the passage of this bill that Hall made his comment, 'the most parte of the Commons were the kynges servauntes'. He added that 'the other were so labored to by other, that the bill was assented to': a seeming refutation of his own earlier statement, since if the king's servants were a majority they could have passed the bill without putting pressure on the other members. Edward Hall, *Hall's Chronicle*, 767.

burgess for London, defended the act before the Mercers' Company. He related the king's promise 'that oonles right urgent causes move hym (which shalbe evident to all his said subgiectes) his Grace woll never demaunde peny of them duryng his lyff naturall, and further, in case they coulde study any thyng that myght be for the publique welth of this his roialme and citie of London, his Grace wold right gladly condescende therunto'. Thus beguiled, the mercers 'all admytted the same to be very well done'.[1] The common reaction, according to Hall, was quite different. Almost all who had participated in the loans expected repayment; some had included the item in their wills, others had transferred the credit in payment of their own debts, 'and so many men had losse by it, which caused them sore to murmur' against Parliament. 'But there was no remedy', Hall lamented; Parliament could not, or would not, undo its work.

Passage of the bill, however, had two fortunate results. The king attempted to allay the general discontent by granting his subjects a general pardon for their past offences, and he rewarded the Commons for their unpopular support by helping break the log-jam which immobilized the probate and mortuary bills.

Several features of the pardon are interesting.[2] As usual, it excluded some capital offences. In addition, the pardon did not extend to those who pulled down crosses on the highways—a sign of the rising Protestant temper—or to clergy who violated the statutes of provisors and praemunire. The king in effect served notice that he would use these weapons against the churchmen should they prove recalcitrant; Burnet says that the clause was intended both to keep them quiet and to encourage them to use whatever influence they had at Rome on the king's behalf.[3]

Evidently as a result of this warning, the bishops ceased their opposition to the regulation of probate and mortuary fees. New bills were drawn up, perhaps by a joint committee but more likely by councillors, which Hall calls 'so reasonable that the spirituall Lordes assented to them, although thei were sore against there myndes'. Neither mortuaries nor probate charges were forbidden; the acts simply established scales of fees according to the

---

[1] Quoted in Miller, 'London and Parliament', 145.   [2] 21 Henry VIII, c. 1.
[3] Burnet, *Reformation of the Church of England*, 1, 84. The prosecution of Wolsey was also excluded from the act, so that the king could claim the lands of Cardinal's College, Oxford.

means of the payer. No doubt the language of the earlier drafts had been toned down, and the penalties softened.[1]

Emboldened by this success, the Commons proceeded to their third bill against the clergy. This was an omnibus measure, intended primarily to limit pluralism and non-residence. It also prohibited clergy from holding farms, keeping tanning-houses or breweries, and dealing in cattle, corn, or other merchandise.

The Lower House passed the bill enthusiastically and sent it up to the Lords. The churchmen there were so angry that (according to Hall) they 'railed on the Commons, . . . and called them heretikes and scismatikes'. The Lords spiritual utterly refused their assent to the measure.

The Commons now appealed directly to the king. In a petition they asked him to command the spiritual lords to declare plainly the 'lawes of God and holye churche' on pluralism, non-residence, and temporal employment of clergy. In particular they inquired 'whether any spiritual person by the lawe of God or holie churche may use buying and selling for lucre and gayne, and yf he may, then . . . after what manner and in what cases they may do so by the said lawes'.[2]

Henry did not call the bishops to account before him, but he did attempt to loosen the deadlock by ordering a committee of eight members from each House to meet one afternoon in the Star Chamber. Since the bishops were not able to justify their position convincingly, the session produced a clear split between the laity and the clergy. Some saving clauses were finally added to the bill, and the temporal peers persuaded their spiritual brethren to accept it. The next day the Lords passed the measure, to the great rejoicing of the laymen and great displeasure of the priests.[3]

The statute as finally enacted is hedged about with provisos.[4] Unfortunately neither the original act itself nor drafts for it now exist, so that we cannot tell just what qualifications were added by

---

[1] Edward Hall, *Hall's Chronicle*, 767. The acts are 21 Henry VIII, cc. 5 and 6. Their preambles bear little sign of bitterness; that of c. 5 is purely historical, while c. 6 states only that the fees demanded as mortuaries are thought 'over-excessive'.

[2] Cottonian MS. Cleopatra F. II, fol. 257, B.M., incorrectly dated 1532 by *L.P.*, v, 721 (2).

[3] Edward Hall, *Hall's Chronicle*, 767.   [4] 21 Henry VIII, c. 13.

the committee.[1] The chief purpose of the act is to prevent clergy from holding more than one benefice with cure of souls worth eights pounds a year or above, and to enforce their residence upon this benefice for at least ten months of the year. Penalties are established—twenty pounds for illegal pluralism and ten pounds for non-residence, with half in each case going to the king and half to the informer. But the exceptions are so numerous that few priests would have felt the act's full rigour. Up to four benefices could be retained if they were acquired before April 1530. Members of the king's Council might keep three benefices, and royal chaplains two. Chaplains to bishops and temporal peers might hold two benefices; an elaborate gradation allows archbishops and dukes to have six chaplains, marquises and earls five, viscounts and bishops four, and so on down to the warden of the Cinque Ports with one.[2] Priests possessing university degrees in divinity or law might also have two benefices; chaplains, clerics occupied in the king's service, and scholars living at the universities are exempted from the residence requirement. A clause fraught with implications for the future prohibits Englishmen from seeking papal dispensations for non-residence.

The other sections of the bill were probably little modified. Clerics who held farms were allowed to grant them to laymen of their own choosing; they were permitted to have orchards and gardens adjacent to their dwellings and could retain other lands necessary for the support of their own households. Heads of smaller monasteries were allowed to keep whatever lands and farms their predecessors had held. But in the main the clerics

---

[1] It can be argued that during our period most sections beginning 'provided that' were added after the original composition of bills, usually as amendments following debate in the two Houses. The original acts of all sessions of the Reformation Parliament except 1529 are preserved in the House of Lords Record Office, and these often indicate clearly—by changes in handwriting or colour of ink, or by attachment of strips of parchment—what clauses were added after engrossment of the bill. The statute against pluralism presents an unusual situation in that it contains five sections of enacting clauses, each followed by relevant provisos: if the provisos had been added in debate they would appear at the end of the act unless the House ordered it redrafted. The limited evidence therefore seems to suggest that the committee inserted provisos—its own as well as those which came from the Commons and Lords—where appropriate and had the bill recopied.

[2] Archbishops and bishops might in fact have two more chaplains than the number stated above, since a proviso, doubtless added by the committee, recognizes the canonical requirement that archbishops be attended by eight chaplains, and bishops by six, at consecrations.

were effectively barred from taking part in agriculture, manufacturing, or trade. Many of the Commons' complaints had been remedied.[1]

5

Although the Parliament had been preoccupied with charges against the clergy, its members found time to consider a variety of other matters. Several abortive drafts are associated with the session of 1529 even though they did not find their way to the statute books then.

One of these is an important bill which sought to correct difficulties in the land law.[2] Its preamble cites the 'grete trobull, vexacion, and unquietnes' which had arisen: entails, uses, and forged evidences in particular led to litigation, 'intollerable costes and charges, and utter undoyng' of many subjects. For remedy, the bill made three main proposals. Entails were simply to be abolished, so that all lands would be held in fee simple and could be alienated freely or bequeathed by their owners. Uses—the procedure under which lands were held by a continuing group of trustees to the use or profit of another, so as to avoid feudal incidents and other difficulties of inheritance—presented a harder problem. The draft allowed the continuation of uses, despite their obvious inconvenience to the king, but held them valid only if they were recorded in the Court of Common Pleas. To prevent forgeries and secret conveyances, each purchaser was required to have his deed read publicly in the church of the parish where the land lay and to have it registered in the shire town. In a brave but unrealistic attempt to cut off litigation, the bill confirmed the possession of lands to all whose ancestors had held them peaceably for forty years, without regard to earlier defects of title.

The most unusual feature of the bill is a proviso allowing noblemen to retain the practice of entail. Perhaps the anonymous

---

[1] J. J. Scarisbrick has shown that more than two hundred cases alleging infringement of these anti-clerical statutes were brought in the Exchequer court, but few were carried through to a decision: see his dissertation, 'The Conservative Episcopate in England, 1529-1535', 88-95.

[2] SP 1/56, fols. 36-9, P.R.O., calendared in *L.P.*, IV, iii, 6043 (6) and printed in full in Holdsworth, *History of English Law*, IV, 572-4. For a discussion of the bill see *ibid.* 451-3, and E. W. Ives, 'The Genesis of the Statute of Uses', *E.H.R.*, LXXXII (1967), 676-97, where Holdsworth's analysis is challenged.

drafter of the measure realized that large holdings were necessary for the support of peers, and that these could not be guaranteed without the safeguards which entails provided. As a further protection, the bill allowed peers to sell portions of their estates only if they had obtained the king's license under the Great Seal. Professor Plucknett has emphasized the remarkable character of this scheme for an endowed peerage, with a separate body of law for noblemen.[1]

It is unlikely that this draft was part of the government's programme: it contains some naive proposals, and it fails to remedy the evasion of feudal obligations which was the king's chief concern.[2] In any case it did not become law. We know only that the document was thought worthy of preservation, presumably among Cromwell's papers.

This bill has sometimes been considered an early version of the great statute of uses. In fact it bears no direct relation to that act and is more likely a forerunner of the statute of enrolments enacted in 1536. But another document of 1529 does represent an attempt by the government to solve the problem of uses. This is an agreement, signed by the chancellor and thirty peers, which permits the device of land and evasion of feudal incidents on two-thirds of an estate in return for the inescapable obligation to pay the king his full dues on the remaining third.[3] The Crown was to have the wardship of all infant heirs of tenants-in-chief, whether the tenant had a use or legal estate. As before, heirs who were of full age were to pay the king half a year's profits upon suing out livery of their lands. No gift in tail or other scheme to exclude the king from his profits was to be valid, but the king on his part promised to be content with the specified benefits even though

---

[1] T. F. T. Plucknett, 'Some Proposed Legislation of Henry VIII', *T.R.H.S.*, 4th ser., xix (1936), 122–4. Plucknett would seem to exaggerate the uniqueness of the proposal; after all, there had been separate arrangements for tenants-in-chief since the inception of the feudal system.

[2] Ives, 'The Genesis of the Statute of Uses', 677–9, argues convincingly against the official provenance which had been posited by Elton ('Parliamentary Drafts', 132).

[3] Cottonian MS. Titus B. iv, fols. 114–18, B.M., fully calendared in *L.P.*, iv, iii, 6044, printed in Holdsworth, *History of English Law*, 574–7. Plucknett ('Some Proposed Legislation of Henry VIII', 122 n. 3) erroneously says that the articles were signed by the Speaker of the Commons; in fact the Lower House had nothing to do with them, and the Audley whose name appears was of course John Tuchet, Baron Audley. The king and Sir Thomas More, as chancellor, also signed the articles; the list of signatures is one of the few guides to the temporal peers actually present in Parliament during the 1529 session.

his administrators might discover novel devices favourable to him.

This agreement seems to have been drawn up too late for parliamentary action in 1529. The signatories promised nevertheless to abide by it and to procure statutory enactment 'in the next full Court [of Parliament] after the prorogacion'. The paper was filed away for future use.

Another bill grew out of the parliamentary programme of the Mercers' Company and was doubtless drafted by some of the burgesses for London. The mercers had complained that 'protections' granted under the Great Seal allowed many persons to detain large sums of money and goods belonging to others;[1] the draft bill likewise alleges that merchants often claim to be suppliers of victual to Calais, Berwick, or some other royal fortress so as to place themselves in the king's protection and escape their creditors.[2] To insure against future abuses the bill would require merchants claiming protection to make sufficient surety in the Court of Chancery for the payment of their debts. The bill was read in the Lower House and committed to a London member, Paul Withypoll, together with Thomas Cromwell, Edward Hall, John Brenning, and the lawyer Henry See.[3] Although one would suppose them favourable to the bill, nothing further seems to have been heard of it. It may conceivably have passed to the Commons, but it was not enacted.

Two further drafts were of little interest save to their promoters. In one the mayor and other townspeople of Oxford charged that they were 'clearly put from the benyfyte of the lawes of the realme' by the privileges which Wolsey had given to the university in 1526. No doubt they hoped to turn the cardinal's fall to their advantage in the struggle between town and gown; they sought to have his grant cancelled and to prevent university officials from interfering with townsmen.[4] The other draft refers to two London forges which had been destroyed long before in Jack Straw's rebellion. They could not be rebuilt, since they would block Fleet Street, but the prior of St John's was still liable for the payment of fifteen shillings a year to the Exchequer

---

[1] Miller, 'London and Parliament', 143.
[2] SP 1/236, fols. 166–7, P.R.O. (L.P., Addenda, i, i, 663).
[3] Ibid. (the names are listed in an endorsement); Miller, 'London and Parliament', 144.   [4] SP 1/56, fols. 48–58, P.R.O. (L.P., iv, iii, 6046).

on their account. The bill would remit the rent and give the site to the king.[1] Despite the possible justice of these complaints, neither measure was passed.

6

But a number of bills, in addition to the three regulating the clergy, did make their way through both Houses. In all, twenty-six statutes were enacted during the session. Nine of these attempted to regulate economics and trade, and nine more effected changes in the English legal system.

The economic measures emphasize the extent of governmental regulation and paternalism under the Tudors. Three statutes of 1529 involved the country generally: one prohibited the slaughter of calves born during the first four months of the year, in order to increase the supply of mature cattle;[2] another fixed the prices of imported hats, bonnets, and night-caps;[3] the third outlawed the export of latten brass or similar alloys, because of the scarcity of copper within the realm.[4] An additional six bills were intended to benefit commerce in specified areas. London artificers secured the ratification of an earlier Star Chamber decree limiting the privileges of alien craftsmen,[5] and the linen merchants of the City obtained a statute fixing the size of imported cloths called dowlasses and lockrams.[6] Statutory regulations were established for the port at Newcastle-upon-Tyne, and unsatisfactory letters patent relating to trade at York were cancelled.[7] Other acts encouraged the making of ships' tackle at Bridport and the manufacture of worsteds in Lynn and Great Yarmouth.[8]

The legal reforms were more technical but perhaps of greater

---

[1] SP 1/56, fols. 44–7, P.R.O. (*L.P.*, IV, iii, 6043 [8]).

[2] 21 Henry VIII, c. 8.

[3] 21 Henry VIII, c. 9. Chapuys complained that the statute required the sale of French caps at half the price of English ones (*C.S.P., Spn.*, IV, i, 232). An ineffectual earlier act had attempted to limit the use of foreign hats and caps to knights and peers; see Andrew Amos, *Observations on the Statutes of the Reformation Parliament*, 99.

[4] 21 Henry VIII, c. 10.   [5] 21 Henry VIII, c. 16.

[6] 21 Henry VIII, c. 14. The statute, on petition from the linen drapers, enforces the ancient assize of dowlas and lockram, cloths originally made in Britanny.

[7] 21 Henry VIII, c. 18 (a petition from the residents of Newcastle) and c. 17.

[8] 21 Henry VIII, c. 12 (another enacted petition) and c. 21, which extends the life of a previous statute for the same purpose. According to Chapuys these commercial matters kept Parliament very busy during the closing weeks of the session (*C.S.P., Spn.*, IV, i, 232).

significance. Four statutes dealt with criminal procedure. In order to limit the privilege of sanctuary, felons and murderers who had fled to sanctuary within a church were now to be branded on the right thumb with the letter 'A' and were to make their abjuration—that is, swear to depart from the realm—at a time fixed by the coroner rather than after the traditional forty days; if they did not quit the church at the appointed time they were to lose all benefits of sanctuary.[1] Embezzlement by servants of goods which their masters had entrusted to them was declared to be a felony,[2] and felons judged guilty of robbery were required to make restitution of stolen property.[3] Henry VII's famous statute dealing with livery and maintenance, riots, embracery, and untrue demeaning of sheriffs was re-enacted, perhaps in an unsuccessful attempt to revive its special tribunal after years in which Wolsey had handled such crimes in the Star Chamber; the enhanced power of the president of the king's Council was recognized by adding him to the panel of officers prescribed in 1487.[4]

Parliament also altered certain practices in civil matters. Plaintiffs in land suits before the assizes were allowed to abridge their plaints, so as to deal only with convenient portions of the property in question.[5] In cases where some executors refused to sell land although ordered to do so by the will of the deceased, sales and bargains by those executors willing to act were pronounced valid.[6] Tenants who had leased land for a term of years were given protection against ouster by new landlords who had obtained the freehold by fictitious recoveries, and landlords were given the power to collect rents and other dues from tenants even if, because of secret agreements and leases, they did not know who currently lived on their properties.[7] Finally, persons who held the use of lands where Wolsey was one of the feoffees were protected from difficulties which might arise because of his attainder.[8]

---

[1] 21 Henry VIII, c. 2; cf. Amos, *Observations*, 175–6.

[2] 21 Henry VIII, c. 7. The act excluded apprentices and youths under eighteen, and was applicable only if the value of the stolen property exceeded forty shillings. In 1536 Parliament went further and denied sanctuary to servants who stole their masters' goods.   [3] 21 Henry VIII, c. 11.

[4] 21 Henry VIII, c. 20, re-enacting 3 Henry VII, c. 1, the act erroneously called 'Pro Camera Stellata'. Cf. Elton, *The Tudor Constitution*, 160.

[5] 21 Henry VIII, c. 3.   [6] 21 Henry VIII, c. 4.

[7] 21 Henry VIII, cc. 15, 19; cf. Amos, *Observations*, 122–7.

[8] 21 Henry VIII, c. 25.

Three private acts completed the statutes of the session. Two were designed to assure certain lands in Lincolnshire, Hertfordshire, and Suffolk to the duke and duchess of Norfolk and their heirs.[1] The other settled the five-year dispute over the estate of John Roper by granting most of the inheritance to his eldest son William, More's son-in-law and a member of the Commons.[2] The senior Roper had owned land in Eltham and Canterbury; his will proved contentious because he ignored the Kentish custom of gavelkind, under which properties descended to the male heirs in equal portions.

7

Since the Commons showed such interest in condemning churchmen, one might have expected the concurrent gathering of clergy to generate either internal reform of the Church or a staunch defence of the ecclesiastical establishment. In fact no such action occurred. During the first month of the session Convocation met regularly enough, on Monday and Friday, but proved singularly ineffectual.[3]

Warham, presiding on 12 November, discussed those abuses which he thought Convocation might curb. He mentioned mainly the age-old failings of the clergy: they visited taverns, played dice, and attended indecent spectacles; their apparel was excessively elaborate, and they practised simony. The archbishop also suggested some better provision for churches which had been appropriated by monasteries or other bodies. He closed by threatening to excommunicate any cleric who revealed the proceedings of Convocation to persons outside the house, of whatever degree. Perhaps he knew that the Commons were debating the faults of the Church, and was unwilling to add fuel to their fire.

On the following Monday Richard Wolman, the Prolocutor of the inferior clergy, reported their views on the reform of abuses, only to be sent back to the lower house with instructions

[1] 21 Henry VIII, cc. 22, 26.
[2] 21 Henry VIII, c. 23; *D.N.B. sub* William Roper. Depositions concerning the will were still being taken in 1531; see *L.P.*, v, 139.
[3] The following narrative is drawn from C.C. 306, 27–9, and David Wilkins, *Concilia Magnae Britanniae et Hiberniae*, iii, 717. The latter is based on John Heylyn's transcripts of the lost *Acta Convocationis*.

to frame specific articles. Warham was now off on another tack: he asked for a general procession of clergy throughout the province of Canterbury to demonstrate English opposition to the Turks, whose siege of Vienna had just been repulsed. The Convocation itself trooped solemnly through St Paul's on Wednesday, 17 November.[1] Two days later Wolman showed the upper house a 'copious multitude' of reforms, but there could be no debate because Warham had other pressing business: Convocation was to announce, as Parliament had done, that the king need not repay forced loans. The clergy agreed to cancel the sums due to them, freely and voluntarily according to the record, and the archbishop proceeded to settle a controversy between the bishop of Hereford and the prior of St John's. On the 22nd Wolman again presented his list of reforms, and Bishop Booth exhibited some articles for the better behaviour of clerics, but discussion was deferred until the next session. The articles conceived in the lower house were finally read on the 26th, but action was postponed. Warham was now more interested in legislation against heretical laymen than in ordinances to reform the clergy. On the 29th he gave a long address denouncing heretics, and Bishop Clerk produced a long list of heretical books,[2] but nothing concrete was done. One wonders if the episode was related to the discussion of heresy in the Commons. On 3 December specific ordinances against heretics were presented; action was once more put off. For some reason Convocation did not meet again. Parliament had two weeks to run, and Warham himself may have anticipated further meetings since he did not prorogue Convocation until 24 December.

It is impossible to be certain why the clergy went home without completing their deliberations or enacting their reforms. No doubt the anti-clerical bills which had presumably passed Parliament by 3 December rendered internal reform pointless: the Commons could not be appeased by a show of action from the Church itself. Or it may be that the bishops and mitred

---

[1] The pope and Charles V were asking England to join in a crusade against the Turk; Chapuys feared that nothing more than a procession and bonfires would result and wondered if Henry intended to 'pay us out in smoke' (C.S.P., Spn., IV, i, 216).

[2] This may be similar to the list printed in Wilkins, Concilia, III, 719-21. Wilkins assumed that it was from 1529, but internal evidence shows that it cannot be earlier than 1530 and Kelly has assigned it to the 1532 session: 'Canterbury Jurisdiction', 233.

abbots were so busy opposing the parliamentary bill against pluralism and non-residence that they had no energy left for their own articles. In any case Convocation appeared to confirm the Commons' view that reformation of the Church could not be left to the churchmen. The ecclesiastics had held up some small pieces of dirty linen but had done nothing to whiten them.

Bishop Fisher's early biographer set another scene in the Convocation of 1529. The king, he asserted, was already casting greedy eyes on the monasteries, and wished to suppress all houses worth less than two hundred pounds a year. The proposal was argued by members of the Council, 'with all the tirrible shewe that might be of the king's displeasure yf it were not graunted'. Some clergy were willing to yield, thinking that by condescending to this limited demand they could satisfy the king's appetite, but Fisher spoke out against such appeasement. He told the clergy a fable,

howe the axe that lacked a handle came on a time to the wood, and making his moane to the great trees, how that for lack of a handle to worke withal he was faine to stand ydle: he therfore desired of them to graunt him some yonge sapling in the wood to make him one; they mistrustinge no guile forthwith graunted a yong small tree, wherof he shaped himself a handle, and being at last a perfect axe in all points, he fell to worke, and so labored in the wood, that in processe of time he left nether great tree nor small standinge.

If the king were given the small monasteries Fisher believed that he would cut down the large soon after. Convocation supposedly agreed. The king's request was denied, and no more was heard of it so long as Fisher lived.[1]

Despite a certain ring of credibility the story must be treated with scepticism. The only evidence which may corroborate it is Chapuys' report that late in the session the king wished to have Parliament consider a measure which would bleed the clergy.[2] Still, the biographer's account of Fisher's activities in Parliament is confirmed by Edward Hall. His description of the bishop's speech in Convocation may be correct also.

8

The king's divorce and the cardinal's disgrace ran as under-currents

[1] Richard Hall, *Life of Fisher*, 71-2.   [2] *C.S.P., Spn.*, IV, i, 232.

throughout the session. Chapuys had feared for months that action unfavourable to Catherine would be taken, and on 13 December he reported that Henry hoped to lay before Parliament the opinion of the University of Paris, which was expected daily.[1] If that was indeed Henry's desire it was frustrated, for the Paris theologians did not render their sentence for some months.[2] The king had developed no other parliamentary programme for the divorce, and the issue seems never to have reached the surface. It was of course on everyone's mind, and Henry's councillors must have welcomed the anti-clerical legislation of 1529 as a means of weakening the independent position of the clergy, should they oppose whatever steps might prove necessary to secure a favourable decision.

Henry did not wish Parliament to discuss Wolsey's misdeeds. Since the King's Bench had already found Wolsey guilty of praemunire, no parliamentary action was needed, and Henry realized that it would be difficult to pardon the cardinal if Parliament pronounced against him.[3] Indeed the king continued to soften as the session progressed: on 18 November he reversed a portion of the court's judgment and received Wolsey back into royal protection during his pleasure.[4]

But parliamentary discussion could not be damped down so easily. The noblemen who stood to benefit from Wolsey's fall were dismayed at the prospect of his rising again, and a number of them proceeded to draw up articles setting out his 'enormities, excesses, and transgressions'.[5] Norfolk, Suffolk, and Rochford (Anne Boleyn's father, soon to be created earl of Wiltshire) were doubtless the moving spirits; they were joined by nine other temporal peers[6] as well as the chancellor, the two chief justices, and two members of the Commons: Sir William Fitzwilliam and

---

[1] *C.S.P., Spn.*, IV, i, 232.   [2] *L.P.*, IV, iii, 6497.

[3] So reported Chapuys: Chapuys MS., fol. 283ᵛ (*C.S.P., Spn.*, IV, i, 257); the dispatch is translated in full in Bradford, *Correspondence of the Emperor Charles V*, 298–319.

[4] *L.P.*, IV, iii, 6059.

[5] Printed in *Parliamentary or Constitutional History*, III, 42–55; summarized in *L.P.*, IV, iii, 6075; Edward Hall, *Hall's Chronicle*, 767–8; and A. F. Pollard, *Wolsey*, 258–61. The original document has disappeared but copies were made by Edward Coke and Lord Herbert.

[6] Dorset, Exeter, Shrewsbury, Fitzwalter (i.e. Robert Radcliffe, soon to be earl of Sussex), Oxford, Northumberland, Darcy, Mountjoy, and Sandys. Darcy had compiled a list of charges against Wolsey during the previous summer; see above, Ch. 1.

Sir Henry Guildford, both officers of the king's household. Interestingly enough, none of the Lords spiritual served on the committee.

This group produced a torrent of accusation. In forty-four articles they charged Wolsey with violating the liberties of the Church, usurping the jurisdiction of the bishops, despoiling religious houses, claiming equality with the king, exposing Henry to 'the foul and contagious disease of the great pox', interfering with the operation of the common law courts, and generally subverting the 'due course and order' of the king's laws 'to the undoing of a great number of . . . people'.

The articles were cast in the form of a petition and were probably presented to the king on 1 December. They proposed no new action against the cardinal but asked merely 'that he be so provided for, that he never have any power, jurisdiction, or authority hereafter to trouble, vex, and impoverish this your realm'. The aim was evidently to record Wolsey's misdeeds and to impress upon Henry the strength of the feeling against him.

A copy of this petition was sent to the Commons. So far as we know there was no debate; certainly no action was required of the House, glad as its members would have been to attack the author of so many faults in Church and State. Years afterward Cavendish wrote that Thomas Cromwell defended his fallen master before the Commons 'so discreetly, with such witty persuasion and deep reasons, that the same bill could take there no effect'.[1] Unfortunately Cavendish's chronology had become badly confused. He thought that the bill charged Wolsey with treason, and that the indictment at King's Bench occurred only after its failure. Possibly Cromwell did make some attempt to help Wolsey. We know that the cardinal sought his counsel and committed to him certain 'thynges requyryng exspedition'.[2] But Edward Hall, who was probably present in the Commons, made no mention of Cromwell. He recorded simply that the articles were 'red in the Common House, and signed with the Cardinalles hand, . . . confessed by hym; and also ther was shewed a writyng sealed with his seale, by the whiche he gave to the king all his movables and unmovables'.[3] Evidently the petition was sent down only to

---

[1] Cavendish, *Life and Death of Cardinal Wolsey*, 116.
[2] Wolsey to Cromwell, [4 December?], Cottonian MS. Vespasian F. xiii, fol. 147, B.M. (*L.P.*, iv, iii, 6080).   [3] Edward Hall, *Hall's Chronicle*, 768.

inform the Commons, and to demonstrate that all necessary action against Wolsey had been taken.

9

Although it was customary to conclude parliamentary sessions before Christmas, so that members might spend the holidays at home, the exact date of prorogation does not seem to have been determined much in advance. On 6 December Chapuys wrote that Parliament had already been prorogued until after Easter.[1] Perhaps that was Henry's original intention, but the work in hand could not be completed so rapidly. A week later Chapuys said that the king had been trying to close Parliament for a fortnight and that one meeting, at least, continued until late at night with no pause for refreshment.[2] The session was not actually terminated until 17 December.

In the concluding ceremony Sir Thomas More gave the king's assent to the bills which had passed both Houses, including the three anti-clerical measures. When he came to the act freeing Henry from repaying the loans More extended the king's thanks to the Lords and Commons;[3] he approved the other acts with the usual formulas in law French. If the king vetoed any bills we do not know about it.

Members could look forward to no long holiday, for Henry ordered them to meet again on 26 April, the second Tuesday after Easter.[4] At that time, armed with a favourable opinion from the Paris theologians, he expected to lay his divorce before Parliament.

[1] Chapuys MS., fol. 246 (*C.S.P., Spn.*, iv, i, 224).
[2] *C.S.P., Spn.*, iv, i, 232.
[3] Parliament Roll, C 65/138, m. 21, P.R.O.; *S.R.*, iii, 316 n. 3.
[4] Chapuys MS., fol. 260; *C.S.P., Spn.*, iv, i, 241. Chapuys wrote that he was enclosing an account of the Parliament, but it does not survive with his other manuscripts.

6

THE SECOND SESSION, 1531: PRAEMUNIRE AND PARDON

Throughout 1530 Henry was preoccupied with his divorce and planned to utilize Parliament in achieving it. On Easter Monday—11 April—he summoned Chapuys to Windsor for a long interview; as the ambassador was leaving, Norfolk overtook him and asked point blank whether Spain would make war on England should Henry marry Anne with the sanction of the English churchmen.[1] A few weeks earlier the French envoy had reported Henry's intention to settle the matter within England, by the advice of Parliament, omitting all recourse to the pope.[2] No doubt both statements indicate what was to be expected at the session of Parliament scheduled to begin 26 April. But when the day came Henry was not prepared to proceed; he was still awaiting the opinion of the theological faculty at Paris as well as the return of Wiltshire, Stokesley, and Edward Lee, whom he had sent to the Continent in an attempt to conciliate the pope and Charles V.[3] Parliament was prorogued to 22 June, ostensibly on account of the plague raging in London and its suburbs.[4] In June the session was again postponed, this time to 1 October, because of the pestilence.[5]

The plague was perfectly genuine—in September it carried off Chapuys' household priest—but the Spanish ambassador was shrewd enough to doubt that it was the real cause of the prorogations.[6] In fact it served as a transparent mask for governmental indecision. Affairs had not been going well for the king. Unexpected difficulties arose in Paris, and even when a favourable decision was obtained in July it was far from unanimous.[7] Wiltshire's embassy met with small success. In March the pope answered Catherine's appeal with a bull citing Henry to appear in Rome, so that the case might be decided there, and inhibiting all other judiciary process under pain of excommunication and

---

[1] Chapuys MS., fol. 304ᵛ (C.S.P., Spn., IV, i, 290).   [2] L.P., IV, iii, 6307.
[3] Cf. Edward Hall, Hall's Chronicle, 768–9.   [4] L.P., IV, iii, 6356.
[5] Ibid. 6469.   [6] Chapuys MS., fols. 330, 335 (C.S.P., Spn., IV, i, 422, 425).
[7] L.P., V, 3, 6.

interdict.[1] Henry found it hard to decide what to do. Perhaps he agreed for a time with Norfolk's proposal that England ignore the pope, or perhaps he and the duke suggested it only to frighten Charles V and Clement VII. Perhaps he intended to have Parliament grant his divorce, or perhaps he expected it merely to apply pressure to the papacy. In any case Henry finally rejected unilateral action. Whatever steps might ultimately prove necessary, for the present it seemed best to negotiate further with Rome. Henry adopted a policy of temporizing, threatening, cajoling, and hoping.

As part of this programme Henry summoned a number of his leading supporters to appear at court on 12 June. He pointedly passed over the chancellor and those prelates who favoured Catherine. At the meeting he urged those present, most of whom were members of the Lords, to write a letter to the pope pressing for immediate and favourable action. After a three-day recess, during which time the letter was probably composed by Henry's secretaries and advisers, the group met again on Corpus Christi Day. A number of signatures may have been given them; others were gathered by commissioners sent out especially for that purpose.[2] Eighty-three persons finally signed.[3]

The letter[4] asserted that all Englishmen were suffering from the delay in granting Henry's divorce and explained the necessity of his remarriage. In conclusion it threatened the pope: 'If your Holiness ... shall, by refusing to comply herein, esteem us as castaways and resolve to leave us orphans, we can make no other construction of it but that the care of ourselves is committed to our own hands, and that we are left to seek remedy elsewhere.'

---

[1] L.P., IV, iii, 6256.

[2] Chapuys, in C.S.P., Spn., IV, i, 354, 366. Scarisbrick, in Henry VIII, 259, suggests that the magnates were displeased at the belligerent tone of the letter presented to them on 12 June, and refused to sign until it was redrafted.

[3] Only four bishops (besides Wolsey and Warham) and five members of the Commons were among the signatories.

[4] The document itself is in the Vatican Archives; a copy, beautifully written in an italic hand, is in the P.R.O., E 30/1012A. It has been printed, in Latin, by Thomas Rymer, Foedera, XIV, 405–6; Bishop Kennett's English translation is in The Parliamentary or Constitutional History of England, III, 68–73. The authors of this volume state erroneously that the letter was considered at a session of Parliament; for a correct version of the events see Knowles, Religious Orders in England, III, 174–5. The calendar in L.P., IV, iii, 6513, is of little use except for the list of signers, which is more accurate than that in the Parliamentary or Constitutional History.

Such a remedy might be extreme, but sick men were forced to look for relief wherever it might be found.

Clement VII's calm reply, written late in September, blamed Henry himself for causing the delay by his failure to send a lawful proctor to the Roman court. Clement could not understand the reasons for the Englishmen's complaint, 'unless you will venture to say that the services which his Majesty has shown us and the Apostolic See are such that the cause should be determined in his favor, without regard had either to right or justice: for that must be the meaning of your words'. As for extreme remedies, it was no fault of the physician if a patient, weary of his illness, rashly ventured upon measures destructive of his health.[1] The interchange of letters accomplished nothing, since it did nothing to alter the political realities underlying the case.

Henry's ambassadors at Rome—Ghinucci, Bennet, and Casale—were no more successful. Their futile instructions were to argue that an English monarch could not be summoned to appear out of his realm, and if that failed to seek a delay until January.[2] Chapuys believed that Henry would immediately bring the case before Parliament if proceedings were commenced at Rome.[3] On 25 September Wiltshire and Suffolk told the papal nuncio that England cared nothing for popes, even if St Peter should come to life again, since the king's absolute power made him both emperor and pope within his realm.[4] Henry himself was so concerned that he assumed personal direction of his affairs; never before had he devoted so much time to business and so little to sport.[5]

During these months a good deal of time and money was expended in securing the opinions of universities in France and Italy. At home, the government lodged praemunire charges against fifteen leading clerics, who were summoned to answer in King's Bench during Michaelmas term.[6] Among the fifteen were a number of Catherine of Aragon's chief supporters: Bishops

---

[1] Translated in *Parliamentary or Constitutional History*, III, 73–9; poorly calendared in *L.P.*, IV, iii, 6638.

[2] *L.P.*, IV, iii, 6667.　　　　　　　　　　　　[3] *C.S.P.*, *Spn.*, IV, i, 443.

[4] Chapuys MS., fol. 340 (*C.S.P.*, *Spn.*, IV, i, 445).

[5] *C.S.P.*, *Milan*, 818; *C.S.P.*, *Spn.*, IV, i, 422.

[6] Our knowledge of this episode rests upon research by Dr Scarisbrick into the King's Bench controlment roll for 1530; see his article, 'The Pardon of the Clergy, 1531', *Cambridge Historical Journal*, XII (1956), 25–9; his unpublished dissertation, 'The Conservative Episcopate in England, 1529–1535', 114–27; and his *Henry VIII*, 273–4.

Fisher, Clerk, West, and Standish; Adam Travers, the archdeacon of Exeter.[1] But Tunstall was not cited, and three clerics who were summoned had signed the letter to the pope,[2] so it is difficult to view the episode solely as a vindictive act against a selected group of the king's enemies. Whatever Henry's precise aim—and it may have been simply to frighten the bishops and inferior clergy by striking out at a random group of them—these cases were never heard. The trial was first postponed, then cancelled.[3]

These abortive praemunire proceedings, like the parliamentary prorogations, demonstrated the government's indecision. As Cromwell wrote to Wolsey on 21 October, 'the prelattes shal not appere [in the] premunire. Ther ys another way devysyd, . . . as your Grace shall ferther know'.[4] Henry's advisers seem to have decided that praemunire charges should be brought against all the clergy of the realm, not just fifteen of them, on the grounds that all had honoured Wolsey's papal appointment as legate.[5]

The broader approach was perhaps dictated by fear that the cardinal was about to rise again. In April he at last made his way to the borders of his archdiocese, and he had laid plans for his enthronement as archbishop at York minster on 7 November. He summoned the Convocation of the northern province to meet on the same day; Tunstall had to inform him that Parliament and the Convocation of Canterbury had been postponed, and to remind him that the Convocation of York customarily waited to see what the southern province had done 'and theropon to consent or dissent as the case hath requiryd'.[6] None of the magnates in London wished Wolsey to regain glory in an imposing ceremony or to exert authority in Convocation, and they may have feared that he would publish some papal bull at York, since he was

---

[1] Clerk and Travers were among the six clerics who opposed Henry in the Convocation of 1533 by voting that Catherine's marriage to Arthur was not proved to have been consummated. Nicholas Pocock, *Records of the Reformation*, II, 457-8.

[2] Bishop Sherburne of Chichester and the abbots of Waltham and Bury.

[3] Scarisbrick, 'Pardon of the Clergy', 27.

[4] Merriman, *Life and Letters of Thomas Cromwell*, I, 334.

[5] It is not clear if Henry ever intended to indict the whole body of clergy at King's Bench. Since they did not form a legal entity, it is more probable that from the first he planned to deal with them in Parliament and Convocation. Hall says that 'the spiritual Lordes were called by proces into the Kynges Benche to answer' (Edward Hall, *Hall's Chronicle*, 774), but as Scarisbrick has shown he confused the earlier charges against selected clerics with the later action against them all ('Pardon of the Clergy', 28).

[6] SP 1/58, fol. 133, P.R.O. (*L.P.*, IV, iii, 6679).

known to have been in communication with Rome. Accordingly, on 1 November they sent out a groom of the king's chamber with instructions to arrest the cardinal. Three days later Wolsey was taken into custody as he ate dinner at Cawood. He would doubtless have faced charges of high treason, but before he could reach London he was removed from all earthly jurisdiction. He died at Leicester on 29 November.[1]

Meanwhile the parliamentary session had been put off yet again, to January 1531. Chapuys emphasized the inability of the king and his advisers to develop an effective programme when he wrote, late in December, 'Parliament is prorogued from time to time, as if they do not know their own minds about the measures to be proposed therein'.[2]

I

Even when Parliament met it was given little to do with the development of high policy. The dramatic scenes and important actions were reserved instead for Convocation.

The clerics, dismayed by the praemunire charges and fearful of a general attack, gathered on 12 January at St Paul's.[3] There was now no splendid ceremonial; instead Warham and the members of the upper house conferred at length about the difficult situation which faced them. The archbishop enjoined strict secrecy, a customary admonition now fraught with uncommon urgency. At the second meeting Stokesley, who had replaced Tunstall as bishop of London, reiterated the warning and threatened to excommunicate anyone who might reveal what was said in the two houses.

On 19 January, before any serious business had been concluded, Stokesley ordered the session transferred to the Chapter House of Westminster Abbey.[4] The move facilitated communication with

---

[1] A. F. Pollard, *Wolsey*, 292–301; Cavendish, *Life and Death of Cardinal Wolsey*, 177–86; Edward Hall, *Hall's Chronicle*, 774. Chapuys reported Wolsey's death in a dispatch of 4 December: *C.S.P., Spn.*, IV, i, 522.

[2] *C.S.P., Spn.*, IV, i, 555.

[3] The following narrative is based on C.C. 306, 31–40, and Wilkins, *Concilia*, III, 724–6. See also Kelly, 'Canterbury Jurisdiction', 215–31.

[4] Wilkins, *Concilia*, III, 724–5, prints the abbot's formal protestation that the Abbey was exempt from the jurisdiction of bishops and Warham's denial that there was any intent to interfere with this independence.

the king and Parliament but tended to compromise the independent position of the synod; it was probably dictated by Henry's advisers. On the same day Chapuys and the papal nuncio attempted to attend Convocation. According to the Savoyard, they hoped to exhort the clerics to uphold the honour and immunity of the Church and to inform them of the state of the queen's case at Rome. But when the nuncio entered their chamber the churchmen were scandalized; they would not listen to his business and begged him for God's sake to leave them in peace. No doubt they feared that he would attempt to deliver a papal decretal, contrary to royal proclamation, or that conferring with a papal messenger might constitute another breach of praemunire. The nuncio did speak with Stokesley, who was presiding, but Chapuys thought him a principal promoter of Henry's affairs and believed that he would report the conversation to the king, not to Convocation.[1]

Very early in the session—we cannot be sure of the exact date—the king's demand for a very large sum of money was made known. As Fisher's early biographer reported,

it was ... declared what great charges the king had wrongfully bene at (as it was tearmed) about the matter of divorce in suit to the Court of Roome, and obtayning of sundrie instrumentes of forraine universities, and draughtes of many learned men's opinions, amounting, as it was declared, to the somme of one hundred thowsand pounds and more; the cheefe and only cause wherof was (as they said) the falshood and dissimulacion of the Cardinall, and certain others of the cheefe of the clergie; in consideracion wherof it was there demanded to be paid amonge them.[2]

Fisher spoke out boldly, saying that it was not the fault of Convocation if Henry had paid such sums; there was no reason why he should have spent a penny about the business. The other prelates may secretly have agreed, but they realized that there was no stopping the king, and they feared his wrath.

Although Henry claimed expenses of £100,000, the clergy at first hoped that he would be content with £40,000. Compromise, however, proved impossible; the king swore that he would punish the priests with extreme rigour if they did not grant the full

[1] Chapuys MS., 1531, no. 6 (C.S.P., Spn., IV, ii, 615).
[2] [Richard Hall], The Life of Fisher, 75.

sum.[1] There seemed to be nothing that the clerics could do. At noon on 24 January, with no great show of resistance, they agreed to pay.[2]

The churchmen lost no time in drawing up the terms of this grant. Their prologue to the subsidy makes no mention of the king's expenses in the divorce or of the priests' allegiance to Wolsey.[3] Instead, the clerics thought it propitious to laud Henry's services to the Church:

for lyke as he thes other dayes, most studiouslie with his pen, and most sumptouslie in bataill, defended the unyversall churche (whose humble membres we be) agenst enemies, ... so also at this present, many our enemyes, speciallie the Luterans, conspiring the mischief and distruction of the church and clergie of England (whose protector and highest hed he is), and of late raging agenst the same and personages of the prelates of the clergie with their famous lyes and cursed bokes and workes everywhere dispersed to th'intent to blemisshe and hurte the estimacion of the said prelates and clergie and to bring them into commen hatred and contempt: hys most wise and excellent majeste ... hath [so] confounded and repressed them, that now their presumptuous boldnes beginnith to rebate.

In appreciation they professed willingness to grant Henry the £100,000; 'most humblie prostrate' upon their knees they begged that he would 'graunte to all and singuler the prelates and clergie of the provynce of Canterbury, and to all the registers and scribes of whatsoever prelates which were mynisters in th'exercising of spiritual jurisdiction within the province of Canterbury, his generall and gracious pardon of all their trespaces of penall lawes and statutes of this realme'.

The draft left a blank where the dates of payment were to be

[1] The existing records of Convocation do not mention this manœuvre; our only source is Chapuys' dispatch of 23 January. Chapuys MS., 1531, no. 6.

[2] The mendicant friars and the prior of St John of Jerusalem had earlier protested their immunity to charges levied by Convocation, but it is not clear whether their exemption was allowed to stand or not: C.C. 306, 33–7. The sum originally agreed to was £100,044 8s. 8d., but it was soon rounded off.

[3] SP 1/56, fols. 84–8, P.R.O. (L.P., IV, iii, 6047 [3], where erroneously dated 1529). The draft does not state specifically that it was composed by the leaders of Convocation, but its general tone suggests that origin. Laymen, particularly advisers like Audley and Cromwell who were active in Parliament, would not have been likely to produce such bitter criticism of those who attempted to 'blemisshe and hurte the estimation of the said prelates and clergie'. Moreover, the records of Convocation speak of changes made by the king's councillors in the general pardon 'drawn up by the clergy' ('a clero conceptam'): C.C. 306, 39.

inserted. The clergy wished instalments to be spread over a five-year period. Henry at first agreed, but later he sought to have the entire amount payable immediately in case of war. This the Convocation was unwilling to grant—quite reasonably, considering the likelihood of conflict and the enormous sum involved. Chapuys reports that they withdrew their grant altogether, and that they asked for certain guarantees before offering it anew.[1] These demands were embodied in a petition which the clergy sent Henry, probably at the end of January: it sought restoration of ancient clerical rights and privileges and a declaration of the precise meaning of the statue of praemunire.[2] It may have been in connection with this enterprise that an English translation of Richard II's act was prepared,[3] but it did no good. Henry denied both requests, agreeing only to allow the full five years for collection of the subsidy.

The sparring was far from complete. Having rejected the clergy's demands, Henry now issued his own in the form of five articles to be added to the subsidy prologue.[4] The first and most important called upon the clergy to recognize Henry as 'sole protector and supreme head of the Anglican church and clergy'[5]— the king, or one of his advisers, had evidently picked up the innocuous 'highest hed' from the priests' own prologue and turned it into a declaration of supremacy with far-reaching implications. Henry now claimed what Norfolk had described to Chapuys as the 'right of empire within his realm, without recognizing any superiors':[6] should not an emperor hold supreme power over all institutions and subjects within his realm? The

[1] Chapuys MS., 1531, no. 7 (*C.S.P.*, *Spn.*, iv, ii, 619).
[2] Cottonian MS. Cleopatra F. ii, fol. 240, B.M., quoted in Scarisbrick, 'Pardon of the Clergy', 32.
[3] SP 2/L, fols. 81-2, P.R.O. (*L.P.*, v, 721 [3]).
[4] These are printed in Wilkins, *Concilia*, iii, 725.
[5] 'Ecclesiae et Cleri Anglicani (cujus protector et supremum caput is solus est)': C.C. 306, 33.
[6] 'Que le Roy avoit droit d'empire en son Royaume sans recognoystre superieux': Chapuys MS., 1531, no. 5. *C.S.P.*, *Spn.*, iv, ii, 615, makes no mention of empire in its rendering of the passage; a better summary is in *L.P.*, v, 45. On the significance of the empire theory see Richard Koebner, ' "The Imperial Crown of this Realm": Henry VIII, Constantine the Great, and Polydore Vergil', *B.I.H.R.*, xxvi (1953), 29–52; Koebner, *Empire*, 52–5; Mattingly, *Catherine of Aragon*, 190–3; Elton, *England under the Tudors*, 160–2; G. L. Harriss, 'Medieval Government and State-craft', *Past and Present*, xxv (1963), 9–12; Elton, 'The Tudor Revolution: A Reply', *ibid.* xxix (1964), 28–36; Harriss, 'A Revolution in Tudor History?', *ibid.* xxxi (1965), 87–90; Scarisbrick, *Henry VIII*, 268–73.

second section credited the king with spiritual jurisdiction, even the cure of subjects' souls; the third confirmed those privileges of the Church (if there were any) which did not detract from the royal prerogative and laws of the realm. Article four recorded the king's pardon of the clergy for violating the statute of praemunire but did nothing to explain the act, and the last section stated that the laity were likewise pardoned: a matter of which more was being heard in the Commons.[1]

Warham introduced the king's articles into Convocation on 7 February. An extremely critical week followed. The urgency of the situation can be deduced from the fact that Convocation met on five successive days—7 to 11 February, Tuesday to Saturday— and from the frequent appearance of councillors in the upper house, presumably in violation of Convocation's traditional rights.

Despite the arguments of Audley and some other councillors who were present during part of the meetings on Tuesday, Wednesday, and Thursday, the supremacy clause encountered stiff opposition. The lower house was unable to decide how to proceed, and the Prolocutor repeatedly asked for more time. In the upper house Fisher was doubtless the king's chief antagonist; according to his biographer 'he opened before the bishops such and so many inconveniences by grauntinge to this demaund' that it was for a time flatly rejected.[2] This was most likely on the Wednesday. Probably on Thursday, Henry's councillors tried to calm the clerics by explaining that Henry did not intend to assume any more power or authority over them than his predecessors had exercised, or to meddle in spiritual affairs, but Fisher was not satisfied. 'What yf he should shortly after chaunge his mind and exercise in deed the supremacie over the church of this realm?' the bishop inquired.

Or what yf he should die, and then his successor challenge the continewance of the same? Or what yf the crowne of this realme should in time fall to an infant or a woman that shall still continewe and take the same name upon them? What shall we then doe? Whom shall we serve [?sewe: sue] unto? Or where shall we have remedie?[3]

The councillors once again tried to set minds at ease. Even if the supremacy were granted as fully and absolutely as Henry

---

[1] Scarisbrick, 'Pardon of the Clergy', 34–5, has further discussion of these articles.
[2] Richard Hall, *Life of Fisher*, 79.　　　　　　　　　　　　　[3] *Ibid.*

wished, they argued, 'yet it must needes be understoode and taken that he can have no further power or authoritie by it then *quantum per legem Dei licet'*—as far as the word of God allows.[1] The limitation was apparently introduced informally, in the hope that the clergy would accept the supremacy with the mental reservation that their act could not set aside God's order.

We do not know who first suggested this saving phrase. It has often been credited to Fisher, but more likely—and ironically—it was Audley or Cromwell. Fisher did, however, make the proposal that the phrase be inserted in the grant, 'for a more trewe and plaine exposition of your meaninge towards the Kinge and all his posteritie'.[2] Only with the qualification would he agree to the article.

On Friday morning Thomas Cromwell appeared in Convocation and had a secret conference with Warham. After his departure the bishops spoke their minds by turns, and it was finally decided that the archbishop and the bishops of London, Lincoln, and Exeter should be sent to see the king. Presumably they hoped to secure his acceptance of the qualifying phrase, but they could not gain admittance to the royal presence. Instead they were referred to some councillors, who insisted that Convocation must accept the first article as it stood before other matters could be discussed. Warham delivered this news to Convocation and adjourned the meeting to 2 o'clock.

In the afternoon the clergy again discussed the supremacy clause but could reach no accord. Anne Boleyn's brother, Lord Rochford, came to deliver several tracts on the supremacy; one which has survived emphasizes the king's power to repress heresy and error, and concludes that his 'supreme auctorite grounded on God's worde ought in no case to be restrayned by any frustrate decrees of popish lawes or voyed prescriptes of humane traditions, but that he maye both order and minister, yea and also execute the office of spiritual administration in the church wherof he ys heed'.[3] Henry's advisers hoped that Convocation would be convinced and that Rochford would carry its answer to the king, but members were reluctant to deal with him. They again attempted to send a delegation, this time including members of the lower house, but were told that they could com-

[1] Richard Hall, *Life of Fisher*, 79. [2] *Ibid.* 80.
[3] SP 6/2, fols. 94–6, P.R.O. (*L.P.*, v, 1022, where misdated 1532).

municate with Henry only through Rochford. When the committee returned to Convocation the lower house still could not acquiesce in the title. Warham adjourned the meeting and sent Henry word of its indecision.

On Saturday morning the archbishop did not appear at the usual hour, and Clerk, acting in his place, was about to order a further recess. Then, at 10 o'clock, Warham arrived, fresh from a conference at court. He had received the king's agreement that the limiting clause might be inserted in the grant, so that it would recognize the king as singular protector and supreme lord of the Church, and even, so far as the law of Christ allows, its supreme head.[1] After Warham's request for discussion was greeted by stunned silence he quoted the common dictum: 'He who is silent seems to consent.'[2] '*Itaque tacemus omnes*', replied an unidentified cleric: 'then are we all silent'. His words, if not his name, have gained an immortal place in the history of the English Reformation.

During the afternoon Warham received the signatures of all the members of the upper house who were present.[3] The lower house held out somewhat longer, but about 6 o'clock the Prolocutor presented a schedule bearing the names of members who were willing to subscribe. Although a majority had probably been obtained, the inferior clergy were still not unanimous in their consent.[4] Indeed a number of them signed protests asserting that they did not intend the king's new title to impugn their loyalty to Rome or the authority of ecclesiastical ordinances and canons.[5]

The crisis was now past, but further details remained to be hammered out. On 23 February the clergy agreed to pay the king £20,000 on the feast of the Annunciation, 1532, and the remainder

---

[1] 'Ecclesiae et Cleri Anglicani, cujus singularem protectorem, unicum et supremum dominum, et quantum per Christi legem licet etiam supremum caput ipsius majestate recognoscimus etc.': C.C. 306, 35.

[2] 'Qui tacet consentire videtur': *ibid*. A more common form of the saying was 'Qui tacet consentit'.

[3] The signatory bishops were Warham, Stokesley, Blyth, Fisher, West, Veysey, Longland, Standish, and Clerk (*ibid*.). The bishops of Chichester, Hereford, Bangor, Llandaff, Salisbury, St David's, and Worcester were absent; Winchester was vacant. The absent bishops of Salisbury, Worcester, and Llandaff were foreigners, Campeggio, Ghinucci, and Athequa.

[4] Cf. Kelly, 'Canterbury Jurisdiction', 219–22.

[5] Dr Scarisbrick located the sole surviving copy of these protests in the Vienna Archives (see 'The Conservative Episcopate', 176–87 and App. III; *Henry VIII*, 277); it was sent to the emperor by Chapuys.

in four annual instalments. Two days later Henry accepted certain additional changes in the prologue. These represented further compromise, for the king abandoned his claim to exercise cure of souls; in addition, the article extending pardon to the laity was deleted. Convocation's certificate of the subsidy, written on parchment and incorporating all the changes, was presented to Henry by Warham, Stokesley, and Veysey on 8 March.[1] Convocation emerged, if not unscathed, at least less battered than has sometimes been suggested. The clergy had parted with an unparalleled sum of money, but they had hedged the royal supremacy about with a qualification which defied human analysis, and they had persuaded the king to retract several other odious demands.[2]

2

Despite the urgency of the praemunire and pardon Convocation found some time for other matters. On 15 February Bishop Stokesley, who was presiding, had opened the session to discussion of reforming canons and constitutions. A good many criticisms may have been aired, especially by the proctors of the clergy; it was probably one of them who wrote a surviving tract denouncing the negligence of bishops, avarice of archdeacons, and carnal affection of those in monastic orders.[3] During the next six weeks a number of specific subjects were considered: feast days, vestments and clerical apparel, convict clerks, licensing of books, teaching in grammar schools, excommunication, appropriated benefices, the institution of vicars, simony, the evil life of clergymen, the manner of studying in the universities, and the abuses of sacraments in such privileged chapels as that of the order of St John of Jerusalem.[4] It is not clear how many measures were actually enacted, or how drastic they were. On 20 March 'certain constitutions' were publicly read and the clergy agreed that they might be promulgated.[5] Our records mention the formal recitation of other articles later in the session. Perhaps this was sufficient to make the reforms binding; they do not seem to have

---

[1] Printed in Wilkins, *Concilia*, III, 742–4. Unlike the first version, the final grant is in Latin.

[2] This point was first made by Scarisbrick, 'Pardon of the Clergy', 35; see also *Henry VIII*, 275.

[3] Cottonian MS. Cleopatra F. II, fols. 223–6, B.M. (*L.P.*, v, 49).

[4] C.C. 306, 36–40; Wilkins, *Concilia*, III, 725–6, 746.   [5] C.C. 306, 37.

been published.[1] In any case they effected no fundamental changes in ecclesiastical administration or discipline.

As in 1529, heresy fascinated Convocation more than reform. The lower house was particularly incensed by the last will and testament of William Tracy, a gentleman of Gloucestershire who had died in 1530. His will, which expressed belief in justification by faith and stoutly refused to make any bequests to the clergy, had encountered trouble in the ecclesiastical courts, and on 25 February the Prolocutor exposed its errors before Convocation. After considerable discussion Tracy's son Richard, a member of the Commons and friend of Cromwell, was called before the churchmen and asked whether he had circulated copies of the will; although he admitted giving away only one, which he had written with his own hand, the will was clearly becoming one of the reformers' favourite texts. Before the end of the session Convocation pronounced a formal sentence of reprobation, and early in the following year it ordered the elder Tracy's body exhumed, since as a heretic he was unworthy of Christian burial. This was not the end of the matter: the bishop of Worcester's chancellor overzealously burned the exhumed remains at the stake, and with Cromwell's help Richard Tracy later forced him to pay a fine of £300. The main effect of Convocation's action was probably to draw attention to the will. Both Tyndale and Frith wrote comments on it.[2]

Richard Tracy, who continued to disseminate his father's beliefs, was an Oxford man. Four Cambridge reformers also found themselves in difficulty with Convocation: Edward Crome, Thomas Bilney, Hugh Latimer, and John Lambert or Nicholson. All had probably been members of the group which discussed Lutheran theology at the White Horse Tavern, and all had attracted attention through their unorthodox sermons. The examination of Crome, Bilney, and Latimer was suggested on 3 March, and on the 14th Stokesley led a long discussion of Crome's errors; Lambert was interrogated by the clerics on the 28th. But Convocation took no action. Crome escaped because of an earlier recantation, Latimer because of his favoured position

[1] Cf. Kelly, 'Canterbury Jurisdiction', 230.
[2] C.C. 306, 36–40; Wilkins, *Concilia*, III, 725, 746–7; *D.N.B. sub* Richard Tracy (d. 1569); Clebsch, *England's Earliest Protestants*, 107–8. Tracy's will was printed by Edward Hall, *Hall's Chronicle*, 796–7.

at court. Lambert went free for the time being only to be tried by Warham in 1532 and before Henry VIII himself six years later; he was then burned. 'Little' Bilney was executed in August 1531, but on the authority of the bishop of Norwich rather than Convocation.[1]

Heretical books, too, were discussed. On 2 March Stokesley read 'a certain famous book against the clergy': probably part of Tyndale's *Practice of Prelates*, which had been published on the Continent the previous year. 'Take heed, . . . wicked prelates,' Tyndale had written, 'blind leaders of the blind; indurate and obstinate hypocrites, take heed.' His invective continued:

Ye will be the chiefest in Christ's flock, and yet will not keep one jot of the right way of his doctrine . . . But whatsoever soundeth to make of your bellies, to maintain your honour, whether in the Scripture, or in your own traditions, or in the pope's law, that ye compel the lay-people to observe; violently threatening them with your excommunications and curses, that they shall be damned, body and soul, if they keep them not. And if that help you not, then ye murder them mercilessly with the sword of the temporal powers.[2]

Doubtless the prelates would have enjoyed exposing the book's errors, as they had already done for Tyndale's earlier writings. But Tyndale ended by criticizing Henry's lascivious desire for a divorce. Did the clergy abandon condemnation when they found that, for once, many of them agreed with the heretic?

3

We turn our attention at last to Parliament. Perhaps because he had nothing important to ask of its members, Henry did not attend the opening of the session on 16 January. He did send the French ambassador in order that he might be impressed by the colourful ceremony.[3]

---

[1] C.C. 306, 36–40; *D.N.B.* After Bilney's death there was considerable argument about the nature of his last words. A conservative alderman of Norwich, John Curatt, maintained that he had recanted, but Edward Rede, the mayor and a member of the Commons, denied hearing any such statement. Their depositions and a record of Rede's examination before Sir Thomas More are in the P.R.O., SP 1/68, fols. 45–52, 81–9 (*L.P.*, v, 522, 560, 569).

[2] William Tyndale, *Expositions and Notes . . . together with The Practice of Prelates*, 242–3.

[3] Chapuys MS., 1531, no. 9 (*C.S.P., Spn.*, IV, ii, 635).

A few days later a bill ratifying the clerical subsidy and pardoning the clergy for having violated the statute of praemunire by honouring Wolsey's legatine authority was introduced into the Lords. This was signed by the king and had obviously been drafted by his advisers. Chapuys reports it in a dispatch of 23 January, and Edward Hall says that the Upper House passed it 'in tyme convenient' and sent it down to the Commons.[1]

Once in the Lower House the measure encountered difficulties. According to Hall, 'divers froward persones would in no wyse assent to it except all men were pardoned, saying that all men which had anything to do with the Cardinal wer in the same case'. Despite the counter-arguments of what Hall terms 'the wyser sort' the Commons determined to send their Speaker with a delegation to present their views to the king. At court, Audley 'eloquently declared' to Henry 'how the Commons sore lamented and bewayled their chaunce to thynke or imagyne themselves to be out of his gracious favor, because that he had graciously geven his pardon of the premunire to his spiritual subjects and not to them'. Henry had evidently been disposed to pardon the laity, since he had added such a proviso to the subsidy prologue in Convocation. But when Audley said that the Commons were unwilling to pass his pardon of the clergy unless all laymen were included, Henry retorted that no one could force his mercy. He could, if he chose, pardon the priests under the Great Seal without the help of Parliament, so that he was not dependent upon them; he would be 'well advised' before he pardoned the laity. With this answer the delegation departed, 'very sorowful and pensive'. The conference had done nothing to satisfy the Commons, and they took no action on the bill. Some men thought that Thomas Cromwell had disclosed the Commons' secrets to Henry and caused him to adopt a severe tone.[2]

While the pardon hung fire Parliament occupied itself with lesser matters. Early in March Chapuys reported that it had been considering nothing more important than sumptuary laws, quarrels between towns and villages, and complaints against the clergy.[3] These last may have concerned chiefly the reluctance of

[1] Chapuys MS., 1531, no. 6 (*C.S.P., Spn.*, IV, ii, 615); Edward Hall, *Hall's Chronicle*, 774.
[2] Edward Hall, *Hall's Chronicle*, 774; Chapuys reports the same events in his dispatch of 2 April: Chapuys MS., 1531, no. 18 (*L.P.*, V, 171; not in *C.S.P., Spn.*).
[3] Chapuys MS., 1531, no. 12 (*C.S.P., Spn.*, IV, ii, 648).

the churchmen to allow an English translation of the Bible. A year earlier, in a proclamation prohibiting the possession of Tyndale's writings, Henry had held out hope that the Scriptures might be translated by 'learned and catholic persons' at a convenient time.[1] In the interim some anonymous writer had circulated 'An Invectyve againste the Clergye for hinderinge the translacion of the Byble';[2] he mentioned the king's promise and added, 'lett not these worldly [clergy] make your Grace believe that [the Scriptures] will cause insurrection, envye, and such myscheves as they imagen of their owne mad braynes'.[3] Finally a bill calling for the Bible in English was drafted; while it was probably not actually before Parliament, its ideas may have been discussed in 1531.[4]

In order to comply with the terms of the proclamation and to allay fear of unrest, the draft suggested that the king appoint a council 'to hear the reasons and opynyons of all them that wyll it were good to have [the Bible] in the mother tonge'. If these councillors perceived that 'the seid desire commeth of mekenes and charytye of the people, and of a love that they have to vertue and to knowledge of the trouthe', they were to report to the king, who would order a translation to be set forth.

The document which includes this proposal did not confine itself to the English Bible. Indeed, it is a mixed bag of barely related clauses; this, and its scrappy character—there are a number of blank spaces, and at one point five items are listed only in outline form—suggests that it was the work of several writers, either in or out of Parliament.[5]

Some of its other proposals are of considerable interest. The standing 'council', itself a novelty which later found its way into three abortive bills, was to continue until the conclusion of the next Parliament. Besides considering the need for a translation of the Bible, the council was to examine suspected heretics, thus depriving bishops of that power, and to consider what spiritual laws and usages required reformation by Parliament: a foretaste of the submission of the clergy in 1532. Other provisions carried

---

[1] Paul L. Hughes and James V. Larkin, eds., *Tudor Royal Proclamations*, I, 196.

[2] At least two copies are extant: SP 6/7, 301-8 and 189-204, P.R.O. The beginning of the second copy is gone.   [3] SP 6/7, 195, P.R.O.

[4] SP 6/7, 55-75, P.R.O. (*L.P.*, v, 50). The draft, as usual, is undated.

[5] Cf. Elton, 'A Further Note on Parliamentary Drafts in the Reign of Henry VIII', *B.I.H.R.*, XXVII (1954), 198-200.

further the legislation of 1529. Priests were to bury their deceased parishioners without any fee, and were to sing dirige and requiem for all Christian souls once each month without any charge to the people. Vicars and, after their death, their executors, were to be responsible for dilapidations if they failed to keep their houses in good repair. To increase the love between the clergy and laity, a section prohibited 'to all laymen . . . to say or reporte that there is no good pryste, . . . and to all spirituell men that non shall say that laymen love not prestes'. A penalty was also prescribed for anyone found arguing that the statutes of pluralism, non-residence, and mortuaries infringed the liberties of the Church.

Finally, a series of articles proposed a surprisingly progressive poor law. Public works, particularly the construction and repair of highways, were to provide employment for vagabonds and beggars, the cost to be met partly by the king and partly by a graduated tax on householders. The standing council was to oversee this programme and to establish punishments for those who refused to work. It would also see whether workmen employed as weavers, fullers, shearmen, or in other common occupations, were paid a living wage. In addition, holders of impropriated benefices were to devote at least a twentieth of their revenues to poor relief within the parish.

While we have no direct evidence to show who framed this impressive measure, we do possess one very intriguing clue. *The Newe Addicions* to Christopher Saint German's *Dialogue Between Doctor and Student* are clearly related to the draft, for they uphold the power of Parliament to legislate about precisely the matters comprehended in it.[1] Since these are so various, the parallel can hardly be accidental. The *Addicions*, published by Thomas Berthelet in 1531, bear no author's name but are almost certainly by Saint German himself.[2] Although he was not a member of Parliament, Saint German had earlier been associated with John Rastell at the Middle Temple;[3] possibly the two lawyers were the

---

[1] S.T.C., nos. 21562 ff. The B.M. holds a manuscript, Cottonian MS. Cleopatra F. II, fol. 247, as well as a printed copy, C. 54, aa. 13.

[2] Franklin Le Van Baumer assumed that Saint German wrote *The Newe Addicions*: 'Christopher St. German: The Political Philosophy of a Tudor Lawyer', *A.H.R.*, XLII (1937), 631–51.

[3] Pearl Hogrefe, 'The Life of Christopher Saint German', *Review of English Studies*, XIII (1937), 402. Miss Hogrefe corrects the tradition that Saint German was a member of the Inner Temple.

chief framers of the document, and Rastell its advocate in the Commons. The likelihood is increased by our knowledge that Rastell later promoted Protestant reforms and opposed the forced collection of tithes from the poor.[1]

Whatever their provenance, the proposals failed to find their way to the statute books. No doubt they were too advanced and costly. Moreover, some dealt with matters, like the English Bible, which Henry preferred to handle without parliamentary interference. But it is fascinating to see what ideas were being considered. Some of them, in particular the programme for poor relief, would crop up again later in the Parliament.[2] Possibly Thomas Cromwell, like Rastell, was concerned with the paper in 1531; after its failure he may well have put it away for future use.

Although the proposal for public works was not enacted, a poor law did reach statutory form in 1531.[3] Much less ambitious than the draft, which may have opened the subject, the act is none the less a landmark, for it is the earliest statute to face the necessity of providing for the impotent poor.[4] It ordered the justices of the peace to make diligent search for all 'aged, poor, and impotent persons which . . . of necessity be compelled to live by alms'. Such persons were to be given licences to beg within limited areas, and to be registered by the justices; if they attempted to beg elsewhere they were to be set in the stocks for two days and ordered to return to their assigned territories. Impotent poor found begging without a licence might be stripped half naked and whipped, or set in the stocks for three days with nothing to eat but bread and water.

These clauses ring little of compassion, and they fail to explain what is to be done for the poor if alms prove inadequate or how the impotent are to find transportation to their assigned areas. Still, the act does recognize that some beggars were unable to work and that the State needed to make provision for them.

The framers of the act regarded idleness as the 'mother and

---

[1] *L.P.*, x, 247; cf. above, Ch. 2. Although he was Sir Thomas More's brother-in-law, Rastell came to hold radical Protestant views and died in prison.

[2] See below, Ch. 10; cf. Elton, 'An Early Tudor Poor Law', *Economic History Review*, 2nd ser., vi (1953), 55–67. The draft discussed above is that which Elton was at that time unable to locate: 56 n. 1.

[3] 22 Henry VIII, c. 12.

[4] Sidney and Beatrice Webb, *English Local Government: English Poor Law History: Part I. The Old Poor Law*, 45. Earlier statutes had dealt with vagrancy rather than genuine relief.

root of all vices', and they took a much harsher line against sturdy beggars. Any person 'whole and mighty in body and able to labour', if found idle, might be brought before the justices of the peace, who could order him 'to be tied to the end of a cart naked and be beaten with whips throughout the ... town ... till his body be bloody'. He was then to depart to the place of his birth, or the place where he had last lived for three years, upon pain of further whipping. The act did not say what was to happen if the sturdy beggars could not find employment; it made no provision for public works. Except for its severer penalties and generally harsher tone, this section is little different from the beggars' act of 1495.[1]

Further sections prescribed fines for towns and parishes which neglected to enforce the act and established punishment for university students, unemployed mariners, hawkers of pardons, and persons pretending knowledge of physic or palmistry, if found begging without authority. The act was to endure until the end of the next Parliament; in fact it was superseded by the more liberal statute of 1536, but was revived under Edward VI[2] and not finally repealed until 1572.[3] Several of Henry VIII's proclamations were intended to enforce it.[4]

A related act tried to rid the realm of another sort of idle wanderers, the 'outlandish people calling themselves Egyptians'.[5] These gypsies used subtle and crafty means to deceive the people, especially by claiming to tell fortunes, and they frequently committed robberies and other felonies. Under the terms of the statute no more 'Egyptians' were to be allowed into the country, while those already in England were given sixteen days after the proclamation of the act to quit the realm. Goods which they had stolen were to be restored to the rightful owners; other property confiscated from gypsies was to be divided between the king and the justice of the peace or other arresting officer.[6]

---

[1] 11 Henry VII, c. 2.

[2] By 3 & 4 Edward VI, c. 16.   [3] By 14 Elizabeth, c. 5.

[4] Hughes and Larkin, *Tudor Royal Proclamations*, I, nos. 131 and 132 (for beggars in London and within the realm generally) and no. 141 (for vagabonds following the court). A fuller text of no. 141, including a preamble mentioning the act of 1531, is in the B.M., Additional MS. 9835, fol. 1; it may well date from the summer of 1531, not 1533 as suggested by Hughes and Larkin.

[5] 22 Henry VIII, c. 10.

[6] The statute was evidently not effective, for 1 & 2 Philip & Mary, c. 4, complained that Egyptians were again plying their 'devlish and naughty practices and devices'.

A number of additional economic and social measures occupied the Commons. One important act, possibly suggested by the draft's proposal for public works, ordered the justices of the peace to keep bridges in repair and gave them authority to levy taxes for that purpose.[1] Another, which originated as a petition of the Commons, limited the fees which could be required of apprentices on entering guilds.[2] The Commons also secured enactment of their petition that all persons born abroad, even if later made denizens, should pay the customs charged aliens: the London merchants had sought such a bill since 1515 but now resented a proviso, attached by the Lords, which gave officials of the government some control over the rates of scavage charged foreign merchants by the City.[3] A statute of 1489 forbidding forestalling and regrating of wool was re-enacted and extended to ten additional counties.[4] Other bills stated that butchers should not operate tanning houses, prohibited the export of horses without licence, and declared that bakers, brewers, surgeons, and scriveners would not, for legal purposes, be considered handicraftsmen.[5]

Some economic measures were essentially local in application. The perennial problem of draining Plumstead marsh, adjoining the Thames east of London, was tackled by a statute imposing rates for drainage works and providing for sale of lands if such charges were not paid.[6] It was perhaps a petition to the king, signed only 'Prentysse',[7] which produced the act making it a felony to damage Powdike or other dikes in Norfolk and the Isle of Ely; the over-worked justices of the peace were once again made responsible for enforcement.[8] A petition from the mayor

In consequence it was made felony, punishable by death, for Egyptians to remain in England. During the sixteenth century attempts were made to expel gypsies from France and Spain as well as England; cf. Amos, *Observations*, 154–7.

[1] 22 Henry VIII, c. 5. For centuries this act provided the legal basis for regulation of bridges, and Sir Edward Coke discoursed on it at length in his second *Institute*.

[2] 22 Henry VIII, c. 4; original act, H.L.R.O. The act strengthened an earlier statute, 19 Henry VII, c. 7.

[3] 22 Henry VIII, c. 8; original act, H.L.R.O.; Miller, 'London and Parliament in the Reign of Henry VIII', 146. This act was being debated in mid-March; see Chapuys, in *C.S.P., Spn.*, IV, ii, 664. It also reinforced a statute of Henry VII.

[4] 22 Henry VIII, c. 1; cf. 4 Henry VII, c. 11.

[5] 22 Henry VIII, cc. 6, 7, 13. The export of horses was already prohibited by 11 Henry VII, c. 13; the clarification about handicrafts was necessary because foreigners were forbidden to enter the handicraft trades.

[6] 22 Henry VIII, c. 3.

[7] SP 1/65, fols. 96–7, P.R.O. (*L.P.*, v, 53).   [8] 22 Henry VIII, c. 11.

and burgesses of Southampton, presented to the Commons by their member John Mille, led to statutory remission of a forty mark fee with which the town had been burdened.[1]

Of the several alterations in the legal system ordered in 1531, much the most interesting arose from an untoward incident in Bishop Fisher's household at Lambeth marsh. In mid-February nearly all of Fisher's servants, as well as some beggars who had been fed out of charity, became violently ill; one retainer and one poor widow died. Richard Roose, a friend of Fisher's cook, was immediately arrested. When examined, Roose admitted that he had placed 'a certain venom or poison' in a pail of yeast used for preparing potage or gruel. He believed that the powder would cause sickness but not death: Chapuys reported that it would *tromper* the servants, and according to the intelligence received in Ghent, Roose had administered a purgative as a jest. Fortunately Fisher had not eaten of the porridge. If Roose intended to poison him, he bungled the job.

The king, always fearful of poison himself and perhaps afraid that he would be suspected of having hired Roose to kill the bishop, became greatly disturbed. On 28 February he took the unusual step of appearing in the Lords, where he spoke for an hour and a half, mostly about the poisoning. Shortly thereafter a bill prepared by royal councillors was introduced into the Upper House: it recited the story of the poisoning and decreed that murder by poison be accounted high treason, the offender to be punished by being boiled to death. Despite its barbarity the bill seems to have passed both Houses easily. Roose was duly executed by boiling at Smithfield on 5 April; Fisher, who may have been nauseated by the episode as well as by events in Convocation, obtained the king's licence to leave London and return to his diocese before the end of the session. The statute was, mercifully, repealed in 1547.[2]

Two more acts affected legal procedure. By one, persons accused of felony were denied the right of foreign pleas and were

---

[1] 22 Henry VIII, c. 23. Mille evidently had the assistance of Sir William Fitzwilliam, Sir Henry Guildford, and the duke of Suffolk in urging the measure, for he gave small presents to them or their wives (H.P.T. biography of Mille).

[2] 22 Henry VIII, c. 9; original act, H.L.R.O.; Chapuys MS. 1531, no. 11 (*C.S.P., Spn.*, IV, ii, 646; *L.P.*, V, 120); Edward Hall, *Hall's Chronicle*, 780–1; Amos, *Observations*, 52–4; *C.S.P., Venetian*, IV, 668; Richard Hall, *Life of Fisher*, 72–3.

ordered to be tried in the county where arrested.[1] The other concerned those who had been forced to abjure sanctuary and leave the realm, in accordance with an act of 1529. The government now feared that such persons, who were often expert mariners or 'apt for the wars', might aid England's enemies; they were commanded to remain in sanctuaries of their choice for life. 'Higher offences in the law'— the term was left undefined, but presumably comprehended treasons—were excluded and could be punished by banishment, as before.[2]

Six private acts, or seven if one counts the act for Southampton already mentioned, were passed in 1531. Of these the most important regulated the king's household, giving it first claim on Crown revenues up to £19,394, and established landholdings for Henry's illegitimate son the duke of Richmond. Other acts had to do with Lady Derby's jointure, the lands of Sir William Fyllol and Lord Montague, and annuities which Wolsey had granted out of the revenues of the bishopric of Winchester.[3] Although these measures were technical and of limited impact, they must have consumed considerable time, for members were intent on safe-guarding their own rights and those of their constituents. In particular the act for the duke of Richmond had to be hedged about with suitable restrictions. The Lords added twenty-one provisos to the original bill, and the Commons a further fifteen.[4]

4

With all these minor matters the Lords and Commons busied themselves while the king completed his negotiations with Convocation. Finally, late in the session, a new bill for the pardon of the clergy was introduced into the Lower House of Parliament.[5]

The most important feature of this measure is its failure to mention Wolsey's legatine power or the fault of the clergy in

---

[1] 22 Henry VIII, c. 2.   [2] 22 Henry VIII, c. 14; cf. Amos, *Observations*, 176–7.

[3] 22 Henry VIII, cc. 17–23. On the act for the King's household see Elton, *The Tudor Revolution in Government*, 407.

[4] 22 Henry VIII, c. 17; original act, H.L.R.O. Chapuys mentions the act in his dispatch of 22 March (*C.S.P., Spn.*, IV, ii, 664). Among the other papers relating to the 1531 session are a partial draft of a treason law (SP 1/65, fols. 87–91, P.R.O. [*L.P.*, v, 52 (2)]). Although clearly prepared for this meeting of Parliament the bill was probably not introduced. See below, Ch. 9.

[5] It survives with the original acts in the H.L.R.O.; like the first bill it was signed by the king.

acknowledging it. Instead, the bill states that the bishops and other clergy have acted 'contrary to the order of [the king's] lawes, and specially contrary to the statutes of provysours, provisions, and praemunire', because they have exercised their spiritual jurisdiction, particularly in ecclesiastical courts.[1] Henry and his advisers had conceived a charge which would not involve the laity, and they doubtless expected easy passage of the bill.

In one section of the new measure eight clerics were specifically exempted from the pardon. Six of these were leaders of the opposition in the lower house of Convocation,[2] and they were subsequently prosecuted on praemunire charges in the King's Bench.[3] A proviso added by the Lords and accepted by the Commons denied the benefits of the act to the clergy in the province of York unless they agreed to pay a sum equal to at least two years' revenues from their offices. All other clerics were pardoned; those who had been involved in the earlier praemunire suits could plead the benefit of the statute and go free upon payment of a shilling to the clerk who recorded their discharge.

This second bill has recently been described as a challenge to the clergy on an issue far more fundamental than Wolsey's legacy: an attack on the cherished independent jurisdiction of the Church.[4] When seen in context it appears somewhat less dramatic. The vaguer charge, affecting only the clergy, was doubtless intended to mollify the Commons; since it was generally believed that the statute of praemunire existed to provide a means of punishing the exercise of jurisdiction independent of the king, the new complaint did little but gloss the old act. Furthermore, the clerics' own draft of the prologue had mentioned the need to

[1] 22 Henry VIII, c. 15.

[2] These included Peter Ligham, dean of the Arches and proctor of the clergy for Canterbury and St David's; Rowland Phillips, proctor of the clergy for Hereford; Thomas Pelles, chancellor of Norwich and proctor for the clergy there; Adam Travers, archdeacon of Exeter; John Baker, proctor for the clergy of Salisbury; and Robert Cliff, archdeacon of London and proctor for the clergy of that diocese. The archbishop of Dublin, John Allen, and the bishop of Hereford, Charles Booth, were also exempted, perhaps because of their association with Wolsey. Both later paid very large fines (L.P., v, 657).

[3] All but Ligham, who was evidently regarded as the most serious offender, were pardoned in November 1531 (L.P., v, 559 [33–7]); Ligham's pardon was delayed until the following June (ibid. 1139 [10]).

[4] Scarisbrick, 'Pardon of the Clergy', 25. Kelly ('Canterbury Jurisdiction', 227) terms it 'a crude betrayal of the clergy'.

pardon scribes who had assisted the bishops 'in th'exercising of spirituall jurisdiction'.[1] Henry had hit upon an indictment which could indeed have sweeping implications—one which fit perfectly his claim to an emperor's supremacy—but it is doubtful if he appreciated its force.

The Commons indeed passed the bill, but they were not entirely at ease. We know nothing of their discussions, but they must have feared that laymen might still be covered by the charge. Many had been parties to suits in ecclesiastical courts or had proved wills there, thus tacitly accepting the Church's jurisdiction. The Commons continued to seek an act for the pardon of temporal subjects, and the king at length agreed to grant it. It was passed first by the Lords[2] and brought into the Lower House on 29 March by Christopher Hales, the attorney general. The knights and burgesses speedily assented and lovingly thanked the king.[3] The statute granted to all laymen a free pardon for all offences against the statutes of provisors and praemunire committed before 30 March. It is of interest chiefly because of its novelty; as J. R. Tanner once remarked, 'a statutory pardon of a whole people has no parallel in history'.[4]

Members of Parliament were customarily allowed to return to their homes for Easter. Since Holy Week began on 2 April, they must have hoped that the session could be completed by the end of March. There seemed to be little reason for them to remain at Westminster, especially after Henry granted the pardon of the laity. Chapuys had earlier reported their irritation that nothing of importance was brought before them, and he noted that a number of members had received royal permission to depart.[5]

On Thursday, 30 March, it was clear that preparations were being made for the end of the session. Sir Thomas More, the chancellor, appeared first in the Lords. He had been commanded by the king to rebuke those who said that Henry pursued the divorce out of love for some lady, or that his motives were false and libidinous. After More's speech Brian Tuke, the clerk of Parliament, read a number of the opinions which Henry had

[1] SP 1/56, fol. 86ᵛ, P.R.O.   [2] 22 Henry VIII, c. 16; original act, H.L.R.O.
[3] Edward Hall, *Hall's Chronicle*, 775; the date is from Chapuys, in *L.P.*, v, 171.
[4] J. R. Tanner, *Tudor Constitutional Documents*, 20.
[5] Chapuys MS., 1531, no. 11 (*C.S.P., Spn.*, iv, ii, 646), a dispatch written 1 March.

collected from the European universities. A disputation followed, with Bishops Stokesley and Longland supporting the king, Standish and Clerk arguing that the time was too short to demonstrate the justice of Catherine's position. Norfolk interrupted, saying that the king had ordered the documents read only for the information of members, without authorizing any debate. Someone asked the chancellor for his opinion, but More would only say that he had given it to the king many times. Lord Talbot was similarly interrogated but also declined to be drawn into argument.[1]

When this scene had been finished a number of the principal actors—More, Tuke, Norfolk, Stokesley, Longland, and some others—trooped down to the Commons. There the episode was re-enacted. 'You of this worshipful House,' More told the knights and burgesses, 'be not so ignorant but you know well that the kyng our soveraigne Lorde hath married his brother's wife, for she was both wedded and bedded with his brother Arthur.' He continued:

If this mariage be good or no many clerkes do doubt. Wherfore the kyng like a vertuous prince willing to be satisfied in his conscience and also for the suretie of his realme hath with great deliberacion consulted with great clerkes, and hath sent my Lord of London here present to the chiefe universities of all Christendome to knowe their opinion and judgement in that behalfe. And although that the universities of Cambridge and Oxford had been sufficient to discuss the cause, yet because they be in his realme and to avoyde all suspicion of parcialitie he hath sent into the realme of Fraunce, Italy the Pope's dominions, and Venicians to knowe their judgement in that behalfe, whiche have concluded, written and sealed their determinacions according as you shall heare red.

Tuke again read the opinions of twelve French and Italian universities; more than a hundred books written by foreign scholars in support of the king's cause were exhibited but not read, since the day was far spent. 'Now you of this Comen House may reporte in your countreys what you have seen and heard,' More concluded, 'and then all men shall openly perceyve that the kyng hath not attempted this matter of wyll or pleasure, as some

[1] Chapuys MS., 1531, no. 18 (L.P., v, 171; not in C.S.P., Spn.); C.S.P., Milan, 861; C.S.P., Venetian, iv, 664.

straungers reporte, but only for the discharge of his conscience and suretie of the succession of his realme.'[1]

At 5 o'clock on Friday the king attended the concluding ceremony in the Lords. Speaking for him, More told the parliamentarians that he was very well satisfied with them. Assent was given to bills, and Parliament was prorogued to 13 October. According to Chapuys the date was a surprise: most observers had thought that Parliament would continue in May, after an Easter recess.[2]

On Saturday, 1 April, the session of Convocation was terminated. Bishop Stokesley, acting as commissary for the archbishop, read the final version of the articles granting the king his £100,000. After the clergy gave their formal assent Convocation was prorogued to 16 October.[3]

The sessions of Parliament and Convocation must have been disappointing in some sense to nearly everyone: to the king and his councillors, because nothing tangible had been done to procure his divorce; to the clergy, because of their forced submission; to the members of Parliament, because they had been kept from their homes but given little significant work to do; to Catherine of Aragon, because of the propagandizing for the king's cause and the unhappy treatment of her adherents. Viewed in a longer perspective they may seem more useful, indeed a necessary stage in Henry's proceedings. The independent position of the clergy had been challenged, the marriage question openly discussed, the writings favouring the king read and circulated. Frustrating as it must have been to defer action, Henry's divorce would come more easily because of the events of 1531.

---

[1] Edward Hall, *Hall's Chronicle*, 774-80. Chapuys' account is similar, but he adds that the Commons were displeased and unconvinced. Much of the material presented to Parliament was printed later in the year by Thomas Berthelet under the title *The determinations of the moste famous and mooste excellent vniuersities of Italy and Fraunce, that it is vnlefull for a man to marie his brothers wyfe, that the pope hath no power to dispence therwith.*

[2] *Statutes at Large*, I, 779. Chapuys gives 14 October (Chapuys MS., 1531, no. 18), while Edward Hall says that Parliament was prorogued until the last day of March (*Hall's Chronicle*, 780). Evidently he meant to write that it was prorogued *on* the last day of March.

[3] C.C. 306, 40; Wilkins, *Concilia*, III, 746.

7

THE THIRD SESSION, 1532: ANNATES, SUPPLICATION, AND SUBMISSION

Although Parliament had been prorogued to October 1531, it did not meet again until January 1532. The delay must have been decided on at the last moment, for on 8 October, a mere five days before the session was scheduled to begin, Henry had issued a warrant for the 'dressing and trimming' of the Parliament chamber with red cloth, canvas, and gilt nails.[1] Chapuys reported that Parliament was postponed, originally to early November and then to mid-January, because no word had come from Rome and Henry's ministers had not decided on a course of action.[2] It is hard to set much store by the official reason, that the air in London was too insalubrious for such a meeting.[3]

The months since the prorogation of Parliament in 1531 had seen little change in the divorce proceedings and English diplomacy. Catherine of Aragon had been sent away from court in July, never to see Henry again, while the king openly went hunting with Anne Boleyn and allowed her to employ an almoner and other officers of state.[4] Sir Thomas Elyot, a former clerk of the Council who had just published his famous *Boke named the Gouernour*, was sent to the Low Countries in October with instructions to persuade Charles V not to meddle with his aunt's case. Naturally he failed.[5] Henry's dispatches to Rome continued to emphasize the injustice of a trial there and to threaten the recall of English envoys if the pope persisted.

The significant changes had been in personnel, not policy. Wolsey's ecclesiastical positions were at last filled in December, when Edward Lee was consecrated archbishop of York and Stephen Gardiner bishop of Winchester. Both had served the king, Lee as an ambassador abroad and Gardiner as Henry's secretary, and although both were religious conservatives they were eager not to displease their sovereign. Gardiner was especially active at court, and when he was sent to France for several

---

[1] L.P., v, 470. [2] Chapuys MS., 1531, nos. 39 and 53 (L.P., v, 472 and 614).
[3] L.P., v, 515. [4] Ibid. 340, 361, 375.
[5] Lehmberg, *Sir Thomas Elyot, Tudor Humanist*, 95–102.

months Henry complained that his absence was 'the lacke of my right hand'.[1]

But it was the rise of Thomas Cromwell, not Gardiner, which was ultimately to alter the course of English policy. A member of the Council since the beginning of 1531, Cromwell had by the year's end joined its inner ring and been entrusted with the dispatch of most government business. In November the former Venetian ambassador, reporting to the Signory, placed Cromwell seventh in a list of leading councillors headed by such noblemen as Norfolk, Suffolk, and Wiltshire.[2] Several months earlier Cromwell had written the first of a long series of memoranda relating to Parliament: in preparation for the coming session he was to make ready bills dealing with treason, apparel, wards and primer seisin, forestalling and regrating, and the regulation of wines and textiles.[3]

Cromwell's new position as the principal manager of parliamentary affairs is made even clearer by the spate of requests for permission to be absent from the coming session, nearly all of which were addressed to him. The abbot of St Mary's, York, the earl of Essex, Lords Audley and LaWarr, Sir Thomas Deny, Lord Stourton and his son Sir William, Sir John Fitzjames, and Reginald Lytilprow all secured the king's licence through Cromwell's mediation, and several sent him blank proxies.[4] Most pleaded illness—both Deny and Fitzjames had sore legs—but Lord LaWarr as usual made poverty his excuse. The abbot of Evesham received licence to absent himself, apparently without Cromwell's help,[5] and Reginald Pole was given permission to leave the realm after implying that he would oppose the king in Parliament if it were withheld. Bishop Tunstall of Durham, an outspoken critic of Henry's policies, was evidently wise enough not to risk attending. Fisher, whose absence would have been equally pleasing to the king, was unwilling to remain at home, but he fell ill soon after the session began and had to return to Rochester.[6]

---

[1] Cromwell to Gardiner, SP 1/69, fol. 42, P.R.O. (*L.P.*, v, 723).

[2] *C.S.P., Venetian*, IV, 694.

[3] Cottonian MS. Titus B. I, fols. 481–3, B.M. (*L.P.*, v, 394).

[4] SP 1/68, fols. 94–5, 115–16, 119–20, 143; SP 1/69, fols. 10–11, 12, 56, 69–70, 72–3, P.R.O.; Cottonian MS. Titus B. I, fol. 366, B.M. (*L.P.*, v, 578, 612, 621, 625, 644, 708, 709, 710, 728, 734, 741).

[5] Harleian MS. 283, fol. 73, B.M. (*L.P.*, v, 699).

[6] Before the session opened Fisher was summoned for an audience with Henry, but he managed to leave before the king could demand his silence in Parliament.

With Cromwell in charge one might have expected that the session of Parliament would run smoothly, and that the long-awaited divorce would be achieved in 1532. But events dictated otherwise. There was an unusual amount of opposition, and matters of great importance had to be left unresolved.

I

The third session of Parliament began on 15 January 1532. Financial matters were first brought before the members: despite the unprecedented clerical grant of the previous year, and the earlier remission of forced loans, Henry needed money. At the end of the month Chapuys reported that Parliament had been asked for a subsidy, a request which Henry justified on the grounds that an attack from Scotland was imminent. The Commons were unconvinced and reluctant to yield; the government could do little but allow the demand to lie fallow for a time.

Next councillors pressed for passage of a bill regulating primer seisin and uses. This had been prepared by the king's legal advisers under Cromwell's supervision, and in all probability it was based on the agreement which had been signed by the noblemen in 1529. That contract, it will be recalled, had given the king assured feudal rights over a third of each estate, allowing for device by will of the remainder, with the provision that lesser feudal lords might similarly demand feudal dues on a third of the land of their tenants. For some reason Henry directed Cromwell to delete this last 'clause concerning the lordes'.[1] It is possible, too, that Cromwell raised the king's share to half rather than a third: in the absence of a draft bill we cannot be certain, but Edward Hall has it that 'everye man myght make his wyll of the halfe of his lande, so that he left the other halfe to the heyre by

---

Chapuys MS., 1532, no. 3 (L.P., v, 737; C.S.P., Spn., iv, ii, 688: the nearly literal renderings of these dispatches in L.P. are preferable, for this period, to the more inflated versions in C.S.P., Spn.). Another change in the composition of the Lords was caused by the death of Geoffrey Blythe, bishop of Coventry and Lichfield, late in 1531. His successor was not named until 1534; in the meantime Cromwell collected the revenues of the bishopric (Elton, *The Tudor Revolution in Government*, 90). On Tunstall's opposition see L.P., v, 819 and 820; SP 6/9, fols. 112–19, P.R.O.

[1] Cottonian MS. Titus B. I, fol. 483ᵛ, B.M.

discent'.[1] Hall supported the measure, and reported that the other 'wyse men' in the House would have joined him had the king been content with the feudal profits from a third or fourth part of the estate rather than half, a reversion to the agreement of 1529 which he had been 'credebly informed' Henry would accept. But, as Hall continued, 'Lorde how the ignoraunt persones were greved, and howe shamefully they spake of the byll and of the kynges learned councell' who had prepared it. Chapuys, too, heard of the 'estranges parolles' spoken against the king and Council.[2] The Commons remained unwilling to acquiesce, and the bill was abandoned.

The session was generating little but heat, and on 14 February Chapuys reported that nothing had been passed except a bill regulating the import of French wines, designed partly to insure that they would be carried in English ships.[3] Behind the scenes there was more activity. Norfolk assembled a group of influential persons—we do not know who, or how many—to discuss Henry's marital plight: he argued that matrimonial cases belonged to the temporal, not spiritual, jurisdiction, and could be settled by the king as emperor within his realm. The duke asked whether those present would not employ themselves and their estates in preserving the royal prerogative; Lord Darcy replied that although his goods and person were at Henry's disposal he had always believed matrimonial causes to be spiritual. The other magnates were equally apprehensive about being drawn into the matter, and little was accomplished. At about the same time Norfolk and Wiltshire were reported in communication with Warham, whom they regarded as pope of England, doubtless attempting to persuade him to grant the divorce on his own authority. According to Chapuys Warham was warned of this move and refused steadfastly.[4] Next the king's advisers evidently toyed with the idea of securing a decision from some other power within the English Church. On 6 March Chapuys reported that Parliament was discussing the abolition of archiepiscopal

---

[1] Edward Hall, *Hall's Chronicle*, 785. Ives argues, in 'The Genesis of the Statute of Uses', 682-3, that Hall was in error and that the draft retained the agreement for royal rights over a third.

[2] Chapuys MS., 1532, no. 6 (*L.P.*, v, 805; *C.S.P., Spn.*, IV, ii, 899).

[3] Chapuys MS., 1532, no. 6. The statute is 23 Henry VIII, c. 7; a draft, in the hand of a Cromwellian clerk, is SP 2/L, fols. 97–105, P.R.O.(*L.P.*, v, 721 [7]). The bill originated in the Commons (H.L.R.O., original act). [4] Chapuys MS., 1532, no. 6, *loc. cit.*

jurisdiction over bishops and its transference to the king, probably in an attempt to obtain the divorce from the English prelates without Warham's interference.[1] A parallel approach, this time towards having Convocation decide the case, is reflected in a bill, drafted by Cromwell and Audley, which would ratify such a decree and cut off the possible effects of papal denunciation.[2] The ideas gave a foretaste of things to come, but they were not followed out; their medicine was too harsh.

Instead, the king decided to confront the pope by mounting an attack on annates. The papacy's most important source of revenue from England, annates or first fruits amounted to the major portion of one year's income paid to Rome by each newly appointed bishop or archbishop in order to obtain his bulls of confirmation.[3] Since the charges were too great to be met out of ordinary income during the period allowed, the bishops were forced to resort to loans, often from Italian bankers, or to subsidies levied on the diocesan clergy. Wyclif had decried annates as being simony, and a statute of 1404 had called them a horrible mischief and damnable custom,[4] but there had been little outcry against them during the intervening century.

Discussion of annates must have begun during the first month of the session. A surviving document, addressed to the king, probably represents the outgrowth of the Commons' debates: it evinces little sympathy with the bishops but asserts that the treasure of England has been conveyed out of the realm so that subjects 'be brought to great penury' and bishops are prevented from fulfilling their obligation to repair churches and dispense alms and hospitality. The petition asks Henry 'to cause the said unjuste exactions of annates to cesse and to be fordoen forever by act of this his Grace's high coort of Parliament'. Should the pope make any process against the realm in an attempt to retain his

---

[1] *Ibid.* no. 11 (*L.P.*, v, 850; *C.S.P., Spn.*, iv, ii, 915).

[2] SP 2/N, fols. 163–4, P.R.O. (*L.P.*, vi, 311 [5]). The bill is in Cromwell's hand, with interlinear additions by him and Audley. It is undated, but references to Catherine as princess dowager suggest that it belongs to 1532.

[3] Actually the term is ambiguous. The payments to secure papal confirmation for bishops and archbishops were originally referred to as services, and annates were paid in certain cases where services were not due. By the sixteenth century, however, annates were generally understood to include services. For a detailed discussion of services and annates see W. E. Lunt, *Financial Relations of the Papacy with England 1327–1534*, 169–445.

[4] 'Horrible malveise & dampnable custume': 6 Henry IV, c. 1.

revenues, the petitioners suggest that the king renounce papal authority altogether:

Forasmuche as the exaction of the said annates is against the law of God and the pope's own law, forbidding the bying or selling of spiritual giftes or promotions, and forasmuch as al good Christen men be more bound to obey God than any man, and forasmuche as Sainct Paule willeth us to withdraw ourselfes from al suche as walke inordinately, it may please the kinges moost noble grace to ordeyne in this present Parliament that than the obedience of him and his people be withdrawen from the sea of Rome.[1]

This petition is couched in a clumsy style and does not bear the marks of Cromwell's incisive mind.[2] Cromwell may, of course have been responsible for raising the matter in the Commons, and he may have added to the debate such financial details as the assertion that annates paid since 1489 had amounted to £160,000.[3] He almost certainly produced the bill to abolish annates which Chapuys reports in Parliament by late February.[4] This repeats most of the complaints found in the petition: 'annates have risen, grown, and increased by an uncharitable custom, grounded upon no just or good title; . . . great and intolerable sums . . . have yearly been conveyed to . . . Rome . . . to the great impoverishment of this realm'. The payment shall therefore 'from henceforth utterly cease'; clergy shall pay no more than 5 per cent of their first year's revenue, to meet the cost of writing and sealing their bulls. If the pope in retaliation refuses to grant bulls for the consecration of any prelate nominated by the Crown, that bishop shall be consecrated without them; if the pope attempts to vex England with excommunication or interdict he shall not be

---

[1] Cottonian MS. Cleopatra E. vi, fols. 274-5, B.M. (*L.P.*, v, 721 [5]).

[2] Merriman (*Life and Letters of Thomas Cromwell*, I, 133) thought that the supplication 'was addressed to the King . . . through Cromwell's agency', and was not sure whether it was put forth by Convocation or Parliament. Actually there is nothing to connect the petition with Convocation: the points made are quite different from those which would have struck the bishops themselves, and the wording ('. . . the subjectes of this realme . . . be forced to make their most humble complainct . . .') seems clearly to indicate a lay origin.

[3] Edward Hall, *Hall's Chronicle*, 785. The act (23 Henry VIII, c. 20) carried over this figure but made it refer to annates paid since 1486. Lunt believed that it was an exaggeration and added that the exact sum cannot be determined (*Financial Relations of the Papacy*, 299-300).

[4] Chapuys MS., 1532, no. 9 (*L.P.*, v, 832; *C.S.P.*, *Spn.*, iv, ii, 907). No copy of the bill in this form survives, and its contents must be inferred from the statute and from other evidence.

obeyed, and clergy 'without any scruple of conscience' shall continue to administer sacraments and sacramentals.

In this bald form the annates bill was probably introduced in the House of Lords. It was hotly debated, and despite its favourable financial implications all the prelates opposed it. Passage seemed uncertain. Even Cromwell wrote, 'to what ende or effecte it will succeede suerlie I know not'.[1] Then, perhaps in response to the opposition, Henry changed his tactics. Cromwell was ordered to draft a new clause which would delay the effect of the act until Henry confirmed it by letters patent: an obvious attempt to avoid the rupture with Rome, at least for a time, while placing great financial pressure upon the pope.[2] As Norfolk wrote to the English envoy at Rome, 'nothyng hurtful' would be done unless the pope persisted 'in procedyng wrongfully and ungrately agaynst the Kyng', for Henry retained power to 'stop all such effectes, and woll so do onles ill and unkynde handlyng enforce hym to consent to the same'.[3]

The conditional clause was to prove useful to Henry,[4] but it did little to smooth the bill's way in Parliament. The king himself had to appear in the Lords on three occasions, and when the final reading was given on 19 March all the bishops and two abbots—probably the only regular clergy present—voted no. So did the earl of Arundel, but about thirty other temporal peers supported the king and carried the day.[5] Norfolk must have been busy politicking: he told Chapuys that he was completely occupied with Parliament and could discuss no other affairs.[6]

The Commons were equally unco-operative. Henry's agents used several arguments, among them the assertion that annates were not paid in Spain, and after continued complaint Henry promised that he would take no further measures against the pope for a year. In the end it was clear that nothing approaching unanimity could be reached, and a sort of division was ordered. Chapuys reports this as a novel procedure devised by the king

[1] SP 1/69, fol. 41ᵛ, P.R.O. (L.P., v, 723).
[2] The draft clauses are Harleian MS. 6849, fols. 60–1, B.M. (not in L.P.); see Elton, 'A Note on the First Act of Annates', B.I.H.R., xxiii (1950), 203–4.
[3] SP 1/69, fols. 137–8, P.R.O. (L.P., v, 831).
[4] It probably accounts for the papal concession over Cranmer's bulls; see below, Ch. 8.
[5] Chapuys MS., 1532, no. 12 (L.P., v, 879; C.S.P., Spn., iv, ii, 922). The act is printed in Burnet, Reformation of the Church of England, i, App. 106.
[6] Chapuys MS., 1532, no. 12, loc. cit.

himself and, we may think, heavily loaded in his favour: Henry ordered the members who would stand for his success and the welfare of the realm to one side of the House and those who opposed the measure to the other. Several who had earlier been in opposition joined the 'yeas' for fear of the king's indignation, and a majority was obtained.[1] The act in conditional restraint of annates thus passed both Houses before the end of March.

2

Although the attack on the pope had to be forced through an unwilling Parliament, criticism of English prelates was popular in the Commons. Edward Hall's first mention of the session reports a discussion of general grievances, among which the Lower House 'sore complayned of the crueltie of the ordinaries' in *ex officio* proceedings for heresy. 'For the ordinaries woulde send for men and ley accusacions to them of heresye, and say they were accused, and ley articles to them, but no accuser should be brought furthe, which to the Commons was very dredeful and grevous: for the partie so assited [cited] must either abjure or be burned, for purgacion he might make none.'[2] Other abuses of the church courts were 'long debated'. On 28 February Norfolk wrote of the 'infenyte clamor of the temporaltye here in Parlement agaynst the mysusyng of the spiritual jurysdiccion', adding that no previous Parliament had complained a tenth so much about ecclesiastical abuses.[3]

According to Hall the Commons at length agreed that 'all the griefes which the temporall men were greved with shoulde be putte in writyng and delyvered to the kyng, whiche by great advyse was done'.[4] It is probable that several members were reminded, not unnaturally, of the similar complaints which they had discussed in 1529, and they may have inquired whether the documents drawn up in that session had survived. Evidently they

---

[1] Chapuys MS., 1532, no. 13 (*L.P.*, v, 898; *C.S.P.*, *Spn.*, iv, ii, 926). Sir Goronwy Edwards regarded these proceedings as 'an improvisation for dealing with one particular bill' and tentatively dated the earliest procedural division to the early 1550s, just after the Commons moved to St Stephen's chapel ('The Emergence of Majority Rule in the Procedure of the House of Commons', *T.R.H.S.*, 5th ser., xv [1965], 165–87).   [2] Edward Hall, *Hall's Chronicle*, 784.
[3] SP 1/69, fols. 137–8, P.R.O. (*L.P.*, v, 831).
[4] Edward Hall, *Hall's Chronicle*, 784.

did—Cromwell or some other member had been shrewd enough to save them—and they became the basis of the famous Supplication against the Ordinaries or Commons' Supplication of 1532.

Professor Elton has argued that the Supplication had been put into virtually final form by the government, operating behind the scenes, before the discussion of clerical abuses was opened in Parliament.[1] Certainly this may be so: Cromwell's careful preparation of documents and strategy suggests its likelihood. But in the absence of definitive evidence other explanations are also possible. It may be that Cromwell took upon himself the drafting of the Supplication only after the Commons opened the subject, perhaps acting on hints which he had dropped or speeches which he had prompted. Or it may be that clerical abuses, mainly those considered in previous sessions, were discussed quite spontaneously in Parliament; that a committee of members learned in the law, perhaps with the help of 'great advyse' from Cromwell and other government officials, took the 1529 drafts and turned them into a new, more comprehensive document; and that this Supplication was accepted by the Commons and presented to the king virtually unchanged.[2]

However it had been prepared, the Supplication against the Ordinaries now contained a preamble and nine charges. A great

[1] Elton, 'The Commons' Supplication of 1532: Parliamentary Manœuvres in the Reign of Henry VIII', *E.H.R.*, LXVI (1951), 507–34.

[2] This view—that 'the drafting [took] place in the Commons, under the supervision of the councillors there'—was advanced by Elton (*ibid.* 514) only to be rejected for reasons which do not seem entirely compelling. His argument depends upon the hypothesis that the draft which he labels 'D' (SP 2/L, fols. 193–202, P.R.O.) was drawn up before the agitation in the Commons began, which hinges in turn upon two further propositions: (1) that the debate in the Commons was delayed until late February, and (2) that the draft was completed before 14 February. The first of these points rests primarily upon Chapuys' failure to mention the matter earlier, while the second depends on an analysis of memoranda in Audley's hand found on the back of the first folio of the draft. It is hard to see how these notes can give certain evidence of the draft's date; if they could, one might accept Elton's second proposition and argue that the draft was already before the House and used by the Speaker for memoranda when he could find nothing else to write on. It is true that Parliament's own papers have been lost, and that only those preserved by Cromwell or other individuals survive, but a parliamentary draft might of course have been filed privately if it were no longer needed by the House. The whole matter of the drafts and their dating is exceedingly complex, and it is impossible to feel confident about any explanation. The view suggested here accords well enough with that of J. P. Cooper, 'The Supplication against the Ordinaries Reconsidered', *E.H.R.*, LXXII (1957), 616–41, although reached independently and based on rather different arguments.

discord and division had arisen between the clergy and laity, the introductory section asserted, partly because of the 'new fantasticall opynyons' contained in heretical books but also on account of the 'uncharytable behaveour and dealyng of dyverse ordynaries, their commyssaries and substitutes'.[1] Since this division led to 'the grett inquyetacion and breche of your peace within this your most catholique realme', the Commons prayed Henry to remedy the clerical abuses which had widened the gulf. Among these they cited first the independent legislative power of Convocation, then the unjust character of *ex officio* proceedings; the subtle interrogatories which often trapped ignorant men in heresy trials; the expense and inconvenience caused when laymen were cited to appear in ecclesiastical courts outside their own dioceses; the use of excommunication for small and light causes; the excessive fees collected in church courts; the great charges made by ordinaries for institution of clergy into their benefices; the conferring of ecclesiastical offices upon young persons whom the bishops called their nephews; the large number of holy days, kept with small devotion; and the secular offices held by clergymen. All these abuses, they hoped, would be remedied by such effectual laws as Henry might devise. The Commons closed with a protestation of their 'mervelous fervent love' towards the king.[2]

On 18 March the Speaker, accompanied by a number of knights and burgesses, delivered the Supplication to the king.[3] Audley declared 'howe the temporal men of [the] realme were sore agreved with the cruel demeanoure of the prelates and ordinaryes, which touched bothe their bodyes and goodes', and begged the king to take what order he thought convenient. Changing the subject, Audley also expressed the displeasure of the Commons at the length of the Parliament; 'he besched the King to consider what payne, charge and cost his humble subjectes of the Nether House had susteyned syth the begynnynge of this Parliament', and asked Henry to dissolve it so that his subjects might return to their homes.

Edward Hall's account of the audience continues:

---

[1] The ideas in this prologue were expanded and published later in the year by Christopher Saint German as *A treatise concernyng the diuision betwene the Spirytualitie and temporaltie.*

[2] Quotations taken from 'D', SP 2/L, fols. 193–202, P.R.O.

[3] This was presumably the fair copy which survives at the P.R.O., SP 6/1, fols. 90–103 (*L.P.*, v, 1016 [1]).

When the kyng had receyved the Supplication of the Commons, he paused a whyle and then sayde: It is not the offyce of a kyng which is a judge to be to[o] lyghte of credence, nor I have not, nor wyll not use the same: for I wyll heare the partie that is accused speake or I geve any sentence. Your booke conteyneth dyvers articles of great and weyghtye matters, and as I perceyve it is agaynste the spirituall persones and prelates of our realme, of whiche thynge you desyre a redresse and a reformacion, whiche desyre and request is mere contraryant to your last peticion. For you requyre to have the Parlyament dissolved and to departe into your countreys, and yet you woulde have a reformacion of your griefes with all diligence. Although that your payne have ben great in tariyng, I assure you myne hath ben no lesse then yours, and yet all the payne that I take for your wealthes is to me a pleasure; therefore if you wyll have profyte of your complaynte, you must tary the tyme, or els to be without remedy.

The king was happy that the Commons wished to remove the causes of discord between them and the clergy, but he felt even more strongly that they should not foster dissension with him, as they had done in the case of the bill touching uses and primer seisin. He thought himself 'greatly wronged', for he had offered good reasons and gained the support of the Lords. 'Therefore I assure you, if you wyll not take some reasonable ende now when it is offered, I wyll serche out the extremitie of the lawe, and then wyll I not offre you so moche agayne.' With this cool answer to their petition and naked threat concerning uses, the Speaker and his followers were forced to depart.[1]

Action on the Supplication was delayed for several weeks. We do not know if further anti-clerical measures were discussed or passed before the end of March, but ultimately four such acts found their way to the statute books. Of these the citations act, prohibiting bishops from citing laymen out of their own dioceses except in certain specified cases, most likely antedated the recess, for it closely parallels one of the charges in the Supplication.[2] Indeed it was probably the 'urgent matter' which Warham discussed secretly with the upper house of Convocation on 15 February.[3] The act prohibiting the permanent settlement of

---

[1] Edward Hall, *Hall's Chronicle*, 784-5.
[2] 23 Henry VIII, c. 9. I have been unable to confirm Scarisbrick's note (*Henry VIII*, 301 n.) that all the lords spiritual voted against the bill: his citation from *L.P.* does not mention the matter. It is, of course, most probable that they voted no.
[3] C.C. 306, 42.

lands to the use of parish churches and chapels[1] is closely related to the troublesome primer seisin bill, since it too was designed to insure that the king's rights and revenues would not be prejudiced by feoffments to uses, and it probably dates from the earlier months. There is less reason to connect the two bills limiting benefit of clergy with the earlier part of the session, but they may have originated then. One was intended to prevent the release of clerics found guilty of murder, robbery, or petty treason, while the other made it felony for clerks convicted to break prison.[2]

3

The session of Convocation in 1532 was of unusual importance because it saw the continuation of the assault begun in 1531. The clerics reassembled at Westminster on 16 January.[3] A week later Warham ordered a group of nine proposed ordinances to be read, and at the following meeting some further canons were brought before the upper house. Although most of these had been discussed in previous sessions, the inferior clergy spent several weeks examining them and made numerous interlinear and marginal alterations. Interestingly enough, the king himself had made a few changes in one draft, perhaps indicating the ecclesiastical authority which he now claimed. By 9 February both houses had given their assent to seventeen new constitutions, and Warham ordered them inscribed in a formal statute book.[4]

The new canons began with a pious exhortation urging the bishops to set a good example. Other sections concerned admission to holy orders, non-residency, the education of monks, abuses in immune chapels such as that in the Tower, and simony. Penance was prescribed for clerics who had lapsed into fornication and turpitude. A long list of heretical books formed part of one

[1] 23 Henry VIII, c. 10. The act noted that this practice differed little from the alienation of lands into mortmain, which had been prohibited in 1279.

[2] 23 Henry VIII, cc. 1, 11.

[3] Records of this session are in C.C. 306, 41–4, and Wilkins, *Concilia*, III, 746–7.

[4] Two drafts of these survive: SP 1/57, fols. 112–35, and SP 6/1, fols. 20–35, P.R.O. The former includes Henry's minor emendations. The statute book is in the B.M., Cottonian MS. Cleopatra F. II, fols. 45ff.; its contents are printed in Wilkins, *Concilia*, III, 717–24. Wilkins erroneously attributed these statutes to 1529 because of the list of heretical books, but in 1529 several of the writings had not yet been published.

canon; among the writers mentioned were Luther, Zwingli, Melanchthon, Bucer, Tyndale, Francis Lambert, and William Roy.

A group of more controversial statutes was left for further discussion and never enacted.[1] Several of these dealt with matters which were also under consideration in Parliament—*ex officio* proceedings and clerks convict; they were no doubt dropped when it became evident that the laymen intended to pass their own legislation. Other abortive proposals concerned clerical dress, appropriated churches and hospitals, preaching throughout the dioceses, and heresy in the universities: Oxford was to be examined by the bishop of Lincoln, and Cambridge by the bishop of Ely, for if the fountains did not run clear the clergy could not imbibe pure doctrine.

Although there were few novelties in the statutes promulgated in 1532, their most recent student has termed them 'an important landmark in the history of English ecclesiastical legislation'.[2] Nothing of comparable scope had appeared since Archbishop Peacham's constitutions of 1281 or Stratford's canons of 1342. But the timing of the statutes was unfortunate. However laudable the impulse towards reform of the Church from within which they demonstrated, and however bland their contents, they pointed up the independent legislative power of Convocation at the exact moment when it was being criticized in Parliament.

Even as the canons of 1532 were being passed the government opened a curious attack on the clergy. On 8 February the attorney general, Christopher Hales, laid *quo warranto* charges in the King's Bench against a number of prominent clerics including the archbishop himself. These indictments questioned the prelates' right to claim such ancient privileges, all but forgotten by the sixteenth century, as the view of frankpledge or the franchise of infangenetheof.[3] Although suits had been filed sporadically against churchmen for violating the anti-clerical acts of 1529, such a mass indictment is unparalleled, and it seems impossible not to view it as a deliberate attempt to intimidate the prelates. It may have helped pave the way for their approaching submission.

[1] SP 6/7, fols. 87–94, and SP 6/12, fols. 167–9, P.R.O.
[2] Kelly, 'Canterbury Jurisdiction', 240. Cf. also Kelly, 'The Submission of the Clergy', *T.R.H.S.*, 5th ser., xv (1965), 97–102.
[3] KB 9/518, fols. 1ff., P.R.O. My attention was drawn to this matter by Dr Scarisbrick's dissertation, 'The Conservative Episcopate in England, 1529–1535', 194–212. See also Scarisbrick, *Henry VIII*, 296–7.

Once opened, the breach between the archbishop and the government widened steadily. On 24 February Warham took the surprising step of issuing a formal protestation dissociating himself from any statutes which Parliament might pass derogating the power of the pope or the liberties of the Church.[1] Within Convocation itself, Warham antagonized the courtiers by summoning one of their favourite preachers, Hugh Latimer, to answer renewed heresy charges. Latimer appeared on 11 March, refused to subscribe to the required articles, and was pronounced contumaceous. Warham then excommunicated the reformer and ordered him into safe custody at Lambeth.[2] Latimer was soon exonerated: on the 21st he appeared before Stokesley, who was presiding in Warham's absence, confessed that he had 'misordered [himself] very farre' by over-bold preaching, and begged forgiveness on bended knees. After he had sworn to two of the articles his sentence was lifted.[3]

Meanwhile, on 15 March, Warham had spoken against the king in the House of Lords. Henry himself was present and is reported to have used foul language, saying that the archbishop would be made to repent his words were it not for his advanced age.[4] But even his years did not save him. Probably in March or April, Warham was threatened with a praemunire suit because he had consecrated Henry Standish as bishop of St Asaph before Standish had exhibited his bulls to the king or performed the ceremony of homage and fealty. The charge was highly arbitrary, since the consecration had taken place nearly fourteen years before and, as Warham pointed out in his defence, 'it standeth not with good lawe or reason that a man shuld be punisshed for a dede by the which no man hath damage or wrong'.[5] The legal

---

[1] Printed in Wilkins, *Concilia*, III, 746.

[2] The fifteen articles administered to Latimer are in Harleian MS. 425, fols. 13-14, B.M. (*L.P.*, V, 860); they merely reiterate conservative theology.

[3] Latimer's speech is printed in Wilkins, *Concilia*, III, 747. The articles which he accepted were perhaps the ones he would have objected to most: no. 11, 'That the Lent and other fasting daies commanded by the canons, and used with the Christians, are to be kepte, except necessytie require otherwyse', and no. 14, 'That yt is laudable and proffitable, that the images of the crucifix and saintes are to be had in ye church in memory, honor, and woorshipe of Jesus Christ and his saintes.'

[4] *C.S.P.*, *Venetian*, IV, 754. This was doubtless one of the days on which Henry appeared to oversee the annates bill, although Carlo Capello, the Venetian ambassador, wrote that the divorce itself was under discussion.

[5] SP 1/70, fols. 236-43, P.R.O. Cf. Kelly, 'Canterbury Jurisdiction', 247-8.

action was not carried through, but Warham may have been saved only by his death.

No other matters of importance arose in Convocation before the end of March. The lower house brought up the case of William Tracy again, requesting that his body be exhumed and burned, and it asked Convocation to condemn the heretical will of Thomas Browne of Bristol; the archdeacon of Hereford exhibited a bill against the canons of that cathedral.[1] But no action resulted. Probably the prelates were too busy manning their forts in the House of Lords to have much time for Convocation after mid-February.

On 28 March—Maundy Thursday—Parliament was prorogued for the Easter recess. Neither it nor Convocation had accomplished much. Most important matters were left hanging for further discussion and possible settlement after the holiday.

4

Parliament reconvened on 10 April, Convocation on 12 April. Sometime during the prorogation Henry must have presented the Commons' Supplication to Warham and asked for a formal reply. Certainly the petition was the first item of business in Convocation; Warham exhibited its contents to the prelates, asked the lower house to consider it immediately, and reported that the king expected a rapid and mature answer.[2] At the next meeting, three days later, Gardiner read the preface to the Supplication, which stressed the division between the clergy and lay subjects, together with a proposed answer to it. He had also extracted two 'particulars' from the Commons' first article, concerning the authority of Convocation to make canons, and he read rejoinders to them. The prelates accepted these answers at once and sent them to the inferior clergy, who added their assent on 19 April.

The subsequent moves of Convocation are unclear. Possibly the clergy intended originally to send the king only Gardiner's answer, incomplete though it was; it is the only reply which we know to have been entered formally in the register of Convocation.[3]

[1] This occurred on 15 March. The bill is mentioned in C.C. 306, 43, and printed in Wilkins, *Concilia*, III, 747–8.
[2] The records of Convocation for these meetings are in C.C. 306, 44–9, and Wilkins, *Concilia*, III, 748–9.
[3] Printed in Wilkins, *Concilia*, III, 750–2.

In it Gardiner held that there was no such division between the clergy and laity as the Commons had maintained. If there was some discord, it had been stirred up by the 'uncharitable behaviour of certain evil and seditious persons' infected with heretical opinions.

And albeit we perceive and know right well, that there be as well disposed and as well conscienced men of your Grace's Commons, in no small number assembled, as ever we knew in any Parliament; yet we be not so ignorant, but that we understand that sinister informations and importunate labours and persuasions of evil disposed persons, pretending themselves to be thereunto moved by the zeal of justice and reformation, may induce right wise, sad, and constant men to suppose such things to be true, as be not so indeed.

In upholding the legislative power of the clergy Gardiner adduced the support of Scripture and ecclesiastical tradition. He saw no reason why the king's assent should be required, but praised Henry's wisdom and offered to be guided by his recommendations in passing future statutes.

Although Warham had ordered Gardiner's answer written out so that it might be dispatched to the king '*cum celeritate*,' some of the churchmen evidently realized that Henry would require their defence against the other points raised by the Supplication. The records of Convocation do not mention the amplification of the answer; they show that the meetings of 19 and 22 April were given over to another examination and exoneration of Latimer, who had appealed to the king.[1] But a fuller reply survives and was probably the document finally presented to Henry.[2] It begins with Gardiner's answer, somewhat softened, and proceeds to argue that if there were abuses in heresy trials or other administrative matters they were the 'defaults of . . . particular men and not of

---

[1] On 19 April, William Peto, provincial head of the Observant Friars, and Henry Elston, warden of their house at Greenwich, appeared in Convocation to accuse Richard Curwen of preaching at the convent without permission. The matter probably helped drive the wedge between the king and Convocation, for on Easter Monday Peto had preached against the divorce in Henry's presence, and Curwen, a royal chaplain, had been sent out by the court to refute Peto. We have no record that Convocation took action in the case; Peto and Elston had been arrested at the king's order, and Warham commanded them to remain in the custody of Bishop Standish. CC. 306, 46; Chapuys MS., 1532, no. 16 (*L.P.*, v, 941; *C.S.P., Spn.*, IV, ii, 934).

[2] SP 6/7, 239–84, P.R.O., printed in Henry Gee and W. J. Hardy, *Documents Illustrative of English Church History*, 154–76.

the hole ordre of the clergie, nor of the lawes wholesomely by them made'.[1] Warham inserted a personal rejoinder to the charge that his courts demanded exorbitant fees: he had (he said) instituted certain reforms a year earlier and had made other changes 'within these ten weeks' since the Commons had begun their onslaught.[2] The answer yields nothing, but attempts to cloak its hardness in servile language; the clergy, 'lowly upon [their] knees', beseech the king to assist them in the execution of their spiritual office.

According to his own account Henry received the answer about 27 April.[3] By this time some bitter words had been spoken in Parliament to match those in Convocation. The unpleasant subject of taxation had been reopened on 16 April when the lord chancellor came down to the Commons, accompanied by an impressive delegation of peers. The king was still worried by the prospect of a Scottish attack. He had been informed by his councillors, More said, that Scotsmen could easily invade the English borderland, for there was 'very lytell habitacion on the Englysh syde, but on the Scottysh syde was great habitacion, and the Scottes dwelled even just on the border'. Henry intended to strengthen the boundary, 'to the great commoditie of all his people'.[4] Perhaps to please the southerners who cared little about Scotland, More spoke also of improving the harbour at Dover,[5] and he may have mentioned further public works in other parts of the realm. For these causes the councillors thought it convenient that the Commons should grant the king 'some reasonable ayd'.

There was evidently considerable opposition. Chapuys reported that two worthy members declared the fortifications needless, for the Scots could cause no serious trouble without foreign aid. The best fortifications, they said, were the maintenance of justice at home and friendship abroad.[6] This argument probably led to the matter of the divorce, which was poisoning English relations with the emperor. Thomas Temys, a burgess for the small Wiltshire town of Westbury and a loyal supporter of Catherine of Aragon, expatiated on the difficulties which the divorce would bring, 'as in

[1] SP 6/7, 253-4, P.R.O.   [2] *Ibid.* 263.
[3] Edward Hall, *Hall's Chronicle*, 788.   [4] *Ibid.* 785.
[5] Chapuys MS., 1532, no. 16, *loc. cit.* The Dover harbour project was still before Parliament in 1581: cf. 23 Elizabeth, c. 6.
[6] Chapuys MS., 1532, no. 22 (*L.P.*, v, 989; *C.S.P.*, *Spn.*, iv, ii, 948).

bastardyng the Lady Marie, the Kynges only childe', and moved the Commons to sue the king 'to take the Quene again into his compaignie'.[1] Although no formal supplication was sent, the king heard of Temys' words and was displeased. The Commons did grant Henry a fifteenth—considerably less than he desired—without undue delay, but Chapuys heard some men express the opinion that its collection would lead to a mutiny.[2]

Several of these matters came to a head on 30 April, when the Speaker and many of the Commons were summoned to an audience with the King. Henry began by handing Audley the clerics' answer to the Supplication, which he had not been able to obtain 'till within three days last past'. Hall recorded the king's comment so succinctly that generations of historians have quoted his words: 'We thinke their answere will smally please you, for it semeth to us very slender. You bee a greate sorte of wise men; I doubt not but you will loke circumspectly on the matter, and we will be indifferent between you.' The anti-clerical chronicler could not resist adding his own view that the answer was 'for a truth . . . very sophisticall, and nothyng avoydyng the greves of the lay people'.[3]

The king then passed to the Temys affair. He said

that he marveiled not a litle, why one of the Parliament house spake openly of the absence of the Quene from hym, whiche matter was not to be determined there, for he saied it touched his soule, and wished the matrimony to be good, for then had he never been vexed in conscience; but the docters of the universities, said he, have determined the mariage to be voyde, and detestable before God, whiche grudge of conscience caused me to abstein from her compaignie, and no folishe or wanton appetite. For I am [said he] forty yere old, at which age the lust of man is not so quicke, as in lustie youth: and savyng in Spain and Portyngall it hath not been seen, that one man hath maried two sisters, the one beyng carnally knowen before: but the brother to mary the brother's wife was so abhorred emongest all nacions, that I never heard it, that any Christen man did it but myself. Wherfore you se my conscience trobled, and so I praie you reporte.[4]

---

[1] Edward Hall, *Hall's Chronicle*, 788.
[2] Chapuys MS., 1532, no. 16, *loc. cit.* The fifteenth must have been granted between 2 May (cf. Chapuys MS., 1532, no. 22, *loc. cit.*) and 8 May, when Convocation was told of it (C.C. 306, 47).   [3] Edward Hall, *Hall's Chronicle*, 788.
[4] *Ibid.* Chapuys thought that Henry had promised to support the Commons against the Church if they would not interfere in the divorce (Chapuys MS., 1532, no. 22, *loc. cit.*).

When the delegation had returned to the Commons' chamber Audley related the events of the interview to the whole House. Hall did not record the reaction to Henry's speech about the divorce, but he does tell us that the clergy's 'slight answere displeased the Commons'.

At this point our attention must once again be directed, as Henry's was, to Convocation. During the first week in May the prelates appeared devoid of leadership; Warham attended only one session, evidently a brief one, and Gardiner found himself in great disfavour with the king.[1] Fisher remained at Rochester. The lower clergy may have attempted to fill the vacuum—we know that they prepared a number of treatises on the power of ecclesiastics to legislate for the suppression of heresies.[2] But it is doubtful if they realized how serious their situation had become.

On 8 May Stokesley, who was presiding in Warham's absence, told a joint session about Parliament's grant of a fifteenth, adding that the clergy should show themselves no less ready to help the king meet the realm's needs. The lower clergy retired, as ordered, to discuss taxation, but soon returned with a new proposal. They wanted the bishops of London and Lincoln, the abbots of Westminster and Burton, the dean of the chapel royal, and Edward Fox, the king's almoner, to go to Henry as suppliants for the entire clergy, beseeching him to preserve and protect the liberties of the Church.[3] The clerics named, all royal favourites, agreed to go, but they accomplished nothing.

Indeed their interview, if it actually occurred, may have been the occasion on which the king presented his peremptory demand that the clergy abandon their legislative power. When Convocation next met, on 10 May, Fox exhibited a schedule of three articles which the king had sent to Convocation: the Church was to renounce its authority to make canons without royal licence;

---

[1] Cf. his undated letter to Henry, printed in Wilkins, *Concilia*, III, 752 (*L.P.*, v, 1019). Kelly comments that Gardiner's opposition almost certainly cost him the succession at Canterbury: 'Submission of the Clergy', 111.

[2] One of these may have been SP 6/2, fols. 23–42, P.R.O. (*L.P.*, v, 1021), headed 'Clerici sunt exempti de jurisdictione laicorum, etiam de jure divino'. A treatise by Fisher, 'That the bysshoppys have immediate autoryte to make suche lawes as they shall thynke expedient for the weale of men sowles' (SP 6/1, fols. 38–41, P.R.O. [*L.P.*, v, 1020]), was also circulating at this time.

[3] Their petition may be Cottonian MS. Cleopatra F. II, fol. 249, B.M. (*L.P.*, v, 1017), although this document is undated and could as plausibly be assigned to 1531.

it was to submit existing canons to the scrutiny of thirty-two persons appointed by the king, half from Parliament and half clergy, abandoning all canons which this committee found offensive; it was to retain the remaining canons with the king's consent.[1]

Warham, sensing the emergency which had arisen, immediately adjourned Convocation to the remote chapel of St Catherine, a part of the Abbey infirmary, where the articles were read again. The archbishop next prorogued the formal session of Convocation for three days and led the prelates to St Dunstan's chapel for a private conference. Fisher's counsel was evidently missed, so much so that the bishops decided to send a delegation to interview him at Rochester.[2] They may have shown him a second answer to the Commons' Supplication, for it includes a few corrections which are probably in his hand. Unyielding in tone, it argues that spiritual jurisdiction proceeds immediately from God and offers to present for royal confirmation only such canons as do not concern the correction of sin or maintenance of faith.[3]

Fisher doubtless counselled firm resistance to the king's demands. But before Convocation could hold another meeting Henry renewed the attack in Parliament. On 11 May he sent for the Speaker again. When Audley arrived, accompanied by twelve members of the Commons, he found the king flanked by his noble councillors. Edward Hall may have been one of the Commons' delegation; he has left us the gist of Henry's speech, which must have been delivered in a tone of horrified surprise.

Welbeloved subjects, [said the king,] we thought that the clergie of our realme had been our subjectes wholy, but now wee have well perceived that they bee but halfe our subjectes, yea, and scarce our subjectes: for all the prelates at their consecration make an othe to the pope, clene contrary to the othe that they make to us, so that they seme to be his

---

[1] SP 6/6, fols. 108–9, P.R.O. (*L.P.*, vi, 276 [2]); printed in Wilkins, *Concilia*, iii, 749.
[2] Members of this group were the bishops of Lincoln and Bath and Wells, the abbot of St Benet's Hulme, Edward Fox, two doctors of theology, and two proctors of the clergy (William Cliff and John Raynes). They were to report to Warham in his dining chamber within Westminster palace at 8 o'clock the next morning. C.C. 306, 48.
[3] Cottonian MS. Cleopatra F. 1, fols. 101–3, B.M. (*L.P.*, v, 1018 [1]). This paper may have been written by Gardiner; we do not know if it was ever presented to the king. It is clearly couched as a reply to the first article of the Commons' petition, not to the king's 'schedule' which superseded it.

subjectes, and not ours. The copie of bothe the othes I deliver here to
you, requiryng you to invent some ordre, that we bee not thus deluded
of our spirituall subjectes.[1]

Audley returned immediately to Parliament and ordered the oaths
read to the whole House. Hall—perhaps like many other
members—was greatly impressed by them; he set them out in
their entirety, commenting that 'the openyng of these othes was
one of the occasions why the pope within two yere folowyng lost
all his jurisdiccion in England'.

Despite his charge to the Commons, Henry does not seem to
have anticipated parliamentary action against the clergy. Instead,
he pressed the ultimatum which Fox had delivered to Convocation; he had probably devised the scene at court as a means
of terrifying the churchmen. The surviving records of Convocation sound deceptively calm, for they show that the prelates
spent part of their meeting on 13 May over the old affair of
William Tracy.[2] But Warham and his fellows must have been
gravely concerned with their response to the king's articles. At
length they agreed to suggest a compromise which had doubtless
been drafted behind the scenes: Convocation would make no
more canons without the king's consent, and it would submit all
existing canons to the king himself—not a committee—for
rejection or ratification. The inferior clergy were willing to
bargain away their legislative power only 'during the kinges
naturall lif', and they added a proviso to uphold the force of
existing canons and ecclesiastical jurisdiction until Henry should
declare his pleasure therein.[3]

Warham probably looked forward to further discussion,
ending perhaps in genuine concord. But matters now took another
unexpected turn: Henry suddenly ordered the archbishop to
terminate the session. When the prelates assembled for their last
meeting on the morning of 15 May Warham read the brief
proroguing Convocation to 4 November. The necessity for
immediate action was further dramatized by the appearance of
some leading councillors—Norfolk, Exeter, Oxford, Sandys,
and the Boleyns—who demanded the submission of the clergy
without any limitation or reservation. Indeed they probably

[1] Edward Hall, *Hall's Chronicle*, 788.
[2] C.C. 306, 48; Wilkins, *Concilia*, III, 749.
[3] Cottonian MS. Cleopatra F. I, fols. 97–9, B.M. (*L.P.*, v, 1018 [2]).

introduced a new form of the king's articles which included the novel assertion that Convocation 'alway hath bin and must bee' assembled only by the king's command.[1]

After an hour's confrontation the peers departed and the inferior clergy entered the Chapter House. They had been polled on the king's three articles: eighteen voted 'no' on the first, renouncing independent legislative authority, and nineteen refused to accept the second and third, dealing with existing canons. In each case the number of abstentions brought the total to twenty-six. Unfortunately neither the total attendance nor the number of affirmative votes is recorded. If the king had obtained a majority in the lower house it must have been a slender one.

Warham heard this news from the Prolocutor, then admonished the inferior clergy to retire since the king's emissaries might reappear at any moment. Norfolk and some others did return at lunch time, but after talking with Warham they left again.

In the afternoon a vote was taken in the upper house. Standish, Stokesley, and Longland gave their voices for the king, but only with considerable reservations which were written into the *acta*. Bishop Clerk was totally opposed. The votes of the other prelates are not recorded. Only three more bishops—Warham, West, and Veysey—are likely to have been present, together with what was probably a small number of mitred abbots. But a majority of the clergy present in the upper house yielded to the king, and Convocation was formally prorogued.[2] The churchmen, wrote Chapuys, were now of less account than shoemakers, for cobblers could still assemble and make their own statutes.[3] The clergy had abandoned their independent power to legislate.

On 16 May the Submission was officially subscribed before a group of special commissioners.[4] The abbots of St Albans, Bury, and Waltham and the prior of Merton were now listed as representatives of the regular clergy. Warham, Standish, Longland, and—strangely—Clerk signed for the bishops. Stokesley's name is not recorded; perhaps he had decided that his reservations were too great. Nor is there any mention of the inferior clergy. The

---

[1] SP 1/70, fol. 38, P.R.O. (*L.P.*, v, 1023); Kelly, 'Submission of the Clergy', 115.

[2] C.C. 306, 49; Wilkins, *Concilia*, III, 749.

[3] Chapuys MS., 1532, no. 23 (*L.P.*, v, 1013; *C.S.P.*, *Spn.*, IV, ii, 951).

[4] Bergavenny, Hussey, Mordaunt, Fitzwilliam, and Cromwell. Cf. Elton, 'Parliamentary Manœuvres', 533.

articles purport to have been ratified 'by these and other bishops, abbots, and priors of the upper house of Convocation',[1] a vague phrase which must have covered a mass of discord and confusion. As Michael Kelly has put it, the Submission of the Clergy was enacted by a rump Convocation.[2]

5

Although Parliament had not been directly involved in the Submission, it seems likely that the king's advisers intended at one time to outlaw clerical legislation by means of a parliamentary statute. Our evidence comes only from a surviving draft bill, written in a common clerk's hand and corrected by Cromwell and at least one other writer.[3] One of the earliest pieces of proposed legislation to display Cromwell's skill at composing an elaborate preamble, the bill expounds the political theory that England is composed of three estates, the clergy, the nobility, and the commons, each labouring in its degree and calling as ordained by God, yet all compact into 'one body polytyke lyvyng under the alegyuns, obedyens, tuycion and defens of the kynges royall megeste being there allonly supreme emperyall hede and soverayn'. The power of making laws belongs alone to the king (Cromwell deleted a phrase requiring 'the assent of the said prelates, nobilles and comens') 'which auctoryte and jurysdiccion roiall ys so unyted and knytt by the hye provydens of God to the imperiall crowne of this realme that the same ys not under the obeyens or appellacion of eny worldly fforen prince'. The bill therefore orders that no ordinances or constitutions made by the clergy contrary to the laws and customs of the realm or the king's jurisdiction and authority shall be of any effect unless confirmed by Parliament. Those who violate the act shall incur the penalties specified in the acts of provisors and praemunire.

We do not know if this bill was actually introduced into

---

[1] The 'Instrumentum super admissione cleri' is printed in Wilkins, *Concilia*, III, 754–5, from Warham's register. Among the MS. copies are SP 6/3, fols. 62–3, and SP 1/70, fols. 34–7, P.R.O. (*L.P.*, v, 1023).

[2] Kelly, 'Submission of the Clergy', 117.

[3] SP 2/L, fols. 78–80, P.R.O. (*L.P.*, v, 721 [1]). SP 2/P, fols. 17–19, P.R.O. (*L.P.*, VII, 57 [2]) is a fair copy incorporating the changes in the first draft. Kelly believes that the bill dates from the period between 11 and 14 May ('Submission of the Clergy', 113 n.).

Parliament or not: probably not, since the king decided to force the Submission of the Clergy within Convocation. Alternatively, the bill may have been sent to Parliament only to be abandoned because of unexpected opposition, perhaps motivated by fear that the king really did intend to claim all legislative power for himself: if so, Parliament would be no better off than Convocation. In any case Cromwell must have saved the papers for further use later. We will see their political theory and several of their phrases reappearing in the great appeals act of 1533; the bill itself was altered and finally passed in 1534. No further attempt was made, for the time being, to have the Submission ratified by statute, and Henry showed no disposition to appoint the sixteen parliamentarians who were to help examine canons.

We lack exact chronology for Parliament's activities during April and May. It was probably at this time that one John Stanton, a servant to a London merchant named Thomas Patmer, complained to Parliament that his master had been imprisoned and badly treated by the bishop of London. Sir Thomas More, answering the charge, brushed off Stanton as hardly fit to represent his master in the Parliament house and suggested, perhaps falsely, that Stanton himself was a favourer of heresy. We hear no more of the matter; a year later Patmer was still in prison.[1]

Since More was involved, this scene had probably occurred in the Lords. In the Commons, members had granted a fifteenth by 7 May, and they had talked of Henry's divorce and the bishops' oaths. By mid-May they had also given their assent to a number of acts designed to improve legal procedures and support economic stability.

Three statutes dealt with civil suits. By the first, penalties were set for perjury by sheriffs guilty of partiality in empanelling juries and by jurors who reached untrue verdicts.[2] Lord Herbert of Cherbury commented that the act 'was to the singular benefit of the subject, there being no mischiefs so easie to be done, so irreparable in their consequence, or unlimited in their extent, as those of this kind',[3] and there is considerable evidence to suggest that sheriffs were often bribed to select biased or corruptible

---

[1] L.P., v, 982; vi, 573; cf. Elton, 'Sir Thomas More and the Opposition to Henry VIII', B.I.H.R., xli (1968), 23.

[2] 23 Henry VIII, c. 3.

[3] Lord Herbert of Cherbury, King Henry the Eighth, 357.

jurymen.[1] Subjects were also benefited by an act ordering unsuccessful plaintiffs in a wide variety of suits to pay the defendants'
costs; such damages had previously been available only to
plaintiffs.[2] Judges were empowered to set other punishments for
plaintiffs suing *in forma pauperis*; most likely they ordered whipping. A third statute improved the procedure in actions of
trespass, annuity, and covenant, providing that in the last resort
the defendant could be outlawed.[3] All of these acts originated in
the Commons. They must have been prepared by the king's
counsel learned in the law, perhaps with some help from Cromwell: we know that he was concerned with juries which gave
'veredicte[s] . . . untrewlie agenst the King'.[4]

The legal position of creditors was strengthened by a statute
allowing them to control the lands of their debtors until the
obligation was satisfied.[5] In criminal suits, the trial of murder
cases in towns was expedited by a statute which set more appropriate qualifications for jurors: ownership of movable property
worth forty pounds was substituted for the old freehold requirement.[6] Corporate towns were ordered to maintain their own
gaols, or to build them if none existed, and provision was made for
erection of gaols in other needful areas, the justices of the peace
being authorized to levy taxes for that purpose.[7]

Much the most important piece of economic legislation was the
statute of sewers, which Cromwell had 'studied, ingrossed, and

---

[1] Cf. Amos, *Observations*, 133–8, and Holdsworth, *History of English Law*, IV, 515–17.
The statute of 1532 mitigated the over-severe common law punishment in cases of
attaint for false verdicts by establishing a scale of fines related to the sum in
dispute; it expired in 1533 but was continued twice under Henry VIII and made
perpetual in 1571.

[2] 23 Henry VIII, c. 15; cf. Amos, *Observations*, 138; Holdsworth, *History of English
Law*, IV, 536–8.

[3] 23 Henry VIII, c. 14; cf. Holdsworth, *History of English Law*, IV, 534.

[4] Original acts, H.L.R.O.; Henry's instructions to Cromwell in Michaelmas term,
1531: Cottonian MS. Titus B. 1, fol. 487, B.M. (*L.P.*, V, 394).

[5] 23 Henry VIII, c. 6. Merchants had previously been able, under the Statute
Staple, to holds the lands of their debtors until the obligation was satisfied; this
remedy was now extended to all creditors, provided that they had recorded
the recognizance. Lord Herbert commented that 'this not only enlarged contracts,
but strengthened much the sinews of them' (*King Henry the Eighth*, 358). Cf. Amos,
Observations, 128.

[6] 23 Henry VIII, c. 13.

[7] 23 Henry VIII, c. 2. The bill originated in the Commons; the Lords added a
proviso, sec. 6 of the statute, extending the provisions of the act to Derbyshire
(original act, H.L.R.O.).

put in a redynes agenst the begynnyng of . . . Parlyament'.[1] The typically Cromwellian preamble sets out the 'great damages and losses which have happened in many and divers parts of this . . . realm' because of flooding of fenlands 'and other low places heretofore through politic wisdom won and made profitable for the great common wealth of this realm'. The act provides for the appointment of commissioners who shall be responsible for the proper maintenance of dikes and removal of obstructions in watercourses. In one of the earliest instances of delegated legislative authority the commissioners were given power to make appropriate laws, ordinances, and decrees; they could also levy taxes and punish offenders.

Other economic measures were more limited in scope. Henry's fear of war with Scotland was reflected in a statute forbidding the sale of horses to Scots.[2] Coopers were protected by an act which prevented brewers and soap makers from manufacturing their own barrels.[3] A petition from the inhabitants of Plymouth and other West-Country ports was worked up by Cromwell and turned into an act prohibiting the extraction of tin by 'stream works' which choked harbours with sand and silt.[4] Similarly, the mayor and commonalty of York secured enactment of their petition calling for destruction of pikes and fishgarths in the Ouse and Humber.[5] Parliament further ordered that no wool be wound unless it had been sufficiently washed, and that no foreign objects be placed in the fleece to increase its weight.[6] Finally, it enacted that no toll should be charged for the use of towpaths along the Severn, which 'time out of mind' had been free to all subjects.[7]

---

[1] Cottonian MS. Titus B. 1, fol. 486ᵛ, B.M. (*L.P.*, v, 394). The act is 23 Henry VIII, c. 5; cf. Amos, *Observations*, 188–200.

[2] 23 Henry VIII, c. 16.

[3] Henry VIII, c. 4. The long act sets prices for barrels and fixes their capacity and weight; it orders every cooper to mark his barrels with a recognizable sign.

[4] 23 Henry VIII, c. 8; the surviving draft, corrected by Cromwell, is SP 2/L, fols. 106–11, P.R.O. (*L.P.*, v, 721 [8]). It lacks the provisos in secs. 3 and 4.

[5] 23 Henry VIII, c. 18. Such bills may have involved the expenditure of considerable sums of money; Sir John Mablisten, writing about bills proposed for the order of St John of Jerusalem, commented, 'Yf we had money inoughe I suppose sum of them might be brought to passe: and without grete plenty therof nothyng here passythe.' SP 1/69, fol. 95, P.R.O. (*L.P.*, v, 775).

[6] 23 Henry VIII, c. 17. An abortive draft (SP 2/L, fols. 115–17, P.R.O.) would give the master and wardens of the London woolmen authority to examine all fleeces in order to carry out the provisions of the act.

[7] 23 Henry VIII, c. 12. The act mentions particularly that owners of boats carrying wine 'now of late' had been forced to give a draught or bottle of wine as a toll.

The Lords and Commons also ratified the pardon of the clergy within the province of York, which Henry had granted after the Convocation of York promised to pay him £18,840,[1] and they passed a belated bill of attainder against Rhys ap Griffith, Norfolk's brother-in-law, who had been beheaded the previous December on the charge that he had not told the government of a project to unite the Scots and Welsh for a conquest of England.[2] Private bills were enacted for the two countesses of Oxford, the countess of Wiltshire, and the earl of Surrey. In addition, Parliament confirmed exchanges of land between the king and the duke of Richmond, Lord Lumley, the prior of St John of Jerusalem, the provost of Eton, the abbots of Waltham, Westminster, and St Albans, and Christ's College, Cambridge.[3]

Having enacted this substantial body of legislation, Parliament was prorogued on 14 May. The king's action appears to have been sudden, and it is not easy to explain. In recording the prorogation itself Hall gave no reason; he had earlier written that the Commons' grant of a fifteenth 'was not enacted at this sessyon, bicause that sodeinly began a pestilence in Westmynster, wherefore the Parlyament was proroged tyll the nexte yere'.[4] But there are no other references to an outbreak of the plague in May.[5] Certainly Chapuys made no mention of it, nor did he say why the session was brought to an end. In a dispatch of 13 May he reported that the chancellor and the bishops were opposing a bill which would have stripped the prelates of their authority to lay hands on men's bodies in heresy cases;[6] Pollard's slight inflation

---

[1] 23 Henry VIII, c. 19; a draft, containing several interlinear additions by Cromwell is SP 2/L, fols. 83–96, P.R.O. (*L.P.*, v, 721 [4]). The Convocation of York had met in May 1531; it was stage-managed for Cromwell by Brian Higdon. See SP 1/65, fols. 255–6 and 261–2, P.R.O. (*L.P.*, v, 224, 237); Cottonian MS. Cleopatra E. vi, fols. 216–25, B.M. (*L.P.*, v, App. 9); Wilkins, *Concilia*, iii, 744.

[2] 23 Henry VIII, c. 34; cf. *L.P.*, v, 563, 657, 724. Griffith's widow, who was Norfolk's half-sister, married Lord Daubeney, later the earl of Bridgwater.

[3] 23 Henry VIII, cc. 21–33. Cromwell had arranged most of the exchanges: Cottonian MS. Titus B. i, fol. 486, B.M. A draft of 23 Henry VIII, c. 26, concerning the exchange of lands between the king and the prior of St John's, survives in the P.R.O., SP 2/L, fols. 118/21 (*L.P.*, v, 721 [1]); it is heavily revised by one of the Crown's legal experts, possibly Christopher Hales, the attorney general.

[4] Edward Hall, *Hall's Chronicle*, 789, 786.

[5] In October Audley did remark on the plague, however; he believed that it was still spreading (SP 1/71, fols. 170–1, P.R.O. [*L.P.*, v, 1476]). The Venetian ambassador noted it at the same time, commenting that it, together with a comet and an unusually high tide at Greenwich, had made the people superstitious (*C.S.P., Venetian*, iv, 816).   [6] Chapuys MS., 1532, no. 23, *loc. cit.*

of this remark[1] has been puffed further by Cooper into the suggestion that Henry disbanded Parliament because he had lost control of the Lords.[2] Another recent writer believes that he may have wished to disperse disgruntled members of both Houses.[3] Certainly there had been an unusual amount of discord, but less dramatic explanations seem more likely. Perhaps the king ordered the end of Parliament and Convocation in order to force the clergy into a speedy submission. Or—more likely—the king simply yielded at last to the Commons' plea that they be allowed to return to their homes. The session of 1532 had lasted for four months with a recess of less than a fortnight at Easter. It was the longest gathering in the life of the Parliament, and must have been unusually burdensome to individual members as well as to the counties and towns which were liable for their expenses.

Contrary to custom, Henry did not attend Parliament on the last day of the session. Presumably More, as Chancellor, gave his assent to the legislation which had passed both Houses, with the exception of the subsidy bill. This Henry declined to accept or reject. Despite Hall, it is difficult to believe that the sudden prorogation determined this rather curious action. Chapuys thought that the king intended to wait until the clergy agreed to pay a tenth,[4] but it is much more likely that he was dissatisfied with the smallness of the Commons' grant and decided to bid for a larger sum at a later session. Henry's fear of a Scottish attack may also have abated, while the rise of Thomas Cromwell was offering more efficient use of the resources already at the king's command.[5]

---

[1] A. F. Pollard, *Henry VIII*, 235.
[2] J. P. Cooper, 'The Supplication against the Ordinaries Reconsidered', 633-4.
[4] Kelly, 'Submission of the Clergy', 118.
[3] Chapuys MS., 1532, no. 24 (*L.P.*, v, 1046; *C.S.P., Spn.*, iv, ii, 952).
[5] Perhaps because the session was abruptly terminated, a number of bills remained 'dependyng in the Comen Hous', and we are unusually fortunate in having a list of them (SP 1/74, fols. 146-7, P.R.O. [*L.P.*, vi, 120]). Some of these, such as the primer seisin bill, were unacceptable to the Commons, but others would probably have passed had there been more time. Two readings had been given to measures dealing with bankruptcy, regrating of corn, portions in lieu of mortuaries, and the 'saving of young spring of woods', and eight other bills had been read once. In addition, we know that a new treasons bill had been prepared for consideration in 1532. It was to come into effect on 6 January—when it was drafted Cromwell evidently still expected Parliament to meet in October or November 1531— and would have made it treason to hold any castle or fort against the king, to leave the realm without the king's licence, to hinder the king's ambassadors abroad, to give allegiance to any foreign power, or to publish foreign writings

Although the Venetian ambassador at first heard that Parliament would meet again in a fortnight,[1] it was prorogued to 5 November. Later the new session was further postponed to 4 February 1533. It must have been a bleak November day when Audley wrote to Cromwell, 'it was moche to my sute to bryng it to that tyme, . . . for it ys about the myddes of Hillary terme and the dayes then shal wax sumwhat fayer ageyn'.[2]

6

Two days after Parliament was prorogued Sir Thomas More delivered the Great Seal to the king at Westminster. He had long wished to resign, and his loathing of the Submission of the Clergy had evidently forced the issue. Chapuys very perceptively wrote that had More continued to serve as chancellor he would have been obliged to act against his conscience or to incur the king's displeasure. 'There was never a better man in the office', Chapuys added.[3] Few will disagree with his judgment.

Another high office was vacated in August, when Archbishop Warham died at his nephew's house near Canterbury. It is hard to exaggerate the effect of these losses, by resignation and death, upon Parliament. Neither More nor Warham played his greatest scenes upon the parliamentary stage. Neither can be credited with guiding the course of Parliament to any considerable extent, for both opposed its anti-clerical activities as well as the king's anti-papal programme. Nor were More and Warham able to become really effective leaders of the opposition: their dependence upon the king was too great. Their policies promised no solution to Henry's problems. The way of the future was not theirs. But they defended the old order with dignity and courage.

The interval between the sessions of 1532 and 1533 marks the

prejudicial to the king. It was once thought that Parliament rejected the measure (I. D. Thornley, 'The Treason Legislation of Henry VIII [1531–1534]', *T.R.H.S.*, 3rd ser., XI [1917], 100), but since treasons are not included in the list of 'matters dependyng' one may wonder whether it was actually introduced. Such doubts are strengthened by the absence of any draft which would have become effective later in the year; an act passed in May to affect deeds done the previous January would have been an unusual exercise in *ex post facto* legislation.

[1] *C.S.P., Venetian*, IV, 767.
[2] SP 1/72, fols. 16–17, P.R.O. (*L.P.*, V, 1514).
[3] Chapuys MS., 1532, no. 24, *loc. cit.*; cf. Elton, 'Sir Thomas More and the Opposition to Henry VIII', 31–4.

watershed in the history of the Reformation Parliament. The later sessions have a different character for several reasons, but not least because of the absence of two of the greatest men of Henry's reign.

8

THE FOURTH SESSION, 1533:
THE GREAT MATTER SETTLED

After four years of skirmishes and flanking operations, the king and his advisers were ready by the beginning of 1533 to mount a frontal attack on Henry's marriage. In this assault a principal role was reserved for Parliament.

Changes in personnel, rather than any fundamental alteration in policy, signalled the coming of effective action. So long as Warham lived there was no certain prospect of achieving the divorce by referring Henry's case to the archbishop of Canterbury; with him dead Henry could appoint a new primate known to be sympathetic to the king's cause. So long as More remained chancellor the king could not call on his highest ranking officer for help in his most important suit; after his retirement the post could be manned by a councillor of demonstrated loyalty.

More's position was the first to be filled. He had delivered up the Great Seal on 16 May 1532; four days later Henry presented it to Thomas Audley, who had earned the king's respect for his management of the Commons during the first three sessions of the Parliament. Norfolk, Gardiner, Cromwell, and some other councillors attended the ceremony in which Audley was made Lord Keeper and authorized to execute all functions normally performed by the chancellor. He was knighted on the same day and took his oath of office on June 5, at the beginning of Trinity term in the Chancery.[1] Just before the reassembly of Parliament, on 26 January 1533, the king raised Audley to the higher dignity of Lord Chancellor.[2] He was to preside over the House of Lords in the remaining sessions of the Reformation Parliament; his experience as Speaker of the Commons must have prepared him well for his duties in the Upper House.

The king hesitated longer over the appointment of a successor to Warham: quite naturally so, considering the great weight that hung on his choice. Gardiner had earlier been regarded as the

[1] L.P., v, 1075.
[2] Ibid. vi, 73. This ceremony, like the earlier one, took place at Greenwich. The L.P. calendar contains the erroneous date 26 June.

archbishop's heir apparent, but he had opposed Henry at a critical stage of the Submission of the Clergy and was now evidently considered too unreliable. From the point of view of their positions Edward Lee of York or Stokesley of London seemed naturally in line for Warham's post; Longland of Lincoln was widely respected and probably sufficiently subservient; Edward Fox, the king's brilliant almoner, was prominent at court and a likely choice if Henry wished to by-pass the entire bench of bishops. But the king chose instead a Cambridge don who was at the time serving him as ambassador in Austria. Thomas Cranmer himself had no inkling of his appointment until November 1532, when he was ordered to return home with all possible speed. He reached London about 10 January, was rushed to the king's presence, and according to one account was named archbishop at a bear baiting.[1] Several weeks later Chapuys commented on the general astonishment which greeted the news: not only had the king made a surprising selection, but he had also broken with the profitable custom of leaving bishoprics vacant for a year so that he could collect the revenues.[2]

Henry's agents at Rome began immediately to seek papal provision for Cranmer—if the English Church were carried into schism it was desirable that it should be done by a papally approved primate—and they soon met with unusual success. Perhaps because they threatened to bring the annates act into force, Clement VII issued the bulls with remarkable speed and waived the normal charge of fifteen hundred florins. The new archbishop was consecrated on Passion Sunday, 30 March, in the Chapter House at Westminster. Since Parliament was in session at the time, a number of its members were probably present to hear Cranmer protest that his oath to the pope could not bind him to violate the laws of God or Henry's prerogative.[3]

[1] Jasper Ridley, *Thomas Cranmer*, 50–3.
[2] Chapuys MS., 1533, no. 6 (*L.P.*, VI, 89; *C.S.P.*, *Spn.*, IV, ii, 1043). Only four days after Warham's death the Venetian ambassador had written that Cranmer was one of the king's possible choices; one would marvel at his insight were not Pole, whose implacability should have been quite obvious, given as the alternative. *C.S.P.*, *Venetian*, IV, 799.
[3] Ridley, *Thomas Cranmer*, 54–5. A contemporary copy of his protestation, possibly in the hand of one of Cromwell's clerks, is in the B.M., Cottonian MS. Cleopatra E. VI, fol. 251 (*L.P.*, VI, 291 [3]). Both Cranmer and Audley experienced financial difficulties in supporting their new dignity; the archbishop borrowed £1000 from Henry, a loan which he was unable to repay for many years, and the chancellor

The king's new appointments made a quick divorce possible; his deepening commitment to Anne Boleyn made it necessary. In September 1532 Henry created her marquis of Pembroke in her own right, granting her lands in Wales and an annuity of £1000 for life.[1] A month later she accompanied him on an expedition to Boulogne, where she danced with Francis I and was treated as a queen.[2] There were rumours that the king had married her abroad, and Hall has it that the marriage was celebrated secretly on St Erkenwald's Day—14 November—immediately after the king's return to England.[3] This is evidently not correct; in his anxiety to protect Anne's character the chronicler probably advanced the date by several months. Cranmer, a more reliable witness, said that the marriage took place about 25 January 1533, although he denied officiating at it.[4] By this time Anne was expecting a child. If it were to be the legitimate male heir which Henry had desired for so long, the marriage had to be validated beyond all legal doubt within three or four months.

This the king's advisers were ready to do. Cromwell, who had further consolidated his position since the Parliament met in 1532, appears to have spent the months which followed its prorogation drafting and redrafting a bill which would cut off all appeals to Rome, thus making it possible for ecclesiastical authorities within England to render a final decision in the king's case. Precise plans were far advanced by January. We can probably discount the common view that Anne's pregnancy caused the preparation of the Act in Restraint of Appeals. It is much more likely that the king's intimacy with her followed from his knowledge that an effective bill had been drafted and a workable programme devised.[5]

I

Eight surviving drafts and four fragments show the stages

had to press Cromwell for the £100 due to him as Speaker of the 1532 session as well as for a loan and the grant of lands formerly held by the dissolved priory of Christ Church, London. Ridley, *Thomas Cranmer*, 54; *L.P.*, VI, 2.

[1] *L.P.*, V, 1370 (1–3).
[2] Edward Hall gives a very full account of the festivities and interviews: *Hall's Chronicle*, 789–94. A number of the great noblemen, including Richmond, Norfolk, Suffolk, Rochford, and Bishops Stokesley, Gardiner, Longland, and Clerk, travelled in the king's train.
[3] *Ibid.* 794. St Erkenwald (d. 693) was one of the earliest bishops of London.
[4] Ridley, *Thomas Cranmer*, 54.   [5] Cf. Elton, *England under the Tudors*, 132.

through which the Act in Restraint of Appeals passed.[1] As usual none of these papers is dated, but we cannot be far wrong in assigning the earliest ones to September 1532. At this stage Cromwell had already devised the opening fanfare of his famous preamble, which reached the statute books with very little change. He must have had in mind the legends about King Arthur, Constantine, and empire which Norfolk had related to Chapuys in 1531; indeed it is possible that Norfolk had a larger role in suggesting the main lines of the bill than has usually been thought.[2] However that may be, the first draft claimed total independence for England because 'in dyvers sundry old authentike storyes and cronicles it is manifestlie declared and expressed that this realme of England is an Impier, and so hath byn accepted in the world'.[3] Moving rapidly from pseudo-history to political theory, the bill asserted that this empire was 'governed by one supreme hedde, having the dignitie and roiall estate of the Imperiall crowne of the same, under whom a body politik compact of all sortes and degrees of people devided in termes of spiritualtie and temporaltie bere and owen to bere next to God a naturall and humble obediens'. Three elements can probably be discerned here: the title of supreme head already granted by the clergy, the Commons' assertion of division between the clergy and laity, and a theory of monarchy recently voiced by Sir Thomas Elyot, the former clerk of the Council and ambassador to Charles V. 'A publike weale is a body . . . compacte or made of sondry astates and degrees of men', Elyot had written, all ruled by 'one soveraigne governour'.[4]

From this theory of total monarchical power Cromwell and his aides deduced that all jurisdiction within England, whether spiritual or temporal, depended from the king, whom even popes had called God's vicar. Temporal laws were administered by temporal judges within the realm, with no possibility of appeal to any external authority, and all spiritual matters should be handled

[1] These have been studied by Elton, in 'The Evolution of a Reformation Statute', *E.H.R.*, LXIV (1949), 174–97. The present writer has examined the manuscript material with some care and concluded that it fully supports Elton's reconstruction.

[2] Chapuys MS., 1531, no. 5 (*L.P.*, v, 45); Koebner, ' "The Imperial Crown of this Realm": Henry VIII, Constantine the Great, and Polydore Vergil', 29–52.

[3] SP 2/N, fols. 78–90, P.R.O. (*L.P.*, IV, 120 [7]). This is Elton's draft 'E'. Most of the corrections on it appear to be Audley's.

[4] Elyot, *The Boke Named the Gouernour*, Book I, Chs. I, II.

by the body spiritual or English Church, which was fully competent to determine them. Earlier kings—Edward I, Edward III, Richard II, and Henry IV—had secured the passage of statutes to prevent the papal see or any other foreign power from vexing English subjects.[1] But appeals to Rome continued, bringing great inconveniences, charges, and delays to many Englishmen.

A long, bitter attack on the papacy followed:

The see appostolik, most ambiciously aspiring to be suppreme lordes of all the world, forgetting the holy steppes and examples of their good predecessoures which nothing els desired but the advauncement of the lawes of God, th'encrease of the catholik faithe and of vertue, good example, and good lif in the people, have now within fewe yeres devised and practysed as well to amplifie their worldly honor and possessions as their auctoritie, power, prehemynence, and jurisdiccions, nott only within this realme but in many other sundry provinces and contreys of the worlde.[2]

This the popes did by appointing foreigners to ecclesiastical positions in England, by collecting annates, by requiring oaths which ran counter to subjects' natural obedience to their king, by 'pretending ... to hier and determyne the spirituall causes of contencion incept and begon within this realme', and finally by

attempting to have power and auctorite to declare and adjudgge when marriages of this realme shalbe lauffull and unlawfull, by which it hath byn sene in tymes past when the primates and prelates of this realme have adjudged a mariage lawfull yet nevertheles by reason of pursute to Rome their judgementes hath byne repealed and onlauffull mariages contynued by the power of the see appostolik agaynst the lawes of God and determynacion of our Englisshe churche of this realme, who owen to be judges of the same.

Popes were not even 'abasshed ne asshamed to take uppon theym the hole pouer and auctorite to declare and adjudge the succession and procreacion, as well of princes and potentates as of all other subjectes of the world'.

The enacting clauses of this early draft deal with the king's

[1] The reference is to the statute of Carlisle (35 Edward I, c. 1), the statutes of provisors and praemunire (25 Edward III, c. 4; 27 Edward III, c. 1; 13 Richard II, c. 2; 16 Richard II, c. 5), and to their confirmation by 2 Henry IV, c. 3, and 9 Henry IV, c. 8.

[2] This passage is reminiscent of, and perhaps derived from, the preamble to the abortive bill for submission of the king's divorce to the English archbishops (SP 2/N, fols. 155–62, P.R.O.; L.P., VI, 311 [4]); see above, Ch. 6.

divorce quite specifically. Noting the warfare and effusion of blood which had been caused in England by 'uncertenty of the posterite and succession of the kinges of the same', the bill insisted that the apostolic see must not be allowed to judge the legitimacy of Henry's offspring. Thus no papal summons or sentence affecting the king or any of his subjects should be obeyed, and all causes, both spiritual and temporal, should be determined within England in accord with 'the auncient customes of this realm'. Papal citations or interdicts were pronounced void; persons who attempted to procure foreign judgments in English cases were declared liable to the penalties of high treason: death and loss of goods.

Cromwell and the other councillors who helped him must have realized almost immediately that these enacting clauses were too vague. Certainly they did not specify a course of appeals which would satisfy the lawyers in Parliament. The councillors' next draft was more precise;[1] it provided that English spiritual cases should be appealed from archdeacons' courts to the diocesan bishop, and from him to the archbishop of Canterbury; a commission appointed by the king under the Great Seal was to be the court of last resort.[2] This version also softened the prescribed penalties: violation of the act was to constitute praemunire, not high treason.

Had Parliament met in November it would perhaps have been presented with the bill in something approaching this form. But Audley secured a prorogation until February, and he and Cromwell were given three more months in which to perfect their proposal. The bill now passed through several closely related stages.[3] In these the bitterly anti-papal charges of the original version were deleted; a passage noting the 'great enormyties of ambicyon and vayneglorie still persevering in the churche of

---

[1] SP 2/N, fols. 103–108, P.R.O. (L.P., VI, 120 [8]; Elton's draft 'G'). This draft was evidently intended to replace only a portion of the original bill, for it lacks a preamble and ends in mid-sentence.

[2] Cromwell evidently paid little attention to a paper which was sent him by an anonymous civil lawyer (Cottonian MS. Cleopatra F. I, fols. 86–7, B.M. [L.P., V, 121]); it spoke derogatorily of the large number of appeals allowed by canon law and argued that only one appeal, to the next higher court, should be permitted.

[3] SP 2/N, fols. 91–102, P.R.O. (L.P., VI, 120 [7]; Elton's 'F'); SP 2/N, fols. 55–65, P.R.O. (L.P., VI, 120 [7]; Elton's 'C'); Cottonian MS. Cleopatra E. v, fols. 178–202, B.M. (L.P., VI, 120 [6]; Elton's 'H'). The last of these is the only draft to bear corrections in the king's hand.

Rome'[1] was added only to be struck out by Cromwell. A lengthy addition defended the king and his councillors against 'evyll interpretours' by protesting 'that in the faythe catholike accepted by the unyversall churche of Cristendome and used as they thinke in Rome there be no faster roted men in Cristen faithe then there be within this realme'.[2] The whole tone of the bill was made more comprehensive than before; instead of referring specifically to Henry's divorce and succession it now included generally 'all causes testamentorie and causes of matrymonye, rightes of tithes, oblacions and obvencions . . . commyng in contencion, debate or question within this realme'.[3] The course of appeals was also altered: the provisions of the previous draft were to apply to subjects only, while cases touching the king or State were to be appealed from the archbishop's court directly to the upper house of Convocation. The archbishop of York, who had been forgotten earlier, was now given authority parallel to the archbishop of Canterbury's to hear cases originating in his province.[4]

Henry himself studied a fair copy of the bill in this form, and he added a few phrases: foreign appeals had occurred 'only by necligence or usurpation, as we take it and estime'; spiritual and temporal jurisdiction proceeded 'off and frome the sayde imperiall crowne and non other wyse'.[5] The king's changes, and Cromwell's, were incorporated in the draft and two more fair copies made.[6] One must have been intended for introduction into Parliament—by this time the calendar had probably reached January 1533—and the other for retention in Cromwell's office.

But before sending the bill to Parliament Cromwell evidently decided to submit it for examination by a number of leading prelates and specialists in canon and civil law. A list prepared by one of his clerks shows who was present—Cranmer, Gardiner, Longland, Standish, the abbots of Hyde and Burton, Edward Fox, Rowland Lee, two prominent doctors of canon and civil

---

[1] SP 2/N, fol. 58, P.R.O.

[2] *Ibid.* fol. 57. This clause was deleted from the act as finally passed, but a similar statement reappeared in 1534 as a proviso to the act for Peter's Pence and dispensations.

[3] Cottonian MS. Cleopatra E. v, fol. 190, B.M.

[4] *Ibid.* fol. 202. This section shows evidence of considerable alteration by Cromwell.

[5] *Ibid.* fols. 180, 185.

[6] SP 2/N, fols. 32–44, P.R.O. (*L.P.*, vi, 120 [7]; Elton's 'A'); SP 2/N, fols. 66–74, P.R.O. (*L.P.*, vi, 120 [7]; Elton's 'D').

law, the dean of the Court of Arches, and the 'fryer Carmely-tane'[1]—and a passage in one of Chapuys' dispatches probably fixes the date of the meeting at 5 February, the day after the opening of Parliament.[2] We have no reliable evidence to indicate exactly what these ecclesiastical officials discussed; according to Chapuys they talked of the divorce, examined some papers, and concluded that the king should proceed to his purpose by the authority of the archbishop of Canterbury. But Professor Elton has suggested that they were shown the draft appeals bill, to which they proposed various amendments.[3] Certainly the next draft contains changes which the churchmen would have been likely to demand: it deletes some of the excessive claims for the royal origin of spiritual jurisdiction and takes from the king the final word in ecclesiastical suits.[4] The course of appeals which finally evolved was complex but well suited to the requirements of the situation. Cases commenced before an archdeacon could be appealed to the diocesan bishop.[5] Cases commenced before a bishop could be appealed to the archbishop within whose province they arose. In neither instance could subjects ordinarily appeal from the decision of the archbishop, nor was any further process possible in suits commenced before an archbishop himself. Only a case touching the king might be carried from an archbishop to the upper house of Convocation, and such a meeting of Convocation could be summoned only by the king. All appeals were to be made within fifteen days after the decision of the lower court.[6] The changes were in the direction of precision and administrative simplicity; the king's advisers may have been quite willing to abandon the royal

[1] These names are the ones pricked on the memorandum. It lists also eleven other men, among them Archbishop Lee and Bishop Stokesley, who were evidently considered but not called or who, if summoned, did not attend. The list is in the P.R.O., SP 1/74, fol. 170 (*L.P.*, VI, 150), and is printed by Elton, 'Evolution of a Reformation Statute', 191. Elton transcribes one name as 'Doodrige', but it is surely 'Goodrige' and refers to Thomas Goodrich, a royal chaplain who succeeded West as bishop of Ely in 1534.

[2] Chapuys MS., 1533, no. 11 (*L.P.*, VI, 142; *C.S.P., Spn.*, IV, ii, 1047).

[3] Elton, 'Evolution of a Reformation Statute', 192.

[4] SP 2/N, fols. 45–55, P.R.O. (*L.P.*, VI, 120 [7]; Elton's 'B'). This draft is based on 'D', which Cromwell corrected at this stage, and on several fragments relating to the course of appeals, especially SP 2/N, fols. 112–13, which is corrected by Audley and may possibly have been drawn up at the meeting itself.

[5] Cases commenced before an archbishop's archdeacon—that is, in the dioceses of Canterbury and York—could be appealed to the appropriate Court of Arches, and from it to the archbishop.

[6] SP 2/N, fols. 52–5, P.R.O.

commission, with all the difficulties which it might entail, as a court of last resort in subjects' suits.[1] Since the archbishops were royal appointees, just as the special commissioners would have been, there was little likelihood that the king's interests would be violated. Indeed it was unwise to suggest that archbishops might fail to render justice at a time when one of them was about to sit in judgment on Henry's great case.

These alterations presumably helped win the support of some clerics. Others remained opposed: later in February Chapuys wrote that Gardiner and Archbishop Edward Lee had refused to subscribe to a 'strange' bill[2] drawn up to fit the king's fancy. The reference is obscure, but it probably indicates a continuing effort to secure the assent of prominent churchmen to the appeals bill before its introduction in Parliament.

2

In addition to hammering out the great appeals bill, Cromwell directed some attention towards securing a docile assembly. A list of 'those who are Burgesses in the Parliament house', catalogued among Cromwell's manuscripts in 1533,[3] shows his interest in studying the personnel of the Commons. The entry probably refers to an existing list of the men elected in 1529, with 'mortuus' written against the names of those who had died before the end of the 1532 session.[4] Cromwell evidently arranged to fill these vacancies through a number of by-elections held late in 1532 or early in 1533. We have a memorandum of his order for the election of two knights of the shire for Essex, to fill the void left by Audley's elevation and the death of Thomas Bonham,[5] and an intriguing letter, unsigned and dated only 9 January, which seems to refer to the vacancy in Huntingdonshire caused by the death of Sir Nicholas Harvey in 1532. The writer had been asked

---

[1] In any case, the possibility of appeal to a royal commission was reinstated in 1534, by 25 Henry VIII, c. 19, sec. 4.
[2] Chapuys' word is *billet*; this appears as 'document' in *L.P.* and 'letter' in *C.S.P., Spn.*: Chapuys MS., 1533, no. 14; *L.P.*, VI, 180; *C.S.P., Spn.*, IV, ii, 1053.
[3] *L.P.*, VI, 137.
[4] This is the list printed in the official *Return of Members of Parliament*, Part I, 368–71, and in *L.P.*, IV, 6043 (2), from SP 1/156, fols. 2–10, P.R.O.; cf. A. F. Pollard, 'Thomas Cromwell's Parliamentary Lists', 42–3.
[5] *L.P.*, VII, 341; A. F. Pollard, 'Thomas Cromwell's Parliamentary Lists', 42.

by Cromwell to stand for the seat, but he found that even his own friends were already committed to Thomas Hall, a burgess for the town of Huntingdon who evidently fancied his promotion to the greater dignity of a county member.[1] There were also by-elections in Yorkshire, Yarmouth, and London, where William Bowyer was chosen to fill the vacancy created by John Petit's death.[2] Our extremely defective evidence does not record any further polls, but a parliamentary list drawn up by Cromwell early in 1533 gives us seven more names of members who were probably elected at this time: Sir Henry Long for Wiltshire, Charles Bulkley for Wycombe, Edmund Page for Rochester, John Brenning the younger and John Hilsey for Worcester, Thomas Bromley for Lancaster, and Thomas Polstead, a servant of Lord Dacre of the South and brother of one of Cromwell's financial assistants, for Bedwin, Wiltshire.[3] In addition, we can deduce that John Tudbold had been named to replace John Pyne at Lyme Regis.[4] It is probable that Cromwell took care to secure the return of new men favourable to the king's policies, and he may have made a special effort to guarantee the attendance of reliable older members. Thus Robert Acton, a burgess for Southwark, wrote Cromwell that he had laid ill since the expedition to Boulogne, but 'yf your mastership doe send me worde to com to the Parlyament I wyll surely com, whatsoever becom of me'.[5]

There is some suggestion of similar attention to the Lords. The abbot of Burton, who had been present at the meeting of ecclesiastics and was presumably sympathetic to royal policy, was admitted to Parliament by virtue of a writ issued the previous April, and Lords Rochford, Maltravers, and Talbot, the eldest sons of the earls of Wiltshire, Arundel, and Shrewsbury respectively, were summoned for the first time in February 1533.[6]

[1] SP 1/74, fol. 26, P.R.O. (L.P., VI, 31).

[2] Return of Members of Parliament, Part I, App., xxix. Philip Bernard was elected in place of John Ladde, deceased, for Yarmouth, and Sir John Neville 'de Cheyte' in place of Lord Latimer for Yorkshire. The latter had succeeded to the Lords in 1531, following his father's death.

[3] SP 1/99, fol. 234, P.R.O. (L.P., IX, 1077); the list has been printed and analysed by A. F. Pollard, 'Thomas Cromwell's Parliamentary Lists', 31–48. The thirty-four men named in the list, not all of whom were chosen in by-elections, have little in common, and Cromwell's purpose in compiling it remains obscure.

[4] A. F. Pollard, 'Thomas Cromwell's Parliamentary Lists', 41.

[5] SP 1/74, fol. 133, P.R.O. (L.P., VI, 106).   [6] L.P., VI, 119, 123.

Cromwell also persuaded Lord Monteagle to attend despite his license to remain in Yorkshire.[1]

3

When Parliament assembled on 4 February its first business was the selection of a Speaker to replace Audley. The king attended the opening of the session and came again from Greenwich four days later to accept the Commons' choice, Humphrey Wingfield, a burgess for Yarmouth. The new Speaker was knighted in a colourful ceremony, witnessed by the papal nuncio and the French ambassador as well as the Lords in their scarlet robes.[2] Doubtless a royal nominee, Wingfield was a lawyer and had served the government in various administrative posts, especially in Norfolk and Suffolk. He was the first burgess to be named speaker, a sign that the knights of the shire were losing some of the pre-eminence which had traditionally been theirs.[3]

Chapuys thought that the papal nuncio had been paraded in the Lords only to overawe the prelates and demonstrate that the king was still on good terms with Rome. A few days later Henry asked him to attend a meeting of the Commons; the nuncio hesitated, but finally agreed to go after Norfolk assured him that nothing touching the papacy would be discussed. When he arrived he found the Commons debating an insignificant bill against thieves: probably the measure providing that persons who killed thieves or murderers in self-defence should be fully acquitted and discharged at law.[4] The nuncio did not stay long in the House, but went on to a sumptuous banquet in Fitzwilliam's lodgings.

[1] On 3 February Monteagle wrote Cromwell that he could not be ready at once but would come: SP 1/74, fol. 138, P.R.O. (*L.P.*, VI, 112).

[2] Chapuys MS., 1533, no. 11, *loc. cit.*

[3] Sir Thomas Fitzwilliam had nearly robbed Wingfield of this distinction: elected as a London burgess in 1488, Fitzwilliam was named Speaker in January 1489, but had meanwhile become a knight of the shire for Lincolnshire. A. F. Pollard, 'Thomas Cromwell's Parliamentary Lists', 36 n.

[4] 24 Henry VIII, c. 5. The act resolved an ambiguity under which such persons might have forfeited their goods. Chapuys believed that the bill under consideration would have denied ecclesiastical immunity to thieves, but no such act was passed. Chapuys MS., 1533, no. 13 (*L.P.*, VI, 160; *C.S.P., Spn.*, IV, ii, 1048). Another legal reform (24 Henry VIII, c. 8) altered civil procedure by denying costs to defendants in cases where they had been involved in suits with councillors. Cf. Amos, *Observations*, 138.

We have little other evidence of chronology for the earlier part of the session. The Venetian ambassador reported on 10 February that the government had requested a large sum of money for the war against Scotland, and two weeks later he wrote that no other momentous matter had been raised.[1] Henry was still spending heavily on border defences, and was fitting out four ships for a blockade of the Scottish coast,[2] but he was more concerned with his divorce than with finance and was probably reluctant to antagonize the Commons by pressing for a subsidy. Certainly no tax bill was passed during the session.

It appears certain that the appeals bill was held back for six weeks, either out of careful strategy or simply because it took that long to confer with the clerics and incorporate their emendations. Thus Parliament probably spent February and early March dealing with economic and social legislation, perhaps primarily with the statute of apparel. This bill was sponsored by the government and had been prepared by Cromwell before the session of 1532, but it failed to complete its parliamentary course in that year and was held over for passage in 1533.[3] Its preamble notes the 'inordinate excess daily more and more used in the sumptuous and costly array and apparel accustomably worn in this realm'; a number of earlier laws attempting to regulate dress were openly flouted, and 'the outrageous excess therein [had] rather ... increased than diminished'.

The act went on to specify what clothes might be worn by persons of each social rank: purple silk and cloth of gold were allowed only to the royal family and, within limits, to dukes and marquises; husbandmen were not allowed to wear cloth costing more than four shillings a yard. The long list of classes, with specified apparel for each, emphasizes the Tudor respect for order and degree, while the admission that previous acts had not been successful testifies to the general love of ostentation and display. Anyone violating the statute was to forfeit the offending garment and 3s. 4d. for each day's violation, half the penalty going to the king and half to the informer. Players in interludes were specifically exempted from the requirements of the act, and women

---

[1] C.S.P., Venetian, IV, 850, 858.   [2] Chapuys MS., 1533, no. 11, loc. cit.
[3] 24 Henry VIII, c. 13; cf. Cromwell's memoranda, Cottonian MS. Titus B. I, fols. 486–7, B.M. (L.P., v, 394). This act originated in the Lords (H.L.R.O., original act). It is discussed in Amos, Observations, 208–18.

seem to have been exempted by implication, since there are no provisions for their attire. Not even a Tudor Parliament, presumably, dared interfere with so delicate a subject as feminine fashion.

Several acts provided for further regulation of the realm's economy. The high cost of meat and wine seems to have been causing unusual distress; prices for both were set by statute, and penalties provided for butchers and wine merchants who refused to abide by them.[1] The act regulating the price of beef, pork, mutton, and veal also required that these meats be sold by weight, in pieces of reasonable size. In an attempt to remedy the shortage of cattle, which had driven up meat prices, Parliament prohibited the slaughter of calves born between 1 January and 1 May, or of any animals under the age of two years.[2]

Two more bills had been drawn up in the hope of improving agriculture. One, which passed through several stages in Cromwell's office, complained of the 'wonderful and marvelous great quantity of corn and grain of all kinds' devoured by crows and rooks; it ordered subjects to do their best to destroy the pests, especially by maintaining crow-nets, and offered a bounty of twopence for each dozen birds captured.[3] The second, intended to promote increased employment in the domestic linen industry, ordered all farmers occupying sixty acres or more 'apt for tillage' to sow one rood with flax or hemp seed.[4]

The leather and woollen industries, too, were beneficiaries of economic legislation. Tanned leather, Parliament enacted, should be sold only in open fairs and markets, where it might be examined

---

[1] 24 Henry VIII, cc. 3, 6.

[2] 24 Henry VIII, cc. 7, 9. These measures proved ineffective. Repeated proclamations issued between 1534 and 1536 suspended the schedule of prices, because farmers and butchers would not bring cattle to market unless they could expect larger profits. The act forbidding the slaughter of calves less than two years old was also suspended, since in the short run it merely increased the scarcity. See Hughes and Larkin, *Tudor Royal Proclamations*, I, nos. 144, 148, 154, 159, 162, 164; cf. nos. 146 and 149.

[3] 24 Henry VIII, c. 10. The extant drafts are SP 2/N, fols. 26–9 and fols. 30–1, P.R.O. (*L.P.*, VI, 120 [4, 5]). Both are in the usual clerk's hand and are corrected by Cromwell; the first lacks the preamble, and both omit some sections of the statute.

[4] 24 Henry VIII, c. 4. A fragmentary draft survives in the P.R.O., SP 2/N, fols. 23–5 (*L.P.*, VI, 120 [3]). A rood is one-quarter acre. The act includes a definition of the acre, an interesting testimony that measurements had not yet reached uniformity. Both of these acts were introduced in the Commons (H.L.R.O., original acts). Cf. Amos, *Observations*, 79–82.

to prove its quality; in and near London all leather was to be 'searched and sealed' by officials of the curriers.[1] Since foreigners had introduced a 'false . . . and deceivable way of dyeing, . . . to the hurt and slander of woollen clothes dyed within this realm, which are the most substantial woollen cloths of all realms christened', Parliament prohibited the use of brazil wood as a scarlet colouring agent and insisted that all woollen cloths be 'perfectly boiled, grained, or maddered'. Wardens of the craft of dyers were authorized to conduct searches in dye-houses, in order to enforce the act.[2]

A bill ordering the paving of the Strand might be considered private legislation, since it affected only the landowners on each side of the way from Strand Cross to Charing Cross, but the statute attempted to demonstrate national relevance by citing the frequency with which subjects from all parts of the realm passed along the Strand to Westminster 'about the needs of [the king's] laws there kept in term season'.[3] Genuinely private bills were passed for the butchers of London, for the town of Hull, and for the jointure of Lady Compton.[4] Two of the London burgesses— Bowyer and Withypoll—brought in another private act which would have confirmed the establishment of a court of requests in the City, but their bill failed to secure passage.[5]

Finally, on 14 March, the appeals bill was presented to the Commons.[6] There seems to have been very substantial opposition, not motivated primarily by religious scruples but rather by fear of economic retaliation.[7] One of the London burgesses, evidently worried that Catholic princes might place an embargo on English wool, suggested that Parliament offer the king £200,000 if he would

[1] 24 Henry VIII, c. 1. The act also provided penalties for searchers who corruptly set their seals to leather insufficiently tanned; cf. Amos, *Observations*, 107.

[2] 24 Henry VIII, c. 2.

[3] 24 Henry VIII, c. 11. Cf. Amos, *Observations*, 198–9.

[4] 24 Henry VIII, cc. 14, 15, 16.

[5] Miller, 'London and Parliament in the Reign of Henry VIII', 145.

[6] Chapuys MS., 1533, no. 18 (*L.P.*, VI, 235; *C.S.P.*, *Spn.*, IV, ii, 1056). It is certain that the bill originated in the Lower House: H.L.R.O., original act, 24 Henry VIII, c. 12. Although Chapuys detested the bill he realized that it would pass, since Henry set so much store by it; the king had just taken Chapuys for a two-hour walk in his gardens and had said 'a thousand things' against the ambition and usurped power of the popes.

[7] Chapuys MS., 1533, no. 20 (*L.P.*, VI, 296; *C.S.P.*, *Spn.*, IV, ii, 1057). It is unfortunate that Hall tells us virtually nothing about the session of 1533; perhaps the press of legal business prevented him from attending regularly.

drop the bill and submit his marriage to a General Council.[1] This proposal would have pleased neither the king nor the pope, and would have burdened subjects with a sum twice the annual revenue of the Crown: small wonder that no more was heard of it.[2] Henry's adherents in Parliament saw no such likelihood of economic troubles. Indeed they argued that continental monarchs would be only too happy to follow Henry's lead in throwing off the papal yoke.[3]

If the Commons, as Chapuys reported, were still resisting the appeals bill on 31 March, Parliament must have moved very rapidly in April. Easter again dictated the termination of the session. Palm Sunday was 6 April, and Parliament was prorogued on the 7th. By this time the measure had cleared both Houses. Its final version differed little from Cromwell's last draft. Most of the changes brought greater clarity without altering the sense of the bill: 'dyvorces', for instance, was inserted after 'causes of matrimony', although they would have been subsumed under the latter head. The only significant alteration allowed cases touching the king to be appealed directly to the upper house of Convocation, while in the earlier version they would have proceeded 'gradatim' through the full range of ecclesiastical tribunals. No doubt the king favoured such a change, and Elton may well be correct in theorizing that Cromwell had obtained it while the bill was in a committee of the Commons.[4] No amendments or provisos were attached to the bill after it had been engrossed, and it passed the Lords without alteration.[5]

The Act in Restraint of Appeals was doubtless the most important single piece of legislation to be enacted by the Reformation Parliament: it forms a climax, with the earlier anti-clerical measures preparing its way and the subsequent ecclesiastical regulation flowing from it. Like the Parliamentary Reform Act of 1832 it was a turning-point opening the door to more sweeping change than its authors foresaw or its supporters intended. There is no way of knowing how many members of Parliament had any idea that they were voting for a permanent break with the

---

[1] Chapuys MS., 1533, no. 21 (L.P., VI, 324; C.S.P., Spn., IV, ii, 1058). Chapuys did not name the burgess but said that he had spent some time in Spain, a qualification which so far as we know was true only of Paul Withypoll.

[2] Cf. Elton, 'Evolution of a Reformation Statute', 193.

[3] Chapuys MS., 1533, no. 20, loc. cit.

[4] Elton, 'Evolution of a Reformation Statute', 193–5.   [5] H.L.R.O., original act.

papacy, but the number may have been small. One may guess that even Cromwell and Cranmer, not to say Henry himself, would have been surprised at the continuing results of their policy.

4

In Convocation, as in Parliament, the most important matters were held off until late in the session.[1] Since the archbishopric was vacant when Convocation assembled, the upper house lacked a presiding officer. Several days earlier the prior of Canterbury cathedral had sent Cromwell a blank commission appointing a temporary president.[2] The king chose Standish of St Asaph, the province's senior bishop, for this office; his name was duly inserted into the commission, and he opened the session on 5 February. Stokesley continued to preside, as he had done in 1532, at most of the routine meetings.

Virtually the only business to come before Convocation in February involved exemption of the universities and certain regular clergy from payment of the clerical subsidy.[3] Despite Gardiner's protest this was easily granted. On 17 March the prelates were required to submit their certificates of assent to Cranmer's consecration. Later in the month they once again set to talking about Hugh Latimer. The irrepressible reformer had delivered some indiscreet sermons in Bristol, contrary to his earlier promises; his subscription to a set of orthodox articles concerning such thing as purgatory and pilgrimages was now sent to the West Country, so that it could be exhibited should he venture on new preaching missions.

Not until 26 March was the issue of the divorce brought before Convocation; once it had been raised the clergy were hardly given time to eat or drink.[4] Stokesley opened the subject, and Gardiner produced a number of books and other documents which he urged his fellows to examine. Someone objected that Convocation should not consider the case while it was pending at Rome, but Stokesley countered by reading an apostolic brief,

---

[1] The account in Wilkins, *Concilia*, III, 756–7, summarized in *L.P.*, VI, 317, begins only with the meeting on 26 March, but we know of Convocation's earlier activities from C.C. 306, 53–8.
[2] SP 1/74, fols. 136–7, P.R.O. (*L.P.*, VI, 108).
[3] C.C. 306, 53–4.   [4] Chapuys MS., 1533, no. 20, *loc. cit.*

issued several years earlier while Cranmer was collecting sentences from the universities, which allowed free expression of opinions in the matter. Two days later Stokesley exhibited the original instruments sealed by the faculties of Paris, Orleans, Bologna, Padua, Bordeaux, and Toulouse. After a long discussion he pressed the prelates to declare their own minds, but some sought more time for deliberation in so weighty a matter. The session was adjourned until 4 o'clock.

When the upper house reassembled its members were asked whether they agreed with the Paris theologians that marriage with a deceased brother's wife was prohibited by divine law against which no papal dispensation could prevail. Stokesley, Standish, Longland, and thirty-six monastic prelates gave their voices in support of the proposition. No other votes were recorded, but Gardiner and Veysey later announced their approval and Clerk his dissent. The *acta* for 29 March add that the abbots of Gloucester, Thorney, Bermondsey, Crowland, Valle Crucis, and Lilleshall assented to the judgment provided that the widow had been carnally known. Fisher's name nowhere appears. According to Matthew Parker's collection of ecclesiastical antiquities he led the opposition in the upper house of Convocation, debating chiefly with Stokesley; Chapuys says that no one else dared to open his mouth, so that Fisher's single voice was of no avail.[1] Perhaps he was persuaded to absent himself when the vote was taken.

So far Cranmer had not appeared in Convocation. He was consecrated on 30 March, and on the 31st he commissioned Stokesley, Gardiner, and Longland to preside in his absence. On 1 April he finally took the chair, and on the 2nd he ordered the members of the lower house to present the opinion of the theologians there on the sentence already accepted by the upper house. The Prolocutor told Cranmer that the major part were in agreement that such marriages created indispensable impediments; according to a schedule presented by his registrar fourteen theologians consented, seven dissented, and two had doubts or reservations.

By this time another proposition had been directed to the canon lawyers in Convocation: had carnal knowledge between Arthur

---

[1] Matthew Parker, *De Antiquitate Britannicae Ecclesiae*, 381 (cf. Burnet, *Reformation of the Church of England*, I, 129); Chapuys MS., 1533, no. 20, *loc. cit.*

and Catherine been sufficiently proved? On 3 April they announced their decision. All agreed that sufficient proof had been given, although an unspecified number held reservations. Richard Wolman, the Prolocutor, may have felt that he did not wish to be associated with such proceedings, for he asked to be relieved of office on the grounds of an illness which may or may not have been diplomatic. Edward Fox, the royal favourite who sat in Convocation as archdeacon of Leicester, was named in his place.

Cranmer again presided on 5 April. While the upper house was discussing payment of the subsidy John Tregonwell, the civil lawyer and member of the King's learned council, entered and relayed Henry's demand that the judgments of Convocation be embodied in a public legal instrument. This was done immediately. The resulting document gives a further voting record, although without names.[1] Sixty-six theologians, holding proxies for 197 more votes, had assented to the first proposition, with nineteen dissenting. On the second question, submitted only to the canon lawyers, there were forty-four assents, three favourable proxies, and five or six negative votes.[2]

The work which had been reserved for Convocation was now done. On 8 April its session was prorogued.

5

Parliament had given the English Church authority to render a final decision in Henry's case, and Convocation had pronounced its judgment that Henry's marriage to Catherine was invalid. It remained only to go through the motions of holding a formal trial. Since the case was not on appeal from a lower court, there was no need to invoke the act's provision for trial before the upper house of Convocation. The clergy there had rendered their opinion on the questions of theology and fact placed before them, in much the same manner as the universities consulted earlier,

---

[1] It is printed *verbatim* in Wilkins, *Concilia*, III, 757–9; it indicates that Convocation was now meeting at St Paul's rather than the Abbey. Early in May the same questions were presented to the Convocation of York, with similar results. To the first question there were twenty-seven assents and twenty-four favourable proxies; to the second, forty-four assents and five or six proxies. Two dissenting votes were recorded in each instance. *Ibid.* 765–8.

[2] The foregoing section is based upon the extracts from the *acta* preserved in C.C. 306, 53–8, and Wilkins, *Concilia*, III, 756–7.

but they had not attempted to sit as a court or deliver a binding judicial verdict.

That task was set aside for the new archbishop. Four days after the prorogation of Parliament Cranmer petitioned the king for permission to judge the validity of his marriage to Catherine.[1] On 12 April Henry assented.[2] The trial, held at Dunstable rather than London in order to avoid the possibility of disturbances, began on 10 May and lasted less than two weeks. Catherine did not appear; Cranmer pronounced her contumaceous and heard no witnesses, relying instead on depositions of the testimony presented to Wolsey and Campeggio four years before. On 23 May, after a delay necessitated by the spring rogation days and the feast of the Ascension, Cranmer rendered his verdict that the marriage was contrary to divine law and therefore invalid. On 28 May he pronounced the king's union with Anne Boleyn lawful.

The new queen was crowned on 1 June. In preparation for the ceremony she was escorted to the Tower by the lords spiritual and temporal, in barges on the Thames.[3] Many members of the Commons must have been in attendance as well, and at least four were knighted in celebration of the occasion: John Horsey and Henry Faryngton, knights of the shire for Dorset and Lancashire, and Thomas Rush and Edward Madyson, burgesses for Ipswich and Hull.[4] One's view of the festivities depended upon one's attitude towards Catherine and Anne; Chapuys thought the coronation cold and meagre, but an anonymous native chronicler called it 'a tryhumfantt syght to se and to heare'.[5] On 7 September Anne bore the long-awaited heir, who three days later was christened Elizabeth.

6

The session of 1533 appears to mark a climax of loosely-organized opposition to the king's policies. We need not credit Chapuys'

---

[1] In the original letter Cranmer beseeched the king 'most humbly upon my knees', but this was not considered subservient enough and he was made to send a second petition describing himself as 'prostrate at the feete of your Majestie'. Harleian MS. 6184, fol. 4, B.M.; SP 1/75, fols. 86–9, P.R.O. (*L.P.*, vi, 327); cf. Ridley, *Thomas Cranmer*, 59.
[2] His letter is in the B.M., Harleian MS. 283, fol. 97 (*L.P.*, vi, 332).
[3] *L.P.*, vi, 563.   [4] *Ibid.* 601 (4).
[5] Chapuys MS., 1533, no. 30 (*L.P.*, vi, 653; *C.S.P., Spn.*, iv, ii, 1081); *L.P.*, vi, 563.

comment that Richard III was never so universally hated as Henry, for the ambassador was trying to persuade Charles V that a few Spanish troops could spark a general uprising.[1] But it does seem that Catherine's partisans and some other opponents of the divorce met with fair regularity to discuss the situation and consider their reactions. Chapuys' lodgings were an obvious haven for such pro-Spanish malcontents, and the ambassador was a ready receptacle for information or gossip. Another group of men, all members of the Commons, dined regularly during sessions at the Queen's Head Tavern. Sir George Throckmorton, their leader, voiced open opposition to the appeals act and was summoned to appear before the king: when Henry spoke of his troubled conscience Throckmorton said that he would be even more distressed if he married Anne, since he had meddled with her mother and sister. Under interrogation by Cromwell, Throckmorton listed some other habitués of the Queen's Head, among them Sir William Essex, Sir William Barentyne, Sir Marmaduke Constable, and Sir John Gifford.[2] Throckmorton also spoke of being encouraged by Sir Thomas More and Bishop Fisher; More had once called him a good catholic man and added, 'if ye do continue in the same way that you began and be not afraid to say your conscience, ye shall deserve great reward of God'. More himself was too circumspect to frequent the Queen's Head, but as Cromwell later alleged he may have attended other policy meetings which 'arrived at conclusions very different from what the peace and interest of the realm required'.[3] Despite all the talk the group did nothing concrete, and Throckmorton soon quit the field. In the autumn of 1533 he wrote that he would take Cromwell's advice, stay at home, serve God, and meddle little in politics.[4]

The former chancellor and the bishop of Rochester were more formidable opponents, but they could do little to injure the king. After his resignation More had retired to his home in Chelsea, hoping to weather the storm by living in quiet obscurity. Fisher, who had criticized the king more openly, was placed in Gardiner's custody on Palm Sunday and later kept under house arrest.[5] These mighty souls were destined to meet a tragic end, but not to fan the flames of rebellion.

[1] Chapuys MS., 1533, no. 20, *loc. cit.*   [2] *L.P.*, XII, ii, 952.
[3] Elton, 'Sir Thomas More and the Opposition to Henry VIII', 27–31.
[4] *L.P.*, VI, 1365.   [5] *Ibid.* VI, 324; *C.S.P., Venetian*, IV, 870.

A few great men could not reconcile their consciences to the break with Rome which the appeals act implied. Some lesser figures grumbled in taverns and gossiped with foreign envoys. But on balance there was surprisingly little evidence of serious opposition to the king's new marriage or to the steps which had been taken to validate it. Seldom has so momentous a change, affecting the religious life of a whole people, been initiated so easily.

9

THE FIFTH AND SIXTH SESSIONS, 1534:
SUPREMACY IN ACTION

The two sessions of Parliament which met during 1534 were in every way a contrast to the session of 1533. No longer faced with the divorce crisis itself, the burgesses, knights, and peers now needed to consider bills recognizing the new succession to the throne and regularizing the new order in the Church. Pressure for routine legislation, too, had built up while attention was riveted on the king's great matter. In a conscientious, workman-like fashion the two Houses dealt with these affairs in 1534. By the end of December sixty acts had reached the statute books, including a greater bulk of public legislation than the Reformation Parliament passed in any other year.

The earlier session of 1534 is unique among the meetings of the Parliament in that its Lords' Journal has survived.[1] This means that we have precise information about the attendance of peers and about chronology, at least in the Upper House. The survival is fortunate, for our other sources now become less useful. Hall's chronicle gives only a brief outline of events in Parliament, and one suspects that the burgess for Wenlock was too busy with his legal career—he was named common serjeant in 1533—to attend Parliament as assiduously as he had done earlier. We know, too, that he completed the finished form of his chronicle only to 1532; the narrative of the later years was printed by Richard Grafton from Hall's rough notes. The Venetian ambassadors' reports are of no use after 1533, and even Chapuys' ubiquitous dispatches must be handled with greater care since he was now totally hostile to royal policy.

In anticipation of the fifth session Lord Windsor, master of the great wardrobe, was ordered to deliver nine pieces of red cloth,

---

[1] *L.J.*, I, 58–83. Comparison with the MS. Journal preserved in the H.L.R.O., I, 127–77, indicates no discrepancies of any significance, although A. F. Pollard referred to the editorial changes in the printed Journals as 'little short of a scandal': 'The Authenticity of the "Lords" Journals in the Sixteenth Century', *T.R.H.S.*, 3rd ser., VIII (1914), 17–39. The B.M. holds a Jacobean copy of the MS. Journal, Cottonian MS. Tiberius D. I, fols. 31–40, and an English translation of excerpts from it, Additional MS. 26,634, fol. 12.

sixty ells of canvas, and 'as much gilt nail . . . as shall suffice' for the refurbishing of the Parliament chamber.[1] Cromwell made ready for the session in a different way; his memoranda bristled with lists of bills to be drafted.[2]

Chapuys would have us believe that Henry himself undertook to secure a favourable assembly by countermanding the attendance of those who opposed him, especially Fisher, Tunstall, Edward Lee, and Lord Darcy.[3] There is probably some truth in this. Fisher certainly did not come to Parliament, excusing himself on grounds of illness.[4] Tunstall had already set out for London when he received a letter from Cromwell allowing him to stay at home because of old age: in fact he was about sixty, but he had another twenty-five years to live.[5] The Journals confirm the absence of Lee and Darcy.[6]

We know of some other peers who stayed at home. Bishop Nix of Norwich had good reason to be absent, for he was nearly ninety and blind, but in addition he had been charged with praemunire. The suit was ostensibly based on his infringement of the liberties of the town of Thetford, but more likely it arose because of his part in the execution of Bilney.[7] Lords LaWarr and Latimer begged off on grounds of poverty, not principle: the latter wrote Cromwell, 'my being at everie prorogacion of the Parliament thies foure yeres haith bene painfull, costlie, and chargeable to me'.[8]

In the Commons, Sir George Throckmorton had already promised to abstain from political activity.[9] His friend, Sir Marmaduke Constable, was also sufficiently intimidated to seek an excuse from Cromwell.[10] Another absentee, Sir Piers Edgecombe,

---

[1] L.P., VII, 53.

[2] Cottonian MS. Titus B. I, fols. 161–2, 427, 453–4, 462–3, B.M. (L.P., VI, 1381; VII, 48, 50, 108).

[3] Chapuys MS., 1534, nos. 6, 10 (L.P., VII, 83, 121; C.S.P., Spn., v, i, 4, 8).

[4] Cottonian MS. Cleopatra E. VI, fol. 162, B.M. (L.P., VII, 239).

[5] During Tunstall's absence his study at Bishop Auckland was ransacked for evidence of his opposition to the divorce. See L.P., V, 986, 987 (misdated 1532, actually of May 1534); Scarisbrick, 'The Conservative Episcopate in England, 1529–1535', 308.

[6] L.J., I, 58–83.

[7] Nix was found guilty but pardoned upon promising to give the king 300,000 crowns a year. SP 1/82, fols. 163–6, P.R.O.; Chapuys MS., 1534, nos. 13, 19 (L.P., VII, 158, 171, 296).

[8] SP 1/83, fol. 69, P.R.O.; L.P., VII, 12, 438.

[9] L.P., VI, 1365. [10] SP 1/82, fol. 46, P.R.O. (L.P., VII, 31).

had no political reason to stay away and can probably be reckoned as a supporter of the government; he remained in Cornwall because his wife had the measles.[1]

A few changes in personnel were advantageous to the king. Nicholas West, bishop of Ely, had died in April 1533 and lay buried in the beautiful chantry chapel which bears his name. The bishop of Bangor, Thomas Skeffington, died a few months later. These sees remained vacant during the earlier of the 1534 sessions, but on 19 April Thomas Goodrich was consecrated bishop of Ely and John Salcot, or Capon, bishop of Bangor. Both were favourable to the king's cause: Goodrich was a royal chaplain, and Salcot had been active in Parliament since 1529 by virtue of his position as abbot, first of Hulme and later of Hyde.[2] In the same ceremony Rowland Lee, another royal chaplain, canon lawyer, and administrator, was consecrated bishop of Coventry and Lichfield. Geoffrey Blyth, the previous bishop, had been dead since 1531.[3] Among the abbots the most important change was the elevation of William Boston or Benson, the former abbot of Burton-on-Trent, who took his seat as the abbot of Westminster on 21 January.[4]

I

Parliament reconvened for its fifth session on Thursday, 15 January. Despite rumours that Henry intended to take prompt and drastic action against the Church—'some presuppose the

---

[1] SP 1/83, fol. 9, P.R.O. (*L.P.*, VII, 365).

[2] The life of Salcot in the *D.N.B.* (under Capon) notes that his consecration took place in defiance of a papal veto. He did not relinquish his abbacy, but in 1538 surrendered the monastery to the Crown.

[3] In the list of attendances for the first day of the session (H.L.R.O., MS. Journal, I, 129; *L.J.*, I, 58–9) a black dot has been placed in front of the listing for the bishops of Salisbury, Ely, Bangor, and Coventry and Lichfield, apparently to indicate that these sees were vacant. Such a mark appears also for the abbot of Reading: curiously, since Hugh Cook, the notorious abbot, had five years to live and attended half the meetings of the fifth session. A different sign is visible following the listing of thirty-five other peers; it evidently indicates that these members had given proxies, although the correspondence with known proxies is imperfect. In the MS. Journal the names of Lords Morley, Powys, Scrope, and Stourton were inserted after the list had been prepared. The omissions were probably simple clerical errors; none of these peerages was a new creation.

[4] His writ of summons, also dated 21 January, is printed in *L.J.*, I, 61. Boston's predecessor, the great John Islip, had died in May 1532. In 1538 Boston surrendered his abbey to the Crown; he lived to be the first secular dean of Westminster.

spirytualtye shall depart with ther temporaltyes, wherof many be glad and fewe bemone them'[1]—the session began with a flurry of routine bills, and most great matters of state were held back until February or March. The Commons acted first on measures to protect the pewterers, the printers, and certain worsted makers from what they considered unfair competition.[2] A bill of attainder to punish John Wolf and his accomplices for the murder of two foreign merchants also passed the Lower House rapidly and was sent up to the Lords on 22 January.[3]

The first bill to be considered by the peers had been drafted by the judges to provide punishment for the 'detestable and abominable vice' of buggery or sodomy. This measure, which made the vice a felony, may have been aimed especially at the Church, and perhaps at the impending visitation of the monasteries, since it provided that offenders could not avail themselves of benefit of clergy. On 22 January the solicitor general and the clerk of the Crown carried the engrossed bill to the Commons, where it passed by 7 February.[4] Benefit of clergy was also denied, by another act passed later in the session, to those who stood mute or refused to answer directly to charges of robbery or other felony.[5]

Several minor bills concerned the Church more directly. With papal authority gone, it was natural that the Italian bishops of Salisbury and Worcester should follow. Accordingly, Campeggio and Ghinucci were deprived;[6] after a year's vacancy the sees were filled by the reformers Nicholas Shaxton and Hugh Latimer. Another act, brought in to remedy a defect in the statute of 1529 which had limited the employment of domestic chaplains, allowed one beneficed but non-resident chaplain to each high

---

[1] John Hussee to Lord Lisle, 7 January: SP 3/5, fol. 16, P.R.O. (L.P., VII, 82).

[2] L.J., I, 60. These bills became 25 Henry VIII, cc. 9, 15, 5. The bills to encourage printing by prohibiting the sale of imported books was rewritten in the Lords (ibid. 69); the other measures passed the Upper House without incident. Cf. Amos, Observations, 98–9. A draft of the preamble to the act for pewterers has survived as SP 2/P, fol. 23, P.R.O. (L.P., VII, 62).

[3] 25 Henry VIII, c. 34. The strange tale of Wolf, who used his harlot wife to lure the merchants into a boat where he was concealed, is told by Edward Hall, Hall's Chronicle, 815. Wolf's wife later escaped from the Tower but was recaptured; she and her husband were hanged in chains 'upon Thames at low water mark' (L.P., VII, 384).

[4] 25 Henry VIII, c. 6; L.J., I, 59–61; Holdsworth, History of English Law, IV, 504.

[5] 25 Henry VIII, c. 3.

[6] 25 Henry VIII, c. 27.

court judge as well as to the attorney general and solicitor general and the chancellor and chief baron of the Exchequer.[1]

The matter of heresy, raised early in the session, was more divisive. For years the Commons had been critical of the manner in which bishops proceeded against supposed heretics, never allowing them to confront their accusers or indeed defining the views which constituted heresy, but in 1534 they were especially incensed by the case of Thomas Phillips. A Londoner, Phillips was an early possessor of the English New Testament and had been arrested on charges of denouncing the real presence, purgatory, pilgrimages, and fast days. He denied the accusations but was nevertheless clapped in prison by Bishop Stokesley; because Sir Thomas More remembered Richard Hunne and wished to avoid another death in the Lollards' Tower, Phillips was shortly transferred to the Tower of London, an unusual place for a suspected heretic.[2] After three years of imprisonment, Phillips petitioned the Commons for redress of grievances, reasserting his innocence and claiming that the bishop 'intended nothyng els, but to make hym as it were a shep, redye in the bocher's lesure to slaughter when so ever it shuld please the bocher to send for hym'.[3]

Thus aroused, the Commons set out on the offensive: by 7 February they had sent Phillips' attack on Stokesley up to the Lords. Here it was brushed aside as a frivolous matter, not fit to be considered in such an 'illustrem Senatum'.[4] Upon hearing that this thrust had failed, the Commons adopted a more general approach. Probably after studying extracts from previous heresy acts,[5] they drafted a bill which repealed the existing law of 1401

[1] 25 Henry VIII, c. 16; cf. 21 Henry VIII, c. 13.

[2] SP 2/P, fols. 139–40, P.R.O. (L.P., VII, 155 [1]). Cf. Elton, 'Sir Thomas More and the Opposition to Henry VIII', 24. Phillips is mentioned in More's *Apology*.

[3] SP 2/P, fols. 142–3, P.R.O. (L.P., VII, 155 [2]).

[4] L.J., I, 65–6, 71. The Journal, charmingly blending Latin and English, says that Phillips was 'de Herysi suspectus'. In the end Phillips did well enough: by 1538 he was a gaoler in the Tower, converting at least one prisoner by giving him the English Bible (Edward Hall, *Hall's Chronicle*, 827).

[5] These are collected in SP 1/82, fols. 63–73, P.R.O. (L.P., VII, 60), with the anticlerical gloss, 'In this forsaid acte was forgotten to declare what ys an heretyk, what the poyntes of heresy, what ys the determination of holy churche, what be called the rights and liberties of the churche, whiche be called myschevous prechinges, . . . what articles, besydes the xij articles of the faith, shalbe objected to any man to aunswere unto.'

and re-enacted the earlier statute of 1382.[1] Heresy and orthodoxy remained undefined, except that speaking against the 'pretended power of the bishop of Rome' was not to be deemed heresy, but open trials were established, convicted heretics were given opportunity to recant, and relapsed heretics were ordered burned by the secular powers, according to the writ *De heretico comburendo*.[2] The Lords received this measure on 26 March, sent it to the chancellor for emendation, and finally gave their assent two days before the end of the session.

Parliament considered, too, a group of bills which extended the government's paternalistic regulation of the economy. Although we usually think of the price revolution as beginning about 1540, it is clear that foodstuffs were in short supply and prices rising as much as a decade earlier. Retail meat prices had already been fixed by statute in 1533, but many butchers 'wilfully and obstinately' refused to abide by these established rates. Parliament therefore assented to a new act permitting mayors of cities and market towns, as a last resort, to sell the offenders' meat themselves.[3] Forestalling and regrating, motivated by 'the greedy covetousness and appetites of the owners of such victuals', was blamed for all economic ills, and another act of 1534 hit at the practice by extending the government's authority to set 'reasonable prices' to such commodities as cheese, butter, and chickens.[4] An attempt was made to preserve the supply of wild fowl—ducks and geese, primarily—by ordering that they not be caught in nets during the summer, when the 'old fowl be moulted, and not replenished with feathers to fly, nor the young fowl fully feathered perfectly to fly'.[5] Since fish were also scarce, Parliament forbade the taking of eels and salmon in nets, or by other 'engines

---

[1] The act, 5 Richard II, St. 2, c. 5, was never accepted by the Commons, so Hales called it a pretended statute; see Amos, *Observations*, 162 n.

[2] 25 Henry VIII, c. 14. The Lords reworked the bill, so that we are presented with the anomaly of an act phrased as a Commons' petition but technically originating in the Upper House (original act, H.L.R.O.). Unfortunately we have no copy of the Commons' version; even in the engrossed act one clause has been erased, and there are several other alterations.

[3] 25 Henry VIII, c. 1. The statute further provided that farmers who would not sell their cattle at rates which would allow butchers to follow the established retail prices might be brought to trial in the Star Chamber.

[4] 25 Henry VIII, c. 2. The bill was perhaps suggested by a surviving petition, SP 2/N, fol. 22, P.R.O.(*L.P.*, VII, 59), although this differs considerably from the act. The original Commons' bill was rejected by the Lords, who framed the final act (*L.J.*, I, 74, 850). [5] 25 Henry VIII, c. 11.

and devices',[1] and it sought to curb regrating by limiting the right to sell salt fish at the Stourbridge Fair to members of the Merchant Adventurers to Iceland, or to the fishermen themselves.[2]

Particularly severe economic distress was reported to Parliament by the citizens of Worcester and the surrounding towns of Droitwich, Kidderminster, and Bromsgrove. Dependent for centuries upon the manufacture of woollen cloth, the boroughs were now decayed and depopulated because of the workshops which had grown up in the villages and hamlets of Worcestershire. Such activities were prohibited when Parliament turned the clothiers' petition into statute law; the manufacture of worsteds was limited to the specified towns, under penalty of forty shillings for each cloth illegally produced. Weavers were further protected from economic peril by another clause, which prohibited the raising of rents on houses in the great cloth towns.[3]

Of much greater importance was a new effort to contain the enclosure movement by limiting the size of flocks grazed on enclosed land. The bill, introduced into the Upper House late in January, provided that no tenant farmer should keep more than two thousand sheep, under a penalty of 3s. 4d. for each additional animal; it carried a preamble blaming excessive concentration on sheep for the rapid rise in rents of arable land and in prices of other agricultural commodities. The original measure was somewhat emasculated by provisos added in both Houses—the Lords insisted that the act should not apply to spiritual persons, and the Commons appended a series of technical clauses, one of which called for enumeration of sheep by 'long hundreds', six score rather than five. Cromwell exaggerated when he told Henry that the act was the most beneficial thing to be done in England since the time of Brutus, but it did remain the most useful of the statutes against enclosure. It was in effect long after other

---

[1] 25 Henry VIII, c. 7.   [2] 25 Henry VIII, c. 4.
[3] 25 Henry VIII, c. 18. Parliament did not pass a more drastic bill which would have attempted to halt urban decay by compelling all artificers to dwell in towns or cities and by prohibiting the sale of merchandise except at market towns and fairs. The surviving draft of this measure (SP 2/P, fols. 133–6, P.R.O. [L.P., VII, 67]), is endorsed 'Mr. Gybson—A bill concernyng cyttes, borowhs, towns, and portes'. This has been taken to mean that the bill was introduced in the Commons by Richard Gibson, a burgess for Romney. But more likely the bill was never before Parliament, and the Gibson was Thomas, a protégé of Latimer's whom Professor Elton has suggested as author of the bill ('Parliamentary Drafts, 1529–1540', 122–3, 126).

acts had expired or been repealed, and it was the basis of Star Chamber proceedings as late as 1639.[1]

Minor acts dealt with a wide variety of matters. In keeping with the Tudor reverence for archery, as well as earlier statutes requiring all men and boys to own longbows, Parliament ordered that no one worth less than £100 a year should keep crossbows or hand-guns.[2] It strengthened the statute of sewers by extending these commissions to Calais and by establishing a fine of five marks for refusal to serve as a commissioner, once appointed.[3] It improved conditions in London by ordering paving in Holborn and Southwark; it pardoned the bishop of Norwich's praemunire; it passed private acts for the town of Plymouth, the abbot of Waltham, the duke of Norfolk, Lord Lumley, Lord Scrope, and Sir Richard Southwell; it assured to the king the monastery of Christ Church, London.[4] In all it wrote thirty-four acts into the statute books during the eleven-week session. The work was exhausting: by 5 March the pressure of business had grown so great that the Lords took the unusual step of assembling daily at 8 a.m.[5]

---

[1] 25 Henry VIII, c. 13; *L.J.*; SP 1/82, fol. 98, P.R.O. (*L.P.*, VII, 73); Holdsworth, *History of English Law*, 365–6; Amos, *Observations*, 74–9. The original act, in the H.L.R.O., makes clear the origin of the provisos and also contains, written on the back, a list of names: 'Mr Baynton, Mr Slyemore, Mr Wygston, Mr Portman, Mr Magdalyn, Mr Vachell, Mr Halles.' These men, several of whom were lawyers and who sat in the Lower House for Wiltshire, Herefordshire, Coventry, Taunton, Wells, Reading, and Winchester respectively, doubtless formed the Commons' committee to consider and amend the Lords' bill. Possibly this committee examined a list of eighteen 'inconveniences that may ensue by the byll of fermes if yt shulde procede as it is proposed', now preserved as SP 2/P, fols. 20–1, P.R.O. (*L.P.*, VII, 58); crosses or the word 'examinat.' have been written against some of the objections.

[2] 25 Henry VIII, c. 17; cf. Lehmberg, *Sir Thomas Elyot*, 65.

[3] 25 Henry VIII, c. 10. The bill as originally written was rejected by the Lords; it passed only after emendation by Christopher Hales, the attorney general. *L.J.*, 1, 79–80.

[4] 25 Henry VIII, c. 8 (the act was extended to Southwark by a proviso added in the Lords: original act, H.L.R.O.), cc. 25, 29, 23, 26, 24, 30, 31, 32, 33.

[5] *L.J.*, 1, 72. Even so not all bills were passed. The Journal tells us that measures concerning glove-makers and horses apt for war were rejected outright by the Upper House; new provisions for aliens, for hounds, and for tithes in Romney marsh were allowed to die without final action (*L.J.*, 1, 78, 76, 79; cf. *L.P.*, VII, 592, where Cranmer wrote that he had restrained the bill for Romney marsh). The aldermen of London had attempted, also, to secure statutory enactment of a tithe rate, but Parliament evidently declined to be drawn into so controversial an area and the rate was later ordered by royal proclamation (Miller, 'London and Parliament in the Reign of Henry VIII', 147–8; Hughes and Larkin, *Tudor Royal Proclamations*, 1, 215–16).

2

Alongside these routine measures the two Houses were called upon to consider high affairs of state. These concerned the Church, the king's marriage, and succession to the throne.

Probably the first great bill to come before Parliament was that dealing with annates. It had grown out of Cromwell's desire to abolish all payments to Rome and bolster royal finances by assigning them to the king; some time before the beginning of the session the secretary had prepared a list of 'actes necessarie to be made at this Parliament', one entry in which read:

Item, an acte that if the pope attempte to vexe our soveraigne lorde the king of this realme, by interdiction, excommunicacion, or otherwise for the said marriage, which is ratified and establisshed by this realme, that then no subject of this realme after suche attempt shall paye to the pope eny maner of annates, porcions, pensions, Peterpens, ne other proffite that the pope now hath owt of this realme, but that the same shalbe payed to our said soveraigne to reteyn for his defence and the realme, till it shall please his Highnes otherwise to dispose and order the same to the pope or see apostolik.[1]

Accordingly, a bill transferring annates from the pope to the king was introduced into the Commons early in the session.

Unfortunately we have no copy of the bill in this form. It seems to have met little opposition in the Lower House, perhaps because of Cromwell's effective advocacy, but it fared less well in the Lords. Following the second reading on 11 February the bill was entrusted to the chancellor, who was to confer with the king about it. The reasons for this scrutiny are not entirely clear—the Journal says merely that Henry was to see the bill 'for certain reasons' (*pro certis causis*)[2] but it may be that the lords spiritual

---

[1] Cottonian MS. Titus B. I, fol. 161, B.M. (*L.P.*, VI, 1381 [3]). The list is undated but is certainly earlier than January 1534; the editors of *L.P.*, calendared it under October 1533. An anonymous memorandum which probably passed through Cromwell's office early in 1534 had recommended such a bill, for 'the temporaltye' were beginning 'to skanne the possessions encroched by the spiritualtye, thinkyng verayly they have a great dele more thenne reason wold require' (Cottonian MS. Cleopatra E. VI, fols. 212–13, B.M. [*L.P.*, VII, 1380 (1)]). Another writer had suggested that fixed salaries be allocated to all bishops and archbishops, the residue of their possessions being assigned to the king 'for the defense of his realm and mayntenance of his roiall estate' (Cottonian MS. Cleopatra E. VI, fols. 207–8, B.M.; *L.P.*, VII, 1355; an alternate form of one section is in the P.R.O., SP 1/86, fol. 145). 　　　　　　　　　　　　　　　　　　　　[2] *L.J.*, I, 67.

objected to the retention of annates, even if paid to the Crown. After all, the act of 1532, giving Henry conditional power to withhold annates from Rome, had complained of their intolerable burden, whereby many bishops and their friends were 'utterly undone and impoverished'.[1]

All this is speculation. What we do know is that the original bill was dropped and a new measure introduced into the Upper House on 27 February. It passed the Lords on 9 March, the Commons a week later.[2]

The bill as finally enacted was of no financial use to the king. Its preamble played down the grievance of annates, emphasizing instead that the 'gentle ways' in which Henry had earlier attempted to deal with the papacy had elicited no response from the 'bishop of Rome, otherwise called the pope'. The cessation of annates was therefore confirmed. But no provision was made for their payment to any domestic English authority: for once the clergy seem to have won a round in their sparring match. The act did, however, provide in detail for the method of electing bishops. Cathedral chapters were to hold elections as before, but were now bound to choose the candidate nominated by the king in his letter missive. Should they fail to do so, or should the ecclesiastical authorities refuse to consecrate a royal nominee, the act invoked the penalties of praemunire. Royal domination of episcopal elections, long a tradition, had become an enforceable legal right.[3]

The second great ecclesiastical bill sprang from another phrase in Cromwell's memorandum, the reference to 'Peterpens'. Peter's Pence, originally an annual tribute to the pope consisting of a penny from each householder owning land of a certain value, had been collected in England since the time of King Alfred; in the twelfth century it had been fixed at two hundred pounds a year for the whole country. It was not one of the larger payments to Rome, but since it was theoretically paid by laymen it may have been regarded as more onerous than charges affecting clerics only. The bill, obviously drafted in Cromwell's office, is unusual in

---

[1] 23 Henry VIII, c. 20.　　　　　　　　　　　　　[2] L.J., 1, 70–6.

[3] 25 Henry VIII, c. 20. As J. R. Tanner noted, the legal position was 'exactly defined in Lord John Russell's reply to a member of the Cathedral Chapter of Hereford, who wrote to him in 1848 to say that he could not conscientiously vote for Dr Hampden: "Sir,—I have the honour to acknowledge your letter of the 20th instant in which you announce your intention of breaking the law." ' (Tudor Constitutional Documents, 29 n.)

that it is cast in the form of a petition from the Commons to the king. Its preamble is interesting because it is one of the earliest documents to speak of a papal usurpation, because it restates the theory that England has 'no superior under God, but only your Grace', and because it argues that the authority of the king's 'imperial crown' is diminished by 'the unreasonable and uncharitable usurpations and exactions' of the Roman pontiff. The enacting clauses cover a curious mixture of matters. In addition to abolishing Peter's Pence the bill cut off all other financial payments to Rome and granted to the archbishop of Canterbury power to issue dispensations formerly given by the pope. It set the fees which might be charged for dispensations and required the royal assent, confirmed by the Great Seal, in matters for which the usual fee exceeded four pounds.

By 12 March the Commons had passed the bill, no doubt with enthusiasm. They are probably responsible for several provisos, perhaps inspired by Cromwell: one of these insists that the act shall not be interpreted as implying that the king's subjects intend to decline from the 'very articles of the catholic faith of Christendom', while a more important section gives the Crown authority to conduct visitations of monasteries which had been exempt from the archbishops' jurisdiction and orders English clergy not to attend religious assemblies held abroad. Further provisos were attached by the Lords, some following the second reading and others, somewhat unusually, after the third. The bill was passed on fourth reading 20 March, the Commons assenting to its provisos immediately, but on the last day of the session one more proviso was added: the king might, at any time before 24 June, abrogate the entire act or any part of it, as he saw fit. Perhaps he was still eager to have some leverage in bargaining with the pope, especially since the French king was attempting to reconcile Henry and Clement.[1] This final proviso was never invoked, for the French efforts came to naught; its addition to a bill which had already passed both Houses is, however, an extraordinary bit of parliamentary procedure.[2]

[1] 25 Henry VIII, c. 21; L.J., I, 74–81; Chapuys MS., 1534, nos. 13, 22 (L.P., VII, 171, 373; C.S.P., Spn., v, i, 10, 13). The provisos added by the Lords, secs. 17–23 of the act as printed in S.R., III, 470–1, are written on two sheets of parchment attached to the original act at the H.L.R.O.

[2] On 23 March the pope finally declared Henry's marriage to Catherine valid: see below and L.P., VII, 363.

A third important ecclesiastical measure confirmed the earlier Submission of the Clergy and called once again for a commission of thirty-two, half clerics and half chosen from the ranks of Parliament, to examine the existing canon law.[1] It is difficult to see why this act was thought necessary, and it may well have been desired by the Commons rather than Cromwell. At any rate the subject produced an unusual conference between the king and parliament; a contemporary memorandum relates that:

The vth day of Marche the Commyn Howse wente before the kyng into his palayse, and the Speker made a professyon to the kyng . . . in the name of all hys subgytes, desyryng hys Grace of reformacion of the actes made by the spiritualtye in the Convocacion agenste hys Grace and hys subgyetes, in callyng many of hys subgettes to their cortes ex ofycio and not knowyng there accuser, and to cawse them to abyowr [abjure] or elles to borne [burn] them for pure malys and apon there abhomynabyll cursys, takyng of tythes and offrynges contrary to justyse, and that they were jugges [judges] and partyes in their owne cawsys. Therfor at that tyme hyt was ordeyned that viij[te] of the Lower Howse and viij of the Hyer Howse and xvj bysshoppes with hothyr of the clergye shulde dyscusse the mater, and the kyng to be umpere, and so to be concludyd.[2]

The actual bill was substantially that which had probably been prepared two years earlier. There are some signs that Cromwell reworked it, for it includes a seemingly irrelevant reference to the course of ecclesiastical appeals: suits might be carried from the archbishops' courts to a commission appointed by the king in Chancery, an arrangement which Cromwell had favoured in 1533 but temporarily abandoned under clerical pressure. A proviso added in the Lords, most likely at the behest of the abbots, established the possibility of appeal from certain monasteries and other religious houses directly to a royal commission, since these houses were by tradition exempt from archiepiscopal jurisdiction.[3]

[1] 25 Henry VIII, c. 19.
[2] Harleian MS. 2252, fols. 34–5, B.M. (L.P., VII, 399). John Rokewood mentioned the same audience in a letter to Lord Lisle dated 8 March; he reported that both Houses of Parliament met with Henry at York House for three hours, and afterwards the Lords sat in the Council House at Westminster until 10 p.m. SP 3/7, fol. 18, P.R.O. (L.P., VII, 304).
[3] Draft act, SP 2/P, fols. 17–19, P.R.O. (L.P., VII, 57 [2]); original act, H.L.R.O.; L.J., I, 80–1; above, Ch. 7. The bill was given its first and second readings in the Lords on the same day, 27 March; the MS. Journal (H.L.R.O.) records the second

On 21 February the Lords received a bill of attainder prepared by the government to silence Elizabeth Barton, the so-called Holy Maid or Nun of Kent.[1] First cursed with a nervous ailment and then, after a miraculous cure, blessed with visions, she had foretold the king's deposition or death if he persisted in taking a second wife. Urged on by Edward Bocking, a monk of Canterbury, and two Observant friars, Hugh Rich and Richard Risby, she approached Bishop Fisher, Sir Thomas More, and other prominent persons with her prophecies. Fisher had listened to her tales but thought them unworthy of mentioning to the king, thus injudiciously laying himself open to a charge of misprision of treason; More, always careful of legal niceties, had more shrewdly refused to hear such predictions as touched the sovereign and had counselled her to avoid talking of 'eny suche maner thinges as perteyne to princes' affeirs, or the state of the realme'.[2]

When Henry finally heard of the Nun's auguries he reacted with a natural enough mixture of fear and anger. He cared little for Elizabeth's obviously demented state and resolved to have her executed, with her supporters, on a charge of high treason. Unfortunately for him, her acts did not constitute treason as legally defined by existing statute, so it was necessary to proceed against her in Parliament, by an act of attainder rather than a trial. Cromwell drafted the necessary bill; one of his remembrances lists those who 'shalbe atteynted of highe treason and suffer dethe except the kynges majesty do pardon [them]'— Elizabeth herself, Dr Bocking, Rich, Risby, and several more— and those who 'by the act shalbe atteynted of mysprision and have imprisonament at the kynges will and lose all their goodes'.[3] Fisher and one of his chaplains headed this second list. More was not named, possibly because Cromwell realized how weak the legal grounds for charging him were. But Henry was not to be

reading in an interlinear insertion. Cf. Elton, 'The Evolution of a Reformation Statute', 195; Kelly, 'The Submission of the Clergy', 117.

[1] *L.J.*, I, 68. Edward Hall was so struck by Elizabeth's offences, 'so greate and wicked, that the like was never heard nor known before', that he recounted her story at unusual length: *Hall's Chronicle*, 803–15.

[2] More to Elizabeth Barton, in E. F. Rogers, ed., *The Correspondence of Sir Thomas More*, 466. More quoted this admonition in his letter to Cromwell written in March 1534: *ibid*. 485. Cf. Chambers, *Thomas More*, 396.

[3] SP 1/82, fol. 81, P.R.O. (*L.P.*, VII, 70). This undated memorandum clearly antedates the bill, for it includes the note, 'Md., to get the name of Adyson, clerk.' Dr John Adyson, Fisher's chaplain, was cited in the bill.

stopped. His affection for More had turned to hatred, and he insisted that the fallen chancellor be included.

The bill, thus prepared, was introduced into the Upper House on 21 February. It was given second reading on 26 February; on the 27th Fisher wrote letters to the king and to the Lords, explaining his limited contact with the Maid and lamenting the 'periculouse diseases' which kept him from defending himself in person. 'If I might have bene present myself, I dowbte not but the greate weaknes of my bodie, with other menyfold infirmities, wold have moved yow much rather to have pitie of my cause and matter', he told the Lords.[1]

More, too, hastened to defend himself. He first wrote to Cromwell to ask for a copy of the attainder bill so that he could detect its 'untrue surmises'.[2] Later, having studied his text, he explained that he had spoken with Elizabeth but had declined to hear her mention the king; he had also refused to listen to the stories carried by Rich and Risby.[3] More wished to have his suit heard before the Lords; Henry preferred to have him interrogated by a group of commissioners, among them Norfolk, Audley, Cranmer, and Cromwell. These commissioners broadened the charges against More, accusing him of having persuaded Henry to uphold papal authority in his now embarrassing treatise against Luther's position on the sacraments. More met all their complaints so well, Roper tells us, that he returned home 'very merye'. He had 'never remembred' to ask if his name had been 'put out of the Parliament bill'.[4]

In fact it had not been. But the Lords were reluctant to condemn their former presiding officer unheard: on 6 March they sent to ask the king whether More might appear before them in the Star Chamber.[5] Henry himself seems to have been willing enough, for he intended to be present personally and trusted that he could overawe the Lords; but in the end his advisers convinced him that his prestige would suffer irreparably should he fail.[6] So More's name was deleted.[7] The amended bill passed the

---

[1] Cottonian MS. Cleopatra E. vi, fols. 156-9, 161-3, B.M. (L.P., vii, 239-40).
[2] Rogers, *Correspondence of Sir Thomas More*, 470. The letter is dated only 'Saturday'.
[3] *Ibid.* 480-8. [4] Roper, *Lyfe of Sir Thomas Moore*, 64-9.
[5] L.J., i, 72. [6] Roper, *Lyfe of Sir Thomas Moore*, 70-1.
[7] Cromwell, meeting Roper in the Parliament House on the following day, informed him that his father-in-law's name had been deleted and asked him to tell More. Roper, *Lyfe of Sir Thomas Moore*, 71.

Lords on fourth reading 12 March and the Commons on the 17th. Sent to Audley for some reason, it was returned to the Upper House on 21 March, nine days before the end of the session. Fisher's name had remained in the bill, but he bought pardon for £300.[1] No doubt Henry had resolved to deal with him and More in another way. Elizabeth, together with Bocking and three of his confederates, was executed at Tyburn in April.

The Nun of Kent died because she questioned the king's marriage. To prevent others from falling into the same error, the government needed to announce by statute that Catherine had no further claim to the title queen and that the succession now rested in the king's issue by Anne. Bills to this purpose were included in the legislative programme which Cromwell had conceived as early as 1533; his lists of 'thinges to be moved on the king's behalf unto his attorneye to be put afterwardes in order and determynacion by the lerned councell agenst the next assemblie of his Parliament' contain the entries:

Furst, a bill to be conceyved for the order and state of the succession of this realme . . .
Item, a bill to be made for the establisshement of the Princes Dowagier for the order and establisshement of her lyvyng.[2]

The second of these bills, designed to reduce Catherine of Aragon to princess dowager, as the widow of Prince Arthur, appeared first in Parliament. The government's draft, written on paper, was brought into the Lords on 11 February. It experienced minor difficulties in both Houses; after third reading the Lords ordered the chancellor to make certain emendations, and the Commons added a proviso. Even so the bill passed rapidly, completing its course by 7 March.[3]

Late in February Chapuys heard that this bill was before Parliament, and that the succession would soon be discussed. Since he regarded himself as Catherine's principal advocate, he sought leave to argue her case in Parliament: not because he thought that

[1] 25 Henry VIII, c. 12; [Richard Hall], *The Life of Fisher*, 85–6.
[2] Cottonian MS. Titus B. I, fols. 478, 453, 161, B.M. (*L.P.*, VI, 1381 [1–3]). For some reason Cromwell crossed out the item referring to the princess dowager in the earliest of these memoranda, and it does not appear in the later redactions. Possibly he once intended to deal with both matters in the succession bill.
[3] 25 Henry VIII, c. 28; *L.J.*, I, 67–73. Catherine had already been deprived of the royal style by proclamation; see Hughes and Larkin, *Tudor Royal Proclamations*, I, 209–11.

Henry would grant permission, but because the king's refusal would demonstrate the injustice and obstinacy of condemning Catherine and Mary without a hearing. On 24 February Chapuys spoke with Norfolk, and later with the king himself, only to have Henry inform him that English custom did not allow foreigners to enter Parliament. The ambassador retorted that not all the Parliaments in England could make Mary a bastard, but in the end he was forced to leave Henry with nothing more than an exhortation to treat Catherine and Mary better.[1]

The ecclesiastical implications of Catherine's new title were clear enough: anyone recognizing her as princess dowager accepted Cranmer's verdict on the divorce and thus denied papal authority in England. The same points appeared even more openly in the succession bill. This was delayed until the end of the session, perhaps because Cromwell's strategy dictated that the more limited bill dealing only with Catherine be passed first to prepare the way, perhaps (as Chapuys believed) because of negotiations with Scotland which involved the claim of the Stuarts to a place in the succession.[2] Whatever the reason, the Lords received the very important bill 'ratifying the King's marriage with the Lady Anne' only on 20 March.

The measure had been drafted with great care by Cromwell and the learned council. We are fortunate in having an unusual memorandum reporting the work of this drafting committee; it shows that the councillors suggested several changes in Cromwell's original version. They thought that 'the oppynyon of the levyticall law' concerning Henry's first marriage 'were better owt then in' the succession act, since it had been sufficiently laboured elsewhere, and (among other things) they were dubious about Cromwell's proposal that 'woord, wryting, or dede' attacking the king's new marriage and succession be made treason. As Cromwell noted, 'they be contentyd that dede and wryting shal be treason, and worde to be mysprisyon'.[3]

[1] Chapuys MS., 1534, no. 18 (L.P., VII, 232; C.S.P., Spn., V, i, 19).
[2] Chapuys MS., 1534, no. 25 (L.P., VII, 393; C.S.P., Spn., V, i, 32). The memorandum of the drafting committee's discussion lends some support to this view: it noted 'that the Kynge of Scottys sholde in no wyse be named, for that it might gyve hym other a corage or elles cause hym to take unkyndnes'. Cottonian MS. Titus B. I, fol. 425, B.M.
[3] Cottonian MS. Titus B. I, fol. 425, B.M. (L.P., VII, 51), analysed in Elton, 'The Law of Treason in the Early Reformation', Historical Journal, XI (1968), 221-2.

All of these changes were accepted, and the act was made ready for Parliament. Considering its official origin one is rather surprised to note that the committee cast it as a petition from both Houses to the sovereign. A preamble recalled the civil strife which had resulted from uncertain succession to the throne.[1] Cranmer's verdict on Henry's marriage to Catherine was cited, as was the king's good and lawful union with Queen Anne. The enacting clauses followed naturally from these premises. Catherine was to be called princess dowager; the succession was fixed in the king's male heirs by Anne, or failing them, by a subsequent wife; in default of such male heirs Anne's daughter, Princess Elizabeth, was to succeed, followed by her children, other daughters to be born to Henry VIII, and their descendants in due order. The bill made no further provision for the succession, thus holding open the possibility that the Scottish descendants of Henry's sister Margaret might one day claim the throne and encouraging—so Henry hoped—peace between the two realms. Curiously enough, the act also avoided any mention of Henry's older daughter Mary. Since her place in the succession was not defined, she was implicitly excluded for the time being; she was not, however, bastardized. Probably neither Henry nor Cromwell wished to settle the question of her legitimacy, which Cranmer too had skirted in his divorce decree. It might later prove desirable to give Mary a place in the succession, and theoreticians could argue, as Chapuys did on occasion, that she was lawfully born since her parents were unaware at the time of any impediment to their union.[2]

Most of these enacting clauses reiterated obvious points, although it was useful to have them established by statute. But the bill did not end here; it went on, rather fortuitously, to generalize the decision in Henry's case by enacting that no persons marrying within the degrees of consanguinity proscribed by Scripture were lawfully joined, or their children legitimate, regardless of dispensations which might have been secured. The Church had no power to override God's laws.[3]

---

[1] One cannot help noticing the similarity of these arguments to those put forward, unsuccessfully, by councillors who wished Elizabeth to fix the succession in the 1560s; cf. Neale, *Elizabeth I and Her Parliaments, 1559–1581*, 101–13, 129–64.

[2] For a fuller discussion of this point see Mortimer Levine, 'Henry VIII's Use of His Spiritual and Temporal Jurisdictions in His Great Causes of Matrimony, Legitimacy, and Succession', *Historical Journal*, x (1967), 5–7.

[3] A proviso, probably added by the Lords and written in darker ink at the end of the

The teeth of the measure lay in the mechanism for enforcement and in the penalties provided for opposition. All subjects could now be required to swear an oath affirming the 'whole effects and contents' of the succession act—and by implication the reconstitution of the Church. Deeds or writings which maliciously imperilled the king, disturbed his title to the crown, or slandered his marriage were to be considered high treason, while (as the legal council had recommended) the like offences by words only now became misprision of treason. In neither case could the offender avail himself of sanctuary.

All of these provisions must have been generally acceptable, for the bill passed speedily. Even with a day out for Passion Sunday it cleared the Upper House by 23 March and was sent to the Commons. Three days later it returned with the assent of the Lower House.[1]

By this time the approach of Easter dictated a speedy termination of the session. The formal closing, in the king's presence, took place the day after Palm Sunday, at 2 o'clock on 30 March. Speaker Wingfield made an oration, which Henry graciously accepted; Chancellor Audley gave the royal assent to Parliament's acts. In a brief speech Audley stressed the importance of the Act of Succession, adding that Henry had given commission to him, together with Cranmer, Norfolk, and Suffolk, to receive the oaths of all members of Parliament. After they had sworn 'to bear ... faith, truth and obedience alonely to the king's majesty, and to the heirs of his body according to the limitation and rehearsal within [the] Statute of Succession', they departed for their homes. Parliament was prorogued to 3 November.[2]

3

During the summer of 1534 general unrest prevailed in England. The papal declaration that Henry's marriage to Catherine had been

MS. act (H.L.R.O.), stipulates that this section is applicable only where the marriages which might create impediments 'were solemnized and carnal knowledge had'.

[1] 25 Henry VIII, c. 22; L.J., I, 77–80. The act was printed, probably immediately, by the king's printer Thomas Berthelet; twenty copies survive at the P.R.O., SP 2/P, fols. 33–127.

[2] L.J., I, 82; Additional MS. 4622, fol. 297, B.M.; MS. Journal, H.L.R.O., 174–5.

valid, issued on 23 March, was received in London shortly after the prorogation;[1] Henry was so irate that he ordered the preachers to denounce the pope in their Easter sermons. When presented with the succession oath More and Fisher agreed to swear to the act itself but not to its preamble. Cranmer believed this sufficient, but Henry was adamant. By the end of April both were in the Tower and Chapuys was convinced that they would be executed.[2] In July the peers were reassembled for the trial and subsequent acquittal of Lord Dacre of the North, who had been charged with treasonable communications with the Scots.[3]

In August the convents of Observant friars were dissolved, since members of the order had been involved with Elizabeth Barton and had refused the Oath of Succession.[4] While the Observants were unusual in their staunch opposition to the divorce and in their continuing Roman sympathies, they were not alone in their protests. In September one William Copley, a lay brother of a Cistercian house in Yorkshire, was indicted under the succession act for calling Cranmer a heretic and Anne a bawd, as well as proclaiming that the king's new marriage was adultery.[5] In the same month Pope Clement VII died, but the election of Alessandro Farnese as Paul III offered no hope of reconciliation; Chapuys called on his master to raise 'the banner of the Crucifix', insisting that Lords Darcy and Dacre were ready to lead an insurrection.[6] Even Protestant minds were unsettled. As a fragmentary chronicle kept at St Augustine's, Canterbury, recorded, 'the same year thear were many heretiques in sundry places of England which did blaspheme the saintes and the worshipping of them, barking agaynst tithes, which neyther wold have fastinges nor pilgramagies'.[7]

[1] The sentence is printed in Wilkins, *Concilia*, III, 769.

[2] *L.P.*, VII, 499, 500, 530.

[3] Chapuys reported that twenty-four lords and twelve judges were present (*ibid.* 1013); according to Edward Hall 'the commons excedyngly joyed and rejoysed [at his acquittal], insomuche as there was in the hall at those woordes, not giltie, the greatest shoute and crye of joye that the like no man livying may remembre that ever he heard' (*Hall's Chronicle*, 815). See also the *Third Report of the Deputy Keeper of the Public Records*, 234–6; Lord Herbert of Cherbury, *The Life and Reign of Henry the Eighth*, 407–8; and above, Ch. 3.

[4] *L.P.*, VII, 590, 1057, 1095; Knowles, *Religious Orders in England*, III, 201–11.

[5] Cited by Elton, 'The Law of Treason in the Early Reformation', 225–6, from K.B. 9/529/39, P.R.O.

[6] *L.P.*, VII, 1206, 1257.

[7] Harleian MS. 419, fols. 112–14, B.M.

4

Against this background Parliament convened for its sixth session on 3 November. As usual a number of peers had obtained licence to be absent, or simply stayed at home: Lord Darcy ostensibly because of his 'aygge [age] and debelities', Lord Conyers because of the gout, Lord LaWarr because of poverty, Bishop Rowland Lee because of his duties in Wales, Bishop Kite because he was bedfast, the abbot of St Albans because of the plague, and the abbot of St Mary's, York, because 'suche a long jorney in this wynter season shuld not onely be chargeable to me and our house but also put me in daunger of my lyfe'.[1] Stephen Gardiner was probably another absentee. He had fallen from favour because of his religious conservatism, had yielded his secretaryship to Cromwell, and had been sent to his diocese of Winchester under orders not to return until he was summoned.[2]

In the Commons there was a vacancy created by the death of Sir Edward Ferrers, one of the county members for Warwickshire. Roger Wigston, a burgess for Coventry, told Cromwell that 'secret suyte and labor' was being made for the seat, which he may have coveted himself.[3] But there is no indication that he obtained it, or indeed any definite evidence about a by-election in Warwickshire. We do know, however, of three other elections held in October. In Kent Sir Edward Guildford, who had died during the summer, was followed by his ward and son-in-law Sir John Dudley. Son of the Edmund Dudley whom Henry had executed in 1510, John was destined to rule England as the duke of Northumberland and to beget Elizabeth's favourite the earl of Leicester. In London Robert Pakington was chosen by the Common Council to fill the seat vacated by William Bowyer upon his election as alderman; at Exeter one former mayor followed another when Robert Hooker succeeded the ailing John Blackaller.[4]

If Cromwell prepared a memorandum setting out his parliamentary programme for the November session it has not survived.

---

[1] SP 1/86, fols. 23, 111, 142, and SP 1/87, fols. 27, 37, P.R.O.; *L.P.*, VII, 1426, 1439, 1513, 1353, 1463, 1324, 1242.

[2] *L.P.*, VII, 441, 483; J. A. Muller, *Stephen Gardiner and the Tudor Reaction*, 55.

[3] SP 1/85, fol. 205, P.R.O. (*L.P.*, VII, 1178).

[4] *Return of Members of Parliament*, Part I, App., xxix; MacCaffrey, *Exeter, 1540–1640*, 287; SP 1/84, fol. 161, P.R.O. (*L.P.*, VII, 789).

Events, however, soon demonstrated that the government desired five great statutes: acts ratifying royal supremacy in the Church, establishing a precise oath of succession, strengthening the law of treason, granting first fruits and tenths to the king, and levying a subsidy.

Edward Hall singled out the act of supremacy as 'one special estatute' among the 'many and sondry good, wholsome, and godly statutes' of 1534 because it 'auctorised the kynges highnes to be Supreme Head of the Churche of England, by the whiche the pope and all his college of cardinalles with all their pardons and indulgences was utterly abolished out of this realme, God be everlastingly praysed therefore'.[1] Such a pæan exaggerates, for the bill merely declared what was by then a well-established fact. Still, it gave legal expression to the king's ecclesiastical powers: he was to be taken as the only Supreme Head in earth of the Church of England, to have all dignities and jurisdictions properly belonging to the same, and from time to time to correct errors and enormities in the Church, by visitation or otherwise. Considering the monastic survey which Cromwell intended, the last clause may be regarded as especially significant. There was no mention of the pope, but the act did proclaim its disregard for any contrary 'usage, custom, foreign laws, or foreign authority'.[2]

We know little about the circumstances under which the act was passed. It was introduced into the Lords and evidently cleared both Houses without amendment.[3] Chapuys reported its passage on 17 November, two weeks after the beginning of the session.[4] Although it is often thought of as ratifying the title granted Henry by Convocation in 1531, it has little direct relation to that clerical pronouncement; it omits the saving clause, 'so far as the law of Christ allows', substituting instead the more precise but more limited qualification 'in earth'. It is thus much more clearly directed against Rome than was the earlier statement: it allows God, or Christ, to hold some variety of supremacy, but not the pope. The judgement that the Roman pontiff had no more jurisdiction in England than any other foreign bishop, now accepted not only by the two Convocations but also by religious houses,

---

[1] Edward Hall, *Hall's Chronicle*, 816.   [2] 26 Henry VIII, c. 1.
[3] Original act, H.L.R.O.; *L.P.*, VII, 1437.
[4] *L.P.*, VII, 921, 1024, 1025, 1121, 1216, 1347, 1594. These signatures were collected between June and December.

cathedral chapters, university colleges, and the parish priests of each deanery, was more closely linked with the act than was the acknowledgment of 1531.

The bill establishing a definite oath of obedience to the king and his heirs was necessitated by a defect in the act of succession passed in March. Although that act had imposed an oath it had not prescribed the wording to be used. It will be recalled that members of Parliament had been sworn as the spring session was prorogued; the oath administered to them was intended as the oath which the act required, but it went beyond the act in several particulars, especially in its requirement that the persons sworn renounce the power of any 'foreign authority or potentate' and repudiate any oath previously made to such a ruler. The discrepancy was well noted by Sir Thomas More, who told his daughter that he had been committed to the Tower 'for refusinge of this oath not agreable with the statute'; he thought that Cromwell and Audley 'did of their owne heads adde more words unto it,' so that they were unable 'by theyr owne lawe . . . to justifye my imprisonement'.[1] Fisher's early biographer, too, commented that the oath was never 'warranted by lawe, nether yet any man compellable by the law to take yt'.[2]

Government policy clearly required that the oath be ratified by statute. This was done in November. The new act, introduced in the Commons[3] and very probably sponsored by Cromwell, set out essentially the wording used at the end of the spring session, declared this to be the oath intended in the earlier act, and ordered that the names of all who might refuse it be certified into the King's Bench. The effect was to confirm the imprisonment of More and Fisher; as the bishop's life says, 'yt was now ordered that his wrongfull imprisonment was to be judged and accounted rightfull from the beginninge'.[4]

These acts allowed the government to detain More and Fisher, but a new treason statute was thought necessary if they and other

---

[1] Roper, *Lyfe of Sir Thomas Moore*, 78.   [2] Richard Hall, *Life of Fisher*, 100.

[3] 26 Henry VIII, c. 2; original act, H.L.R.O.

[4] Richard Hall, *Life of Fisher*, 100. Amos also emphasized the 'effrontery and injustice' of the new act: *Observations*, 32–6. Flowing from this general statute are the acts (26 Henry VIII, c. 22 and c. 23) attainting Fisher and More of misprision of treason because of their refusal to swear the oath. One of Cromwell's memoranda, 'To remember the bill of the othes in the Upper House', may indicate a troubled passage through the Lords. (Cottonian MS. Titus B. 1, fol. 422, B.M.; n.d., placed in *L.P.*, VII, 1436, at 17 November.)

opponents of royal policy were to be executed. The resulting bill proved to be much the most contentious measure of the session. Henry's advisers had been drafting treason bills since 1531, but so far as we know no earlier version had appeared before Parliament. The new bill, prepared mainly by Audley, was substantially different from its predecessor. It dropped the elaborate historical preamble written in 1532[1] and instead noted succinctly the necessity of restraining slander or peril to the king, queen, and their heirs, condemned the 'cankered and traitorous hearts' who should not be given 'too great a scope of unreasonable liberty', and reiterated Parliament's love for Henry. The enacting clauses made it high treason maliciously to 'wish, will, or desire, by words or in writing', or to attempt by deed, any harm to Henry, Anne, or their heirs, or to deprive them of their titles (such as Supreme Head), or to call the king a heretic, tyrant, or usurper, or to keep from his service any forts, ships, or ammunition belonging to him. Sanctuary was denied to offenders in high treason, provision was made for trial of treasons committed by subjects outside the realm, and a final clause called for forfeiture of all lands which the offenders held in use or in possession: a subtle attempt to keep successors to convicted abbots, for instance, from regaining their predecessors' lands.[2]

The bill was introduced into the Lords.[3] We do not know what reception it received there, but we have ample testimony that a flood of criticism greeted its appearance in the Commons. John Rastell, a member for the Cornish borough of Dunheved, later wrote: 'the bill was earnestly withstood, and could not be suffered to pass, unless the rigour of it were qualified with this word *maliciously*; and so not every speaking against the Supremacy to be treason, but only malicious speaking. And so, for more plain declaration thereof, the word *maliciously* was twice put into the act.'[4] Bishop Fisher's brother Robert, a burgess for Rochester,

---

[1] SP 2/Q, fols. 103-9, P.R.O. (*L.P.*, VII, 1381 [5]). This draft was clearly of 1532, for it applied to offences committed after 6 February of that year. This is the version labelled 'A₃' by Isobel D. Thornley, 'The Treason Legislation of Henry VIII (1531-1534)', *T.R.H.S.*, 3rd ser., XI (1917), 89. For a general account of Tudor treason laws see Samuel Rezneck, 'The Trial of Treason in Tudor England', in *Essays in History and Political Theory in Honor of Charles Howard McIlwain*, 258, 288.

[2] The drafts of 1534, corrected by Audley, are SP 2/Q, fols. 90-6, 97-102, P.R.O. (*L.P.*, 1381 [3, 4]). The last draft is virtually identical with the statute, 26 Henry VIII, c. 13.

[3] Original act, H.L.R.O.   [4] Quoted in Chambers, *Thomas More*, 320.

likewise asserted that 'there was never such a sticking at the passing of any act in the Lower House as was at the passing of the same, . . . for now, . . . speaking is made high treason, which was never heard of before. . . . They stuck at the last to have one word in the same, and that was the [word] *maliciously*.'[1] We seem for once tantalizingly close to knowing what was said in the Commons: if only a diarist had preserved the speeches![2]

These accounts suggest that the bill prepared by Cromwell and Audley would have had all words attacking the king, queen, or succession be treason, and that the Commons refused to pass the bill until the adverb 'maliciously' was inserted. That has certainly been the usual interpretation. But, as Professor Elton has noted, the drafts include the word 'maliciously', and it is reasonably clear that the drafts were made in preparation for Parliament: they were never themselves before the Commons.[3] Further, none of the accounts of what went on in the Commons is strictly contemporary, and all are from observers who had some personal stake in the matter.[4] Edward Hall, who might have given us an impartial lawyer's opinion of the act, did not mention it at all. Still, the early accounts probably reflect some semblance of truth. Precisely what happened in Parliament can never be known. Perhaps Cromwell, or some other member concerned to have the act as strong as possible, suggested the deletion of 'maliciously' only to be shouted down. Or perhaps—and rather more likely—some members expressed reluctance to pass so severe a measure, and the bill's proponents answered by stressing that only words spoken maliciously would be actionable. In any case the bill finally passed without significant change.

[1] *L.P.*, VIII, 856. See also Richard Hall, *Life of Fisher*, 101–2.
[2] We also possess a tantalizing list of names, written on the back of a letter to Cromwell, which may just possibly indicate the membership of a committee to consider the treason bill late in the session. Nearly all of the fifty-three men named were members of the Commons, and some of the others were clerks. The list is divided into three unequal columns, but it seems impossible to discover the basis of such classification. A. F. Pollard commented that 'the gathering . . . has many resemblances to a modern parliamentary dinner party' ('Thomas Cromwell's Parliamentary Lists', 43 n.). The list is printed in *L.P.*, VII, 1522, from SP 1/87, fol. 106, P.R.O.
[3] Elton, 'The Law of Treason in the Early Reformation', p. 228. As Elton notes, the act of succession had contained the qualification 'maliciously', so its use was not new.
[4] Cf. *L.P.*, VIII, 856, which would date Robert Fisher's description to February 1535.

The Commons may have salved their consciences by emphasizing an adverb, but in the end it had no effect. Within a year Prior Houghton and the Carthusians, More and Fisher were to be executed under the terms of the statute. The government simply interpreted any denial of Supremacy as being malicious. Thus we have Rastell's acid comment: 'the word *maliciously*, plainly expressed in the act, was adjudged by the King's commissioners to be void'.[1]

Cromwell and Audley laboured long over the bill annexing first fruits and clerical tenths to the Crown. A surviving draft suggests that the chancellor framed the main body of the act, which is very long and full of legal technicalities.[2] The preamble seems to have been Cromwell's special responsibility, for it is heavily corrected by him with a few additions in another hand which may possibly be the king's own, or at least represent his demands.[3] Since Parliament had previously declared first fruits and tenths to be 'intolerable and importable', and since the project of granting them to the king had evidently been dropped during the spring session, it was of unusual importance for the preamble to justify their renewed collection. This it did by praising the king, 'in whom . . . is united and knit so princely a heart and courage, mixed with mercy, wisdom, and justice'; by recalling 'how long . . . his Majesty hath . . . governed . . . his realm . . . in tranquillity, peace, unity, quietness, and wealth'; and by noting his 'excessive and inestimable charges' for maintenance and defence of the realm. The reasoning may be suspicious, as Amos says, but it is hard not to agree with Tanner that the preamble remains 'a triumph of rhetorical skill and ingenuity'.[4]

The enacting clauses grant the king and his successors a sum equal to one year's revenue, to be paid by every spiritual person appointed to a bishopric, abbacy, benefice, or any other office after 1 January 1535, and a tenth of all revenues received by churchmen, first payable at Christmas 1535. Commissioners were

---

[1] Quoted in Chambers, *Thomas More*, 320.

[2] E 175, file 9, P.R.O. (*L.P.*, VII, 1380 [2]). The draft is in the usual clerical script although probably written by two different clerks; the enacting clauses are corrected in Audley's hand.

[3] The changes which may be Henry's emphasize his exalted position and the corresponding meekness of his subjects: the Lords and Commons '*most humblye*' pray for the continuation '*and augmentacyon*' of the king's estate as their '*oonly* supreme hed *in erth*'. (*Ibid.* 1.)

[4] Amos, *Observations*, 288; Tanner, *Tudor Constitutional Documents*, 37.

directed to ascertain the value of all spiritual preferments—their compilation became the famous *Valor Ecclesiasticus*—and bishops were made responsible for the collection of tenths, which they were directed to pay to the treasurer of the Chamber. As a small *douceur* the king remitted a fifth of the £118,840 with which the clergy had bought their pardon in 1531, and he permitted prelates to deduct from their annates any fees which they had been obliged to pay for temporal justice. First fruits were not to be collected for benefices worth less than eight marks a year, and abbots or priors who had been bound to pay pensions exceeding forty pounds to their predecessors were allowed to reduce such payments by half.[1] In spite of such concessions the amount which the clergy were now forced to pay the king proved considerably larger than the sums formerly sent to Rome: Professor Lunt believed after long study that 'the rank and file of the clergy may well have looked back upon the era of papal annates as a golden age'.[2]

If there was now any opposition to the bill we do not know about it. The measure was introduced in the Lords, where the bishops may possibly have suggested the final proviso.[3] The Commons probably passed the bill before 28 November; they must have received it enthusiastically, for it provided substantial revenues at no cost to themselves and it chimed nicely with their desire to milk the Church.[4]

But despite the heavy contributions exacted from the clergy a subsidy appeared necessary.[5] Laymen had not been taxed since 1523, when Wolsey's demands had raised an uproar in the Commons. The Lower House had agreed to levy a fifteenth and tenth in 1532, but that session had been terminated so abruptly that the

---

[1] For evidence that this clause was invoked see Elton, *Star Chamber Stories*, 169.

[2] Lunt, *Financial Relations of the Papacy*, 445. The Court of First Fruits and Tenths was established to handle these clerical payments, which in 1534–1535 averaged about £40,000 (Elton, *The Tudor Revolution in Government*, 190).

[3] The final section of the statute is not included in the draft but appears in the original act, H.L.R.O., 26 Henry VIII, c. 3.

[4] Chapuys reports the bill in his dispatch of 28 November, *L.P.*, VII, 1482. A related bill was drawn up, probably late in the session, to clarify a legal point which had not been covered in the main act. This supplementary statute, 26 Henry VIII, c. 17, declared that in cases where persons leased lands from clergy or ecclesiastical bodies the owner, not the lessee, should be held responsible for paying the first fruits and tenths.

[5] It had been recommended and justified in the proposal to set fixed salaries for bishops, Cottonian MS. Cleopatra E. VI, fols. 207–8, B.M.

grant was never enacted.[1] Since the realm was at peace the government experienced some difficulty in justifying its request for aid in 1534; many still believed that the king should live of his own except in times of national emergency, and previous tax bills had carried preambles speaking of military expenses. Henry's advisers wished to strengthen the realm by rebuilding Dover pier and by repairing a number of fortresses, and Cromwell even drafted a bill justifying taxation by belabouring the king's 'weightie and importable charges' in maintaining these defences.[2] In the end, however, he decided to drop the pretence; he framed a measure which justified the grant by reciting the king's services to his subjects and emphasizing the excellence of his rule. Some mention was made of the 'wilful, wild, unreasonable, and savage' Irish who were troubling Henry, but in the main the preamble sought merely to have Parliament reciprocate the 'entire love and zeal which the king bore to his people'.[3] The new view, that goodwill and calm rule deserved recompense quite as much as military expenses, may be regarded as one of Cromwell's revolutionary innovations.

The act called for the payment of two subsidies and a fifteenth and tenth, with aliens to be charged double and clergy to be rated on their temporal possessions. During debate the Commons added a number of provisos, all favourable to the taxpayers rather than the Crown.[4] The grant nevertheless brought more than £80,000 into the royal coffers.[5] Chapuys believed that all these

---

[1] See above, Ch. 7.

[2] SP 2/Q, fols. 135–6, P.R.O. (L.P., VII, 1611 [1]). The matter of the embankment at Dover, which had been partially destroyed some four years earlier, had begun with a petition from the townspeople requesting aid in rebuilding (L.P., VII, 66 [1]). A draft bill had been prepared for the spring session; Cromwell, in editing it, had inserted some phrases emphasizing the importance of Dover harbour for the realm's defence (SP 2/P, fols. 128–32, P.R.O.; L.P., VII, 66 [2]). But the bill was probably never introduced in the earlier session. On the whole matter see S. P. H. Statham, The History of the Castle, Town, and Port of Dover, 96–102; L.P., IX, 399.

[3] 26 Henry VIII, c. 19. See also R. S. Schofield, 'Parliamentary Lay Taxation 1485–1547' (unpublished dissertation, Cambridge University), 26.

[4] Three slips of provisos are stitched to the original act, H.L.R.O. An act for a separate clerical subsidy survives at the H.L.R.O., but it does not appear on the Parliament Roll, C 65/143, P.R.O.

[5] Schofield, 'Parliamentary Lay Taxation', 156, 416. The fifteenth and tenth had been collected for centuries at a fixed rate for each locality, while the subsidy was a tax of varying rates levied on individuals according to the criteria specified in each act. Schofield notes that the sections of the 1534 act dealing with the assessment were deficiently drafted, a matter of some surprise since Cromwell is known to

financial measures were devised by Cromwell, who had boasted that he would make Henry wealthier than all the other princes in Christendom.[1] In any case the king rewarded his faithful subjects at the end of the session by granting 'his moste gracious and general free pardon' for all past offences save such serious misdeeds as ravishing the king's wards, wasting his woods, or withholding customs and subsidy payments.[2]

5

Almost as significant as these bills—perhaps of equal significance, in the long run—were the five acts relating to Wales. As early as 2 December 1533, Cromwell had recorded the Council's intention of reforming the administration of Wales, so that peace should be preserved and justice done.[3] Attention had been drawn to the area by Rhys ap Griffith's insurrection at Carmarthen in 1529; he was executed two years later, but disorder continued. Doubtless most of the trouble resulted from the shaky control which the central government exercised in Wales, for the principality was dominated by more than a hundred semi-autonomous lords who did little to keep order and gave little heed to the policies promulgated in London.[4] By the spring of 1534 Parliament was expressing its concern at the 'horrible outrages' committed in the counties of Gloucester, Hereford, Shropshire, and the Welsh marches.[5]

The first step in the government's programme of reform came with the appointment of Cromwell's friend Rowland Lee as president of the Council in the Marches of Wales. Although he was bishop of Lichfield and active also in the visitation of religious houses, Lee devoted most of his energy to Welsh affairs. A

have studied earlier subsidy acts. The act of 1534 is unique in having collectors of the subsidy appointed directly by the king (*ibid*. 215, 220). The subsidy act was printed by Berthelet and ran to twenty pages of black letter (SP 1/86, fols. 170–81, P.R.O.).

[1] 'Qui se vante quil fera son maistre plus pecunieux que tous les autres princes de chretiente': Chapuys MS., 1534, no. 70, 19 December (*L.P.*, VII, 1554).

[2] 26 Henry VIII, c. 18; Edward Hall, *Hall's Chronicle*, 816.

[3] SP 1/80, fols. 171–175, P.R.O.; quoted in Elton, *The Tudor Revolution in Government*, 362.

[4] See W. Llewelyn Williams, 'The Union of England and Wales', *Transactions of the Honourable Society of Cymmrodorion*, 1907–1908, 47–117, and William Rees, 'The Union of England and Wales', *ibid*. 1937, 27–100.

[5] SP 1/84, fol. 131, P.R.O. (*L.P.*, VII, 781).

contemporary described him as 'stowte of nature, redie witted, roughe in speeche, not affable to any of the Walshrie, an extreme severe ponisher of offenders, desirous to gayne (as he did in deede) credit with the king and comendacion for his service.'[1]

In June Henry met with the marcher lords at Shrewsbury, securing their assent to a group of reforming ordinances.[2] By September Lee could report that good order had begun, so that thieves grew fearful.[3] But legislation was needed to complete the programme: Lee must have helped Cromwell, Audley, and other councillors learned in the law to frame it.

Of the five related measures passed during the second session of 1534, much of the longest and most significant is the act 'concerning murders and felonies in Wales'.[4] Two drafts survive, the second virtually identical with the statute.[5] They appear to have been edited by Audley rather than Cromwell, perhaps because of their legal character. Only the second includes the preamble, which complains that the people of Wales 'have of long time continued and persevered in perpetration and commission of divers and manifold thefts, murders, rebellions, willful burnings of houses, and other scelerous deeds and abominable malefacts'. As a 'sharp correction and punishment' the bill provides remedy for unjust acts of the marcher lords or their officers, prohibits the bringing of weapons into court, outlaws certain exactions and —amazingly—all games except shooting with the longbow, gives certain powers to justices of the peace and of gaol delivery in the English counties bordering on Wales, and directs that courts shall be kept in 'sure and peaceable' places. The other bills, all introduced in the Commons, were intended to prevent tampering with juries (penalties were established for jurors who gave untrue verdicts by acquitting felons or murderers), to limit passage over the Severn River to daylight hours and to persons of known integrity, to order imprisonment of Welshmen who assaulted residents of Gloucestershire, Shropshire, or Herefordshire, and to set stricter rules for criminous Welsh clerks.[6]

---

[1] Williams, 'The Union of England and Wales,' 82. Cromwell's son Gregory lived with Lee during most of 1534: *L.P.*, VII, 940, 968, 1151, 1194, 1576.
[2] SP 1/84, fol. 131, P.R.O.   [3] *L.P.*, VII, 1151, 1264.
[4] 26 Henry VIII, c. 6.
[5] SP 2/Q, fols. 74–87, P.R.O. (*L.P.*, VII, 1381 [1]).
[6] 26 Henry VIII, cc. 4, 5, 11, 12; original acts, H.L.R.O.

Shortly after their passage Chapuys commented that these acts took away the native laws, customs, and privileges of the Welsh, 'the last thing in the world they can endure patiently'.[1] In fact Henry's Welsh subjects proved amazingly malleable, perhaps because they regarded the Tudors themselves as Welshmen or because forfeitures had brought so many of the Welsh lordships into Henry's own hands. As the efficient Rowland Lee enforced the acts of 1534, Cromwell and Henry could look forward to even more drastic changes which they expected to introduce when Parliament met again.

6

The remaining statutes of 1534 need not detain us long. Two more acts concerned the Church. One reproved clergymen in the archdeaconry of Richmond, Yorkshire, for levying special assessments on the estate of deceased persons.[2] The other provided for the nomination and consecration of suffragan bishops: diocesans who desired to have such assistants were directed to submit the names of two suitable candidates to the king, who would make the final choice and certify the nominee to the archbishop for consecration. Twenty-five towns, together with the Isle of Wight, were listed as appropriate sees of suffragan bishops.[3] Considering the expanded work of ecclesiastical administration and the frequent employment of bishops in diplomatic service, these episcopal assistants were most desirable.

The only important economic measure dealt with the import of French wines. This had been restricted by an act of 1532, which had also required that certain goods be shipped only in English bottoms. But—as Chapuys reported[4]—that act was now thought to violate treaties with France; the king was given the right to revoke the act, and 'all other such acts,' by proclamation, and to

---

[1] Chapuys MS., 1534, no. 70 (L.P., VII, 1554).

[2] 26 Henry VIII, c. 15.

[3] 26 Henry VIII, c. 14. The act originated in the Upper House, possibly with the lords spiritual (original act, H.L.R.O.). The towns mentioned are Thetford, Ipswich, Colchester, Dover, Guildford, Southampton, Taunton, Shaftesbury, Molton (Derbyshire?), Marlborough, Bedford, Leicester, Gloucester (which became a diocese only after the dissolution of the great monastery there), Shrewsbury, Bristol, Penrith, Bridgwater, Nottingham, Grantham, Hull, Huntingdon, Cambridge, Berwick, Perth [sic], and St Germans.

[4] Chapuys MS., 1534, no. 70.

revive the statutes again at his convenience, also by proclamation. It is an interesting instance of delegated legislative power.[1]

Three local acts testify to the hard times being experienced in the clothing towns of Norfolk. The first, for re-edifying Norwich, refers to a great fire which occurred there at about the time of Henry VIII's accession. Many of the houses remained in ruins, and some grounds lay 'desolate and vacant, replenished with much uncleanness and filth'. A bill introduced in the Commons would have given the municipal corporation authority to take over such properties which were not improved by their owners within two years; the Lords added a proviso giving the 'chief lords' from whom these lands were held one year further in which to make a restoration. Properties not re-edified by the city within two years of its entry were to revert to their original owners.[2]

In Lynn, too, many buildings were 'in great decay and desolation', thus allowing the 'flood and rage of the sea' to ravage the town. Upon petition from the mayor and inhabitants Parliament gave the corporation powers similar to those granted Norwich.[3] Since a decline in the worsted industry was responsible, at least in part, for this urban decay, Parliament also re-enacted a statute of 1523 regulating the manufacture of worsteds in Norwich, Lynn, and Yarmouth.[4]

A final local bill permitted the construction of highways in Sussex according to terms already established for the Weald of Kent: if any person was willing to lay out a 'more commodious' route across his lands he might do so, being granted the old way in compensation.[5]

Among the private bills much the most important was the attainder of the Irish earl of Kildare.[6] According to the bill Kildare had plotted rebellion with the earl of Desmond, with the

[1] 26 Henry VIII, c. 10. A draft, lacking the preamble and lightly corrected by Audley, survives at the P.R.O., SP 2/Q, fols. 80–89 (*L.P.*, VII, 1381 [2]). Cf. Amos, *Observations*, 101.
[2] 26 Henry VIII, c. 8, original act, H.L.R.O.
[3] 26 Henry VIII, c. 9, original act, H.L.R.O.
[4] 26 Henry VIII, c. 16, ratifying 14 Henry VIII, c. 3.
[5] 26 Henry VIII, c. 7, extending 14 & 15 Henry VIII, c. 6.
[6] 26 Henry VIII, c. 25. A surviving draft, Lansdowne MS. 159, fols. 36–9, B.M. (*L.P.*, VII, 1382), is cast in the form of a Commons' petition. Since it is in an unusual hand Elton believed that it was the work of the Fitzgeralds' opponents in Ireland ('Parliamentary Drafts, 1529–1540', 120).

French, and with the emperor; even when summoned to England and imprisoned he counselled his son, 'Silken Thomas', to conspire with the pope and with Charles V. Although the old earl had died in the Tower before the beginning of the parliamentary session, he was now declared guilty of treason from 1528, so that his heirs would forfeit all their lands. The bill also attainted 'all such persons which be or heretofore have been comforters, abettors, partakers, confederates, or adherents unto the said Earl in his said false and traitorous acts': a dubious matter, since they were declared guilty without even being named. Although Silken Thomas was not immediately executed, his reprieve was motivated by expediency rather than mercy. In 1537 he was hanged at Tyburn, together with five of his uncles.

Other private acts assured lands to the dukes of Norfolk and Richmond, exempted foreign merchants of the Steelyard from statutes 'in any way prejudicial to them', and ratified an exchange of lands between the king and the abbot of Waltham. This last, like all such exchanges, was doubtless favourable to the king; by it Henry gained the manor of Copthall, Essex, to which he had 'a singular pleasure and affection to repair and resort for the great consolation and comfort of his most royal person'[1].

No doubt wearied from considering so many bills in so short a time, the Lords and Commons must have been relieved when Parliament was prorogued on 18 December. They had a week in which to return to their homes for Christmas; they were to have just over a year before the final session of their Parliament.[2]

7

By 1534 Convocation had ceased to play a significant role in determining national ecclesiastical policy. During the spring session, so far as we know, the only business before the clergy was the question whether the Roman pontiff had any greater jurisdiction within England, according to God's word, than other foreign bishops. On 31 March William Saye, a notary, reported thirty-two negative votes, four affirmative, and one abstention

---

[1] 26 Henry VIII, cc. 20, 21, 26, 24.

[2] On 20 December 1534, the king ordered that Wingfield be paid £100 for his work as Speaker; smaller sums were given to the chief justices, the solicitor and attorney general, and the under-clerk of Parliament. Exchequer, K.R., 421/20, P.R.O. (L.P., VII, 1557).

in the lower house. We have no record of the vote in the upper house, although the opinions of the prelates were ordered written into the *acta*.[1] The Convocation of York, meeting in May, denied papal authority unanimously.[2] Neither assembly seems to have been involved in the discussion of annates, Peter's Pence, heresy, or the succession, despite the obvious ecclesiastical implications of such matters.

On 4 November, at the first meeting of Convocation's sixth session, Cranmer announced the change in his archiepiscopal style necessary to reflect the break with Rome. He was now to be called the metropolitan of England, not the legate of the Apostolic See.[3]

Later meetings were devoted almost entirely to the discussion of heretical books, especially a Protestant *Prymer* which had been published by Cromwell's protégé William Marshall.[4] Perhaps because of its blunt attack on the veneration of saints, the *Prymer* was judged not consonant with the teachings of Holy Mother Church or fit for public use. Tyndale's revised translation of the New Testament, printed at Antwerp in November, also came under fire. But the clergy were not, as has sometimes been thought, wholly opposed to the idea of an English Bible. At their last meeting—indeed after they had heard the king's letter of prorogation read—the bishops and abbots summed up their views in a petition. They asked Henry to appoint a special commission, to which all suspect books should be delivered, and urged him to consider whether the task of translating the Scriptures should be undertaken by men of sound learning and true faith. In addition, the clergy sought a royal proclamation prohibiting the public discussion of theological matters, since even the mystical sacrament of the altar had become a common subject for alehouse arguments.[5]

Our sources do not indicate that Convocation debated first fruits and tenths, supremacy, or any other great issue of the day.

---

[1] C.C. 306, 58-9; Wilkins, *Concilia*, III, 769. Wilkins gives the number of negative votes as thirty-four.

[2] Wilkins, *Concilia*, 782-3; L.P., VII, 769.

[3] C.C. 306, 60; Wilkins, *Concilia*, 769.

[4] Probably S.T.C. 15986. Marshall had been financed by Cromwell through personal loans and had printed an English translation of the *Defensor Pacis* by Marsilio of Padua in the spring of 1534 (Clebsch, *England's Earliest Protestants*, 254-5).

[5] C.C. 306, 61; Wilkins, *Concilia*, 770. Henry complied with the request of Convocation in a proclamation printed in Wilkins, 776-8.

One must conclude that the clergy, having bargained away their independence, were no longer much regarded.

8

Inevitably, some men felt that Parliament had not dealt with all the problems facing the realm in 1534. One anonymous writer drafted a list of 'thynges necessary, as it semeth, to be remembred before the brekyng up of the Parliament'. Probably sent to Cromwell, this memorandum sought statutory ratification of various advanced religious views: 'that the bloode of Christ suffiseth to man's redempcion without the bloode of martyrs; that it cannot be provid by Scripture that the bisshopis of Rome may deliver soulis out of purgatory, ne that there is any purgatory; . . . that it is a more necessary and more cheritable prayor to pray for theym that be alive then for theym that be dedde'. The writer hoped, too, to reverse the enclosure movement, 'to buylde townes agayne that be layd to pastures'. None of his suggestions bore fruit.[1]

Some Lutheran proposals had been sent to Cromwell earlier, evidently by John Rastell.[2] These called for legislation allowing priests to marry and prohibiting offerings to images; turning to secular affairs Rastell also sought reforms in the common law and the Court of Chancery. Another petition, ostensibly from the 'commons' of England, had complained of the expense and delay encountered in legal proceedings. Since the Lower House of Parliament was 'ruled' by lawyers, the writer turned to the king and Lords requesting effectual reform in the law.[3]

A draft bill of considerable interest would have established a court of six 'Conservators of the Common Weal' to enforce penal statutes. These justices, sitting at Whitehall, were to be assisted by serjeants who would act much as modern police in apprehending offenders. The draft went so far as to suggest heraldry for the court's seal—a ship, a plough, carts, a hammer, and a spade

---

[1] Cottonian MS. Cleopatra E. vi, fol. 330, B.M. (*L.P.*, vii, 1383). The memorandum also discusses General Councils and certain Biblical texts which seem to advance the independent power of the Church.

[2] SP 1/85, fols. 99–100, P.R.O. (*L.P.*, vii, 1043); cf. *L.P.*, vii, 1071, 1073; Elton, 'Parliamentary Drafts, 1529–1540', 118 n. 6.

[3] SP 2/Q, fols. 138–140, P.R.O. (*L.P.*, vii, 1611 [3]).

as well as the king's arms—to demonstrate the role of good industry in maintaining the commonwealth.[1]

There is no likelihood that this bill originated with the government: its form is irregular and its ideas are too advanced. Professor Plucknett, who greatly admired the draft, once suggested that it sprang from the pen of Sir Thomas More. Despite some echoes of the *Utopia* this can hardly be the case; Professor Elton's view, that it was conceived by Thomas Starkey and other members of Cromwell's circle, is much more probable. However admirable the proposal may have been, we have no reason to think that it was given serious consideration or presented to Parliament.[2]

Finally, there is Cromwell's own memorandum 'that it may please the kynges highnes that some reasonable wayes may be devised for his wardes and prymer seasyn', presumably an indication that he hoped for a statute of uses in 1534.[3] It was not forthcoming. For reasons which will appear later, legislation had to be put off yet again.

Although these and some other matters remained unresolved, the sessions of 1534 must be ranked among the most productive of the entire Parliament. Succession and supremacy; first fruits and subsidy; treason, economic regulation, and Welsh government: such items stand out among the statutes of Henry's reign. The government had prepared its legislative programme with uncommon efficiency and the two Houses had enacted it with a minimum of delay.

[1] SP 1/88, fols. 25–41, P.R.O. (*L.P.*, VII, 1611 [4]), printed by Plucknett, 'Some Proposed Legislation of Henry VIII', 119–44.
[2] Plucknett, 'Some Proposed Legislation of Henry VIII', 133; Elton, 'Parliamentary Drafts, 1529–1540', 123–24.
[3] Cottonian MS. Titus B. 1, fol. 159ᵛ, B.M. (*L.P.*, IX, 725 [2], where misdated; actually from the autumn of 1534).

10

THE SEVENTH SESSION, 1536: THEIR LABOURS ENDED

Parliament did not meet during 1535. A session had been scheduled to begin on 3 November, but it was cancelled because of the plague which had ravaged London.[1] After some consultation Henry, Cromwell, and Audley decided on adjournment to 4 February, when cold weather should have ended the pestilence.[2]

It may be that the king and his advisers welcomed the prorogation, for the passage of time might blur memories of a singularly unpleasant summer. The plague had been accompanied by constant rain, bad harvests, murrain, high prices of victual, and a depressed market for cloth.[3] In May the saintly Prior Houghton had been sent to the Tyburn gallows along with two fellow Carthusians; Fisher was executed in June, More in July. Whatever the parliamentarians may have thought about royal supremacy, many of them must have been distressed at Henry's handling of their former colleagues.

The autumn proved little better. Catherine of Aragon, whose plight had attracted wide sympathy, was ill throughout the last months of 1535 and died in January 1536: Chapuys suspected poison.[4] By this time Henry was tiring of Anne Boleyn, who miscarried of a male child on the day of Catherine's funeral.[5] Discontent was rife in the Church also, although the clergy had been so well neutralized that they had no effective way of expressing it. Cromwell's appointment as vicegerent in spirituals brought him broad powers to run the Church as Henry's deputy,

---

[1] 'The plage rayneth in every parysh of London', one of Cromwell's servants wrote in August: SP 1/95, fol. 104, P.R.O. (L.P., IX, 156).

[2] SP 1/96, fols. 167–168, P.R.O. (L.P., IX, 370), a letter from Audley to Cromwell.

[3] See L.P., IX, 152, 274, 383, 594, 851. Chapuys noted that the first payment of the subsidy voted in 1534 had come due but that the king had made no attempt to collect it because of the economic distress.

[4] Ibid. X, 59, 141. Chapuys believed that Anne, not Henry, was responsible, although he noted that on the Sunday after Catherine's death Henry showed his joy by dressing in yellow, a great white plume in his hat, and dancing about Greenwich with Elizabeth in his arms.

[5] Ibid. 282, 351.

and he soon proceeded with his great visitation of the monasteries.[1] By the end of the year a few of the smaller houses had
already surrendered, and it was obvious that further spoliation
lay ahead.[2] Nearly every group thus had some reason to be
dissatisfied with the course of events; some of the conservatives
even talked to Chapuys about rebellion. Among the disaffected
peers Professor Mattingly identified Lords Darcy and Hussey,
both Lords Dacre, the earls of Derby and Northumberland, Lord
Sandys, Lord Bray, the marquis of Exeter, and the earl of Rutland.[3]

Perhaps realizing this discontent, the king and Cromwell took
certain steps to assure a co-operative Parliament. To begin with,
Cromwell advised Henry 'to graunt fewe licenses for any to be
absent from the Parlyament'.[4] Doubtless he wished to force the
attendance of members who supported the king's proceedings.
Others could stay at home: indeed it was rumoured that abbots
had been forbidden to attend.[5] While that seems to be untrue, we
know that a number of churchmen and other opposition peers
did not come to the session. In fact Henry drew up a form letter
licensing its recipients to be absent provided that they named a
'sufficient procurator or procurators'.[6] Some peers pleased him
by submitting blank proxies; Lord LaWarr's had 'a wyndoe for to
put in whom yt shall please the kynges highnes to apoynt'—Lord
Rochford, as it turned out—and the Earl of Essex offered to
recall an earlier proxy if Cromwell desired to name his proctor.[7]
Darcy, Hussey, and Northumberland had the good sense to stay at
home. The chance survival of a fragment copied from the Lords
Journal, which has been lost, lets us know that at least ten abbots
and three bishops were licensed to be absent.[8] Others simply
stayed away without formal permission. The archbishop of York,
Edward Lee, remained in the North of England, while Gardiner
was in France on an embassy.[9] The only monastic clergy known

[1] He was probably appointed vicegerent at the beginning of 1535; see Lehmberg,
'Vicegerency and Supremacy: A Re-examination', E.H.R., LXXXI (1966), 225–35.
[2] L.P., IX, 816.　　　　　　　　　　　[3] Mattingly, Catherine of Aragon, 286–90.
[4] SP 1/102, fol. 5, P.R.O. (L.P., x, 254).　　　　　[5] Thus Chapuys: L.P., 732.
[6] SP 1/101, fol. 144, P.R.O. (L.P., x, 159).
[7] SP 1/101, fols. 131 and 235, P.R.O. (L.P., x, 154 and 231).
[8] Harleian MS. 158, fols. 143–4, B.M. This is part of a volume of parliamentary papers
collected by Sir Simonds D'Ewes. See also L.P., VIII, 1107; x, 78, 150, 161, 206.
S[pecial] C[ollections] 10, file 52, P.R.O., contains some of the actual proxies for
this period.
[9] See the correspondence in L.P., x, 172, 413, 521; 235, 255, 374, 725.

to have attended were Whiting of Glastonbury, Fuller of Waltham and Thornton of St Mary's York.[1] Since Parliament was to decide the fate of the religious houses the matter is of some importance.

Five new bishops helped advance the cause of reform. Edward Fox, the scholar and diplomat who had first brought Cranmer to Henry's notice and who had defended supremacy in his book *De vera differentia*, now took his seat as bishop of Hereford. The notoriously Protestant Hugh Latimer followed Ghinucci at Worcester, John Hilsey succeeded Fisher at Rochester, and Nicholas Shaxton, another reformer, took the see of Salisbury after Campeggio's deprivation. William Barlow, a former monastic prior whose future held exile under Mary and the bishopric of Chichester under Elizabeth, was named to succeed the deceased Standish at St Asaph. Norwich was vacant throughout the session and St David's for most of it, Bishop Rawlins dying in mid-February 1536.

Although at least one writer has credited Henry with a 'judicious creation of peers' for this session,[2] no new titles were in fact given. There was one new temporal peer, William Lord Stourton, who had succeeded to the barony on his father's death in December 1535. Another elderly baron, Lord Bergavenny, had died in 1535, but his heir was less than ten years old and was not summoned to Parliament until 1552. No doubt Cromwell would have advised Henry to create new peers had he believed it necessary; as it was, few opponents of his policies were brave enough to attend, and creations were not needed.

We know less about the Commons. There should have been a by-election to fill the seat for Somerset vacated when Stourton was raised to the Lords, but no record of it survives. Two by-elections are documented: Nicholas Quernby was named a burgess for Nottingham in succession to Henry Statham and George Carew replaced Sir William Courtenay as a county member for Devon.[3] Chapuys thought that Carew was ready to take up arms against the king, and his election may be a sign of opposition in the west.[4] All in all the Lower House changed less than the Upper during the thirteen months between sessions, a

[1] Harleian MS. 158, fols. 143–4, B.M.   [2] Fisher, *History of England*, 375–6.
[3] *Return of Members of Parliament*, Part I, App., xxix.
[4] Mattingly, *Catherine of Aragon*, 288.

circumstance which suited the king well enough since the Commons were already inclined to support most of his proposals.

Chapuys realized that preparations for the new session were almost wholly in the hands of Cromwell, whom he described as more powerful than ever Wolsey was: even the chancellor was but his minister.[1] The ambassador once believed that Parliament would be asked to order the execution of Catherine and Mary, presumably under colour of their refusal to swear the oaths. It is highly improbable that either Cromwell or Henry ever considered such action; if they did, they abandoned it after Catherine's death. Chapuys also wrote, accurately but without any special prescience, that some sort of action would be taken against religious houses, so that monks might renounce their vows and enter secular life.[2]

Cromwell himself considered a much broader legislative programme. A set of memoranda probably drafted by one of his assistants prior to November 1535 suggested bills concerning wardship and primer seisin, usury, depopulation of cities and towns, and customs paid by foreign merchants. It argued that all the king's subjects should pay a small sum annually to be applied toward the defence of the realm, in place of the 'smoke-pence' which they had previously paid the pope. Perhaps yielding to the prevalent animus against the legal profession, it urged that 'some good ways may be considered and devised for restraint and utter extinction of the abuses of the lawyers of this realme', and it suggested a reduction in the salaries of the 'men of the long robe' (lawyers) so that the revenues of 'personages of the short robe' (soldiers) might be increased. Most intriguing, if least important, was the eugenic proposal that 'yong men shuld as well be restraynyd from mariage till they be of potent age, as tall and puyssaunt personnes stayed from mariage of olde widowes'.[3]

By the beginning of February Cromwell's own plans were well advanced, and his remembrances list most of the great bills of the session.[4] His entry, 'the abhomynacion of religious persones throughout the realme, and a refformacyon to be devysed therein', presages some attack on the monasteries. He too was angry with

---

[1] L.P., IX, 862.   [2] Ibid. 357, 776, 861; X, 141.
[3] Cottonian MS. Titus B. I, fols. 159ᵛ, 160, B.M. (L.P., IX, 725).
[4] Cromwell himself drew up two memoranda (SP 1/102, fols. 7–9); these were copied, probably by Sadler, into a single remembrance which was further emended by the Secretary (ibid. fols. 5–6; L.P., X, 254).

lawyers and proposed 'dymynyshyng of the attorneys in all the shires throughout this realme, which persons be the cause of gret plee and disencyon'. He anticipated acts for the assurance of first fruits and tenths, for true assessing of the subsidy, for surveying the accounts of the Wardrobe, and for payment of customs duties to the king quarterly, all other revenues twice a year.[1] Rivers and streams were to be protected by bills prohibiting weirs, water mills, or stream works for tin; sanctuaries and special religious liberties were to be abolished; punishment was to be set for forgery or counterfeiting the king's signature; new ordinances were to be established for Calais. Draft bills dealing in detail with many of these matters were prepared for introduction into Parliament.

I

The final session of the Reformation Parliament began 4 February 1536, and ended on Good Friday, 14 April. Surviving indications of chronology within these limits are disappointingly meagre, but there is some reason to think that ecclesiastical matters were attacked first and that an effort was made outside the Parliament chambers to influence the members' attitude. On Sunday, 6 February, Cranmer preached at Paul's Cross for two hours, devoting most of his time to an attempt to prove that the scriptural passages about Antichrist referred to the pope.[2] At the same time several books attacking images, ceremonies, and purgatory were published. Chapuys thought that this propaganda campaign was aimed at destroying belief in purgatory so that the king might more easily confiscate endowments devoted to prayers for the dead.[3] It is not now possible to identify the volumes, but one of them may have been *A lytell boke that speaketh of Purgatorye*, preserved in a single copy at the Huntington Library.[4] Cromwell

---

[1] We have a draft bill, corrected in Cromwell's hand, which orders the payment of customs receipts to the Exchequer on 1 May and 1 November (Harleian MS. 1878, fols. 22–5, B.M.; *L.P.*, x, 246 [18]). No such act was passed in 1536; we do not know whether it was introduced or not.

[2] Chapuys MS., 1536, fol. 29 (*L.P.*, x, 283).

[3] Chapuys MS., 1536, fols. 32–3 (*L.P.*, x, 282). *C.S.P., Spn.*, v, ii, 21, is a summary of the same dispatch; it is misdated, and it refers incorrectly to the publication of 'a pamphlet' although the MS. reads 'plusiers livrez'.

[4] The book, S.T.C. 3360, was published by Robert Wyer. It bears no date, but 1536 (suggested by Clebsch, *England's Earliest Protestants*, 319) seems more likely than the S.T.C.'s '[1550?]'.

may also have sent out some copies of the *Disputacion of Purgatory* by John Frith, whose Protestant views were only now becoming acceptable.[1] After considerable discussion Frith had concluded that 'this their paynefull purgatory was but a vayne imagination, and that it hath of long time but deceaved the people and milked them from their money'.

Some tracts which survive only in manuscript may have circulated as well. One alleges it to be 'most plain, by special and directe wordes in veray many and diverse places of Scripture, that all the possessions, landes, and tenements hertofore given unto the said forsaken Anticrist [the pope] or any of his orders . . . do appertain and belong to the kinges highnes'.[2] A short 'opinion' suggests that, according to the common law and feudal doctrine, monasteries which had failed to observe all the services enjoined at their foundation should escheat to the king; the writer estimated the income from such lands at £40,000 a year.[3] Another tract cites the second Psalm to prove that 'kynges be judges of the worlde', so that they may determine what opinions are heretical.[4] A fragmentary dialogue between doctor and student emphasizes that Scripture alone is necessary to salvation and belittles the notion of apostolic succession: the bishops 'be successours to the apostles, but yet it is no doubte but that the apostles had divers auctorities and powers that they have not'.[5]

The way was thus prepared for several of Cromwell's ecclesiastical bills. According to Chapuys, proposals to deprive the bishops of their tribunals and jurisdiction and to subject all churchmen to temporal courts were introduced on 16 February.[6] Several matters are conflated here. One, the denial of jurisdiction, probably refers to a bill restoring to the king certain rights of making appointments and administering justice in liberties and franchises granted by his predecessors.[7] Not all of these were ecclesiastical, but there can be little doubt that Henry was eager to limit the authority of the bishop of Durham in his palatinate as

---

[1] The *Disputacion* had been printed at Antwerp in 1531, reprinted in 1535; Frith was burned at Smithfield in 1533. See Clebsch, *England's Earliest Protestants*, 88–94.

[2] SP 6/3, fol. 47, P.R.O. (*L.P.*, x, 253). Possibly in the hand of Brian Tuke.

[3] SP 1/101, fol. 248, P.R.O. (*L.P.*, x, 242).

[4] SP 6/1, fols. 105–122, P.R.O. (*L.P.*, xi, 85).

[5] SP 6/2, fols. 45–85, P.R.O. (*L.P.*, xi, 86 [1]).

[6] Chapuys MS., 1536, fols. 42–3 (*L.P.*, x, 308).

[7] 27 Henry VIII, c. 24; cf. Amos, *Observations*, 225–8.

well as the independence of Lancashire and Cheshire: the Crown now assumed all responsibility for punishing felonies, including treason, and for naming justices of the peace.[1] Although the Commons added a number of provisos, they passed the bill by 18 February.[2]

It is not clear just what Chapuys meant by his statement that the clergy were to be subject to temporal courts. There had been talk of removing all causes except matrimony and probate of small estates from church courts,[3] but we have no knowledge that so drastic a proposition was submitted to Parliament. The two Houses were asked, however, to re-enact the Submission of the Clergy which had been forced through Convocation in 1532 and given statutory form by an act of 1534. Once again it was provided that the king should appoint thirty-two persons, half clergy and half laymen from Parliament, to examine the canons and constitutions of the Church, rejecting those which did not stand with the king's authority and the laws of the realm.[4] As the new statute admitted, nothing had yet been done under the earlier act, but since that contained no expiration date it is hard to see why the reenactment was thought necessary. Under the act of 1536 the commissioners' power was to terminate three years after the end of the Parliament. Although this may appear a limitation, Cromwell probably intended it as a means of hastening action. There is some suggestion that a panel of canon lawyers was at work on the project of recodification during the autumn of 1535;[5] possibly the vicegerent hoped that he could bring the matter to a speedy conclusion if armed with a new deadline to emphasize its urgency. In fact, however, the commission was never appointed.

But such matters were of little importance compared to the dissolution of the monasteries. For several years the idea of

[1] It is just possible, too, that Chapuys' phrase 'aucune jurisdiction' refers to the episcopal powers, including visitation and the holding of church courts, which Cromwell had inhibited in 1535 (see Lehmberg, 'Supremacy and Vicegerency', 227–33). But this matter required no further legislative sanction, and it is hard to see why it would have been a subject for parliamentary discussion.

[2] Original act, H.L.R.O.; L.P., x, 337.

[3] SP 1/99, fols. 231–2, P.R.O. (L.P., IX, 1071), a memorandum probably written by William Petre late in 1535. Cf. Lehmberg, 'Supremacy and Vicegerency', 227–8.

[4] 27 Henry VIII, c. 15. The original act (H.L.R.O.) is written in an uncommon spiky legal hand. Chapuys evidently misunderstood the scope of the act; he believed that it transferred the whole authority of Parliament to a committee of thirty-two. Chapuys MS., 1536, fol. 91ᵛ (L.P., x, 699; C.S.P., Spn., v, ii, 43).

[5] L.P., IX, 549, 690; cf. Lehmberg, 'Supremacy and Vicegerency', 229.

confiscating monastic endowments to meet the king's financial needs had been taking shape in Cromwell's mind. Unfortunately we cannot trace successive stages in the development so exactly as we could with the restraint of appeals, for no draft bills survive.[1] Such evidence as we have suggests strongly that Cromwell had decided as early as the beginning of 1535 to seek the eventual dissolution of all religious houses. The methods and timing demanded subtle calculation and were evidently still undetermined when Cromwell's agents began their great visitation of the monasteries in July. Proof is lacking, but one surmises that he fixed on his precise plan late in the year, or possibly early in 1536. Our first mention of it is no more than gossip, although it turned out to be reliable gossip: on 3 March one of Lord Lisle's friends wrote him that abbeys and priories 'under iij' markes by yere and having not xij in convent shall down'.[2] The vicegerent had decided to suppress only the smaller houses, leaving the great abbeys to be dealt with subsequently. The scheme was one of Cromwell's shrewdest: it had the merit of gradualism; it displaced no monks or nuns who had a serious vocation, since they could transfer to the larger abbeys if their own convents were closed; it affected houses that were not likely to have influential friends in either the Lords or Commons. As an added inducement Cromwell was able to dangle the prospect of monastic land before the eyes of his supporters.

[1] We do have a draft (SP 6/1, fols. 123-8, P.R.O.; *L.P.*, x, 246 [16]) suggesting much milder treatment for the monks. It begins by noting the 'heresy, idolatry, superstition, ypocrisy, buggery, adultery and other kyndes of incontinency with other dyvers crymes, enormities, and excesses' which the visitors had found in the monasteries. These had sprung from 'the fontayne and originall of all misery and abomination, the usurped power of the bisshop of Rome'. But the king would 'of his moste abundant goodness' forgive all, requiring only that religious persons not 'allure any man to runne abowte on pylgrymage' and that 'they persuade not the people their pretensed religion to be holynes or piety, nor their simulate povertie to be vertue'. Since such an act would have brought the king no revenue, it is inconceivable that it originated with the government. Its form is not usual, as Elton noted ('Parliamentary Drafts, 1529-1540,' 125), and it is much less precise than the products of Cromwell's office. The draft is uncertain whether existing statutes contain 'express punishment for such cryme', and it sermonizes, likening an idle monk to a drone bee devouring 'suyche allmys and sustentation as shulde be geven to poore, impotent, and miserable persons'. Most likely it emanated from one of the 'commonwealth men' interested in preserving the charity and hospitality of religious houses, perhaps Thomas Starkey. (Cf. W. Gordon Zeeveld, *Foundations of Tudor Policy*, 161-4.)

[2] SP 3/8, fol. 56, P.R.O. (*L.P.*, x, 406).

There is no proof that Cromwell himself drafted the suppression bill; indeed, an anonymous Elizabethan chronicle attributes it to Audley and Rich.[1] The preamble, however, sounds like Cromwell and is framed with considerable rhetorical skill. It begins by lamenting the 'manifest sin, vicious, carnal, and abominable living . . . daily used and committed among the little and small abbeys, priories, and other religious houses' having fewer than twelve members. Continual visitations had failed to reform these, but there were 'divers and great solemn monasteries . . . where, thanks be to God, religion is right well kept and observed'; these could house persons who now 'rove abroad in apostacy'. By some sleight of hand houses lacking twelve professed inhabitants are equated with those having annual incomes of £200 or less—presumably the financial figure was more convenient administratively, and it would prevent monastic superiors from impressing monks merely to prevent dissolution. At any rate the bill called on the king, in the name of the Lords and Commons, to extirpate sin and advance 'the pleasure of Almighty God and . . . the honour of this . . . realm' by confiscating all endowments and properties of monastic houses yielding less than £200 a year. Specialized clauses relieved recently appointed abbots from paying first fruits, provided pensions for the heads of suppressed houses, discharged the Convocations of Canterbury and York from responsibility for portions of their subsidies which would have been paid by dissolved houses, and exempted cells of monasteries which were themselves worth above £200 as well as any other houses which the king might name.[2]

Since the reports of Cromwell's visitors were to supply evidence of the vice and sin mentioned in the bill, there can be little doubt that they were important in his parliamentary campaign. The point is useful in fixing chronology, for the *comperta* covering northern England were not dispatched to London until 28 February.[3] They were filled with accounts of incontinent or

---

[1] D. M. Loades, ed., *The Papers of George Wyatt Esquire*, 159. The chronicler, who was perhaps recording an oral tradition, added that Cromwell had originally advised Henry to undertake the dissolution 'by litle & litle, not sodeinly by Parliament'.

[2] Under this clause seventeen small priories of the exclusively English Gilbertine order were exempted; see G. W. O. Woodward, *The Dissolution of the Monasteries*, 68.

[3] *L.P.*, x, 363–4. A letter written on 22 February confirms that there had been no talk as yet of the dissolution: SP 3/6, fol. 110, P.R.O. (*L.P.*, x, 339).

sodomitic monks and fallen nuns, thus giving Cromwell just what he wanted, but they required editing because they showed the great houses to be at least as bad as the small.[1] This revision accomplished, Cromwell was ready to open the parliamentary debate.

According to the original act the bill was introduced, somewhat surprisingly, into the Lords. This must have occurred about Monday, 6 March. Edward Hall, who tells us nothing about the Commons in 1536, suggests that even those few abbots who attended Parliament were reluctant to oppose the measure:

In this tyme [he wrote] was geven unto the kyng by the consent of the great and fatte abbottes, all religious houses that were of the value of CCC markes and under, in hope that their great monasteries should have continued still. But even at that tyme one said in the Parliament house that these were as thornes, but the great abbottes were putrified old okes and they must nedes follow: and so will other do in Christendom, quod Doctor Stokesley, bishop of London, or many yeres be passed.[2]

This account has the ring of truth, but since Hall was not a member of the Lords it cannot be regarded as necessarily trustworthy.

Neither, unfortunately, can the report of Latimer, who may well have been an eye-witness. He did not record a description of the scene until 1549, when in a sermon preached before Edward VI he referred to the fate of the abbots 'when abbeys were put down. For when their enormities were first read in the Parliament house, they were so great and abominable, that there was nothing but "down with them." '[3] The passage of time may have blurred Latimer's memory, producing the inconsistencies noted by Professor Knowles.[4] Still one is tempted to accept the general tenor of the bishop's story. 'Enormities . . . abominable . . . down with them': it sounds like just the effect which Cromwell had contrived to produce.

If it is uncertain what occurred in the Lords, it is even more

---

[1] These reports or *comperta* should not of course be taken at face value. For a thoughtful discussion of them see Knowles, *Religious Orders in England*, III, 291–303.

[2] Edward Hall, *Hall's Chronicle*, 818–19.

[3] Hugh Latimer, *Sermons*, 123. Latimer was making the point that Edward should not promote chantry priests to bishoprics, as his father had done with some of the abbots.   [4] Knowles, *Religious Orders in England*, III, 292 n. 1.

doubtful how to interpret the unsatisfactory evidence relating to the Commons. This consists mainly of an intriguing but obscure letter sent to the mayor of Plymouth by one Thomas Dorset, vicar of St Margaret Lothbury in the City of London. Dorset claims that Henry himself made an extraordinary appearance in the Lower House:

On Saterdaye in the ymbre weke [i.e. 11 March] the kynges Grace came in amonge the burgesis of the Parliament and delyvered theym a byll and bade theym loke apon it and waye it in conscience, for he wold nott, he saide, have theym passe on it nor on any other thyng because his Grace gevith in the bill, but they to see yf it be for a comyn wele to his subjectis and have an eye thetherwarde, and on Wedynsdaye next he will be there agayne to here their myndes.[1]

Dorset did not specify the contents of the bill; his letter went on to describe the proposed poor law (of which more will appear later), so that some historians have identified that with the bill which Henry introduced.[2] Others have supposed that the king presented the bill for the suppression of the monasteries. As Knowles says, the evidence either way is 'too slender as it stands to take the weight of a firm assertion',[3] but on balance it seems more likely that Henry would have concerned himself with the monasteries. And, although it was certainly unusual for the king to appear personally in the Commons, it seems not improbable that such a confrontation might have been part of Cromwell's plan. By 11 March the bill could well have passed the Lords, and we have Chapuys' word that it cleared the Commons by 18 March.[4] The chronology thus fits perfectly.

Dorset's account holds further interest because it describes other events which may have been associated with Cromwell's propaganda campaign. On Saturday, 12 March, Latimer preached at Paul's Cross, calling the covetous abbots and other superior clergy thieves and knaves. Cranmer also attacked useless church-men, alleging 'that the kynges Grace is at a full poyntt for fryers and chauntry pristis, that they shall awaye all that, savyng them that can preche'. Someone told Cranmer he trusted that they

---

[1] Cottonian MS. Cleopatra E. IV, fols. 131–2, B.M. (*L.P.*, x, 462). The letter was written 13 March; the spring Ember days were 8, 10 and 11 March.
[2] Thus Froude, *History of England*, II, 452.
[3] Knowles, *Religious Orders in England*, III, 299 n. 1.
[4] Chapuys MS., 1536, fols. 58–60 (*L.P.*, x, 494).

might 'serve forthe their lyff tymes, and he said theye shulde serve it out a[t a] cart then for any other service they shuld have bye that'.[1] In fact the act dissolving the religious houses made no reference to chantries: did the archbishop mention them only to emphasize the moderation of the bill under consideration and to suggest that, if it were rejected, more extreme measures would be substituted?

However that may be, the act passed the Commons speedily.[2] To the detailed provisions of the original bill the Lower House added two sections, both intended to support agriculture by requiring that persons who might be granted monastic land maintain husbandry and tillage as had been done in the past.[3] This limitation of enclosure bothered suitors not at all, and by the end of the session at least eight members of the two Houses had asked for a share in the spoils. Some of these—the earl of Essex, Lord Lisle, and Lord LaWarr—had certainly not been present to vote for the dissolution. Others, like the duke of Norfolk, the earl of Westmorland, Sir John Neville, and Sir Piers Edgcombe, may have anticipated a reward for their support. Even Cranmer sought a priory for his brother-in-law.[4]

Despite its carefully drawn details the dissolution statute contained no provision for administration of the confiscated estates. Cromwell had given this matter, too, his attention; he was eager not to have these revenues handled in the Exchequer, where outmoded procedures seemed impossible to reform. Instead, it was decided to establish a new 'Court of the Augmentations of the Revenues of the King's Crown' to take charge of all dissolved houses and their property as well as any other lands acquired by the king. Accordingly a bill was introduced into Parliament—we do not know when, but clearly after the passage of the dissolution statute—erecting the new revenue court, listing its officers, and establishing their duties and perquisites. Although

---

[1] The phrase 'a cart' is puzzling. Evidently it refers to the punishment of beggars prescribed by the poor law of 1531: see above, 123.

[2] Margaret Bowker has drawn attention to the failure of monasteries to name able resident clergy in parishes where they held the patronage: 'If the religious lacked friends at the dissolution, one reason must surely be that they had neglected to make them in the parishes from which the members of parliament were drawn' (*The Secular Clergy in the Diocese of Lincoln, 1495–1520*, 67).

[3] These clauses are written on a separate sheet attached to the original act and signed by the king, presumably to indicate his approval. The act became 27 Henry VIII, c. 28.   [4] *L.P.*, v, 381, 486, 531, 547, 552, 633, 599.

the court represented a bureaucratic department which Professor Elton has described as revolutionary in its efficient independent structure, and although Exchequer officials in particular might have resented its creation, the bill seems to have attracted little opposition. After it was engrossed one clause was erased and a substitute inserted, a rather unusual procedure, and a group of provisos was attached at the end. But these are all technical in nature; they cannot represent compromise to satisfy dissenters.[1]

Several other statutes of 1536 affected the Church. The problem of tithes had come before Parliament during the earlier sessions; it was now settled by an act ordering the full payment of such sums as had been customary, with offenders to be tried by ecclesiastical courts assisted if necessary by the justices of the peace.[2] The act did not apply to London, but another statute ordered its inhabitants to pay according to the rates fixed by proclamation in 1534 until further order.[3]

Other difficulties had arisen from the first fruits act of 1534. That statute had provided no relief from tenths during the year in which churchmen were paying their first fruits. Such double taxation was perhaps never intended; it was clearly abolished in 1536.[4] Another ambiguity concerned the universities and schools, which feared that their officers, masters, and scholars would be required to pay first fruits and tenths. At least two bills requesting exemption were prepared outside of Parliament, one by Oxford and Cambridge, the other by an obscure chantry school in

[1] 27 Henry VIII, c. 27, original act, H.L.R.O.; Elton, *The Tudor Revolution*, 203–19. The anonymous chronicle mentioned earlier credits Audley and Rich with drafting the Augmentations act also: Loades, *Papers of George Wyatt Esquire*, 159. For a thorough study of the bureau see Richardson, *History of the Court of Augmentations*. Richardson says (page 32) that the act creating the new court was 'the penultimate act of the session, passed just before Parliament was dissolved on April 14'. It is true that the Parliament Roll (calendared in *L.P.*, x, 243) lists the Augmentations act as no. 61 out of 62, but this cannot be used as a guide to chronology. The final act on the roll is that establishing new ordinances for Calais, which was probably one of the earliest bills to pass (see below and *L.P.*, x, 336).

[2] 27 Henry VIII, c. 20. The Commons added a proviso that the act would have effect only until ecclesiastical laws should be recodified by the commission of thirty-two. A less significant act, 27 Henry VIII, c. 60, gave collectors of the tenth a slightly longer time in which to present their certificates at the Exchequer.

[3] 27 Henry III, c. 21. The original act is unusually sloppy, suggesting that it was prepared in haste. It does not provide for trial but simply for imprisonment of offenders until they 'have agreed with the . . . curates for the said tithes'.

[4] 27 Henry III, c. 8.

Cornwall.[1] The former was enacted, possibly because it flattered Henry with references to his most excellent goodness, divine charity, and fervent zeal for learning;[2] the latter failed, doubtless because exemption of chantry priests would have been too costly.

Royal revenues were further augmented by a bill ratifying an agreement between the king and William Repps or Rugge, the abbot of St Benet's Hulme, whom Henry intended to make bishop of Norwich. The statute united St Benet's to the bishopric, thus allowing Repps to enjoy his former perquisites, but it alienated to the Crown the lordship and manor of Lynn Episcopi or Bishop's Lynn, together with some smaller properties.[3] The town thus acquired its modern name, King's Lynn. A final statute with religious implications imposed further restrictions on the privilege of sanctuary, requiring sanctuary men to wear badges and to remain within their sanctuaries at night. It is perhaps surprising that sanctuaries were not abolished altogether, considering the complaints against them: having been passed over by the Reformation Parliament they were to continue for nearly another century.[4]

2

An ordinary session lasting only two and a half months might well have been given over entirely to such religious legislation. But the last session of the Reformation Parliament was no ordinary one. Almost as if they realized that extraordinary endeavours were demanded in every field, the members passed seminal economic and social legislation, striking legal reforms, and an unparalleled number of private acts.

The social problems were familiar yet particularly acute: unemployment, vagabonds, beggars, poor relief, enclosures. All

---

[1] SP 1/101, fols. 353–68, and SP 1/104, fols. 151–4, P.R.O. (L.P., x, 246 [11] and 1092). The bill for the universities is elegantly written, with large initial letters.

[2] 27 Henry VIII, c. 42. The statute was made to cover Eton and Winchester as well as the two universities; it required Oxford and Cambridge to establish lectureships in the king's name.

[3] 27 Henry VIII, c. 45. Repps, who had been unusually active in Parliament during the session of 1534, later experienced financial difficulties which may doubtless be traced to this act. He resigned his see, evidently under pressure, in 1550, dying later in the same year.

[4] 27 Henry VIII, c. 19. The right of sanctuary was eliminated by 21 James I, c. 28.

had come before Parliament earlier, and such acts as the poor law of 1531 had been designed to remedy some of them. But the cure proved ineffective; difficulties increased and threatened to be made worse still by the removal of monastic charity. It is perhaps not unreasonable to suggest that the suppression of inefficient monastic charity was closely connected, in the minds of Cromwell and his associates, with the provision of a more modern system operated by the secular government.[1]

Professor Elton has drawn attention to the truly remarkable draft poor law prepared for this session.[2] Its most revolutionary feature is its clear-headed recognition that many able persons who were willing to work found it impossible to obtain employment. Earlier acts merely ordered such sturdy beggars whipped until they took work; the new draft realized that it was the responsibility of the government to provide work when private employers failed. Consequently it proposed a national 'councell to advoide vacabondes', with power to supervise public works: the 'makyng of the haven of Dover, renovacion and reparacion of other havens and harbours for shippes, . . . makyng of the comen high waies and fortresses, skowryng and clensyng of watercourses through the realme'. Unemployed persons were to be summoned to these projects, to be punished—mildly—if they failed to report, and to receive reasonable wages for their work. Those suffering from disease or sickness were to receive free medical care until 'cured and heled, then . . . to be put to labor in the seid workes'. The cost—obviously enormous—was to be borne partly by the king, partly by his subjects through a graduated income tax coupled with contributions gathered in parish churches. The impotent poor, although unable to work, were likewise to be supported by the government, working through local 'censours or overseers of povertie'. Private alms to sturdy beggars were forbidden, under pain of a substantial fine, and all individual relief was discouraged.

We do not know who conceived this comprehensive programme. Clearly the draft did not originate with the government— its form shows that well enough—but equally clearly it found its way into the hands of the parliamentary leaders. Professor Elton

---

[1] On the controversial subject of monastic charities see Knowles, *Religious Orders in England*, III, 264–7.

[2] Elton, 'An Early Tudor Poor Law', 55–67. The draft is in the B.M., Royal MS. 18. c. VI; it is not calendared in *L.P.*

has suggested that it was written by William Marshall, one of Cromwell's protégés, possibly on commission from the secretary.

Whatever its provenance the draft became the basis for the vagabonds act or poor law of 1536. Probably the draft itself was introduced into the Commons: at least Thomas Dorset's letter of 13 March contains a very accurate summary of it.

Sturdye beggars [he wrote] and suche prisonaris as can nott be sett a worke shalbe sett a worke at the kynges charge, some at Dover and some at the place where the water hath broken in on the lande and other mo placis. They yf they fall to idelnes the idelers shalbe had before a justice of the peace and his fawte writen, then yf he be takyn idle agayne in another place he shalbe knowne where his dwellyng is and so at the second monycion he shalbe burnyd in the hande, and yf he fayle the iij^de tyme he shall dye for it. This saide [a] burgis of the Parliament.[1]

But the draft as it stood was too ambitious. Perhaps in Cromwell's office but more likely in a committee of the Commons, the draft was turned into a less radical measure.[2] Although the resulting bill still recognized the necessity of providing employment for sturdy beggars, it abolished the national programme of public works and instead ordered mayors and other officers of towns and parishes to find work for the poor. This course was much less likely to be effective, but it was also much less likely to overtax the central government and its financial resources; the principle that the parish was an important administrative unit was to be extended widely under Elizabeth.[3] Many humanitarian points remained. The act of 1531 had ordered vagrants to be whipped and sent to their places of birth; the new bill allowed them meat, drink, and lodging at intervals of ten miles along these journeys. Lepers and bed-ridden persons were to be relieved wherever they might be. Poor children were to be taught a trade and set to work. Alms were to be gathered locally for the employment of sturdy beggars and maintenance of the impotent, the clergy exhorting the people to give liberally. Common doles were

---

[1] Cottonian MS. Cleopatra E. iv, fols. 131^v–132^r, B.M.

[2] The original act, 27 Henry VIII, c. 25, H.L.R.O., offers the principal reason for thinking that the work was not done by an official clerk: the act is in an uncommon form, written on four leaves stitched together and opening like a book. There are some interlinear additions; the penalty mentioned in section xiv (*S.R.*, III, 561) was inserted in a different colour of ink. On the use of committees see below and *L.P.*, x, 336.   [3] Cf. Holdsworth, *History of English Law*, iv, 155–6.

outlawed, but the poor were allowed to collect broken meats and 'refuce drink'.

The number of provisos attached to the bill probably indicates lively debate in both Houses. The Commons added three clauses, the most important providing that the surplus alms of one parish should be applied to the aid of neighbouring districts. Five provisos originated in the Lords: noblemen and clergy were allowed to give alms as before; friars, shipwrecked mariners, the lame and blind were exempted from the prohibition on accepting private charity. The act as finally passed thus failed to include the visionary national system set out in the draft, but it did enunciate the principle that work had to be found for the unemployed. The significance of this revolutionary change can hardly be exaggerated.

Since enclosures were responsible for some of the vagrants and were often blamed for all of them, the enclosure act of 1536 was closely related to the new poor law. The bill, introduced in the Commons, aimed at preventing rural depopulation by requiring the maintenance of farm houses and of agriculture.[1] This was to be accomplished by giving the king half the profits of land converted from tillage to pasture since 1489 until such time as the land was returned to crops and proper houses were provided for the farm workers. The act was not to take effect until 1538, so that landlords would have time to make the necessary changes. A proviso, evidently added after debate since it is written in a different hand, limits the act to thirteen Midland counties and the Isle of Wight, a useful guide to the areas where depopulation was thought to be most severe.[2] As the king stood to profit from the act, there was some hope that it might prove more effective than its predecessors; in the absence of specialized studies we cannot be sure, but it seems that this act too failed to be enforced with any diligence.

The remaining pieces of economic and social legislation were more limited in their application. A bill 'for reedifying of divers towns' was reasonably comprehensive, covering Nottingham, Ludlow, Bridgnorth, Queenborough, Northampton, Shrewsbury, and Gloucester. Modelled on the act of 1534 for Norwich, it lamented that where 'in times past have been beautiful dwelling

[1] 27 Henry VIII, c. 22.
[2] The counties are Lincoln, Nottingham, Leicester, Warwick, Rutland, Northampton, Bedford, Buckingham, Oxford, Berkshire, Worcester, Hertford, and Cambridge.

houses' there were now 'desolate and void grounds, with pits, cellars, and vaults lying open and uncovered'. The owners of such decayed houses were given three years in which to make repairs, after which the lords from whom the land was held had a further three years. In the last resort the municipal corporations themselves might enter and reedify the properties.[1]

It is surprising that York was not included in this act for urban renewal, since it had instructed its burgesses several years earlier 'to make labour that it may be inacted that all the waists and howling doun of howses boith within the walls of the citie and suburbs of the same shall frome nowefurth be employed and convertyed to the comon use of the same citie unles that the owner of the same ground woll bild them agayn'.[2] But the 'ruin and decay' of York did move Parliament to ratify a reduction of £60 in its annual rent owed to the earl of Rutland. The city had sought this relief since 1532.[3] In London, too, a building in the Cheap had 'fallen down to the ground', creating 'but a void place or plot of ground in the most open and chief place of the same city'. The property had been bequeathed to the mayor and commonalty, with its revenues to be applied toward the maintenance of London bridge; the City now proposed to rebuild, at great cost, and obtained parliamentary remission of certain rent charges.[4]

The maintenance of proper harbours troubled several of the great ports. The Thames itself, 'most commodious and profitable to all the king's liege people', suffered from the 'casting in of dung and other filth' and from unauthorized removal of piles and other material for ballast. As a remedy Parliament ordered offenders fined £5, half to be paid to the king and half to the City.[5] Residents of Plymouth and other ports in Devon and Cornwall complained that the statute of 1532 prohibiting stream works for tin was little regarded; they secured its re-enactment with doubled penalties.[6]

---

[1] 27 Henry VIII, c. 1. [2] Raine, *York Civic Records*, III, 139.

[3] *Ibid.*; 27 Henry VIII, c. 32. Henry See represented York in securing the passage of the act; cf. SP 1/98, fol. 106, P.R.O. (*L.P.*, IX, 705).

[4] 27 Henry VIII, c. 49. The P.R.O. holds a draft, SP 1/101, fols. 384–7 (*L.P.*, X, 246 [14]), evidently prepared by legal counsel.

[5] 27 Henry VIII, c. 18.

[6] 27 Henry VIII, c. 23. A draft, SP 1/101, fols. 326–33, P.R.O. (*L.P.*, X, 246 [8]), was apparently written by the same legal counsel who prepared the act for the plot in the Cheap. The draft requested repeal of the earlier act, 23 Henry VIII, c. 8, and its replacement by a new statute.

Certain crafts and trades, too, promoted the passage of special interest legislation. The fishermen of Norfolk and Suffolk, who alleged that they were utterly impoverished and undone, obtained an act outlawing excessive tolls at Hull.[1] An act 'for true making of woollen cloths' required the clothiers to weave an identifying mark into each cloth and attach to it a lead seal specifying its length.[2] Another act allowed the export of white woollen cloths worth £4 and under and of coloured cloths valued at £3 or less; it modified a statute of 1514 which had prohibited export of cloths worth more than five marks. The justification is interesting as an early proof of inflation: 'wool is risen to a far greater price than it was at the making of the foresaid act, for where a cloth was then commonly sold at five marks [£3 6s. 8d.] it is now sold for four pounds'.[3] The high price of meat necessitated further suspension of acts passed in 1533 and 1534 to require its sale by weight at fixed prices, while scarcity led Parliament to allow the slaughter of calves despite its previous prohibition.[4] Frauds in the exportation of leather were attacked by a statute requiring that tellers and packers of leather be appointed at all ports, as they were in London and Southampton.[5] Finally, a curious experiment in equestrian eugenics required each owner of an enclosed deer-park to keep at least two mares standing above thirteen hands high, these mares to be bred to horses of not less than fourteen hands.[6]

3

Among the problems affecting the English legal system was one which had been discussed in 1529 and 1532 but never resolved. This was the matter of uses and primer seisin. Although the king had failed twice to obtain the legislation which he desired, he was evidently determined that some sort of bill should pass before the Parliament's dissolution. Now, as a result of extraordinary

---

[1] 27 Henry VIII, c. 3.   [2] 27 Henry VIII, c. 12.   [3] 27 Henry VIII, c. 13.

[4] 27 Henry VIII, c. 9, suspending 24 Henry VIII, c. 31, and 25 Henry VIII, c. 1, for four years and 24 Henry VIII, c. 7, for two years. A proclamation to the same effect was issued on 14 April: Hughes and Larkin, *Tudor Royal Proclamations*, I, no. 164.

[5] 27 Henry VIII, c. 14. The government's principal concern was that customs should be paid on the exports.

[6] 27 Henry VIII, c. 6.

court proceedings, he was able to gain more than he had requested earlier.

The story of judicial action relating to uses goes back to the death of Thomas Fiennes, Lord Dacre of the South, in September 1533. Lord Dacre had left a sizeable estate settled in such a way as to rob the Crown entirely of its feudal rights. Cromwell may have had advance notice of the settlement, for Thomas Polstead, a servant of Dacre and a Member of the Commons, was the brother of Cromwell's receiver Henry Polstead.[1] In any case the government set about an attack on Dacre's feoffees which became a test for the validity of all uses. The decision rendered by the judges in the Exchequer Chamber, during the Trinity term of 1534, set aside Dacre's attempt to evade wardship and with it the legality of the use generally.

The Crown's strategy in this matter is of considerable interest. Sir William Holdsworth, who was unaware of these judicial proceedings, thought that Henry gained his desire in Parliament by mounting a sweeping assault on both landowners and lawyers.[2] But E. W. Ives, in suggesting the significance of the Dacre case, has shown that what the government in fact did was to build on the common-law judges' jealousy of the Chancery: since only Chancery would enforce uses, their prevalence tended to derogate the common-law courts as well as the king's feudal prerogative.[3]

The members of Parliament were thus in a desperate plight by 1536. Unless they passed a statute of uses which overrode the judicial decision, the whole mechanism of the use would be valueless and a great many family settlements would fail. Hence the king—and the evidence suggests that Henry himself took the initiative here—could count on success for practically any measure, no matter how drastic.

Three drafts enable us to trace the development of the final bill. Probably first was a measure which provided mainly that uses be subject to the rules of the common law.[4] This might have pleased Henry's allies in the common-law courts, but it was not very advantageous to the Crown financially.[5] Next came the prototype of the

---

[1] Ives, 'The Genesis of the Statute of Uses', 688–691; A. F. Pollard, 'Thomas Cromwell's Parliamentary Lists', 40.
[2] Holdsworth, *History of English Law*, 454.
[3] Ives, 'The Genesis of the Statute of Uses', 686–7.
[4] SP 1/101, fols. 286–291, P.R.O. (*L.P.*, x, 246 [4]), printed in Holdsworth, *History of English Law*, 580–1.   [5] Holdsworth, *History of English Law*, 457.

actual statute, probably prepared by Thomas Wriothesley or another of Cromwell's drafting clerks.[1] Finally, a draft written in a legal script and improved stylistically by Cromwell is virtually identical with the act as passed.[2]

This bill met the problem of uses by proposing a bold innovation: those who were entitled to the use of land were to hold the legal estate, to be seized and deemed in lawful possession. Thus uses were again recognized, but persons who profited from them were made responsible for full feudal incidents. These were not now limited to a third or half of the estate, as had been proposed in earlier sessions, nor was the right to devise land by will restored.

Considering the urgency of the situation, persuasion by preamble was not so necessary as usual. Still the bill began with a section showing that virtually every class of persons suffered from uses: heirs because they might be disinherited; lords because they were deprived of wardships and other feudal incidents; women because they might lose their dowers; the king because he failed to profit from forfeitures; the public because agreements were made craftily and secretly, not in courts of record. This list had probably been suggested by two memoranda, headed 'Inconveniences for sufferance of uses' and 'Damna usum,' which were evidently composed for Audley or Cromwell.[3]

While we know nothing of the bill's reception in Parliament, we can be reasonably sure that it was passed without significant alteration.[4] Its details and its role in the future development of English land law belong more properly to the legal than the parliamentary historian.[5] Our main interest lies in Henry's tactics. Twice frustrated by Parliament, the king seized on an opportunity to press his advantage in the courts, then presented the two Houses with a situation so intolerable that virtually any legislation was preferable. The scheme was brilliant but, as Ives has

[1] SP 1/101, fols. 252–60, P.R.O. (*L.P.*, x, 246 [1]).
[2] SP 1/101, fols. 261–81, P.R.O. (*L.P.*, x, 246 [2]); 27 Henry VIII, c. 10.
[3] SP 1/101, fols. 282–5, P.R.O. (*L.P.*, x, 246 [3]), printed in Holdsworth, *History of English Law*, 577–80.
[4] There are no provisos attached to the original act, 27 Henry VIII, c. 10, H.L.R.O. It is just possible that the final decisions about the statute of uses were made 20 and 21 February: on the 20th Henry conferred with Audley and Cromwell for half an hour in the gallery at Greenwich, and on the 21st all the judges and serjeants-at-law, the barons of the Exchequer, and the king's attorney met with Audley (SP 3/8, fol. 44, P.R.O. [*L.P.*, x, 337]).
[5] See Holdsworth, *History of English Law*, 461–80.

shown, probably unwise. It was partially responsible for the Pilgrimage of Grace, and it produced an unsatisfactory act which had to be modified in 1540 by the statute of wills.[1]

Although the statute of uses complained of secret conveyances, it took no steps to prevent them. This was left to the subsidiary act 'concerning enrollment of bargains and contracts of lands and tenements.'[2] A surviving draft would have given the king power to appoint for each shire or riding special officers who would enter all documents affecting possession of land in a 'roll of record'. Such rolls would be deposited in the Chancery, where they might be searched by anyone willing to pay 6d. All bargains not recorded within forty days were to be void. The enrolling officers were to be given seals; they were allowed to charge set fees and could be tried before a committee of the Council if charged with malfeasance. The draft included a preamble explaining the necessity for such action.[3]

But the act which passed Parliament is less impressive. It lacks a preamble, and it provides for enrolment before existing authorities rather than new officers: the king's courts at Westminster or the justices of the peace within their counties might now record deeds and indentures. A period of six months was allowed for enrolment, and cities which had customarily recorded such transactions were allowed to continue. Holdsworth conjectured that the landowners and lawyers united against the more comprehensive bill, and that the king yielded because his financial interests were not so clearly involved as in the regulation of uses; he lamented the loss of a great opportunity to create a national system of registration.[4] The absence of a preamble suggests that the clauses concerning enrolment were at one time part of the bill for uses but were later removed and watered down for separate passage.

Two further legal reforms were designed to secure stricter punishment for robbers. One was aimed at those who committed theft, piracy, or murder at sea. Such criminals had often escaped because of the civil law applied in admiralty courts; they were now to be tried before royal commissioners, who were instructed

---

[1] Ives, 'The Genesis of the Statute of Uses', 695-697. Ives emphasizes that Henry, not Cromwell, was probably responsible.
[2] 27 Henry VIII, c. 16.   [3] SP 1/101, fols. 303-21, P.R.O. (*L.P.*, x, 246 [6]).
[4] Holdsworth, *History of English Law*, 457-60.

to summon grand juries and treat their indictments according to common law, as if the felonies had been committed on land.[1] The second denied sanctuary or benefit of clergy to servants who stole or embezzled goods worth more than £2 from their masters.[2]

Several important if technical administrative measures were passed in 1536. One of these touched the clerks of the signet and privy seal. Ostensibly designed to insure that these clerks received proper fees for their work, the act was really more significant because it recognized an established bureaucratic procedure and order of seals. Professor Elton has discussed the act and the draft on which it was based at some length; he emphasizes among other things the implication that the signet had now 'gone out of court' or left the king's household to become part of the administration of the State. Since Cromwell was in charge of the signet and privy seal it can hardly be doubted that he was behind the act to regulate their use.[3]

His hand may be discerned, too, in the act for the King's General Surveyors, the chief accounting office in the chamber system of finance. Earlier acts had given the surveyors authority only until the end of the succeeding Parliament; in 1536 the office was made permanent, but it was deprived of the possibility of further revenues. Cromwell wished the General Surveyors to oversee the administration of old Crown lands, but he reserved new acquisitions for his new Court of Augmentations.[4]

Another regulating act, of enormous length, provided new ordinances for Calais. The measure had been prepared by a royal commission, headed by Sir William Fitzwilliam, which surveyed Calais in 1535 and 'founde this towne and marches farre oute of order, and so farre, that it wold greve and petie the hart of any good and true Englisshemen to here or see the same'. The commissioners had examined Lord Lisle, the deputy of Calais, and other officers, but they concluded that they could not 'at this present tyme reforme all thinges which is out of order here, for sum thinges there is that cannot be perfaicted without an acte of Parliament'.[5]

---

[1] 27 Henry VIII, c. 4. A proviso for the Cinque Ports was added in the Lords (original act, H.L.R.O.).   [2] 27 Henry VIII, c. 17.
[3] 27 Henry VIII, c. 11; draft, SP 1/101, fols. 292–302, P.R.O. (*L.P.*, x, 246 [5]); Elton, *Tudor Revolution*, 270–6.
[4] 27 Henry VIII, c. 62; cf. Elton, *Tudor Revolution*, 182–4.
[5] Cottonian MS. Caligula E. II, fols. 213–14, B.M. (*L.P.*, IX, 192).

Although Lord Lisle was greatly interested in the bill, he remained at his post throughout the session: a fortunate circumstance for the historian, since several correspondents in London kept him informed of parliamentary affairs. One of these, Sir William Kingston, wrote a letter which is of unusual interest because of its commentary on the use of committees:

We of the Commen Howse hathe a gud boke for Cales, and it hath bene red and shortly will pass; bot at the redyng ther was won that wold have had it commytted (as the manner ys). And then yf it shuld be comytted, it be commytted to sum blynd men, soe it ys far from our knowlage. Bot I assure your lordshyp it ys a gud boke.[1]

Evidently the bill was not committed—another correspondent reported that it passed the Commons on 18 February, very early in the session.[2] But Kingston's comments imply strongly that referral of bills to committees was common practice by 1536. In the absence of journals we have little evidence on such procedural points, and chance references like Kingston's are especially valuable.

The bill itself begins with a brief preamble explaining the king's intention to improve the administration and fortification of Calais after a period of great decay and neglect. Succeeding sections list the officers for Calais, with oaths for chief administrators and tables of fees for soldiers, archers, masons, and carpenters; the act deals also with the decay of houses, the keeping of wells, the taking of tolls, the paying of customs, and the sale of corn, cattle, bread, beef, and beer. Finally, there is the provision that Calais shall send two burgesses to Parliament, one to be chosen by the deputy and council, the other by the mayor and burgesses.[3] Had efficient administrators governed in accordance with the act, and had they received support from London, England's continental toehold might have lasted a good deal longer than it did.

4

The granting of burgesses to Calais and the reassertion of royal power in liberties and franchises show that Henry and his

---

[1] SP 3/6, fol. 20, P.R.O. (*L.P.*, x, 336).   [2] SP 3/8, fol. 44, P.R.O. (*L.P.*, x, 337).
[3] 27 Henry VIII, c. 63. The act occupies eighteen folio pages in *S.R.*, III, 632–50, sixteen pages in MS. (original act, H.L.R.O.).

advisers wished to incorporate these areas more fully into the fabric of English life and government. The same policy was extended, with much more significant results, to Wales.

The acts of 1534 had made a start by ordering stricter law enforcement, in accordance with some of the principles of English law. These measures had been supported and enforced by Rowland Lee, bishop of Lichfield and president of the Council in Wales. Early in 1536 the king asked Lee to devise further 'articles for the helping of Wales', but Lee could see no necessity for drastic change. He recommended only two acts, one compelling negligent or corrupt legal officers in the Welsh lordships to compensate parties who had been wronged by lack of justice, the other prohibiting the discharge of felons, by fine or otherwise, except in open court.[1]

Such limited reforms had little appeal to Henry and Cromwell. They had decided, probably well before the opening of Parliament, that Wales should be divided into counties, on the English pattern. These would be represented in Parliament and governed by its laws; order would be maintained by justices of the peace and other officers as in the English shires.

By 12 March Lee had heard that 'the Kinges pleasure was to make Wales shireground and to have justices of the peace and off gaole delyvery as in Englande'. He was aghast. Shiring brought no benefits: the areas of Wales which had been shired, Merioneth and Cardigan, were 'as ill as the worste parte'. If juries of Welshmen were empanelled, one thief would try another. 'And . . . for justices of the peace and of gaole delyvery to be in Wales, I thinke hit not moche expedient, for there be very fewe Welshemen in Wales above Brecknock that may dispende ten pounde[s in] lande, and to saye truthe their discretion [is] lesse then their landes. . . . Wolde God I were with you oone houre', he wrote to Cromwell, 'to declare my mynde therein at full.'[2]

But Cromwell was not moved. Three bills had been prepared and were probably already in Parliament when Lee wrote. The most important ordained that Wales should be 'incorporated, united, and annexed to and in this . . . realm of England', so that the singular usages and customs of the Welsh might be extirpated and English law perfectly observed. Five new counties were

---

[1] SP 1/102, fols. 63–4, P.R.O. (*L.P.*, x, 330).
[2] SP 1/102, fols. 199–200, P.R.O. (*L.P.*, x, 453).

erected—Monmouth, Brecon, Radnor, Montgomery, and Denbigh—and some existing counties were extended to include adjacent lordships or feudal enclaves. Welsh lands were to be held according to the rules of English tenure; joint citizenship was decreed; all courts were ordered to use the English tongue.[1] Parliamentary representation was to be supplied by two knights for the county of Montgomery, one for every other county, and one burgess for each county town except Merioneth. Twenty-four Welshmen were thus added to Parliament: a very substantial number considering the sparse population of Wales.[2] One of the subsidiary bills provided for the appointment of justices of the peace and of gaol delivery; the other prohibited unreasonable tolls and tributes or seizure of cattle in Welsh forests.[3] All three bills were introduced into the Commons, where there was evidently serious debate since a proviso was added to exempt some areas from the English principle of primogeniture.[4]

While the lasting importance of these measures can hardly be overestimated, some writers have exaggerated the enlightened liberalism and far-sighted vision of their authors.[5] Much more immediate considerations were probably responsible: the authority of Parliament had to be extended to Wales if the Welsh monasteries were to be dissolved under the statute of 1536, and the anomalous position of the Church in Wales had to be resolved by the legal extension of royal supremacy. Whatever its final results, the great reorganization of Wales and its annexation to the realm of England may thus be seen as an inevitable part of Henry VIII's ecclesiastical reformation.[6]

---

[1] This provision was repealed in 1942.

[2] 27 Henry VIII, c. 26; cf. Rowse, *The Expansion of Elizabethan England*, 52-4; Rees, 'The Union of England and Wales', 27-100. Rees' article includes a carefully annotated transcript of the statute as well as an excellent map. The *Return of Members of Parliament* suggests that some of the Welsh counties and boroughs did not avail themselves regularly of the privilege of sending members.

[3] 27 Henry VIII, c. 5, c. 7.

[4] 27 Henry VIII, c. 26, original act, H.L.R.O.; cf. Rees, 'The Union of England and Wales', 70. It was common practice in Wales to divide land among heirs.

[5] Cf. Williams, 'The Union of England and Wales', 47-117.

[6] This view has been put forward by Rees, 'The Union of England and Wales', 44-5. It should be noted that the acts of 1536 established the general principle of Welsh annexation but omitted many necessary administrative details. These were supplied by an act of 1543, 34 & 35 Henry VIII, c. 26. On the whole matter of union with Wales see the Cambridge dissertation (1965) by P. R. Roberts.

5

In 1536 Parliament was required to deal with an enormous quantity of private legislation. While statute-counting may not be the most analytical method of assessing parliamentary accomplishment, some interest attaches to sheer bulk of legislation. On this basis only one session of the Tudor period surpasses our present gathering, and one ties with it. Thirty-five private bills were passed in the last session of the Reformation Parliament, thirty-five in the freshly elected Parliament of June 1536. The highest figure, rather surprisingly, is thirty-eight for Henry VII's Parliament of 1495. No Elizabethan session approached this volume of work.[1]

As one would expect, few of the private bills are of general interest. A handful, such as the ordinances for Calais and the bills for York and London, have already been mentioned. Most of the others concern land: they sanction exchanges, ratify jointures, and generally assure that the beneficiaries of the acts shall enjoy their holdings in spite of legal ambiguities or obstacles. The king himself stood to benefit from ten of these bills, which granted him among other things the manor of Wimbledon, Suffolk Place in Southwark, and, in reversion, all the properties of the earl of Northumberland.[2] Queen Anne's possession of lands in Essex and Northamptonshire was confirmed for the term of her life: not, in the event, very long.[3] Others who secured the passage of similar bills were Norfolk's sons Lord William Howard and Lord Thomas Howard, Lord Chancellor Audley, Lady Vaux, Lady Clifford, Sir Charles Willoughby, Sir Thomas Pope, Sir Piers Dutton, and a London mercer, Richard Hill.[4]

Three bills call for fuller notice.[5] The first charged that Sir Thomas More, before committing his 'abominable and detestable high treasons', contrived to convey away his lands in Chelsea so that they should not be forfeited to the king. Parliament now frustrated his scheme, granting the property to the Crown. Another noteworthy measure was a bill of attainder against John Lewis, who had taken part in a Welsh revolt, broken out of

[1] These figures are based on *S.R.*, II, III, and IV.
[2] 27 Henry VIII, cc. 29, 31, 33, 34, 38, 39, 50, 52, 53, 61.
[3] 27 Henry VIII, cc. 41, 51.
[4] 27 Henry VIII, cc. 30, 35, 36, 40, 46, 48, 54, 56, 57.
[5] 27 Henry VIII, cc. 37, 58, 59.

prison, and committed heinous murders. Before Lewis was executed for treason his hands were to be cut off, as a punishment for the murders and an example to other mischievously disposed persons. A final act pardoned Henry VIII's wild and improvident brother-in-law, Charles Brandon, duke of Suffolk, and released him from certain debts owed to the king.

It should not be thought that these private bills were passed as a matter of routine, without close examination by Parliament. We know of some bills which were not enacted, perhaps because they were rejected by one of the Houses.[1] At least half of the successful measures contain provisos or other changes originating with the Lords or Commons. The act to make Henry VIII heir to the earl of Northumberland, for instance, includes seven sheets of provisos, each written in a different hand, added by the Lower House to protect the rights of persons who had purchased lands from the earl. The bill for Sir Piers Dutton and others, which confirms a settlement made by the king after a Star Chamber inquiry into a disputed inheritance, is signed by Sir Roger Cholmeley, William Horwood, William Portman, and Henry See: all lawyers who sat in the Commons. Presumably they had served as members of a committee to examine the bill. It may be interesting to note, too, that some of the private bills are cast in the form of petitions to the king; these and some others bear Henry's signature, possibly affixed to indicate royal approval before the bills were sent to Parliament.[2]

6

A good many members may have heard the sermon preached in the Chapel Royal on Passion Sunday, less than two weeks before the end of the session. John Skip, Queen Anne's scholarly chaplain and almoner, spoke at length about the rapidity of change in the Church and commonwealth, which he said caused great murmuring among the people. He commended the example of 'a certen nacion called Locrenses,' which had been 'moych trow-

---

[1] These are the bills to exempt chantry schoolmasters from first fruits, mentioned above, to reform Sherbourne hospital, near Durham (SP 1/96, fols. 206–7, P.R.O. [L.P., x, 401]), and to limit the activities of those who purveyed fish to the king and noblemen (SP 1/239, fols. 278–81, P.R.O. [L.P., Addenda, 1, Part i, 1049]). Unfortunately it is not certain whether these bills were actually introduced or not.

[2] Original acts, H.L.R.O.

bulled and vexed withe innovacions and alteracions in civill matters'. After alteration upon alteration and statute upon statute they devised a cure: anyone who introduced a bill into their Parliament was required to wear a rope about his neck, 'and the peple shuld lay their handes apon the roepe to th'intentt [that] when the bill was redde they myght pull the roepe and straungle hym yff they perceved that hitt weyre agaynste their commyn welthe'. Thus they were delivered from unnecessary alterations for a hundred years and more.

Someone seems to have taken offence at the tale, complaining that Skip had slandered the king, his councillors, and the entire Parliament. Preparations were made for the preacher's interroga- tion, and he was required to submit a copy of his sermon for examination. This included his pseudo-history of the Locrenses, but also comments on Parliament which were decidedly flattering. Nothing was done in the English Parliament but for the general good, Skip asserted; its members were 'the moest noble men of this realme, the moeste prudentt and awncient fathers, the moeste hyght lerned men'. Parliamentary procedure could hardly have been better:

There is no onquietnes, no tumultuus fashion, their is no cheking or tawntyng of eny man for shoyng his mynde, their is no man that will stande up and saye that hitt is the pleyssuire of any person that this or this hitt shuld be, their spekithe nott paste one att ons, and yff his reson be good hitt is alowed. And yff hitt be otherwise he is answered with gentle maner and fashion. Their is no man spekithe for eny carnall affections or lucre of the promocions of this worlde. Butt all thing is done for zeill of the commyn weilthe. This I thincke and other men ought to thyncke the same.

Evidently this text laid criticism to rest. No action was taken against Skip. Indeed he weathered the storm of Anne's fall well, receiving preferments which culminated in the bishopric of Hereford. The incident is unimportant, but Skip's description of the decorous debates is one of our valuable scraps of evidence about early Tudor parliamentary procedure.[1]

7

Convocation played no part in the government's plans, and its

---

[1] SP 6/1, fols. 8–11; SP 1/103, fols. 78–87, P.R.O. (*L.P.*, x, 615 [1–5]).

session which began on 5 February was of no significance. So far as we know the only subject to be discussed was payment of the remaining portion of the £100,000 for which the clergy had been granted their pardon in 1531. It is difficult to see how examination of the collectors and exhortation to render accounts expeditiously could have consumed fourteen meetings of the clergy, but that is what our very fragmentary records suggest.[1] The session of Convocation which was to begin in June would be of considerably greater importance, partly because Cromwell appeared personally to exercise his authority as vicegerent.[2] He could have done so equally well earlier; evidently he had no desire to work through Convocation in February, and the churchmen had no heart for independent action.

Some of the bishops were kept busy in other ways. Cranmer, Latimer, and Shaxton spent a good deal of time examining John Lambert, whose heretical views had aroused the duke of Norfolk and the earl of Essex. Lambert had been imprisoned by Warham in 1532 but had been released on the old archbishop's death; he was now in trouble for having said that it was sinful to pray to saints. The bishops agreed that such prayers were unnecessary but refused to call them sinful; even Latimer, whose views most nearly accorded with Lambert's, was 'most extreme' against him. Finally, in exasperation, the bishops sent him to be dealt with by Audley.[3] He was later, in 1538, to be examined by the king himself before being executed for his faith.

The leading bishops also preached at Paul's Cross during the session of Parliament and Convocation. As we have seen, Cranmer set the tone with his sermon on 6 February. Hilsey and Longland followed; on 27 February the conservative Tunstall proved that he had abandoned all resistance to Henry's policies in an appearance before nine bishops and the public. Shaxton, Latimer, and Salcott concluded the campaign on the first three Sundays of March.[4]

---

[1] Wilkins, *Concilia*, III, 802–3. C.C. 306 contains nothing for this session. According to Wilkins, Convocation was not dissolved until 24 April, on the basis of a royal writ dated 14 April. While it would be unusual for a meeting of Convocation to occur so long as ten days after the dissolution of Parliament, such procedure may be explained by the intrusion of Easter week, during which the churchmen could not have held their final meeting.

[2] *Ibid.* 803; Lehmberg, 'Supremacy and Vicegerency', 233.

[3] Ridley, *Thomas Cranmer*, 94–5, based on Thomas Dorset's letter, Cottonian MS. Cleopatra E. IV, fol. 131, B.M.   [4] Ridley, *Thomas Cranmer*, 98.

8

The Parliament ended, its members were ordered to their homes so that they could assist the king in defending the realm and in collecting the subsidy which they had voted in 1534.[1] While some of the Lords and Commons doubtless enjoyed the amenities of London, most of them must have needed little urging.

Soon after the dissolution the chief officers of Parliament were rewarded by the king. Audley, who had served well in both Houses, received an annuity of £300 and a dissolved priory in Colchester.[2] Speaker Wingfield was paid £100, Chief Justices Fitzjames and Baldwin £40 and 40 marks respectively, Christopher Hales and Richard Rich (the king's attorney and solicitor) also 40 marks each. Another judge, Sir Anthony Fitzherbert, and two of the king's serjeants, John Hynd and Humphrey Brown, received 30 marks; Robert Ormeston, under-clerk of Parliament, £10; the lord chancellor's clerks, £5; the assistants of Edward North, clerk of Parliament, 'and other for their paynes this Parliament', 20 marks.[3] Ordinary members of the Lower House were left to secure their wages from their constituencies, if they could; peers might only hope that they would be remembered when the monastic spoils came to be distributed.

It would be pleasant to record that Henry dispersed his Lords and Commons with special thanks for their uncommon services. Unfortunately the surviving records for April, 1536, tell us nothing about the end of the session, although they cover a myriad of other subjects, from diplomacy to—literally—kitchen sinks.[4] Chapuys did not write to his master until 21 April, by which time he was so full of his meetings with the king and Cromwell that he had little interest in Parliament; Edward Hall, to whom we might have looked for an eye-witness account, either did not attend the concluding ceremonies or thought them not worthy of mention.

---

[1] Additional MS. 9835, fol. 22ᵛ, B.M. The proclamation is undated but probably should be assigned to April 1536. It is difficult to see why it would have been issued in May 1535, as Hughes and Larkin suggest (*Tudor Royal Proclamations*, I, no. 156), since there was no session of Parliament in that year.

[2] *L.P.*, x, 1015 (28, 29).

[3] SP 1/103, fols. 58–9, P.R.O. (*L.P.*, x, 598). These disbursements are mingled with others made by Cromwell at the same time, and it is impossible to be certain whether any other items refer to services in Parliament.   [4] *L.P.*, x, 674.

But we know from the fragmentary Lords' Journals that Henry VIII was present for the final meeting of at least ten sessions during his reign, and that the royal presence was regarded as traditional by Elizabeth's time.[1] Let us, then, supply in the probability of imagination what we are denied in the certainty of record.

We may picture the Lords' chamber on 14 April: perhaps in the morning, since it was Good Friday, although the concluding ceremony more often took place in the afternoon. The Lords, resplendent in their robes, are seated on their benches; the king, his crown imperial glittering, is on the throne; the Commons, led by their Speaker, crowd in behind the bar. Wingfield is heard first, then the lord chancellor, announcing the king's assent to the Parliament's acts. Finally Henry himself, or Audley in his name, dismisses both Houses with profound thanks. The work of the Reformation Parliament was complete.

[1] *L.J.*, 1, 8, 42, 56, 81–2, 101, 124–5, 161, 197, 234, 281; Neale, *The Elizabethan House of Commons*, 419–30.

THE TOTAL REFORMATION

The Reformation Parliament earned its name by its ecclesiastical legislation: this was the Parliament which ushered in the Reformation of the Church of England.[1] No one, whether apologist or detractor, would seriously question the importance of this work. It was dramatic at the time; it gave a great institution its continuing shape. But our survey has revealed other sides to the reforming activity of Parliament. In economic regulation, in social conscience, in legal procedure, in administration and government finance: in all these areas Parliament acted as an organ of reform and renewal. The Parliament which met from 1529 to 1536 could have been linked with reformation had it left religion completely untouched.

It may be useful to reconsider the main areas of legislation one by one, beginning with the ecclesiastical statutes. These may be seen as the product of three stages in governmental policy. In the first, which spanned the sessions of 1529 and 1531, no clear-cut programme of dealing with the Church or the pope had been evolved. Because of this lack of leadership, the Commons were free to chart their own course to an unusual degree, and we may confidently ascribe the anti-clerical legislation of 1529, regulating probate, mortuaries, and non-residency, to the initiative of the Lower House itself. There was more royal direction behind the pardon of the clergy in 1531, with its admission of royal supremacy in the Church. But here again the government seems to have been drifting. In all likelihood Henry cared more for the £100,000 than for the title granted him by the Convocation of Canterbury; if he prized the headship it was for egotistical reasons, not

---

[1] Although the term Reformation was in use by the end of the sixteenth century, the name 'Reformation Parliament' does not seem to have become common until the early twentieth. Froude, searching for an identification when his narrative reached the last session, called this only 'the same old parliament of 1529, which had commenced the struggle with the bishops' (*History of England*, II, 438), and in 1881 William Stubbs termed it 'the Long Parliament of 1529–1536' (*Seventeen Lectures*, 269, 275). But in 1906 Fisher used 'The Reformation Parliament' as a chapter heading in *The History of England*, 289. Amos had published his little-known *Observations on the Statutes of the Reformation Parliament* in 1859.

because he appreciated the use which he might make of it.

By an extraordinary stroke of luck these bills, passed almost by chance, proved enormously useful when an effective policy was devised. Thomas Cromwell became the dominant figure during this second stage, lasting from 1532 to 1534, and the king's divorce became the determining factor in all legislation touching the Church. The chief measures of 1532—the conditional restraint of annates and the submission of the clergy—stemmed from the conscious desire to put pressure upon the pope while weakening the power and resolve of the clergy within England. Here the anti-clerical sentiment of the Commons could be utilized; indeed the Supplication against the Ordinaries may have been a more or less spontaneous outgrowth of the Commons' discussions, helpful though it was in advancing Cromwell's plans. When all attempts at diplomacy proved fruitless the way was fully prepared for the great appeals act of 1533: the English clergy, having already acknowledged royal supremacy, were in no position to resist. The legislation of 1534 completed this phase by cutting away any remaining ties with the papacy and by establishing the constitution of the autonomous English Church.

In 1536 religious policy moved into a third stage. In this post-divorce period the king's advisers began the confiscation of ecclesiastical properties which were deemed superfluous, and they instigated an attack on certain tenets of orthodox theology. This phase was only beginning when the Reformation Parliament was dissolved; the suppression of the smaller monasteries was but a foretaste of the greater changes which were to come.

It is hard to exaggerate the importance of the general antipathy towards the clergy in making these sweeping changes possible. There was, of course, some opposition in Parliament and some pressure on parliamentarians: how much, we will soon consider. Still, few regretted Henry's actions against churchmen. 'Thei digged the diche that thei be now fallen in', Sir Thomas Elyot wrote.[1] His words might be taken as the motto of the bills to reconstitute the Church.

Economic and social measures exceeded the ecclesiastical laws in bulk and nearly matched them in importance. Two points stand out in the economic legislation: first, the amount of governmental regulation and paternalism; second, the attempt to

[1] SP 1/75, fol. 81, P.R.O.

deal with rising prices, especially of meat. It was evidently the workers in various crafts who desired statutory protection, not the government which wished to prescribe rules. Thus the acts dealing with wool, worsteds, leather, pewter, printing, baking, and brewing sprang mainly from petitions and were intended to benefit established craftsmen rather than the public. On the other hand, the laws designed to ensure an adequate supply of mature cattle and to set reasonable prices for beef, veal, mutton, cheese, butter, and chickens represent an attempt by the government itself to deal with the scarcity which had driven prices up rapidly since the beginning of Henry's reign. A recent study has shown that the price of a composite unit of foodstuffs very nearly doubled between 1509 and 1532 while wages, at least those of building craftsmen in southern England, remained stable.[1] As we have noted, these acts proved unsuccessful and were suspended almost immediately, first by proclamation and then by statute. No doubt royal advisers were trying to grapple with modern market conditions while armed only with the inflexible and unenforceable concept of the just price. But the attempt is the important thing. Rather than turn their backs on economic distress, the councillors and parliamentarians recognized a responsibility for directing the economy, however outmoded the theories and inadequate the methods available to them.

Much the same thing must be said about the social legislation of the Reformation Parliament, most of which was also intended to alleviate economic pressure. The statute of apparel should have curbed conspicuous consumption; the acts against enclosure and depopulation should have limited the extent to which sheep were allowed to 'eat up men'; the poor laws of 1531 and 1536 should have provided some solution to the problems of vagrancy, unemployment, and genuine poverty. Given the magnitude of the tasks and the limited resources with which a sixteenth-century government could tackle them, we ought not to be surprised if the success of the acts was limited. The significant thing, especially in the case of the poor law, was the principle that some agency of the

---

[1] E. H. Phelps Brown and Sheila V. Hopkins, 'Seven Centuries of the Prices of Consumables, Compared with Builders' Wage-Rates', in E. M. Carus-Wilson, ed., *Essays on Economic History*, II, 179–96, especially page 194. The index figures are 92 for 1509, 179 for 1532. Admittedly both are exceptional, and the general trend of prices did not rise so rapidly. For further statistics see Joan Thirsk, ed., *The Agrarian History of England and Wales*, IV, 815–70.

people had to be responsible for relieving the destitute. We should not be far off in tracing the development of national social services and public welfare programmes to these tentative beginnings in the 1530s.

A similar interest attaches to the acts for rebuilding in decayed areas of London, Norwich, and other towns. Without exaggerating their modernity or labelling them schemes for city planning and urban renewal one can take their main point, that unenterprising private owners could not be allowed to blight the safety and beauty of urban areas permanently. Neither could ruinous bridges, unpaved highways, or unauthorized interference with watercourses be permitted to hinder the king's subjects in their travel and commerce. The general good came first.

Curiously enough, bills altering the English law drew more opposition than ecclesiastical or social reforms. No doubt the reason was that legal changes were likely to touch individual laymen more closely. Perhaps the most hotly contested measures of the Parliament, and two of the most important, were the treason act and the statute of uses. We have seen the evidence that 'there was never such a sticking at the passing of any act in the Lower House as was at the passing' of the treason bill. If the length of time required for passage is any guide, the regulation of uses was even more bitterly opposed, since bills to this purpose were introduced in the first session, discussed in the third, and accepted only in the last. Here we see the Commons asserting their independence, resisting measures which were avidly desired by the king but regarded as menacing by his subjects. Only after adroit political manipulation did the government succeed.

By contrast, administrative reforms seem to have passed with little difficulty. The main point here is the significance of the changes which they effected. Cromwell's acts for the General Surveyors and the Court of Augmentations heralded a new system (if a transitory one) of financial administration. The provisions for better justice in Wales and its subsequent annexation brought greater unity to the king's domains, as did the bills resuming liberties and regulating Calais. Not the least important feature of these acts, and one which affected Parliament itself, was the extension of parliamentary representation to the Welsh and the burghers of Calais.

Other statutes could be cited, but they would merely enlarge our picture of a Parliament concerned with reform in virtually every area of English government and society. Let us, instead, revert to the question of royal control and parliamentary subservience.

As we come full circle we should perhaps remind ourselves of the charges that the Reformation Parliament was 'parcially chosen', bribed, parasitic, and unrepresentative.[1] We have already dismissed some of these complaints, but we have not attempted to assess the relationship between the king and the two Houses. There was no real question of packing the Commons: what of politicking, propaganda, and pressure? What of the Lords, and what of Convocation?

Without question Convocation was treated very harshly. Its early sessions gave some promise of ecclesiastical reform from within. This was frustrated, partly by Parliament's statutory regulation and partly by royal interference. In 1531 and 1532 naked threats were used to secure the Pardon and Submission of the Clergy, and in 1533 pressure was again applied in the matter of Henry's divorce. Later sessions show us a Convocation which had lost contact with the vital religious issues and sunk into inactivity or ineffectual talk about heresy. The decline of Convocation must be regarded as one of the most important phenomena of our period.

Now for Parliament. Let us take first the interrelated questions of membership and attendance. As we have seen, little or no attempt was made to dictate the original choice of knights of the shire or burgesses. By-elections seem to have been similarly free from interference. There was no mass creation of peers to alter the complexion of the Lords. Only in the case of the bishops were opponents of royal policy gradually replaced by Henrician nominees. But although the presence of these reforming bishops in Parliament proved convenient, it was not the determining factor in their appointments. By tradition the king had the choice of bishops, and he naturally named men who would administer the Church in accord with his policies. The fact that these bishops might also assist him in the Lords—or in Convocation—was only incidental.

The actual attendance of members is another matter. We have considerable evidence to suggest that, especially after Cromwell's

[1] See above, Ch. 2.

rise, opponents of the king were encouraged to stay away from Parliament while supporters were persuaded to attend. In the Lower House the case of Sir George Throckmorton offers the best example of such pressure. Throckmorton opposed the conditional restraint of annates, the appeals act, and the king's marriage to Anne Boleyn. Advised by Cromwell to abandon this meddling in politics, he stayed away from the earlier of the 1534 gatherings but may have found courage to speak against the treason bill in the second session. After the Pilgrimage of Grace he was in further trouble and spent some time in the Tower before retiring to his house at Coughton Court. Sir Marmaduke Constable, another member of the Queen's Head Tavern group, likewise absented himself from Parliament in January 1534. Some others may have feared to take their seats in the later sessions: one wonders in particular about William Roper and Robert Fisher.[1] Lack of evidence may cover a good deal of intimidation.

We know a bit more about the situation in the Lords. Fear or pressure caused Archbishop Lee and Bishops Fisher, Tunstall, and Nix to remain away from Parliament in January 1534. Lord Darcy was similarly absent. Two years later Lee and Darcy stayed home again, as did Northumberland, Hussey, and most of the abbots. Conversely, the king's friends may have been prodded into attending: our main evidence is Cromwell's stated resolve to grant few licences for absence in 1536.

It seems fair to say then that some of the king's chief antagonists were frightened into abstaining from opposition in Parliament. But let us not regard the matter of pressure on individuals as being more serious or unusual than it was. It is difficult to conceive a legislative assembly operating without some sort of pressure: in important divisions today the government would surely attempt to secure the attendance of every possible supporter, and it might well suggest that favour or promotion would be withheld from persistent critics. During Elizabeth's reign (to come to the Tudor period) the Puritan William Strickland was once forbidden to attend Parliament, and Peter Wentworth was thrice imprisoned. *Mutatis mutandis,* the actions of Henry VIII and Cromwell were scarcely different.

Intimidation of an entire House, or a majority of its members, should be considered separately. Here again we can cite some

---

[1] Robert Fisher was spared the problem of the last session, since he died in 1535.

reasonably clear cases and infer the existence of others. In 1531, after the affair of Fisher's cook, Henry appeared personally in the Lords to emphasize his interest in the barbarous act against poisoners. In 1532 he probably forced a novel division in the Commons, implying pointedly that those who opposed the annates bill opposed the welfare of the realm. In the same session he threatened to 'serche out the extremitie of the law' if the Commons rejected his bill for primer seisin and uses. In 1534 he must have applied pressure—we do not know just how—to secure the passage of the treason act. In 1536 he created a legal situation which forced Parliament to accept the statute of uses, and he 'came in among the burgesis' to deliver what was probably the bill for the dissolution of the monasteries. More subtly, he worked through Cromwell and Cranmer to create an atmosphere favourable to the dissolution.

In these cases lie the tangible grounds for believing that the king seriously interfered with Parliament. But this charge too must be considered in context. Let us compare Henry's activities with Elizabeth's, of which Sir John Neale has told us so much. Henry's daughter repeatedly refused to hear of legislation fixing the succession: it was monstrous, she said, for the feet to direct the head. In 1556 she stopped consideration of a Puritan bill for 'sound religion'. In 1571 she vetoed a much-desired bill requiring attendance at Communion. In 1572 she withstood concerted parliamentary pressure for the execution of Mary, Queen of Scots. In 1581 she forced Parliament to tone down a bill against Catholics. In 1587 she confiscated the famous Puritan 'Bill and Book'. In 1589 she commanded Parliament to keep its hands off the prerogative. In 1601 she undercut an attempt to legislate against monopolies.

Elizabeth prevented her Parliaments from enacting some measures which they ardently desired. Henry prodded Parliament into passing some bills which members mistrusted. There is a difference, but not a vast one. And, whatever pressure there may have been, we have no reason to think that a majority of members remained strenuously opposed to any bill which passed Parliament.

If this analysis be correct, the story of the Reformation Parliament should be read in terms of partnership and co-operation rather than antagonism and opposition. In most areas the king and his subjects desired very much the same thing. They wished to reject outmoded institutions and procedures, replacing them with what they hoped would be effective new schemes. Without question hesitations, tensions, and angry words arose as these plans were enacted. Many of them were controversial: reforms usually are. But through the haze of controversy, pressure, and self-seeking gleams the ultimate goal of king and ministers, Lords and Commons. As John Skip had asserted, they acted out of 'zeill [for] the commyn weilthe'.[1] They sought the general good of the realm, the common weal of England.

[1] See above, Ch. 10.

APPENDIX A

ATTENDANCES OF LORDS SPIRITUAL, FIFTH SESSION, 1534

	Days Present
Archbishop of Canterbury (Thomas Cranmer)	41
Bishop of Bath and Wells (John Clerk)	40
Abbot of Winchcombe (Richard Munslow or Ancelme)	40
Abbot of Waltham (Robert Fuller)	39
Abbot of Hyde (John Salcot or Capon)	38
Abbot of Westminster (William Boston or Benson)	37
Abbot of St Augustine's Canterbury (John Essex or Focke)	35
Abbot of St Albans (Robert Catton)	35
Abbot of Battle (John Hamond)	33
Bishop of Winchester (Stephen Gardiner)	31
Abbot of St Benet's Hulme (William Repps or Rugge)	27
Bishop of London (John Stokesley)	26
Abbot of Colchester (Thomas Marshall or Beche)	25
Abbot of Bury St Edmund's (John Melford)	24
Abbot of Reading (Hugh Cook or Faringdon)	23
Abbot of Shrewsbury (Thomas Butler)	21
Abbot of Cirencester (John Blake)	15
Bishop of Lincoln (John Longland)	7
Bishop of Llandaff (George de Athequa)	4
Abbot of Burton (William Edys)	4
Abbot of Glastonbury (Richard Whiting)	1
Abbot of Tavistock (John Penryn)	1
All others	0

APPENDIX B

ATTENDANCES OF LORDS TEMPORAL, FIFTH SESSION, 1534

	Days Present	
Arundel, Earl of	*Days Present*	45
Oxford, Earl of		44
Wiltshire, Earl of		42
Rochford, Lord		41
Latimer, Lord		41
Ferrers, Lord		40
St John of Jerusalem, Prior of (Sir William Weston)		39
Exeter, Marquis of		39
Bergavenny, Lord		39
Dacre of Gisland, Lord		39
Richmond, Duke of		38
Norfolk, Duke of		38
Sussex, Earl of		38
Talbot, Lord		38
Morley, Lord		37
Daubeney, Lord		37
Windsor, Lord		36
Westmorland, Earl of		35
Montague, Lord		33
Lumley, Lord		33
Huntingdon, Earl of		30
Cumberland, Earl of		29
Mountjoy, Lord		29
FitzWarin, Lord		28
Rutland, Earl of		27
Powys, Lord		27
Berkeley, Lord		26
Maltravers, Lord		26
Shrewsbury, Earl of		25
Mordaunt, Lord		25
Suffolk, Duke of		24
Cobbam, Lord		23
Sandys, Lord		23

Derby, Earl of	22
Conyers, Lord	19
Vaux, Lord	18
Northumberland, Earl of	16
Worcester, Earl of	15
Grey de Wilton, Lord	12
Bray, Lord	12
Scrope, Lord	10
Zouch, Lord	7
Burgh, Lord	4
Monteagle, Lord	2
All others	0

BIBLIOGRAPHY

I. MANUSCRIPT SOURCES

London
  British Museum
    Additional Manuscripts
    Cottonian Manuscripts
    Harleian Manuscripts
    Royal Manuscripts

  House of Lords Record Office
    Lords' Journal
    Original Acts
    Parchment Collection

  Public Record Office
    C 54: Chancery, Close Rolls
    C 65: Chancery, Rolls of Parliament
    E 175: Exchequer, King's Remembrancer, Parliamentary and
           Council Proceedings
    KB 8: King's Bench, Baga de Secretis
    KB 9: King's Bench, Ancient Indictments
    SP 1: State Papers, Henry VIII
    SP 2: State Papers, Henry VIII, folio
    SP 3: Lisle Papers
    SP 6: Theological Tracts

Oxford
  Christ Church
    MS. 306, Records of Convocation

Vienna
  Haus-, Hof-, und Staatsarchiv
    Dispatches of Eustace Chapuys, Staatenabteilung England,
      Karton 4, 5, 7

II. PRINTED WORKS AND TYPESCRIPTS

Amos, Andrew. *Observations on the Statutes of the Reformation Parliament*,
  London, 1859.

Ashford, L. J. *The History of the Borough of High Wycombe from its Origins to 1800*, London, 1960.

Aspinall, Arthur, *et al. Parliament through Seven Centuries: Reading and Its M.P.s*, London, 1962.

Baskerville, Geoffrey. *English Monks and the Suppression of the Monasteries*, London, 1937.

Baumer, Franklin Le Van. 'Christopher St. German: The Political Philosophy of a Tudor Lawyer', *A.H.R.*, XLII (1937), 631–51.

Behrens, Betty. 'A Note on Henry VIII's Divorce Project of 1514', *B.I.H.R.*, XI (1933), 163–4.

Benham, W. Gurney, ed. *The Red Paper Book of Colchester*, Colchester, 1902.

Bindoff, S. T. 'Clement Armstrong and His Treatises of the Commonweal', *Economic History Review*, XIV (1944), 64–73.

——. 'Parliamentary History, 1529–1688', *Victoria County History, Wiltshire*, V, 111–70.

Blunt, John Henry. *The Reformation of the Church of England*, London, 1869.

Bond, Maurice. *Historic Parliamentary Documents in the Palace of Westminster*, London, 1960.

Bowker, Margaret. *The Secular Clergy in the Diocese of Lincoln, 1495–1520*, Cambridge, 1968.

Bradford, William. *Correspondence of the Emperor Charles V*, London, 1850.

Burnet, Gilbert. *The History of the Reformation of the Church of England*, 2 vols, London, 1681.

Calendar of Letters, Despatches, and State Papers, Relating to the Negotiations between England and Spain, 15 vols, London, 1862–1954.

Calendar of State Papers and Manuscripts Existing in the Archives and Collections of Milan, London, 1912.

Calendar of State Papers and Manuscripts, Relating to English Affairs, Existing in the Archives and Collections of Venice, 38 vols, London, 1864–1947.

Cavendish, George. *The Life and Death of Cardinal Wolsey*. In *Two Early Tudor Lives*, ed. Richard S. Sylvester and Davis P. Harding, New Haven and London, 1962.

Clebsch, William A. *England's Earliest Protestants, 1520–1535*, New Haven and London, 1964.

C[okayne], G. E. *The Complete Peerage*. New ed., 12 vols, London, 1910–1959.

Cooper, C. H. *Annals of Cambridge*, 5 vols, Cambridge, 1842–1902.

Cooper, J. P. 'The Supplication against the Ordinaries Reconsidered', *E.H.R.*, LXXII (1957), 616–41.

Dasent, A. I. *The Speakers of the House of Commons*, London, 1911.

Dickens, A. G. *The English Reformation*, London, 1964.

——.'Tudor York', *Victoria County History, The City of York*, 117–59.

Dictionary of National Biography, 22 vols, London, 1908–1909.

Dietz, Frederick C. *English Government Finance, 1485–1558*, 2nd ed., New York, 1964.

Dugdale, Sir William. *A Perfect Copy of all Summons of the Nobility to the Great Councils and Parliaments of this Realm*, London, 1685.

——. *Monasticon Anglicanum*, 6 vols, London, 1817.

Edwards, J. G. *The Commons in Medieval English Parliaments*, London, 1958.

——. 'The Emergence of Majority Rule in the Procedure of the House of Commons', *T.R.H.S.*, 5th ser., xv (1965), 165–87.

Ellis, Sir Henry. *Original Letters Illustrative of English History*, 3rd ser., 4 vols, London, 1846.

Elton, G. R. 'A Further Note on Parliamentary Drafts in the Reign of Henry VIII', *B.I.H.R.*, xxvii (1954), 198–200.

——. 'An Early Tudor Poor Law', *Economic History Review*, 2nd ser., vi (1953), 55–67.

——. 'A Note on the First Act of Annates', *B.I.H.R.*, xxiii (1950), 203–4.

——. *England under the Tudors*, London, 1955.

——. 'King or Minister?: The Man Behind the Henrician Reformation', *History*, new ser., xxxix (1954), 216–32.

——. 'Parliamentary Drafts, 1529–1540', *B.I.H.R.*, xxv (1952), 117–32.

——. 'The Commons' Supplication of 1532: Parliamentary Manœuvres in the Reign of Henry VIII', *E.H.R.*, lxvi (1951), 507–34.

——. 'The Evolution of a Reformation Statute', *E.H.R.*, lxiv (1949), 174–97.

——. 'The Law of Treason in the Early Reformation', *Historical Journal*, xi (1968), 211–36.

——. *The Tudor Constitution*, Cambridge, 1960.

——. 'The Tudor Revolution: A Reply', *Past and Present*, xxix (1964), 28–36.

——. *The Tudor Revolution in Government*, Cambridge, 1953.

——. 'Sir Thomas More and the Opposition to Henry VIII', *B.I.H.R.*, xli (1968), 19–34.

——. *Star Chamber Stories*, London, 1958.

——. 'State Planning in Early-Tudor England', *Economic History Review*, 2nd ser., xiii (1960–1961), 433–9.

——. 'Thomas Cromwell's Decline and Fall', *Cambridge Historical Journal*, x (1951), 150–85.

Elyot, Sir Thomas. *The Boke Named the Gouernour*, London, 1531.

Modernized ed., *The Book Named the Governor*, ed. S. E. Lehmberg, London, 1962.

Fabyan, Robert. *The New Chronicles of England and France*, London, 1811.

Fisher, H. A. L. *The History of England from the Accession of Henry VII to the Death of Henry VIII (1485–1547)*, London, 1910.

Froude, J. A. *History of England from the Fall of Wolsey to the Defeat of the Spanish Armada*. Vol. I, new ed., London, 1870; Vol. II, 2nd ed., revised, London, 1858.

Gee, Henry, and W. J. Hardy. *Documents Illustrative of English Church History*, London, 1896.

Greenleaf, W. H. 'Filmer's Patriarchal History', *Historical Journal*, IX (1966), 157–71.

Grieve, Hilda. *Examples of English Handwriting 1150–1760*, Chelmsford, 1954.

Hall, Edward. *Hall's Chronicle*, London, 1809.

[Hall, Richard]. *The Life of Fisher*, London, 1921.

Harpsfield, Nicholas. *The Life and Death of Sir Thomas Moore*, London, 1932.

Harriss, G. L. 'A Revolution in Tudor History?', *Past and Present*, XXXI (1965), 87–90.

——. 'Medieval Government and Statecraft', *Past and Present*, XXV (1963), 9–12.

[Harrod, Henry]. *Report on the Records of the Borough of Colchester*, Colchester, 1865.

Herbert of Cherbury, Edward Lord. *The Life and Reign of King Henry the Eighth*, London, 1683.

Historical Manuscripts Commission. *Third Report*, London, 1872.

Hogrefe, Pearl. 'The Life of Christopher Saint German', *Review of English Studies*, XIII (1937), 398–404.

Holdsworth, Sir William. *A History of English Law*, 14 vols. London, 1903–1956.

Hollis, D., ed. *Calendar of the Bristol Apprentice Book, 1532–1565*, Part I, Bristol, 1949.

Hook, Walter Farquhar. *Lives of the Archbishops of Canterbury*, 12 vols, London, 1860–1876.

Hughes, Paul L., and James F. Larkin, eds. *Tudor Royal Proclamations*, Volume I, New Haven and London, 1964.

Hughes, Philip. *The Reformation in England*, Volume I, London 1952.

Ives, E. W. 'The Genesis of the Statute of Uses', *E.H.R.*, LXXXII (1967), 673–97.

Jay, Winifred. 'List of Members of the Fourth Parliament of Henry VII', *B.I.H.R.*, III (1926), 168–75.

Journals of the House of Lords, Volume I, London, [1888].

Kelly, Michael. 'Canterbury Jurisdiction and Influence during the Episcopate of William Warham, 1503–1532'. Unpublished dissertation, Cambridge University, 1963.

——. 'The Submission of the Clergy', *T.R.H.S.*, 5th ser., xv (1965), 97–119.

Kemp, E. W. *Counsel and Consent*, London, 1961.

Knowles, Dom David. *The Religious Orders in England*, Volume III, Cambridge, 1959.

Koebner, Richard. *Empire*, Cambridge, 1961.

——. ' "The Imperial Crown of This Realm": Henry VIII, Constantine the Great, and Polydore Vergil', *B.I.H.R.*, xxvi (1953), 29–52.

Latimer, Hugh. *Sermons*, Cambridge, 1844.

Lehmberg, Stanford E. *Sir Thomas Elyot, Tudor Humanist*, Austin, 1960.

——. 'Supremacy and Vicegerency: A Re-examination', *E.H.R.*, lxxxi (1966), 225–35.

Le Neve, John. *Fasti Ecclesiae Anglicanae, 1300–1541*, new ed., 12 vols, London, 1962–1967.

Letters and Papers, Foreign and Domestic, Henry VIII, 21 vols, London, 1862–1932.

Levine, Mortimer. 'Henry VIII's Use of His Spiritual and Temporal Jurisdictions in His Great Causes of Matrimony, Legitimacy and Succession', *Historical Journal*, x (1967), 3–10.

Loades, D. M. *The Papers of George Wyatt Esquire*, London, Royal Historical Society (Camden Fourth Series, vol. 5), 1968.

Lunt, W. E. *Financial Relations of the Papacy with England, 1327–1534*, Cambridge, Mass., 1962.

MacCaffrey, Wallace T. 'England: The Crown and the New Aristocracy, 1540–1600', *Past and Present*, xxx (1965), 52–64.

——. *Exeter, 1540–1640*, Cambridge, Mass., 1958.

McKisack, May. *The Parliamentary Representation of the English Boroughs during the Middle Ages*, London, 1932.

MacLure, Millar. *The Paul's Cross Sermons, 1534–1642*, Toronto, 1958.

Mackie, J. D. *The Earlier Tudors*, Oxford, 1952.

Makower, Felix. *The Constitutional History and Constitution of the Church of England*, London, 1895.

Mattingly, Garrett. 'A Humanist Ambassador', *Journal of Modern History*, iv (1932), 175–85.

——. *Catherine of Aragon*, London, 1950.

——. *Renaissance Diplomacy*, London, 1955.

Merewether, H. A., and A. J. Stephens. *A History of the Borough and Municipal Corporations of the United Kingdom*, 2 vols, London, 1835.

Merriman, R. B. *Life and Letters of Thomas Cromwell*, 2 vols, Oxford, 1902.

Miles, Leland. 'Persecution and the *Dialogue of Comfort*: A Fresh Look at the Charges Against Thomas More', *Journal of British Studies*, V (1965), 19–30.

Miller, Helen. 'Attendance in the House of Lords during the Reign of Henry VIII', *Historical Journal*, X (1967), 325–51.

——. 'London and Parliament in the Reign of Henry VIII', *B.I.H.R.*, XXXV (1962), 128–49.

——. 'The Early Tudor Peerage, 1485–1547'. Unpublished thesis, London University, 1950.

——. 'The Early Tudor Peerage, 1485–1547', *B.I.H.R.*, XXIV (1951), 88–91.

Muller, J. A. *Stephen Gardiner and the Tudor Reaction*, New York, 1926.

Nairn, Ian, and Nikolaus Pevsner. *Surrey*, Harmondsworth, Mdx., 1962.

Namier, Lewis B. *The Structure of Politics at the Accession of George III*, 2nd ed., London, 1957.

Neale, J. E. *Elizabeth I and Her Parliaments, 1559–1581*, London, 1953.

——. *The Elizabethan House of Commons*, London, 1949.

Nichols, J. G., ed. *Narratives of the Days of the Reformation*, London, 1859.

Notestein, Wallace. *The Winning of Initiative by the House of Commons*, London, 1924.

O'Donoghue, Edward G. *Bridewell Hospital*, 2 vols, London, 1923.

Ogle, Arthur. *The Tragedy of the Lollards' Tower*, Oxford, 1949.

Park, G. R. *Parliamentary Representation of Yorkshire*, Hull, 1886.

Parker, Matthew. *De Antiquitate Britannicae Ecclesiae*, London, 1572.

Parliamentary or Constitutional History of England, 24 vols, London, 1751–1762.

Parmiter, G. de C. *The King's Great Matter*, New York, 1967.

Phelps Brown, E. H., and Sheila V. Hopkins, 'Seven Centuries of the Prices of Consumables, Compared with Builders' Wage-Rates', in E. M. Carus-Wilson, ed., *Essays in Economic History*, II (1962), 179–96.

Pike, Luke Owen. *A Constitutional History of the House of Lords*, London, 1894.

Plucknett, T. F. T. 'Some Proposed Legislation of Henry VIII', *T.R.H.S.*, 4th ser., XIX (1936), 119–44.

Pocock, Nicholas. *Records of the Reformation*, 2 vols. Oxford, 1870.

Pollard, A. F. 'A Changeling Member of Parliament', *B.I.H.R.*, X (1932), 20–7.

——. 'An Early Parliamentary Election Petition', *B.I.H.R.*, VIII (1930), 156–66.

——. *England under Protector Somerset*, London, 1900.

——. 'Fifteenth-Century Clerks of Parliament', *B.H.I.R.*, xv (1937), 137–61.

——. *Henry VIII*, London, 1951.

——. 'Receivers of Petitions and Clerks of Parliament', *B.I.H.R.*, LVII (1942), 202–26.

——. 'The Authenticity of the "Lords" Journals in the Sixteenth Century', *T.R.H.S.*, 3rd ser., VIII (1914), 17–39.

——. 'The Clerical Organization of Parliament', *E.H.R.*, LVII (1942), 31–58.

——. 'The Clerk of the Crown', *E.H.R.*, LVII (1942), 312–33.

——. *The Evolution of Parliament*, 2nd ed., revised, London, 1926.

——. 'The Reformation Parliament as a Matrimonial Agency and Its National Effects', *History*, XXI (1936), 219–29.

——. 'Thomas Cromwell's Parliamentary Lists', *B.I.H.R.*, IX (1931), 31–43.

——. *Wolsey*, London, 1929.

——. 'Wolsey and the Great Seal', *B.I.H.R.*, VII (1929), 85–97.

Pollard, A. W., and G. R. Redgrave. *A Short-Title Catalogue of Books Printed in England, Scotland, and Ireland, and of English Books Printed Abroad, 1475–1640*, London, 1946.

Porritt, Edward. *The Unreformed House of Commons*, 2 vols, Cambridge, 1903.

Powicke, Sir Maurice, and E. B. Fryde, eds. *Handbook of British Chronology*, 2nd ed., London, 1961.

Raine, Angelo, ed. *York Civic Records*, 8 vols, York, 1939–1953.

Rees, William. 'The Union of England and Wales', *Transactions of the Honourable Society of Cymmrodorion*, 1937, 27–100.

Return of Members of Parliament, 4 vols, London, 1878.

Rezneck, Samuel. 'The Trial of Treason in Tudor England', in *Essays in History and Political Theory in Honor of Charles Howard McIlwain*, Cambridge, Mass., 1936, 258–88.

Richardson, W. C. *History of the Court of Augmentations, 1536–1554*, Baton Rouge, La., 1961.

Ridley, Jasper. *Thomas Cranmer*, Oxford, 1962.

Rogers, E. F., ed. *The Correspondence of Sir Thomas More*, Princeton, 1947.

Roper, William. *The Lyfe of Sir Thomas Moore, Knighte*, London, 1935.

Roskell, J. S. 'Perspectives in English Parliamentary History', *Bulletin of the John Rylands Library*, XLVI (1964), 448–75.

——. *The Commons and their Speakers in English Parliaments, 1376–1523*, Manchester, 1965.

——. *The Commons in the Parliament of 1422*, Manchester, 1954.

Rowse, A. L. *Sir Richard Grenville of the Revenge*, London, 1937.

———. *The Expansion of Elizabethan England*, London, 1955.

———. *Tudor Cornwall*, London, 1957.

Ryan, Lawrence V. *Roger Ascham*, Stanford, 1963.

Rymer, Thomas. *Foedera*, 2nd ed. 17 vols, London, 1727–1729.

Saint German, Christopher. *A lytell treatise called the newe addicions*, London, 1531.

———. *A treatise concernyng the diuision betwene the spirytualtie and temporaltie*, London, [1532].

Scarisbrick, J. J. *Henry VIII*, London, 1968.

———. 'The Conservative Episcopate in England, 1529–1535'. Unpublished dissertation, Cambridge University, 1955.

———. 'The Pardon of the Clergy, 1531', *Cambridge Historical Journal*, XII (1956), 22–39.

Schofield, R. S. 'Parliamentary Lay Taxation 1485–1547'. Unpublished dissertation, Cambridge University, 1963.

Shirley, T. F. *Thomas Thirlby, Tudor Bishop*, London, 1964.

Sims, Catherine Strateman. ' The moderne forme of the Parliaments of England ', *A.H.R.*, LIII (1948), 288–305.

Slavin, A. J. *Politics and Profit: A Study of Sir Ralph Sadler, 1507–1547*, Cambridge, 1966.

Smith, H. Maynard. *Henry VIII and the Reformation*, London, 1948.

Smith, Lacey Baldwin. *A Tudor Tragedy: The Life and Times of Catherine Howard*, London, 1961.

———. *Tudor Prelates and Politics, 1536–1558*, Princeton, 1953.

Snow, Vernon F. 'Proctorial Representation and Conciliar Management during the Reign of Henry VIII', *Historical Journal*, IX (1966), 1–26.

Statham, S. P. H. *The History of the Castle, Town, and Port of Dover*, London, 1899.

Statutes at Large, 8 vols, London, 1758–1771.

Statutes of the Realm, 11 vols, London, 1810–1828.

Stone, Lawrence. *The Crisis of the Aristocracy, 1558–1641*, Oxford, 1965.

———. 'The Political Programme of Thomas Cromwell', *B.I.H.R.*, XXIV (1951), 1–18.

Stow, John. *Survey of London*, London and New York, 1956.

Strype, John. *Life of Sir Thomas Smith*, Oxford, 1820.

Stubbs, William. *Seventeen Lectures on the Study of Medieval and Modern History and Kindred Subjects*, Oxford, 1886.

Tanner, J. R. *Tudor Constitutional Documents*, Cambridge, 1948.

Third Report of the Deputy Keeper of the Public Records, London, 1842.

Thirsk, Joan, ed. *The Agrarian History of England and Wales, 1500–1640*, Cambridge, 1967.

Thornley, Isobel D. 'The Treason Legislation of Henry VIII (1531–1534)', *T.R.H.S.*, 3rd ser., XI (1917), 87–123.

Toms, Elsie. *The Story of St. Albans*, St Albans, 1962.

Tucker, Melvin J. *The Life of Thomas Howard, Earl of Surrey and Second Duke of Norfolk, 1443–1524*, The Hague, 1964.

Tyndale, William. *Exposition and Notes . . ., together with The Practice of Prelates*, Cambridge, 1849.

Veale, E. W. W., ed. *The Great Red Book of Bristol*, Part IV, Bristol, 1953.

Venn, John and J. A. *Alumni Cantabrigienses*, Part I, 4 vols. Cambridge, 1922.

Victoria County History. Bedfordshire, Vol. III, London, 1912.

——. *The City of York*, London, 1961.

——. *Wiltshire*, vol. *V*, London, 1957.

Waugh, W. T. 'The Great Statute of Praemunire', *E.H.R.*, XXXVII (1922), 173–205.

Webb, Sidney and Beatrice. *English Local Government: English Poor Law History: Part I. The Old Poor Law*, London, 1927.

[Wedgwood, Josiah C.] *History of Parliament, 1439–1509*, 2 vols, London, 1936–1938.

Weske, D. B. *The Convocation of the Clergy*, London, 1937.

Whatmore, L. E. 'The Sermon against the Holy Maid of Kent and her Adherents', *E.H.R.*, LVIII (1943), 463–75.

Wheatley, Henry B. *London Past and Present*, 3 vols, London, 1891.

Wilkins, David. *Concilia Magnae Britanniae et Hiberniae*, 4 vols, London, 1737.

Williams, W. Llewelyn. 'The Union of England and Wales', *Transactions of the Honourable Society of Cymmrodorion*, 1907–1908, 47–117.

Woodward, G. W. O. *The Dissolution of the Monasteries*, London, 1966.

Zeeveld, W. Gordon. *Foundations of Tudor Policy*, Cambridge, Mass., 1948.

INDEX

Kite, John, bishop of Carlisle, 39, 74, 201
Knight, William, 69
Knightley, Edmund, 26
Knightley, Richard, 25 n.

Ladde, John, 170 n.
Lambert, Francis, 143
Lambert (or Nicholson), John, 117–18, 246
Land, exchanges of, 157, 213, 243
Land law, 94–6, 98; see also Enrolments; Uses
Latimer, Hugh
  examined in Convocation, 117–18, 146; named bishop of Worcester, 185, 219; mentioned, 38, 40, 176, 188 n., 226–7, 246
Latimer, John Neville, third baron, 57, 58–9, 170 n., 183
Latimer, Richard Neville, second baron (d. 1530), 54 n.
Latton, John, 29
LaWarr, Thomas West, baron, 54 n., 57, 58 n., 132, 183, 201, 218, 228
Lawrence, John, see Wardeboys, John
Lawson, George, 22
Lawyers, in Commons, 8, 24–6
Leather, legislation concerning, 173–4, 235
Lee, Edward, archbishop of York, 28, 38, 45, 74–5, 105, 131, 162, 168 n., 169, 183, 218, 254
Lee, Geoffrey, 28, 30
Lee, Rowland
  and Convocation, 69; named bishop of Coventry and Lichfield, 184; and acts for Wales, 209–11, 241–2; mentioned, 40, 167, 201
Legal reforms, 97–8, 125–6, 154–5, 185–6, 235–40, 252
Leicester, Robert Dudley, earl of, 201
Leo X, pope, 6
Lewis, John, 243–4
Lichfield (or Wych), Clement, abbot of Evesham, 44, 132
Ligham, Peter, 66 n., 70, 71 n., 127 n.
Lincoln, bishop of, see Longland, John
Linen, legislation concerning, 97, 173
Lisle, Arthur Plantagenet, viscount
  and ordinances for Calais, 239–40; mentioned, 48–9, 54, 59, 193 n., 224, 228

Lisle, Edward Grey, viscount, 54
Livery and maintenance, 98
Llandaff, bishop of, see Athequa, George de
London, bishop of, see Fitzjames, Richard; Tunstall, Cuthbert; Stokesley, John
London, City of
  method of electing burgesses, 11; burgesses for, 19–21; legislation concerning, 97, 174, 189, 234, 243, 252; by-elections in, 170, 201
London, Dr John, 71
Long, Sir Henry, 170
Longland, John, bishop of Lincoln, and Convocation, 67, 114, 115 n.; and Submission of the Clergy, 149, 150 n., 152; mentioned, 39, 129, 162, 163 n., 167, 177, 246
Lords, House of
  membership analysed, 36–58; Lords spiritual, 37–45; bishops in, 37–41; abbots in, 41–45; proxies in, 45; attendance in, 48, 54; expense of attending, 58–60; clerks of, 60; writs of assistance, 60; Henry VIII appears in, 125, 137, 255; opposition annates bill, 137; pressure of work in, 189; royal influence in, 254–5; see also Reformation Parliament
Lowys, George, 24 n.
Ludlow, act for, 233–4
Lumley, John, baron
  private acts for, 157, 189; mentioned, 54 n., 57
Luther, Martin, 87, 143, 195
Lynn, Bishop's, later King's Lynn
  acts for, 97, 212; manor of, granted to king, 230
Lyster, Sir Richard, 62
Lytilprow, Reginald, 23, 132

Mablisten, Sir John, 156 n.
Madyson, Sir Edward, 30, 179
Mallet, Baldwin, 62
Maltravers, Henry Fitzalan, baron, 47, 52, 54 n., 170
Malvern, William, abbot of Gloucester 45
Manners, Thomas, see Rutland, earl of
Margaret, queen of Scotland, 198
Marshall, John, 24 n.